Economic Theory and Mathematical Economics

Volume I

Economic Theory and Mathematical Economics

Volume I

Edited by **Derek Beaven**

Clanrye International

New Jersey

Published by Clanrye International,
55 Van Reypen Street,
Jersey City, NJ 07306, USA
www.clanryeinternational.com

Economic Theory and Mathematical Economics: Volume I
Edited by Derek Beaven

International Standard Book Number: 978-1-63240-157-1 (Hardback)

Printed in China.

Contents

Preface

Since it encompasses multiple things, it is difficult to define Economics. Its origins can be traced to ancient times and traditionally, it has been associated with an understanding of production processes such as distribution and consumption of goods and services in an economy. Essentially, Economics is a science of choices in situations of scarcity and abundance. It serves to answer questions related to resource allocation, and how and why it is done. This involves comparisons of costs and benefits and a consideration of alternative available opportunities.

The discipline of Economics perfectly balances theory with practical applications. This is because many economic magnitudes are measurable. In fact, economics has developed models to organize facts and to think about policy alternatives. Economists also play an important role in understanding the relationship between interest rates and bond prices. The subject has broadly been categorised into: Microeconomics, which examines the various forces which go into play for the formation of a market and Macroeconomics, which examines the economy as a whole to explain broad aggregates and their interactions.

I'd like to thank all the researchers who've agreed to share their valuable studies with us in this book. I would also like to thank them for maintaining the timelines and cooperating with me at every step and providing guidance for making this book a valuable text.

Editor

An Empirical Analysis of Retirement and Marriage in Taiwan

Wen-Shai Hung
Department of Business Administration, Providence University, Taichung, Chinese Taipei

ABSTRACT

This paper investigates the factors influencing changes in marriage following retirement in Taiwan. The data used are from the Survey of Health and Living Status of the Middle Aged Elderly in Taiwan. The Weibull models are used to estimate the hazard rates of divorce or separation after retirement. The factors of unobserved heterogeneity are also examined for the influences of divorce or separation after retirement. The main empirical results find that Mainlanders, Aboriginals, people with better educational attainments, people with poor health or poor relationship with family have higher hazard rates of divorce or separation than others. In contrast, people with more children and persons with higher income have lower hazard rates of divorce or separation than others. After considering unobserved heterogeneity, most estimated coefficients on the marriage hazard regressors are larger in magnitude than the corresponding coefficients in the reference model.

Keywords: Divorce; Separation; Weibull Model; Unobserved Heterogeneity

1. Introduction

This paper examines the factors influencing changes in marriages following retirement in Taiwan. According to the 2012 survey of Ministry of the Interior, the highest proportion rates of divorce were concentrated at the 10 - 14 years of marriage duration and the trends gradually declined during the recent 10 years. In contrast, the trends of divorce rates over 20 years were gradually increased during the same period. This implies that the changes in marriages and retirement behavior may have some special relationships and it is interested to do a deeper research.

Most previous studies on retirement behaviour in Taiwan were focused on the health status and health-care utilisation, living arrangements, and the economic well-being of the elderly. For example, Schoenbaum [1] used the Survey of Health and Living Status of the Middle Aged and Elderly in Taiwan data to test the effect of health on labour force transition among the elderly using four different measures[1]. He concluded that health is a major determinant of labour force transition, regardless of how it is measured. Individuals in poor health are significantly more likely to retire than people in good health. In addition, Chen [2] used the 1989 Labour Force Survey by the Directorate-General of Budget, Accounting and Statistics in Taiwan to examine the effect of health status and health-care utilisation among the elderly. He noted that the proportion of old-old population was relatively low. Taiwan's elderly were more inclined to use health-care facilities than elderly in other developed economies.

Chang [3] used the data from the Survey of Health and Living Status of the Middle Aged and Elderly to examine the changes in living arrangements of the elderly in Taiwan between 1989 and 1995. He found that reduction in widowhood would be favorable for the elderly to live with a spouse only. Increases in educational attainments and economic independence will alter the elderly to live alone. In addition, the increasing age at marriage means that unmarried children are likely to be in the parental home for a longer period and thus minimize the strong trend toward independent living of the elderly.

Hermalin, Roan, and Chang [4] also used the data from the Survey of Health and Living Status of the Middle Aged and Elderly in 1996 to test the effect of demographic and socioeconomic trends on the economic well-being of the elderly. The data combined two panels,

[1] The four types of health measures considered in his paper include: 1) a summary measure of limitations on activities of daily living (ADL), such as shopping and lifting; 2) a summary measure of health conditions, such as stroke and dizziness; 3) a summary measure of mood and depression using the Centre for Epidemiologic Studies Depression Scale (CES-D) that can measure how people have been feeling in the past week; and 4) health indices, such as crude birth rate, crude death rate, life expectancy at birth (years) constructed using an instrumental variables framework.

including the first panel 2669 respondents aged 67 and over and the second panel 2462 respondents aged 50 to 66 in 1996. In general, those who relied on children as their major source were reported lower incomes than those who relied on other major sources.

Furthermore, Yu and Chang [5] investigated the retirement behavior of public sector employees. They used the matched data sets from the Taiwan Manpower Utilization Survey from 1986 to 2002. They analyzed the incentive effects of public-sector retirement regulations on the retirement timing of public sector employees. Further, they examined whether the sample attrition bias was serious in their framework. Their empirical results found that the regulations on retirement age and tenure had significant effects on the choice of retirement timing.

Hung [6] examined the determinants of retirement among the middle aged and elderly workers in Taiwan. The data used were from two waves of Survey of Health and Living Status of the Middle Aged and Elderly in Taiwan in 1996 and 1999. He considered the models without and with time-varying covariates on estimated retirement. He found that the model without time-varying covariates, older workers, female workers, Mainlander workers, and workers with eligible pension have higher hazard rates of retirement, and workers with better education have a lower hazard rate of retirement. Furthermore, for the model with time-varying covariates, workers with poor health have a higher hazard rate of retirement, in particular as workers being in poor health increase the hazard rates of retirement, other things being equal.

For the other developed countries, some early studies on the effects of retirement on marital satisfaction provide limited support for the view that retirement has a negative impact on marital wellbeing. For example, Moen, Kim and Hofmeister [7] used two waves of the Cornell Retirement and Well-Being Study in US in 1994-1995 and 1996-1997 to investigate whether couples' employment/retirement circumstances predict marital quality differently for men and for women. They found that initially, the retirement transition led to decreased marital satisfaction and increased marital conflict for men and women. The evidence complements the findings that homemaker wives' marital quality declines temporarily when their husbands retire. It is also consistent with Szinovacz's [8], who used the data from the National Survey of Families and Households in US to explore the impact of couples' employment/retirement patterns on indicators of marital quality, including conflicts, heated arguments, marital happiness. He claimed that marital problems during the retirement behavior are typically temporary and resolved within a few years after retirement.

Vaus and Wells [9] showed the paper from Shaw, Patterson, Semples and Grant [10], those who suggested that after retirement a balance in the relationship must be re-established based on a new set of routines and patterns of communication. The evidence indicates that as couples settle into retirement, a new balance is generally found and the role strain that couples experienced during the retirement transition is reduced.

Pienta [11] used data from the 1992 Health and Retirement Survey to compare the retirement behavior of husbands and wives. He found that the wives' retirement status is related to familial factors, economic resources, and spouses' personal characteristics supporting the new modes of retirement hypothesis. Husbands differ mainly in that familial and spousal attributes have more limited relationships with retirement behavior according to the usual modes of retirement hypothesis.

Smith and Moen [12] investigated factors related to retirees' and their spouses' individual and joint retirement satisfaction using decision-making theory and a life course perspective. The sample included retired respondents (ages 50 to 72) and spouses from the Cornell Retirement and Well-Being Study in US in 1994-1995 and 1996-1997. Although 77% of retirees report retirement satisfaction, only 67% of their spouses are satisfied; even fewer couples (59%) report joint satisfaction. Multivariate logistic regression analyses reveal that retirees' and spouses' individual and joint reports of retirement satisfaction are related to perceptions of spousal influence on the retirement decision, with effects varying by gender.

In sum, few papers analysed the issues of changes in marriages and retirement, particularly for exploring the related questions of the impacts of retirement on the domestic divisions of labour and on marital quality in this domain in Taiwan. This paper will use the duration analysis and micro data to fill this gap. First, it describes the factors influencing changes in marriages, including divorce, separation, or spouse's deceased following retirement in Taiwan. Second, it estimates the hazard rates of changes in marriages among the middle aged and elderly. Third, in addition to investigating the effect of unobserved heterogeneity of changes in marriages following retirement, it is well known that the duration analysis produces incorrect results if unobserved heterogeneity is ignored (Lancaster, [13])[2], and it is to find useful policies for retirement and marriage in Taiwan.

2. Some Facts about Marital Status among the Middle Aged and Elderly in Taiwan

Marital status always affects individual participation in work and retirement behaviour. For instance, once a man is married, he tends to have more opportunities to work,

[2]See Hosmer, Lemeshow and May [14] and Cleves, Gould, and Gutierrez [15] for a description of the frailty models.

and perhaps an increased desire or need to work as he is likely to be the main earner for his family. In contrast, a married woman might do more housework and have a lower desire (less need or opportunity) to work. The survey of Taiwan and Fujian Areas shows that the proportion of the population who are married decreased with increasing age from 85.4% aged 50 to 54 to 39.3% aged 80 and over. In contrast, the proportion whose spouse was deceased increased with age from 5.7% aged 50 to 54 to 57.3% aged 80 and over in 2005. The proportion of the population divorced or separated decreased with increasing age from 6.2% aged 50 to 54 to 1.6% aged 80 and over. In particular, for the Taiwanese traditional society, most people prefer to only marry once during their lives.

Therefore, this paper is interested to examine some hypothesis of changes in marriages following retirement in Taiwan: for example, does marriage improve or get worse following retirement? Do men and women report different marital outcomes following retirement? What happens to the division of labour between married men and women following retirement? May the hazard rates of separated or divorced after retirement be higher than before retirement?

3. Research Methods

3.1 Data Source

The data used are from the Survey of Health and Living Status of the Middle Aged and Elderly in Taiwan (hereafter, SHLS) to analyse retirement and marriage issues. The SHLS is an important and unique survey in Taiwan, the first large-scale panel data set collected and produced by the Taiwan Provincial Institute of Family Planning (TPIFP)[3] and the Population Studies Centre in the University of Michigan (PSC, UM), and is available for the period from 1989 to 2007. The project was initiated in 1989 with a survey of 4049 respondents aged 60 and above. These respondents were interviewed four times including a major follow-up interview in 1993. The SHLS survey was extended by a second panel of individuals aged 50 to 66 in 1996. The two 1996 questionnaires were very similar. The sample size for the first panel was 2669 individuals aged 67 and over, and the second panel had 2462 respondents aged 50 to 66. In 1999 the first panel comprised 2310 respondents aged 70 and over, and the second panel had 2130 respondents aged 53 to 73. In 2003 the first panel comprised 1743 respondents aged 74 and over, the second panel had 2035 respondents aged 57 to 73, and the SHLS survey was again extended by a third panel of individuals aged 50 to 56. Until 2007, the first panel comprised 1268 respondents aged 78 and over, the second panel had 1864 respondents aged 61 to 77 and the third panel had 1402 individuals aged 54 to 60.

[3]The Taiwan Provincial Institute of Family Planning was merged into the Bureau of Health Promotion, Department of Health in July 2001.

The main data used are from the second panel of SHLS and the sample aged 50 to 66 in 1996. In particular, the voluntary retirement can be taken at age 50 if individuals have worked for 25 years, or reached age 55 and worked for more than 15 years. The first panel in 1989 did not cover those aged 50 to 60. For this reason the first panel has been discarded for this study, and instead this uses the second panel. The SHLS data represents a national random sample, the detailed information includes individuals, family, marital status, health, social support, employment, and economic status.

3.2 Variables Specification

3.2.1. Dependent Variable

According to the SHLS data, the sample consists of two groups, namely the currently married and the divorced or separated, except widowed. The former group remains married during the sample period and are known as "right-censored" of marriage duration. The latter group includes those divorced and separated during the sample period, and the date on which an individual started their last marriage and the exact age at which their marriage ended were observed. These are known as the "uncensored" of marriage duration. Therefore, marriage duration includes the period from when an individual first married to the end of the marriage for the "uncensored" duration spells, and they continue married for the "right-censored" duration spells. This variable can be categorized as a dependent variable. The uncensored variable is coded 1 for divorced or separated and 0 otherwise.

3.2.2. Explanatory Variables

The explanatory variables recorded in the SHLS data include 1) Demographic characteristics of respondent: age, gender, race, educational attainment, and health status. 2) Family structure and support: number of children, relationship with family, and residence status. 3) Economic and employment factors: household income and retirement.

First, the demographic characteristics of respondents are explored. The effect of ageing alone is important in explaining why people losing their married status. In particular, as people become older, they are more likely to die or lose their partner. From the SHLS data, age can be categorised into four groups: Age1 (aged 50 to 54), Age2 (aged 55 to 59), Age3 (aged 60 to 64), and Age4 (aged 65 to 66). In addition, females always have a longer life expectancy than males in Taiwan. That is, the numbers of females who lose their husbands are is greater than males who lose their wives. The Gender variable is coded 1 for female and 0 for male. Next, the Race variables have four groups, namely Race1 (Fujianese), Race2 (Hakka), Race3 (Mainlander), and Race4 (Aboriginal). For the education variable is divided into four levels of schooling, namely Edu1 (informal schooling), Edu2 (primary level: 1 to 6 years), Edu3 (high school level: 7 to 12 years) and Edu4 (college level: 13 to 17 years). For the health assessment, the SHLS survey identifies five levels including excellent, good, average, not so good, and poor. The Poorh variable is coded 1 for poor health, including "not so good" and "poor" health, and 0 for otherwise.

Second, the variables of family structure and support: the number of children can reflect marriage duration and living support. In particular, the traditional Chinese culture in Taiwan suggests that people with more children expect more family support in old age. There are 0 to 11 children for this variable. Next, the definition of relationship with family includes that people sharing, concerning, communicating, and caring with their family; particularly for the sickness, if the respondents could not believe or depend on their family and the variable can be defined as Poorla4, that is people with poor relationship with their family. The variables of residence status include Area1 (people living in urban), Area2 (people living in town), and Area3 (people living in rural). Basically, people with more children have lower hazard rates of divorce or separation. In contrast, respondents with poor relationship from their family have a higher hazard rate of losing their marriage.

Third, the economic and employment factors cover household income and retirement. If people have a better economic status or higher income, they might have a lower hazard rate of ceasing to be married. For the employment variables, the Retirement variable is coded 1 for respondent's retired and 0 for otherwise. Basically, if the retired people without earnings or pension benefits have higher hazard rates of losing their marriage.

However, the main limitation of this study is the survey data, the response rates on earnings and pension income were low, reflecting the reluctance of participants to divulge their true income. One more hidden danger of the SHLS data is the unknown accuracy of the responses given by the participants. No obvious means of verifying these responses exists. To solve the limitation of the SHLS is the lack of data on the interviewees' wages and their assets. This paper only uses the household income as an indicator of income to facilitate further analysis of changes in marriages following retirement. The descriptive and summary statistics are given in **Table 1**.

3.3. Estimation Method: Duration Model

Duration analysis has been developed in the field of bio-statistics to describe the timing of events. It has become a subject of increasing interest to applied economics, such as retirement issues in labour economics (Diamond and Hausman, [16]; Hung, [17]), and divorce topics in marriage economics (Hung and Ho, [18]). Therefore, this paper uses duration analysis and considers marriage duration in two groups, including right censoring (individuals who remain married during the sample period), and event or failure time (individuals do not remain married, including divorce or separation during the sample period). From these two sets of marriage duration, we can calculate the hazard rates of divorce or separation.

3.3.1. Model without Unobserved Heterogeneity

Weibull distributions are widely used as models for durat ion analysis. The hazard function of marriage duration without unobserved heterogeneity is specified as

$$h(t|x_i) = \alpha t^{\alpha-1} \cdot \lambda = \alpha t^{\alpha-1} \cdot e^{(\beta_0+\beta_i x_i)}. \quad (1)$$

Empirically, the parameters λ and α in the Weibull distribution can be estimated by maximum likelihood. The parameter λ depends on the explanatory variables x_i, thus providing us with a more flexible hazard function. For example, the hazard function is increasing if $\alpha > 1$, decreasing if $\alpha < 1$, and constant if $\alpha = 1$. For observed duration data, $t_1;t_2,\cdots,t_n$ the log-likelihood function can be formulated and maximized to include censored and uncensored observations. Combining the Weibull model into a general parametric likelihood yields:

$$L(\beta) = \prod_{i=1}^{n}\left\{\left[f(t_i|x_i,\beta)\right]^{c_i} * \left[S(t_i|x_i,\beta)\right]^{1-c_i}\right\} \quad (2)$$

where $\beta = (\lambda, \alpha)$, and $c_i = 1$ represents uncensored observations, $c_i = 0$ represents right-censored observations (Cleves, Gould, and Gutierrez, [15]). To obtain the maximum likelihood with respect to the parameters of interest, β, then maximise the log-likelihood function[4]:

$$\ln L(\beta) = \sum_{i=1}^{n}\left\{c_i \ln\left[f(t_i|x_i,\beta)\right] + (1-c_i)\ln\left[S(t_i|x_i,\beta)\right]\right\} \quad (3)$$

The procedure to obtain the values of maximum likelihood estimation requires taking derivatives of $\ln L(\beta)$ with respect to β, the unknown parameters, setting these equations equal to zero, and solving for β.[5]

3.3.2. Model with Unobserved Heterogeneity

After considering unobserved heterogeneity on estimated individual marriage behaviour, the hazard function can

[4]Since the log function is monotone, maxima of (2) and (3) occur at the same value of β; however, maximizing (3) is computationally simpler than maximizing (2).

[5]See Klein and Moeschberger [19], for a description of the numerical methods for implementing multivariate Newton-Raphson methods.

Table 1. Descriptive statistics of variables.

Variable	Description	Mean	Std. Dev.
Duration	Duration of marriage between 1 and 50 years.	32.032	7.755
Censor	1 = Uncensored, 0 = Otherwise.	0.029	0.167
Age96	50 - 66 years old in 1996.	57.411	4.733
Age1	1 = aged 50 to 54, 0 = Otherwise.	0.323	0.468
Age2	1 = aged 55 to 59, 0 = Otherwise.	0.326	0.469
Age3	1 = aged 60 to 64, 0 = Otherwise.	0.256	0.436
Age4	1 = aged 65 to 66, 0 = Otherwise.	0.093	0.291
Gender	1 = Female, 0 = male.	0.437	0.496
Race1	1 = Fujianese, 0 = Otherwise.	0.728	0.444
Race2	1 = Hakka, 0 = Otherwise.	0.185	0.388
Race3	1 = Mainlander, 0 = Otherwise.	0.072	0.259
Race4	1 = Aboriginal, 0 = Otherwise.	0.013	0.115
Edu1	1 = Informal education, 0 = Otherwise.	0.251	0.433
Edu2	1 = 1 to 6 years of schooling, 0 = Otherwise.	0.463	0.498
Edu3	1 = 7 to 12 years of schooling, 0 = Otherwise.	0.210	0.407
Edu4	1 = 13 to 17 years of schooling, 0 = Otherwise.	0.075	0.263
Health1	1 = Excellent Health, 0 = Otherwise.	0.205	0.403
Health2	1 = Good Health, 0 = Otherwise.	0.237	0.425
Health3	1 = Average Health, 0 = Otherwise.	0.331	0.470
Health4	1 = Poor Health, 0 = Otherwise.	0.203	0.402
Health5	1 = Very Poor Health, 0 = Otherwise.	0.023	0.150
Poorh	1 = Poor and Very Poor Health, 0 = Otherwise.	0.226	0.418
Children	0 - 11 children	3.791	1.453
Poorla4	1 = Poor relationship with family, 0 = Otherwise.	0.052	0.222
Area1	1 = People living in urban, 0 = Otherwise.	0.381	0.485
Area2	1 = People living in town, 0 = Otherwise.	0.265	0.441
Area3	1 = People living in rural, 0 = Otherwise.	0.353	0.478
Income1	1 = Less than NT$99,999, 0 = Otherwise.	0.159	0.366
Income2	1 = NT$100,000 - 299,999, 0 = Otherwise.	0.334	0.472
Income3	1 = NT$300,000 - 599,999, 0 = Otherwise.	0.294	0.455
Income4	1 = NT$600,000 - 999,999, 0 = Otherwise.	0.127	0.333
Income5	1 = Larger than NT$1,000,000, 0 = Otherwise.	0.084	0.277
Retirement	1 = retired, 0 = Otherwise.	0.311	0.463

Note: 1) The effective sample has 1556 observations, including 45 divorced or separated, and 1511 people who remain married. 2) The exchange rate was US$1 = NT$27.457 in 1996.

be defined as

$$h(t_i | x_i, u) = \alpha t^{\alpha-1}\lambda = \alpha t^{\alpha-1} \cdot e^{(\beta_0 + \beta_i x_i + u)} \quad (4)$$

where u can represent unobserved heterogeneity, the differences between observations are introduced via a multiplicative scaling factor. This is a random variable taking on positive values, with the mean normalised to one and finite variance σ^2. A crucial assumption in the model is that u is distributed independently of x_i and t. The other calculation procedures are same with the previous model without unobserved heterogeneity.

4. Empirical Results

4.1. Model without Unobserved Heterogeneity

Table 2 shows the estimated coefficients and hazard ratios of divorce or separation by Weibull model. For the benchmark individuals, all explanatory variables take a

Table 2. Estimation by Weibull model.

Variables	Coefficient	Standard Error	Hazard Ratio	Standard Error
Age96	−0.034	0.035	0.965	0.034
Gender	−0.293	0.359	0.745	0.268
Race2	0.012	0.497	1.012	0.503
Race3	1.365***	0.434	3.916***	1.702
Race4	1.895***	0.629	6.657***	4.190
Edu2	0.866*	0.503	2.377*	1.196
Edu3	1.531***	0.573	4.626***	2.654
Edu4	1.020	0.836	2.774	2.319
Poorh	0.782**	0.329	2.186**	0.719
Children	−0.506***	0.123	0.602***	0.074
Poorla4	1.225***	0.367	3.406***	1.250
Income2	−0.917**	0.397	0.399**	0.158
Income3	−1.339***	0.440	0.261***	0.115
Income4	−1.578**	0.651	0.206**	0.134
Income5	−2.703**	1.107	0.066**	0.074
Retirement	0.196	0.347	1.217	0.422
Constant	−4.317**	2.155		
$/\ln\_\alpha$	0.135	0.142	0.135	0.142
α	1.145	0.163	1.145	0.163
$1/\alpha$	0.872	0.124	0.872	0.124
Log likelihood	−205.652		−205.652	
LR chi2 (16)	83.55		83.55	

Notes: 1) The effective samples are 1,556 observations. 2. Effects are significant at $^*p \le 0.10$, $^{**}p \le 0.05$, $^{***}p \le 0.01$. 3) Goodness of fit: the result of Log-likelihood ratio test can reject the hypothesis that all coefficients except the intercept are 0 at the 0.01 level.

value of zero. That is, the benchmark individuals in all cases are relatively young Fujianese men with lower education attainments, no child, good health, with lower household income, and not retire. The hazard rate of divorce or separation estimates can be derived from the Weibull model of

$$h(t;x_i) = \alpha t^{\alpha-1}\lambda = \alpha t^{\alpha-1} \cdot e^{(\hat{\beta}_0 + \hat{\beta}_i \cdot 0)} = 1.145 * t^{0.145} * \exp(-4.317) \quad (5)$$

In particular, $\alpha = 1.145 > 1$ and $1 \le t \le 50$, which indicates the hazard rate has positive marriage duration dependence, $dh(t)/dt > 0$. And $-\ln(1/\alpha) = 0.135$, the estimate suggests that the hazard rate of divorce or separation is increasing over time. As marriage duration gets longer, the hazard rate increases and people are more likely to divorce or separate.

First, for the age variables of respondents, **Table 2** shows that the estimated coefficient of Age96 is negative and has lower hazard rates *ceteris paribus*, but statistically insignificant. The hazard ratio for Age96 is 0.965. This implies that older Taiwanese have 3.5% lower hazard rates than otherwise and they are less likely to divorce or separate, *ceteris paribus*. The estimated coefficient of Gender is negative and has lower hazard rates *ceteris paribus*, but also insignificant. The hazard ratio for Gender is 0.745. This implies that women have 25.5% lower hazard rates than otherwise and they are less likely to divorce or separate, *ceteris paribus*. In contrast, the estimated coefficients of Race3 and Race4 are positive and statistically significant and have higher hazard rates *ceteris paribus*. The hazard ratios for Race3 are 3.916, and Race4 is 6.657. This implies that Mainlanders have 391.6% and Aboriginals have 665.7% higher hazard rates than Fujianese and they are more likely to divorce or separate, *ceteris paribus*. Furthermore, the estimated coefficients of Edu2 and Edu3 are positive and statistically significant and have higher hazard rates *ceteris paribus*. The hazard ratios for Edu2 are 2.377, and Edu3 is 4.626. This implies that people with primary education have 237.7%, junior and senior high school have 462.6%

higher hazard rates than people with informal education and they are more likely to divorce or separate, *ceteris paribus*. For the variables of health status, **Table 2** shows that the estimated coefficient of Poorh is positive and statistically significant and has higher hazard rates *ceteris paribus*. The hazard ratio for Poorh is 2.186. This implies that people with poor health have 218.6% higher hazard rates than otherwise and they are more likely to divorce or separate, *ceteris paribus*.

Second, for the variables of family structure and social networks, **Table 2** shows that the estimated coefficient of Children (number of children) is negative and statistically significant and has lower hazard rates. Especially, the hazard ratio for Children is 0.602. This implies that respondents with children have 39.8% lower hazard rates than respondents without children and they are less likely to divorce or separate, *ceteris paribus*. Further, the estimated coefficient of Poorla4 (poor relationship with family) is positive and statistically significant and have higher hazard rates *ceteris paribus*. The hazard ratio of Poorla4 is 3.406. This implies that people with poor relationship from their family have 340.6% higher hazard rates than otherwise and they are more likely to divorce or separate, *ceteris paribus*.

Third, for the variables of economic status and employment, **Table 2** shows that the estimated coefficients of Income2, Income3, Income4, and Income5 are negative and statistically significant and have lower hazard rates. The hazard ratios for Income2, Income3, Income4, and Income5 are 0.399, 0.261, 0.206, and 0.066 respectively. These show that people with higher household income have lower hazard rates than otherwise and they are less likely to divorce or separate. In contrast, the estimated coefficient of Retirement is positive and have higher hazard rates *ceteris paribus*, but statistically insignificant. The hazard ratio of Retirement is 1.217. This implies that Retirement has 21.7% higher hazard rates than not retired and they are more likely to divorce or separate, *ceteris paribus*.

4.2. Model with Unobserved Heterogeneity

Frailty is a random component designed to account for variability due to unobserved individual-level factors of divorce or separation that are otherwise unaccounted for by the other predictors in the marriage duration model. Of particular note is the Poorla4 variable, which shows that 5.2% of people with poor relationship from family. When people are sick, they do not believe or depend on their careing.

Table 3 shows that the frailty model of all samples is assumed to follow a gamma distribution with mean 1 and variance equal to theta (θ). The estimate of theta is 0.269. A variance of zero (theta = 0) would indicate that the frailty component does not contribute to the model. A likelihood ratio test for the hypothesis theta = 0 is shown directly below the parameter estimates and indicates a chi-square value of 3.31 with 1 degree of freedom yielding a highly significant p-value of 0.034. Notice how all the parameter estimates are altered with the inclusion of frailty. The estimate for the shape parameter is now 1.143, different from the estimate 1.138 obtained from the model without frailty. The inclusion of frailty not only has an impact on the parameter estimates but also complicates their interpretation. Some estimated coefficients of the variables of Race4 (Aboriginals), Children (number of children), Income2, Income3, Income4, and Income5 are slightly larger in magnitude than the corresponding coefficients in the reference model. The Weibull distribution shape parameter α is also slightly larger in the frailty model than in the reference model. Therefore, the effects of unobserved heterogeneity are important for examining the duration of marriage. Therefore, people need to consider the factors of unobserved heterogeneity and to improve the relationship with their families, they may be able for reducing the rates of divorce or separation in the modern society.

5. Conclusions

This paper investigates the factors influencing changes in marriages following retirement in Taiwan. The data used are from the 1996 Survey of Health and Living Status of the Middle Aged Elderly in Taiwan and the sample aged 50 to 66.

First, for the demographic characteristics, the empirical results show those Mainlanders, Aboriginals, people with better educational attainment, and those in poor health have higher hazard rates and they are more likely to divorce or separate, *ceteris paribus*. Second, for the economic status and employment, people with higher household income have lower hazard rates and they are less likely to divorce or separate. In contrast, respondents retired have higher hazard rates and they are more likely to divorce or separate. Third, for the family structure and social networks, people with more children have lower hazard rates of divorce or separation. In contrast, the respondents with poor relationships from family have higher hazard rates and they are more likely to divorce or separate.

After considering the effect of unobserved heterogeneity from the factors of poor relationship (including difficultly sharing, concerning, communicating, and caring from their family), the estimated theta is larger than the model without unobserved heterogeneity. This implies that the influence of divorce or separation is more affected by the factors of unobserved heterogeneity. Particularly for the sickness, the respondents could not believe or depend on their family. To reduce the rate of divorce or separation, people may consider the factors of unobserved het-

Table 3. Estimation by Weibull models without and with unobserved heterogeneity.

Variables	Without Unobserved Heterogeneity		With Gamma-Heterogeneity	
	Coefficient	Standard Error	Coefficient	Standard Error
Age96	−0.039	0.035	−0.035	0.035
Gender	−0.222	0.352	−0.274	0.356
Race2	−0.027	0.495	0.001	0.496
Race3	1.404***	0.447	1.376***	0.435
Race4	1.842***	0.626	1.885***	0.627
Edu2	0.868*	0.495	0.867*	0.501
Edu3	1.672***	0.571	1.566***	0.573
Edu4	0.971	0.818	1.007	0.831
Children	−0.533***	0.124	−0.512***	0.123
Poorhealth	0.846***	0.324	0.799**	0.327
Income2	−1.111***	0.389	−0.966**	0.397
Income3	−1.538***	0.440	−1.387***	0.442
Income4	−1.957***	0.641	−1.674**	0.654
Income5	−2.879***	1.094	−2.745**	1.103
Retirement	0.180	0.343	0.192	0.345
Constant	−3.689*	2.075	−3.543	2.194
/ ln_ α	0.129	0.142	0.134	0.138
/ ln_ *the*			−1.311	1.196
α	1.138*	0.162	1.143*	0.158
$1/\alpha$	0.878*	0.125	0.874*	0.121
theta			0.269*	0.322
Log likelihood	−210.266		−208.611	
LR chi2 (15)	74.32		65.57	

Notes: 1) The effective samples are 1,556 observations. 2) Effects are significant at $^{*}p \le 0.10$, $^{**}p \le 0.05$, $^{***}p \le 0.01$. 3) Goodness of fit: the result of Log-likelihood ratio test can reject the hypothesis that all coefficients except the intercept are 0 at the 0.01 level. In particular, Log-likelihood ratio test of theta = 0: chibar2 (01) = 3.31, Prob > = chibar2 = 0.034.

erogeneity and how to improve their relationship with their family.

For the future work, this study will continually use the 1996-2007 panel data with the time-varying covariates analysis. People with poor health have higher hazard rates of divorce or separation, in particular as people being in poor health increase the hazard rates after retirement, other things being equal. Few changes in earnings or household's income may provide a stable marriage following retirement.

6. Acknowledgements

The authors would like to thank the Population and Health Research Centre, Bureau of Health Promotion for providing the Survey of Health and Living Status of the Middle Aged and Elderly in Taiwan data. Thanks also to the Korea National Research Foundation for providing partially funding of this research. The number is: NRF-2011-220-B00027.

REFERENCES

[1] M. Schoenbaum, "The Health Status and Labour Force Behaviour of the Elderly in Taiwan," Research Report, University of Michigan, Ann Arbour, 1995, pp. 95-32.

[2] C. Chen, "Health Status and Health-Care Utilisation of the Elderly in Taiwan," In: C. Chen, A. I. Hermalin, S. Hu and J. P. Smith, Eds., *Emerging Social Economic Welfare Programs for Aging in Taiwan in a World Content*, The Institute of Economics, Academia Sinica, Taipei, 1999, pp. 279-303.

[3] M. Chang, "A Longitudinal Study on Living Arrangements of the Elderly in Taiwan," In: C. Chen, A. I. Her-

malin, S. Hu and J. P. Smith, Eds., *Emerging Social Economic Welfare Programs for Aging in Taiwan in a World Content*, The Institute of Economics, Academia Sinica, Taipei, 1999, pp. 43-64.

[4] A. I. Hermalin, C. Roan and M. Chang, "The Economic Status of the Elderly in Taiwan," In: C. Chen, A. I. Hermalin, S. Hu and J. P. Smith, Eds., *Emerging Social Economic Welfare Programs for Aging in Taiwan in a World Content*, The Institute of Economics, Academia Sinica, Taipei, 1999, pp. 157-203.

[5] R. Yu and Y. Chang, "The Retirement Behaviour of Public Sector Employees in Taiwan," Working Paper, The Institute of Economics, Academia Sinica, Taipei, 2004 (in Chinese).

[6] W. Hung, "Duration Analysis for Retirement Decisions in Taiwan," *Journal of Risk Management*, Vol. 10, No.3, 2008, pp. 259-278.

[7] P. Moen, J. E. Kim and H. Hofmeister, "Couples' Work/ Retirement Transitions, Gender, and Marital Quality," *Social Psychology Quarterly*, Vol. 64, No. 1, 2001, pp. 55-71.

[8] M. Szinovacz, "Couples' Employment/Retirement Patterns and Perceptions of Marital Quality," *Research on Aging*, Vol. 18, No. 2, 1996, pp. 243-268.

[9] D. Vaus and Y. Wells, "I Married Him for Better or for Worse But Not for Lunch: Retirement and Marriage," *The 8th Australian Family Research Conference*, Melbourne, 12-14 February 2003, pp. 1-22.

[10] W. S. Shaw, T. L. Patterson, S. Semples and I. Grant, "Health and Well-Being in Retirement: A Summary of Theories and Their Implications," In: M. H. and V. B. V. Hasselt, Eds., *Handbook of Clinical Geropsychology*, Plenum, New York, 1998, pp. 383-409.

[11] A. M. Pienta, "Partners in Marriage: An Analysis of Husbands' and Wives' Retirement Behavior," *The Journal of Applied Gerontology*, Vol. 22, No. 3, 2003, pp. 340-358.

[12] D. B. Smith and P. Moen, "Retirement Satisfaction for Retirees and Their Spouses: Do Gender and the Retirement Decision-Making Process Matter?" *Journal of Family Issues*, Vol. 25, No. 2, 2004, pp. 262-285.

[13] T. Lancaster, "The Econometric Analysis of Transition Data," Cambridge University, New York, 1990.

[14] D. W. Hosmer, S. Lemeshow and S. May, "Applied Survival Analysis: Regression Modelling of Time to Event Data," 2nd Edition, John Wiley & Sons, Inc., New York, 2008.

[15] M. A. Cleves, W. W. Gould and R. G. Gutierrez, "An Introduction to Survival Analysis Using Stata," 3rd Edition, Stata Corporation, College Station, 2008.

[16] P. Diamond and G. A. Hausman, "Individual Retirement and Saving Behaviour," *Journal of Public Economics*, Vol. 23, No. 1-2, 1984, pp. 81-114.

[17] W. Hung, "An Economic Analysis of Retirement Decisions in Taiwan," Ph.D. Dissertation, School of Economics, Finance and Business, University of Durham, Durham, 2009.

[18] W. Hung and S. Ho, "Duration Analysis of Marriage among the Middle Aged and Elderly in Taiwan," *The Empirical Economics Letters*, Vol. 8, No. 1, 2009, pp. 79-87.

[19] J. P. Klein and M. L. Moeschberger, "Survival Analysis: Techniques for Censored and Truncated Data," 2nd Edition, Springer Science Business Medin, Inc., New York, 2005.

2

An Information Theoretic Approach to Understanding the Micro Foundations of Macro Processes

Sofia B. Villas-Boas[1], **George Judge**[2]
[1]Department of Agricultural and Resource Economics, University of California, Berkeley, USA
[2]Department of Agricultural and Resource Economics and Graduate School, University of California, Berkeley, USA

ABSTRACT

In the context of a simple equilibrium macro process we suggest a probability basis for recovering information regarding the unknown and unobservable micro process, and solving the resulting inverse problem.

Keywords: Empirical Exponential Likelihood; Information Theory

1. Introduction

Policy makers often use macro indicators without knowledge of its allocative and distributive micro impacts. Although observations from economic behavior systems are micro and statistical in nature, the world we perceive is a macro one and the data we work with are often single valued in content. In addition, the dynamic transition process between the two worlds-economic systems often remains hidden. Given single valued-point equilibrium outcome data, in this paper we seek a probabilistic way to unlock the corresponding hidden micro content. In the context of an invisible hand economy, we consider a single market process and the aggregate price data provided by a point equilibrium in the price and quantity space. Visualizing an economic-market process that involves agents in the form of buyers and sellers that are driven by an optimization principle, our objective is to use these data to recover information at the micro level and to provide a measure of the stability-order of the process. Following a traditional economic equilibrium approach, leads to imaginary individuals coming to an imaginary market with ready-made bid and offer prices. Traditionally, this leads to conceptual demand and supply functions involving unknown and unobservable parameters and a solution that satisfies a single valued equilibrium concept. In a traditional context, this framework becomes the basis for a range of logical conclusions involving such concepts as excess demand and supply, movements along a demand of supply function, and shifts in the demand and supply functions that are not observable.

Realistically, what evolves data wise from a market equilibrium, is a point in the price-quantity space that summarizes the aggregate data-information regarding buyers and sellers. Assuming a general price-quantity relationship, this macro-aggregate data point is useful in a summary way, but what would be more useful from a market performance standpoint, is information on the price probability-frequency distributions underlying the unknown and unobservable possible micro prices that produced the single macro state equilibrium result. Capturing the unknown underlying discrete micro state space price frequencies from the information gained by observing the aggregate-average price outcome data, requires the solution of an inverse problem. This type of information recovery provides a way of interpreting the outcome of micro market experiments as a probability measure on a defined discrete state space. The resulting discrete price-quantity state space probabilities 1) provide a bridge between the macro and the micro properties of the market process while avoiding the underlying micro details and 2) a basis for understanding agent behavior and the efficiency of market processes-outcomes. The recovered probabilities may be used to indicate how agents' behavior may change the probabilities, and thereby affect the stability, competitive nature, and informational content of the market process, and the resulting macro indicator/outcome.

The paper proceeds as follows: given an aggregate market equilibrium price and quantity, in Section 2 we develop a model for the price state space and Section 3 outlines the conceptual and methodological basis for recovering, in an informational-probability context, the underlying micro distributions of the unobserved possible state space prices. Section 4 presents an illustrative example and in Section 5 we summarize the implications of the micro-macro bridge.

2. Modeling the Price State Space

As a basis for defining the information recovery problem, we model a single market process where the aggregate-average outcome price $\bar{x}$, is a result of market experiments carried out a large number of times. Each experiment reveals one of n potentially equally likely price outcomes $x_i = \{1, 2, \cdots, n\}$. Assume as the market operates, the experiment is repeated a large number of times, but the only thing we know is the average price resulting from these trials. Given this sample of price information, and nothing else, what probability-price frequency p_i should we assign to each of the possible x_i price outcomes? With an average price of $\bar{x}$, the resulting moment constraint

$$\sum_{i=1}^{n} p_i x_i = \bar{x}, \qquad (1)$$

can be satisfied by an infinite number of probability mass functions(pmfs)-price frequencies. In other words, there are a large number of price frequencies that can lead to a mean market price $\bar{x}$. The price information recovery problem is how to choose one of the possible pmfs-price frequencies, to represent the market price behavior. The sample x_i frequencies are not given to us. However, the probability space defines, in exponential form, a unique family of pmfs-price frequencies, $\sum_{i=1}^{n} f_i u(x_i)$, where f_i represents the frequency of the price outcomes equal to the prescribed mean. Consequently, the problem may be solved in a statistical information theoretic context by Lagrange multiplier-extremum methods.

3. An Information Theoretic Approach to Information Recovery

One way to solve this ill-posed inverse problem for the unknown probabilities p_i, without making a large number of assumptions, imposing artificial information to make the problem tractable, or introducing additional information, is to formulate it as an extremum problem. This type of extremum problem is in many ways analogous to allocating probabilities in a contingency table where p_i and q_i are, respectively, the observed and reference distributions of a given event. This is a well developed information theoretic method, and the solution is achieved by minimizing the divergence between the two sets of probabilities, as the data will permit. That is, we optimize a goodness-of-fit (pseudo-distance measure) criterion, subject to the data-moment space constraint. One attractive set of divergence measures (see [1,2]) involves the following Cressie-Read(CR) power divergence distance measure, ([3,4])

$$\text{CR} = I(p,q,\gamma) = \frac{1}{\gamma(1+\gamma)} \sum_{i=1}^{N} \left(p_i \left[\left(\frac{p_i}{q_i} \right)^{\gamma} - 1 \right] \right) \qquad (2)$$

where γ is an arbitrary and unspecified parameter.

In the context of recovering the unknown price probability distribution, if we use the CR criterion (2), this suggests we seek the following extremum solution:

$$\hat{p} = \arg\min_p \Big[I(p,q,\gamma) \mid \sum_{i=1}^{N} p_i x_i = \bar{x}, \sum_{i=1}^{N} p_i = 1, p_i \ge 0 \Big] \qquad (3)$$

where the reference distribution q is specified as a uniform distribution.

In the limit, as γ, ranges from 1 to 1, *a family of CR functionals emerge*. Three variants of $I(p, q, \gamma)$ have received explicit attention in the literature [5]. If we assume for expository purposes that the reference distribution is discrete uniform, $q_i = 1/N \;\; \forall i$, and let the CR statistic $\gamma \to 0$, then $I(p, q, \gamma)$ converges to the maximum empirical exponential likelihood (MEEL the criterion $\sum_{i=1}^{N} p_i \ln(p_i)$. This criterion is also known in the literature as the maximum entropy solution of [5].[1] What emerges with the MEEL solution is a descriptive measure of the corresponding unknown price probability distribution(s), which in our case is consistent with the mean of prices. Solutions for these distance measures cannot be written in closed form and must be numerically determined.

Information Theoretic Formulation

If, consistent with our multinomial formulation, we use the CR criterion with $\gamma \to 0$, we select the probabilities that maximize

$$H(p) = -\sum_{i=1}^{N} p_i \ln(p_i) \qquad (4)$$

subject to

$$\sum_{i=1}^{N} p_i x_i = \bar{x} \qquad (5)$$

and the condition that the probabilities must sum to one

$$\sum_{i=1}^{N} p_i = 1 \qquad (6)$$

The corresponding Lagrangian for the extremum problem is

$$L = -\sum_{i=1}^{N} p_i \ln(p_i) + \lambda\left(\bar{x} - \sum_{i=1}^{N} p_i x_i\right) + \varphi\left(1 - \sum_{i=1}^{N} p_i\right) \qquad (7)$$

Since H is strictly concave, there is a unique interior

[1]When $\gamma \to -1$, then $I(p,q,\gamma)$ leads to the estimation criterion that is equivalent to the [6] maximum empirical likelihood (MEL) criterion $-\sum_{i=1}^{N} \ln(p_i)$. The MEL criterion is consistent with a result that assigns discrete mass across the possible outcomes, and in the sense of objective function analogies, it is closest to the classical maximum-likelihood approach.

solution and solving the first-order conditions yields the exponential result

$$p_i = \frac{\exp\left(-p_i\hat{\lambda}\right)}{\sum_{i=1}^{N}\exp\left(-p_i\hat{\lambda}\right)} \quad (8)$$

for the ith outcome. In this context, the chosen distribution is, out of the possible solutions, the one that is numerically identical with the frequency distribution that can be realized in the greatest number of ways. In other words the frequency distribution can be realized experimentally in more ways than any other distribution that satisfies the mean constraint. We note again that $p(\lambda)$ is a member of a canonical exponential family with mean $\bar{x} = \sum_{i=1}^{N} p_i x_i$.

This price formulation provides one way to express the probabilistic-statistical nature of micro process-data. It recognizes that demand and supply transactions-outcomes may occur, with a different probability, at any place in the price state space ensemble. The monotonic probability distributions are different from quantum economic theory formulations that suggest symmetric mean based distributions (see [7]).

4. An Illustrative Example

As an illustration of an ill-posed economic inverse problem, assume in the context of the previous sections, that the possible price space may be defined by the first six integers, $x_i = 1, 2, \cdots, 6$. The only information given is that the average price outcome for a large number of independent trials is $\bar{x}$. There are an infinite number of probability distributions supported on $\{1, 2, \cdots, 6\}$ that have a mean of $\bar{x}$.[2] In a situation like this, if we follow the MEEL formulation (4) we would select the probabilities that maximize

$$H(p) = -\sum_{i=1}^{6} p_i \ln(p_i) \quad (9)$$

with corresponding Lagrangian

$$\begin{aligned} L(p) &= -\sum_{i=1}^{6} p_i \ln(p_i) \\ &+ \lambda\left(\bar{x} - \sum_{i=1}^{6} p_i x_i\right) + \varphi\left(1 - \sum_{i=1}^{6} p_i\right) \end{aligned} \quad (10)$$

If $\bar{x} \in (1, 6)$, the constraint set is non-empty and compact. Given that $H(p)$ is strictly concave, there is a unique interior solution to the problem. By solving the first order conditions, the MEEL probability exponential distribution places the weight

$$p_i = \frac{\exp\left(-p_i\hat{\lambda}\right)}{\sum_{i=1}^{6}\exp\left(-p_i\hat{\lambda}\right)} \quad (11)$$

The resulting MEEL price frequency distribution estimates for various values of $\bar{x}$ are presented in **Table 1**.

The maximum of the CR functional $H(\hat{p})$ and minimum micro price information occurs with a mean of $\bar{x} = 3.5$ and the corresponding uniform price distribution. Other monotonic distributions of the state space price probabilities are, using a MEEL distance measure, in the form of exponential distributions.

5. Summary

There are well developed economic general equilibrium price and allocation models over space and time. In microeconomics, events decisions-actions take place instantaneously or in a moment in time. In this paper, using information theoretic methods, we have attempted, in a probability context to capture the price implications of this type of action-outcome process. It is important to recognize a world where micro price transactions may reflect non-uniform distributions and to evaluate the resulting allocation and distribution implications. Economic data reflecting average outcomes abounds. Creative use of the information theoretic methods introduced in this paper should permit the recovery, in a probabilistic form, of information from the aggregate data and identify unusual

Table 1. Estimated MEEL distributions for various $\bar{x}$.

$\bar{x}$	$\hat{p}_1$	$\hat{p}_2$	$\hat{p}_3$	$\hat{p}_4$	$\hat{p}_5$	$\hat{p}_6$	$H(\hat{p})$
2.0	0.381	0.295	0.210	0.124	0.038	0.000	1.367
3.0	0.247	0.207	0.174	0.146	0.123	0.103	1.748
3.5	0.167	0.167	0.167	0.167	0.167	0.167	1.792
4.0	0.103	0.123	0.146	0.174	0.207	0.247	1.748
5.0	0.021	0.038	0.072	0.136	0.255	0.478	1.367

$\bar{x}$ is the mean value of the distribution, $\hat{p}_i$ $i = 1, \cdots, 6$ the frequencies, and $H(p)$ a measure of uncertainty.

[2]Those familiar with a theoretical basis for information recovery, will recognize that this could also be [5] variant of a six-sided die problem, where the average is given for a large number of rolls of the die (see [8], p. 12).

price variability and evaluate micro behavior outcomes.

While the focus in this paper has for expository purposes been on a particular problem in economics, the implications are general for all of the behavioral sciences. For example, consider the hidden dynamics of voting systems in political science, as we move from individuals voting to the general results of an election. Or in a general game-decision context the hidden dynamics and an unobservable stochastic-probabilistic micro components.

6. Acknowledgements

We thank the editor and an anonymous referee for the comments and Mike George, Wendy Tam Cho, Alexander Gorban, Leo Simon, and David Wolpert for great comments and suggestions.

REFERENCES

[1] A. Gorban and G. Judge, "Entropy the Markov Ordering Approach," *Entropy*, Vol. 12, No. 5, 2009, pp. 1145-1193.

[2] G. Judge and R. Mittelhammer, "An Information Theoretic Approach to Econometrics," Cambridge University Press, Cambridge, 2012.

[3] N. Cressie and T. Read, "Multinomial Goodness of Fit Tests," *Journal of Royal Statistical Society*, Vol. 46, No. 3, 1984, pp. 448-464.

[4] T. Read and N. Cressie, "Goodness of Fit Statistics for Discrete Multivariate Data," Springer Verlag, New York, 1988.

[5] E. Jaynes, "Information Theory and Statistical Mechanics," In: K. W. Ford, Ed., *Statistical Physics*, W. A. Benjamin, New York, 1963, pp. 181-218.

[6] A. Owen, "Empirical Likelihood," Chapman and Hall, New York, 2001.

[7] E. Smith and D. Foley, "Classical Thermodynamics and Economic General Equilibrium Theory," *Journal of Economic Dynamics and Control*, Vol. 32, No. 1, 2008, pp. 7-65.

[8] A. Golan, G. Judge and D. Miller, "Maximum Entropy Econometrics," John Wiley and Sons, Chichester, 1996.

3

Should We Overlook All Altruistic Behavior by Politicians?

Shunsuke Sekiguchi
Ishinomaki Senshu University, Ishinomaki, Japan

ABSTRACT

Not all policies benefit their intended targets even though they are motivated by political altruism. This paper analyzes how the frequency of altruistic behavior changes depending on whether consumers (*i.e.*, the electorate) or producers (*i.e.*, politicians) bear the responsibility. It compares the strict liability rule, which means the altruist must bear all damages, with the no liability rule, which means the recipient must bear all damages. It finds that under the no liability rule, if politicians are altruist, the frequency of altruistic behavior is less than under the strict liability rule. Therefore, the paper shows that if politicians were altruists, they would prefer the strict liability rule.

Keywords: Altruism; Liability; Caveat Emptor; Caveat Venditor

1. Introduction

Altruistic behavior is that the behavior is motivated in improving the target's welfare. However, in the political context, not all policies benefit their intended targets even though they are motivated by political altruism. For example, although helping the poor is generally considered to be altruistic behavior, some policies do not always help the underprivileged; in the same way, some protection policies for marginal producers also benefit not marginal producers but wealthier producers. This paper thus analyzes how the frequency of altruistic behavior changes depending on which party (*i.e.*, producers or consumers) bears the responsibility for liability.

There are two types of statues. The first type of statue is developed by looking at certain models, such as the disabled, seriously ill patients, and orphans. This is a real image. We know that there are many poor people with many difficulties. The second statue is considered to be a "flight of fancy." Although there is no model in the real world, artists create one and stretch it to suit this purpose. As mentioned, it is convenient for politicians to create and manipulate such statues. If politicians benefit from manipulating public sector, then they aim to expand the public sector through both real and unreal statues, which both make certain goods and/or services public.

Particularly in political situations, we should change our traditional attitude of overlooking all altruistic behavior by politicians. If politicians are altruists, they only offer real statues. If politicians are hypocrites, but also use the word "altruism" in their rhetoric, they also create unreal statues. However, it is hard for us to distinguish whether incumbent and/or candidate politicians are real altruists or not. Therefore, altruistic behavior, at first glance, burdens us with irrevocable costs compared with its benefits.

In this paper, we assume that politicians are altruists rather than selfish individuals or egoists as is generally assumed. In general, it is difficult to distinguish between altruists and selfish individuals because many people seek to gain utility through altruistic behavior. Therefore, there is no difference from the viewpoint of rational choice[1], but only a difference in the approach. For the sake of simplifying the discussion, we distinguish between them based on whether a person is interested in other people or not. Through this assumption, we analyze whether politicians prefer to make self-interested rules.

The remainder of this paper is organized as follows. Section 2 is literature reviews, Section 3 is focused on the relation between a liability and altruistic behavior, Section 4 is the theoretical considerations, and Section 5 is the implications and concluding remarks.

2. Literature Review

2.1. The Benefits of and Motivation behind Altruism

A number of economists have studied altruistic behavior,

[1]We consider that each is rational.

notably the "Rotten Kid Theorem" of Becker [1], the "Samaritan's dilemma" presented by Buchanan [2,3], and Harnay and Marcia no's study of the economics of altruism [4]. These studies analyzed how the welfare state affects a family when policymakers behave altruistically. In general, altruistic behavior is defined as a behavior that supplies a benefit in return for nothing. Supplying in this context includes not only supplying goods and services but also subsidizing some of the costs. However, in the context of studying altruism, what is the benefit of altruistic behavior?

From an absolutism standpoint, it is straightforward to define the concept of "benefit." By contrast, relativists always consider that each sense of value (e.g., what is good, what is bad, and so on) is not always equal but rather situation-dependent. Although these concepts of absolutism and relativism are extreme views, it is easy to imagine all people have similar moral standards: not to steal, not to invade another's property, respect for human rights, and so on. However, it is also easy to imagine that each person has different individual standards.

Buchanan used the principle originally presented by Frank Knight of "relatively absolute absolutes" to advance the study of ethics and/or constitutional choice [5]. Using this principle allows us to focus on the main theme of this paper, namely how to facilitate altruistic behavior, by defining "benefit." In this paper, we confine the term "benefit" as follows: whatever a recipient desires an altruist to do, the altruist does. In other words, we exclude what an altruist believes is useful for a recipient.

2.2. Definition of Altruism in the Political Context

In light of the above definition, altruistic behavior in the political context means devoting resources to the poor, such as marginal consumers/producers or the elderly. However, many politicians seek to divert resources to the poor for the sake of winning an election or abusing public sector. For example, policies for marginal consumers/producers might also make rich people richer rather than improving the situation for the poor. Likewise, although there are some poor elderly people, many elderly people own their own houses and are cash-rich.

Indeed, elderly voters are often targeted by politicians because of their electoral influence compared with other generations. In general, since the voting cost for elderly people is relatively low and the benefit of voting is relatively high, their voting rate increases. Representing those groups that have the most electoral influence is one of the most relevant policies for politicians to attain their objectives. Politicians tend to persuade voters to regard a trivial problem as a serious problem.

3. Liability and Altruistic Behavior

This paper analyzes how the frequency of altruistic behavior changes depending on whether producers or consumers bear the responsibility.

There are risks in the purchase of all goods and services. For example, a car purchased by an individual could have a defect that causes him or her to have an accident. Likewise, purchased food could contain impurities that negatively affect health. Although it is important for producers to prevent these cases in order to build a strong brand image, it is expensive to confirm whether all products are safe or not. Regulating producers to do so would only move the costs to consumers depending on the relative price elasticity of the products in question[2].

Many studies have analyzed this so-called liability problem. Who (consumers or producers) should bear the costs of product defects? A number of studies have focused on this question from the viewpoint of the welfare state. Under the rule caveat emptor, consumers must be aware that they cannot recover damages from the producer (hereafter termed the "no liability rule"). By contrast, under caveat venditor, the consumer is able tore cover damages from the producer ("strict liability rule") (see Buchanan [5]; Brown [6]; Hamada [7]; Tanaka [8]).

We can imagine a similar case in a political situation in the short-term. Although the strict liability rule is rational compared with the no liability rule, it may not always be true in the context of altruistic behavior. This is because, according to Janssen and Mendys-Kamphorst [9], altruistic behavior can be displayed not only by an altruist but also by an egoist[3].

4. Theoretical Considerations

This section presents a simple model in order to analyze whether the no liability rule or strict liability rule encourages altruistic behavior. In this model, we assume that there are two people: a recipient and an altruist. For the sake of simplicity, we also assume that the recipient cannot reject all the altruist's offers.

The recipient cares about his or her own consumption as well as the graces given by the altruist. Thus, the recipient's utility function U_r is given by (r denotes recipient)

$$U_r = U_r(X_r) + B(g_a). \quad (1)$$

Where X_r is his or her consumption of composite goods and $B(g_a)$ is the benefit supplied by the altruist. It is further assumed that $U'(X_r) > 0, U''(X_r) < 0, B'(g_a) > 0, B''(g_a) < 0$ respectively. The recipient's budget constant is thus given by

[2]If the elasticity of the consumer is less than that of the producer, the former bears more costs than does the latter.

[3]In this paper, we rephrase "egoist" as "hypocrite."

$$p_x X_r \le I_r \tag{2}$$

where p_x is the price of X_r and I_r is the recipient's income.

The altruist cares about both his or her own consumption as well as the recipient's consumption. The altruist's utility function U_a is thus given by (a denotes altruist)

$$U_a = U_a(X_a) + V(U_r). \tag{3}$$

Where X_a is the altruist's consumption of composite goods and $V(U_r)$ is the indirect utility, which is found by recognizing the recipient's utility. The altruist's budget constraint is given by

$$p_X X_a + w_g g_a \le I_a \tag{4}$$

where w_g is the cost of the altruist's behavior and I_a is the altruist's income. It is thus assumed that $U'(X_a) > 0, U''(X_a) < 0, B'(g_a) > 0, B''(g_a) < 0$ respectively.

4.1. Without Risks

In this case, the first-order condition for maximizing utility with composite goods and altruistic behavior is

$$\frac{U'}{p_X} = \frac{V^B}{w_g}. \tag{5}$$

This means that the altruist equals the weighted marginal utility of composite goods with the weighted marginal utility of altruistic behavior.

4.2. With Risks

4.2.1. No Liability for Altruistic Behavior

In this case, when the altruist injures the recipient, damage $D(g_a)$ is borne by the recipient. This paper assumes that e represents the probability of the recipient benefitting from the actions of the altruist. The probability *e* is an exogenous variable and indicates the difficulty of altruistic behavior. In other words, the more *e* increases, the higher is the probability of supplying a benefit. The recipient's expected utility function is thus given by

$$U_r = U_r(X_r) + eB(g_a) - (1-e)D(g_a) \tag{6}$$

Substituting Equation (5) into (3), we obtain the following

$$U_a = U_a(X_a) + V\left[U_r(X_r) + eB(g_a) - (1-e)D(g_a)\right] \tag{7}$$

$$\text{s.t.} p_X X_a + w_g g_a \le I_a$$

In this case, the first-order condition for maximizing utility with composite goods and altruistic behavior is

$$\frac{U'}{p_X} = \frac{eV^B - (1-e)V^D}{w_g}. \tag{8}$$

We can thus depict **Figure 1**; V^B and V^D are defined below.

In **Figure 1**, MU_x means $\frac{\partial U_a}{\partial X_a}$ and MU_g means $\frac{\partial U_a}{\partial g_a}$.

The figure shows that the level of altruistic behavior declines $(g0 \to g1)$ under risk rather than under certainty. If $V^B = V^D$, then the probability *e*, at least, must meet $e > \frac{1}{2}$[4].

4.2.2. Strict Liability for Altruistic Behavior

In this case, if the altruist injures the recipient, the damage is borne by the altruist through insurance, which is supplied in a perfectly competitive market. The recipient's utility function is thus given by

$$U_r = U_r(X_r) + eB(g_a). \tag{9}$$

The altruist's utility function and budget constraint are given by

$$\begin{aligned} &U_a = U_a(X_a) + V(U_r) \\ &\text{s.t.} p_X X_a + w_g g_a + r \le I_a \\ &r = (1-e)(g_a) \end{aligned} \tag{10}$$

The first-order condition for maximizing utility with composite goods and altruistic behavior is

$$\frac{U'}{p_X} = \frac{eV^B}{w_g + (1-e)D^g}. \tag{11}$$

From Equations (8) and (11), we can find the function of *e*, which is depicted in **Figures 2-10**. These figures allow us to analyze whether the strict liability rule or no liability rule provides greater incentive for altruistic behavior. Since the altruist acts to equalize the marginal utility between altruistic behavior with risk and the consumption of composite goods, we can illustrate nine patterns depending on V^B and V^D. These figures suggest that the strict liability rule promotes altruistic behavior with a low degree of probability. In other words, if the probability of supplying benefits is low, then the strict liability rule encourages altruistic behavior.

These figures show that real altruists prefer the strict liability rule to the no liability rule in eight of 11 patterns (*i.e.*, 73%), whereas altruists prefer the no liability rule only in one pattern. However, even in this pattern, when the probability of success is low, the altruist prefers the strict liability rule. In other words, if politicians were

[4]This is because the right-hand side of (7), $\frac{eV^B - (1-e)V^D}{w_g} > 0$, must be larger than 0. Solving $\frac{eV^B - (1-e)V^D}{w_g} > 0$ for *e* yields the above condition, $e > 1/2$.

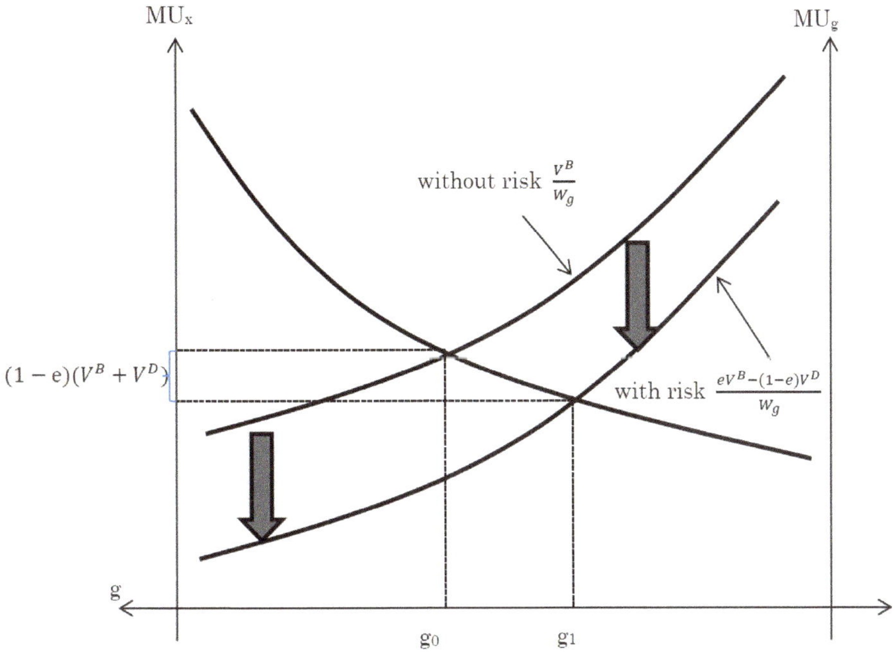

Figure 1. Changing the recipient's marginal utility for composite goods and altruistic behavior.

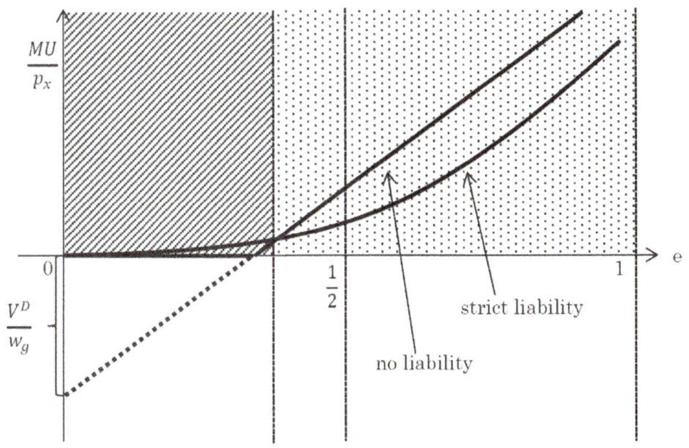

The shaded area illustrates the range where the marginal utility of altruistic behavior under the strict liability rule is larger than that under the no liability rule.

Figure 2. Under $V^B > V^D$.

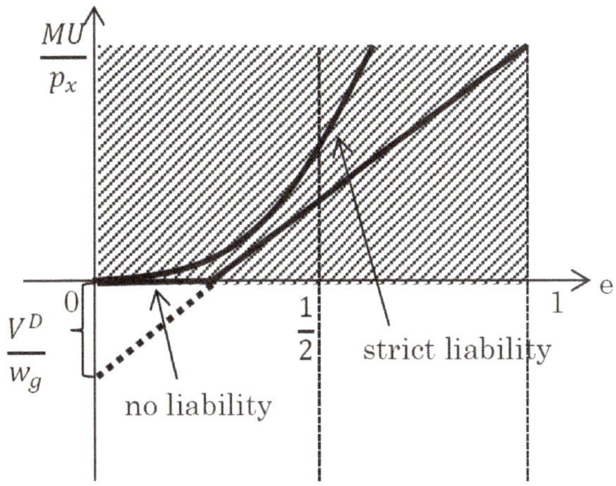

Figure 4. Under $V^B > V^D$.

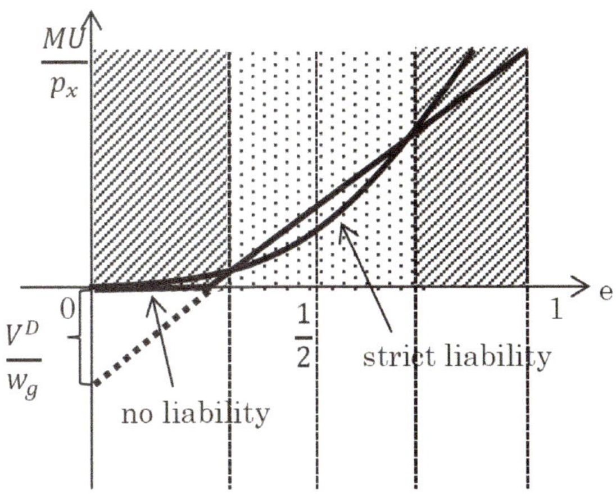

Figure 3. Under $V^B > V^D$.

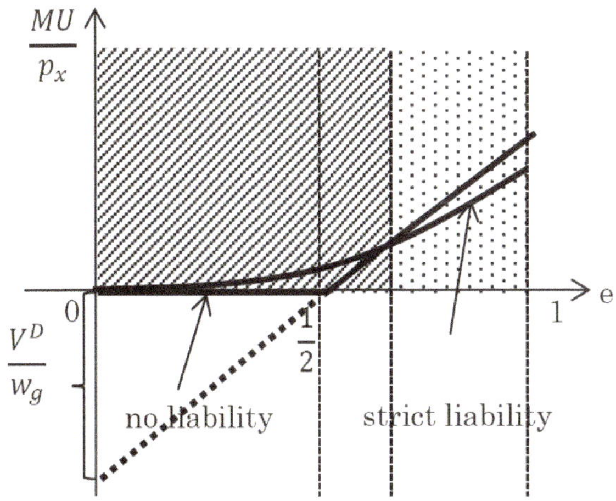

Figure 5. Under $V^B > V^D$.

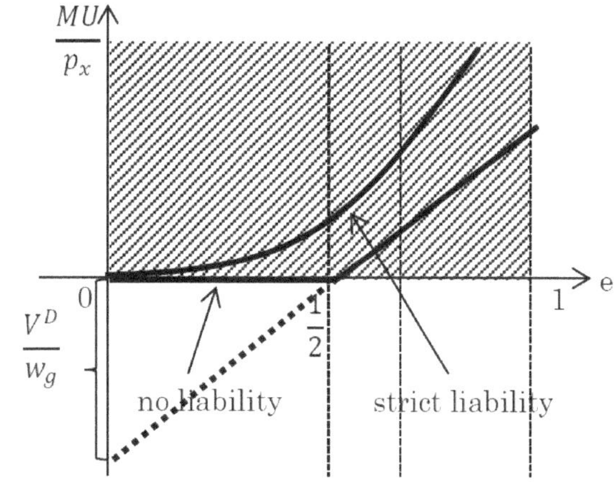

Figure 6. Under $V^B > V^D$.

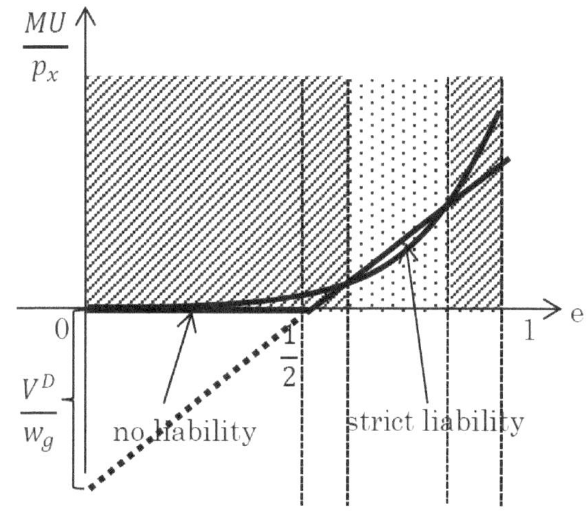

Figure 7. Under $V^B > V^D$.

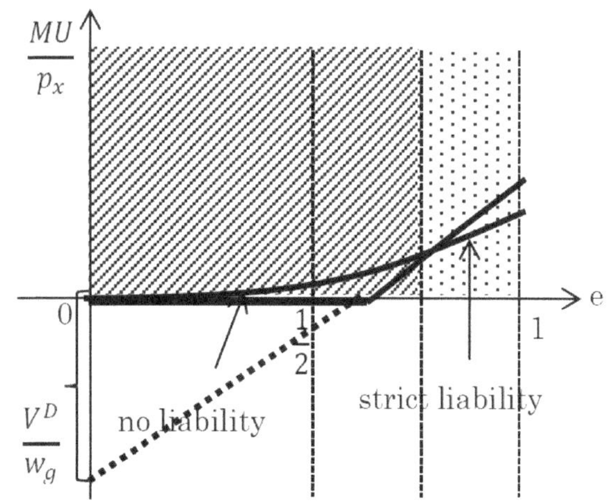

Figure 8. Under $V^B > V^D$.

altruists, they would prefer the strict liability rule.

5. Implications and Concluding Remarks

Not all policies benefit their intended targets even though

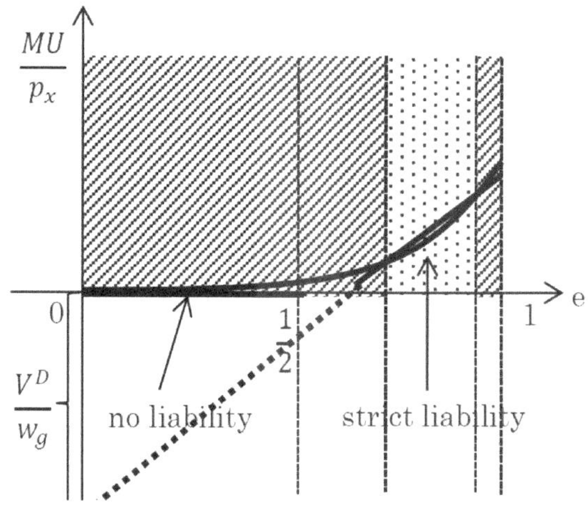

Figure 9. Under $V^B > V^D$.

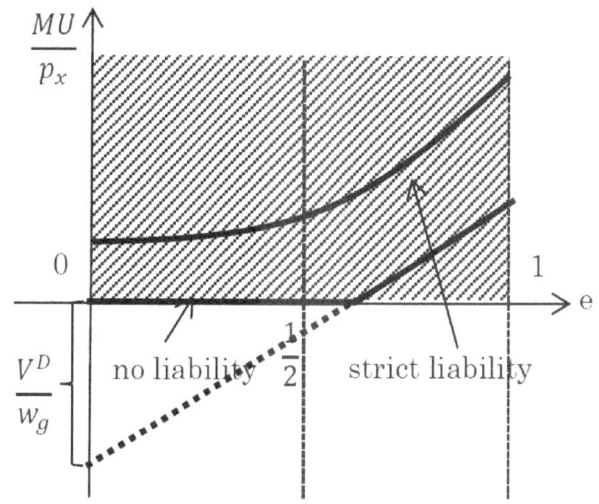

Figure 10. Under $V^B > V^D$.

they are motivated by political altruism (ex. infant death by vaccination for reducing infant mortality, inefficiency by land-use zoning for encouraging the efficient use of land, and so on.). The presented findings suggest that even if the electorate recognizes that certain policies were mistakenly implemented, politicians would not bear personal damage. In this situation, they may be defeated in the next election, but they would not bear the damage themselves. In other words, the no liability rule does not restrain a politician's behavior and overlooks irresponsible activity. This lack of restraint on policymaking would occur regardless of whether politicians use altruism as a means to pushing themselves forward. Most significantly, we cannot anticipate politics by altruists under the no liability rule. According to the presented results, under the no liability rule, even if we hope politicians are altruists, altruism abstains from participation in politics.

While we acknowledge that the concept of altruism is necessary, we should not accept it without reservations. If we desire a realization of politics based on altruism, paradoxically, we must become stricter on the use of altruism.

6. Acknowledgements

I thank the useful comments by anonymous referee, Kazuyoshi Kurokawa (Hosei University), Susumu Nagai (Hosei University), Hayato Nagase (Mitsui Fudosan), and all members of Kurokawa seminar.

REFERENCES

[1] G. S. Becker, "A Theory of Social Interactions," *Journal of Political Economy*, Vol. 82, No. 6, 1974, pp. 1063-1093.

[2] J. M. Buchanan, "In Defense of Caveat Emptor," *University of Chicago Law Review*, Vol. 38, No. 1, 1970, pp. 64-73.

[3] J. M. Buchanan, "Altruism, Morality, and Economic Theory," Russell Sage Foundation, New York, 1975.

[4] S. Harnay and A. Marciano, "Should I Help My Neighbor? Self-Interest, Altruism and Economic Analyses of Rescue Laws," *European Journal of Law and Economics*, Vol. 28, No. 2, 2009, pp. 103-131.

[5] J. M. Buchanan, "Essays on the Political Economy," University of Hawaii Press, Honolulu, 1989.

[6] J. P. Brown, "Toward an Economic Theory of Liability," *Journal of Legal Studies*, Vol. 2, No. 2, 1973, p. 323.

[7] K. Hamada, "Liability Rules and Income Distribution in Product Liability," *American Economic Review*, Vol. 66, No. 1, 1976. pp. 228-234.

[8] K. Tanaka, "The Coase Theorem in Product Liability: Buchanan's Case," *Sophia Economic Review*, Vol. 45, No. 1-2, 2003, pp. 149-152.

[9] M. C. W. Janssen and E. Mendys-Kamphorst, "The Price of a Price: On the Crowding out and in of Social Norms," *Journal of Economic Behavior and Organization*, Vol. 55, No. 3, 2004. pp. 377-395.

Asset Prices, Nominal Rigidities, and Monetary Policy: Role of Price Indexation

Kengo Nutahara[1,2]
[1]Department of Economics, Senshu University, Kanagawa, Japan
[2]The Canon Institute for Global Studies, Tokyo, Japan

ABSTRACT

A recent paper by Carlstrom and Fuerst ["Asset Prices, Nominal Rigidities, and Monetary Policy," *Review of Economic Dynamics*, Vol. 10, 2007, pp. 256-275] finds that monetary policy response to share prices is a source of equilibrium indeterminacy because an increase in inflation implies a high real marginal cost and low share prices in a sticky-price economy. We find that if the New Keynesian Phillips curve has a lagged inflation term caused by price indexation, this effect is weakened. Moreover, equilibrium indeterminacy caused by the monetary policy response to share prices never arises if all the firms that cannot re-optimize their prices follow price indexation.

Keywords: Asset Prices; Monetary Policy; Equilibrium Determinacy; Price Indexation

1. Introduction

A paper by Carlstrom and Fuerst [1] shows that equilibrium indeterminacy arises if monetary policy responds to share prices in a standard sticky-price economy. An increase in inflation reduces firm's profits, and the share prices decline, since they reflect the firm's profits. Then, the monetary policy response to share prices implicitly weakens overall reactions to inflation. This is a source of equilibrium indeterminacy.

In this paper, we extend the model of [1] by introducing price indexation and show that equilibrium determinacy is likely to arise. Under price indexation, the New Keynesian Philips curve is hybrid and has a lagged inflation term. It is shown that the effect of an increase in inflation on real marginal costs is weakened through the hybrid Phillips curve. Moreover, equilibrium indeterminacy caused by the monetary policy response to share prices never arises if all the firms that cannot re-optimize their prices follow price indexation.

An increase in inflation increases the real marginal cost under the sticky-price setting without price indexation, since a fraction of firms cannot change their prices. This increase in the real marginal cost implies low share prices. Then, the monetary policy response to share prices implicitly weakens overall reactions to inflation. Contrary to this, firms following price indexation can keep their real marginal cost constant in the long run since the past inflation reflects this increase in inflation.

[2] emphasize the inflation persistence by empirical analyses, and [3] develop a model with the hybrid New Keynesian Phillips curve. Many state-of-the-art DSGE models a la [4-6] employ price indexation. Therefore, it is important to consider the type of New Keynesian Phillips curve used when we investigate the relationship between monetary policy and share prices.

The rest of this paper is organized as follows. Section 2 introduces our model. Section 3 presents the main results and their interpretation. Finally, Section 4 presents our concluding remarks.

2. The Model

We employ a standard sticky-price model with shares, like [1]. The difference between our model and theirs is that we introduce price indexation in sticky prices.

2.1. Households

The household begins period t with M_t cash balances, B_t one-period nominal bonds that pay R_t gross risk-free interest rate, S_t shares of stock that sell at price Q_t.

The utility function is

$$U\left(C_t, H_t, \frac{M_{t+1}}{P_t}\right) = \frac{C_t^{1-\sigma}}{1-\sigma} - \phi\frac{H_t^{1+\gamma}}{1+\gamma} + V\left(\frac{M_{t+1}}{P_t}\right), \quad (1)$$

where $\sigma > 0, \phi > 0, \gamma > 0, V(\bullet)$ is increasing in and concave, C_t denotes consumption, H_t denotes labor supply, P_t denotes aggregate price level, and M_{t+1}/P_t denotes real cash balances at the end of period *t*. The budget constraint of household is

$$\begin{aligned} &P_tC_t + M_{t+1} + B_{t+1} + P_tQ_tS_{t+1} \\ &\le P_tW_tH_t + M_t + R_{t-1}B_t + P_t(Q_t + D_t)S_t + X_t \end{aligned} \tag{2}$$

where W_t denotes wage rate, D_t denotes dividends of share, and X_t denotes monetary injection.

The first order conditions of households are

$$\phi C_t^{\sigma} H_t^{\gamma} = W_t,$$

$$C_t^{-\sigma} = \beta C_{t+1}^{-\sigma} \frac{R_t}{\Pi_{t+1}},$$

$$Q_t C_t^{-\sigma} = \beta C_{t+1}^{-\sigma} [Q_{t+1} + D_{t+1}],$$

where $\Pi_{t+1} \equiv P_{t+1}/P_t$ denotes gross inflation. The first equation is the intratemporal optimization condition, the second is the Euler equation for consumption, and the last is the Euler equation for share. The last equation can be rewritten as familiar asset prices equations:

$$Q_t = [Q_{t+1} + D_{t+1}] \frac{\Pi_{t+1}}{R_t}. \tag{3}$$

2.2. Firms

There are competitive final-goods firms and monopolistically competitive intermediate-goods firms and.

The production technology of final-goods firms is

$$Y_t = \left(\int_0^1 Y_t(i)^{(\theta-1)/\theta} \mathrm{d}i \right)^{\theta/(1-\theta)}, \tag{4}$$

where θ denotes the elasticity of substitution and $Y_t(i)$ denotes outputs of intermediate-goods indexed by *i*. The profit maximization of final-goods firms implies the demand curve for $Y_t(i)$ as

$$Y_t(i) = \left(\frac{P_t(i)}{P_t} \right)^{-\theta} Y_t, \tag{5}$$

where $P_t(i)$ denotes the price level of intermediate-goods indexed by *i*. Combining Equations (4) and (5) yields the following price index for intermediate goods:

$$P_t = \left(\int_0^1 P_t(i)^{1-\theta} \mathrm{d}i \right)^{1/(1-\theta)}, \tag{6}$$

The intermediate-goods firms are monopolistically competitive, and they produce intermediate-goods $Y_t(i)$ employing labor $H_t(i)$ from households. The production function of intermediate-goods firm is

$$Y_t(i) = H_t(i), \tag{7}$$

The cost minimization problem implies

$$W_t = Z_t, \tag{8}$$

where Z_t denotes the Lagrange multiplier of the cost minimization problem, and it can be interpreted as the real marginal cost.

Intermediate goods firms set their prices subject to Calvo-type price staggeredness with price indexation.

The price can be re-optimized at period *t* only with probability $1-\kappa$. Among κ firms that cannot re-optimize their prices, a fraction η firms index their prices to the past inflation Π_{t-1}. As in [5,6], under this setting, we obtain the hybrid New Keynesian Phillips curve,

$$\pi_t = \frac{\beta}{1+\eta\beta}\pi_{t+1} + \frac{\eta}{1+\eta\beta}\pi_{t-1} + \lambda z_t, \tag{9}$$

where $\lambda \equiv (1-\kappa)(1-\kappa\beta)/(\kappa(1+\eta\beta))$. π_t and z_t denote the log deviations from a steady state of inflation and the real marginal cost, respectively.

2.3. Monetary Policy

We assume that monetary authority follows a Taylor rule:

$$r_t = \tau\pi_t + \tau_q q_t, \tag{10}$$

where r_t and q_t denote the log-deviations from a steady state of R_t and Q_t, respectively. If $\tau_q > 0$, a central bank responds to asset price fluctuations.

2.4. Equilibrium

The market clearing conditions are

$$H_t = \int H_t(i)\mathrm{d}i, \tag{11}$$

$$B_t = 0, \tag{12}$$

$$S_t = 1. \tag{13}$$

The resource constraint is

$$C_t = Y_t, \tag{14}$$

and the aggregate production function is

$$Y_t = \frac{1}{\Delta_t} H_t, \tag{15}$$

where Δ_t is a measure of resource cost of price dispersion:

$$\Delta_t = \left(\int_0^1 \frac{P_t(i)}{P_t} \right)^{-\theta} \mathrm{d}i. \tag{16}$$

In this paper, we ignore effects from the price dispersion for simplicity.

We focus on a equilibrium where all monopolistic competitive firms are symmetric in this paper.

The firm's profits are paid out as dividends to the shareholders. For simplicity, we assume that the measure of firms is equal to the measure of households.

The dividend of intermediate-goods firms is given by

$$D_t = Y_t - W_t H_t. \quad (17)$$

By Equation (8), the dividend is written by

$$D_t = (1 - Z_t) Y_t. \quad (18)$$

2.5. Linearized System

The linearized system is given as follows:

$$(\sigma + \gamma) c_t = w_t, \quad (19)$$

$$\sigma (c_{t+1} - c_t) = r_t - \pi_{t+1}, \quad (20)$$

$$q_t = \beta q_{t+1} + (1-\beta) d_{t+1} + (\pi_{t+1} - r_t), \quad (21)$$

$$d_t = c_t - \frac{z}{1-z} z_t \quad (22)$$

$$w_t = z_t \quad (23)$$

$$\pi_t = \frac{\beta}{1+\eta\beta} \pi_{t+1} + \frac{\eta}{1+\eta\beta} \pi_{t-1} + \lambda z_t \quad (24)$$

$$r_t = \tau \pi_t + \tau_q q_t \quad (25)$$

where the lower letters denote the log-deviations from a steady state.

As shown by [1], the dividend is given by

$$d_t = -A z_t \quad (26)$$

where

$$A \equiv \frac{z(1+\sigma+) - 1}{(1-z)(\sigma+\gamma)}.$$

We employ an assumption on A following [1].

Assumption 1. $A > 0$.

Under this assumption, an increase in the real marginal cost decreases the dividend.

The equilibrium system is reduced to the following matrix form:

$$\begin{bmatrix} 1 & 0 & \chi & 0 \\ \beta/(1+\eta\beta) & 0 & 0 & 0 \\ 1 & 0 & -(1-\beta)A & \beta \\ 0 & 1 & 0 & - \end{bmatrix} \begin{bmatrix} \pi_{t+1} \\ \pi_t \\ z_{t+1} \\ q_{t+1} \end{bmatrix} = \begin{bmatrix} \tau & 0 & \chi & \tau_q \\ 1 & -\eta/(1+\eta\beta) & -\lambda & 0 \\ \tau & 0 & 0 & 1+\tau_q \\ 1 & 0 & 0 & 0 \end{bmatrix} \begin{bmatrix} \pi_t \\ \pi_{t-1} \\ z_t \\ q_t \end{bmatrix}$$

where

$$\chi \equiv \frac{\sigma}{\sigma+\gamma} > 0.$$

The first equation is the consumption Euler Equation (20); the second, the New Keynesian Phillips curve (24); and the third, the Euler equation for share (21).

In this paper, we impose the following restriction.

Assumption 2. $1 < \tau \le 2$.

We make this assumption to easily prove Proposition 1. However, according to our numerical robustness check, the result in this paper is robust even if $\tau > 2$.

3. Main Results

3.1. Results

The main results of this paper are as follows.

Proposition 1. *Under Assumptions* 1 *and* 2 *a necessary and sufficient condition for equilibrium determinacy is*

$$\tau_q < \tau_q^{\max} \equiv \frac{\lambda(1-\tau)(1+\eta\beta)}{A(1-\eta)(1-\beta)}.$$

If $\tau_q > \tau_q^{\max}$, *there is equilibrium indeterminacy or no stationary equilibrium.*

Proof. See Appendix *Q.E.D.*

At a limit of $\eta = 0$, the threshold $\tau_q^{\max}$ is the same as the threshold in Proposition 1 of Carlstrom and Fuerst (2007).

The threshold $\tau_q^{\max}$ depends on the fraction of price indexation firms, η.

Proposition 2. $\tau_q^{\max}$ *is increasing in* η.

Proof. Since $\lambda \equiv (1-\kappa)(1-\kappa\beta)/(\kappa(1+\eta\beta))$, we obtain

$$\tau_q^{\max} = \frac{(1-\kappa)(1-\kappa\beta)(\tau-1)}{\kappa A(1-\eta)(1-\beta)}. \; Q.E.D.$$

Then, in the case where the fraction of price indexation is large, equilibrium determinacy is likely to arise even if monetary policy responds to share prices. Especially, in the case where $\eta = 1$, equilibrium indeterminacy never arises even if monetary policy responds to share prices.

Proposition 3. *Under Assumptions* 1 *and* 2, *if all the firms follow price indexation,* $\eta = 1$, *then equilibrium determinacy arises.*

Proof. $\lim_{\eta \to 1} \tau_q^{\max} = \infty$. *Q.E.D.*

3.2. A Taylor Principle Interpretation

The Taylor principle establishes that a permanent increase in the inflation rate leads to a more-than-proportionate increase in the nominal interest rate. Following [1] and [7], we interpret our results according to this principle.

A one percentage point permanent increase in the inflation rate causes the marginal cost to increase by $(1-\eta)(1-\beta)/[\lambda(1+\eta\beta)]$ percentage point through the New Keynesian Phillips curve. By the definition of λ, this can be rewritten as

$$\frac{\kappa(1-\eta)(1-\beta)}{(1-\kappa)(1-\kappa\beta)}. \quad (27)$$

This decreases dividends and share prices by $A\kappa(1-\eta)(1-\beta)/[(1-\kappa)(1-\kappa\beta)]$. The total effect on the nominal rate is given by

$$\tau-\tau_q\frac{A\kappa(1-\eta)(1-\beta)}{(1-\kappa)(1-\kappa\beta)}. \quad (28)$$

If this total response is greater than unity, the rule satisfies the Taylor principle.

If $0\leq\eta<1$, the coefficient of τ_q is strictly positive. Thus, monetary policy response to share prices weakens the total response to inflation and is a source of equilibrium indeterminacy. However, this effect is decreasing in η since this coefficient of τ_q is decreasing in η. This is because the effect of an increase in inflation on the real marginal cost, through the hybrid Phillips curve, is weakened. In particular, if $\eta=1$, then this coefficient is zero and the total effect on the nominal interest rate of inflation is τ. Therefore, monetary policy response to share prices is not a source of equilibrium indeterminacy in this case.

Under the sticky-price setting without price indexation, a fraction of firms cannot change their prices in every period. Then, a permanent increase in inflation implies a low real marginal cost. Under the sticky-price setting with price indexation, a fraction of firms that cannot re-optimize their prices indexes their prices to the past inflation. In the long run, firms following price indexation can keep their real marginal cost constant since the past inflation reflects this increase in inflation.

Therefore, a permanent increase in inflation does not change the real marginal cost if all the firms that cannot re-optimize their prices follow price indexation.

3.3. A Numerical Example

We have the fraction of firms that follow price indexation η affects the threshold of the central bank's stance to the share prices on equilibrium indeterminacy qualitatively. In this subsection, we investigate the quantitative effects of η on $\tau_q^{\max}$.

For this exercise, we set the parameter values of the model as follows. The discount factor of households, β, is 0.99. The relative risk aversion, σ, is two. The Frisch elasticity of labor, γ, is two. The central bank's stance to inflation, τ is 1.5. The steady-state marginal cost, z, is 0.85, which implies that the steady-state markup is 15%. These values are taken from those employed by [1]. We set the Calvo-pricing price-stickiness parameter, κ, is 0.75 following the literature, which implies that firms can re-optimize their prices about once a year.

Figure 1 shows the determinacy and indeterminacy regions. The vertical axis means the central bank's stance to the share price. The horizontal axis means the fraction of firms that follow price indexation. The equilibrium indeterminacy arises in the upper-left region. The equilibrium determinacy arises in the lower-right region. Then, a stronger stance of the central bank to the share prices induces equilibrium indeterminacy. However, if the fraction of firms that follow price indexation is sufficiently high, equilibrium indeterminacy is not likely to arises if monetary policy responds to share prices.

4. Concluding Remarks

A recent paper by Carlstrom and Fuerst [1] found that monetary policy response to share prices is a source of equilibrium indeterminacy in a standard sticky-price model because an increase in inflation implies a high real marginal cost and low share prices.

In this paper, we investigated a sticky-price model in which the New Keynesian Phillips curve has a lagged inflation term caused by price indexation. We found that if firms follow price indexation, the effect of an increase in inflation on real marginal cost is weakened and equilibrium determinacy is likely to arise. Moreover, equilibrium indeterminacy never arises if all the firms that cannot re-optimize their prices follow price indexation.

Empirical results support the significance of a backward inflation term in the New Keynesian Phillips curve. Therefore, when we discuss the relationship between asset prices and monetary policy, we must consider the type of Phillips curve.

5. Acknowledgements

I would like to thank Timothy Fuerst, Masaru Inaba, and Keiichiro Kobayashi for their helpful comments and

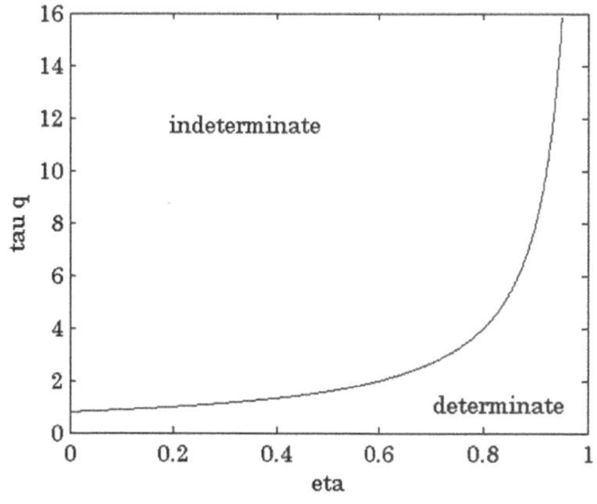

Figure 1. Determinacy and indeterminacy regions.

suggestions. Of course, the remaining errors are mine. This work was funded by a Senshu University research grant ("Analyses of Monetary Policy Responses to Asset Price Fluctuations") in 2011.

REFERENCES

[1] C. T. Carlstrom and T. S. Fuerst, "Asset Prices, Nominal Rigidities, and Monetary Policy," *Review of Economics Dynamics*, Vol. 10, No. 2, 2007, pp. 256-275.

[2] J. Fuhrer and G. Moore, "Inflation Persistence," *Quarterly Journal of Economics*, Vol. 110, No. 1, 1995, pp. 127-159.

[3] J. Gali and M. Gertler, "Inflation Dynamics," *Journal of Monetary Economics*, Vol. 44, No. 2, 1999, pp. 195-222.

[4] L. Christiano, M. Eichenbaum and C. Evans, "Nominal Rigidities and the Dynamic Effects of a Shock to Monetary Policy," *Journal of Political Economy*, Vol. 113, No. 1, 2005, pp. 1-45.

[5] F. Smets and R. Wouters, "Shocks and Frictions in U.S. Business Cycles: A Bayesian DSGE Approach," *American Economic Review*, Vol. 97, No. 3, 2007, pp. 586-606.

[6] F. Smets and R. Wouters, "An Estimated Dynamic Stochastic General Equilibrium Model of the Euro Area," *Journal of the European Economic Association*, Vol. 1, No. 5, 2003, pp. 1123-1175.

[7] J. Bullard and K. Mitra, "Learning about Monetary Policy Rules," *Journal of Monetary Economics*, Vol. 49, No. 6, 2002, pp. 1105-1129.

Appendix: Proof of Proposition 1

For equilibrium determinacy, just one root should be inside the unit circle and others should be outside the unit circle. It is easily shown that one root is $1/\beta$. The three remaining roots are the solutions of a characteristic equation:

$$F(x) = x^3 + F_1 x^2 + F_2 x + F_3,$$

where

$$F_1 \equiv -\frac{1}{\beta\chi}\{\tau_q A(1-\beta) + \eta\beta(\lambda + \chi) + \chi(1+\beta+\tau_q) + \lambda\} < 0$$

$$F_2 \equiv -\frac{1}{\beta\chi}\{\eta\tau_q A(1-\beta) + \lambda\tau(1+\eta\beta) + \eta\chi(1+\beta) + \chi[1+\tau_q(1+\eta)]\} > 0$$

$$F_3 \equiv -\frac{\eta(1+\tau_q)}{\beta} < 0$$

It is shown that $F(0) = F_3 < 0, F'(0) = F_2 > 0$, and

$$F'(1) \equiv -\frac{1}{\beta\chi}\{\tau_q[(2-\eta)A(1-\beta) + \chi(1-\eta)] + \chi(1-\beta)(1-\eta) + \lambda(2-\tau)(1+\eta\beta)\} < 0$$

since $\tau \leq 2$. A necessary condition for equilibrium determinacy is

$$\begin{aligned} &F(1) \\ &= 1 + F_1 + F_2 + F_3 \\ &= \frac{1}{\beta\chi}\{\lambda(\tau-1)(1+\eta\beta) - \tau_q A(1-\eta)(1-\beta)\} > 0. \end{aligned}$$

In the case where all roots are real, it is obvious that this condition is also sufficient.

Next, consider the case where two roots are complex. Suppose that $a \pm bi$ are roots and a norm of $M = \sqrt{a^2 + b^2}$. We have

$$\begin{aligned} &F(x) \\ &= (x - a + bi)(x - a - bi)(x - r) \\ &= x^3 - (2a + r)x^2 + (M^2 + 2ar)x - M^2 r \end{aligned}$$

where r is a real root in $(0,1)$.

For equilibrium determinacy, we will show that $M^2 > 1$. By the form of $F'(x)$, it is easily shown that $F(x)$ reaches a local minimum at

$$x = x^{L\min} \equiv \frac{2a + r + \sqrt{r^2 - 2ar + a^2 - 3b^2}}{3}.$$

Since $F'(0) < 0$ and $F'(1) > 0$, it is shown that $x^{L\min} > 1$. It suffices to show that $x^{L\min} < a$ for for $M = \sqrt{a^2 + b^2} > 1$.

The rest of this proof, we show that $r < a$ at first. Since $r < x^{L\min}$, it is obtained that

$$2(r-a) < \sqrt{r^2 - 2ar + a^2 - 3b^2}.$$

If $r \geq a$, we have

$$4(r-a)^2 - (r^2 - 2ar + a^2 - 3b^2) = (r-a)^2 + 3b^3 \geq 0$$

and it is a contradiction. Then, $r < a$. Finally, $x^{L\min} < a$ is shown as follows. A necessary and sufficient condition for $x^{L\min} < a$ is

$$\sqrt{r^2 - 2ar} + a^2 - 3b^2 < a - r.$$

Since $r < a$, this condition is reduced to

$$r^2 - ar + a^2 - 3b^2 < (a-r)^2,$$

and this is easily shown.

Q.E.D.

The Ambivalent Role of Idiosyncratic Risk in Asymmetric Tournaments

Kerstin Pull[1], Hendrik Bäker[2], Agnes Bäker[1,3]
[1]School of Economics and Business, Eberhard Karls University Tuebingen, Tuebingen, Germany
[2]Mathematics, Eberhard Karls University Tuebingen, Tuebingen, Germany
[3]Department of Economics, University of Warwick, Coventry, UK

ABSTRACT

In our paper, we analyze the interplay of contestant heterogeneity and idiosyncratic risk in rank-order tournaments: While in symmetric tournaments an increase in idiosyncratic risk reduces incentives, in asymmetric tournaments this is not necessarily the case: Rather, we show that increasing the level of idiosyncratic risk in asymmetric tournaments will at first increase and—only after a critical risk level has been reached—reduce incentives. We find this critical risk level to be higher, the larger the degree of contestant heterogeneity. Concerning practical implications, it is more important to reduce idiosyncratic risk in the tournament when contestants are similar and less beneficial when contestants are heterogeneous. In light of the fact that equilibrium effort levels in tournaments with a low level of contestant heterogeneity are by far higher than those in tournaments with high levels of contestant heterogeneity, the advice would be to simultaneously reduce contestant heterogeneity (e.g., by league-building or handicapping) *and* idiosyncratic risk.

Keywords: Tournaments; Contestant Heterogeneity; Idiosyncratic Risk

1. Introduction

Tournament incentives have developed into an important component of organizational reward systems: Employees compete against one another with the best performing employee(s) receiving a predefined tournament prize (e.g. a promotion, a bonus payment, a travel incentive or the like). Given the prevalence of tournament incentives, it is not surprising that beginning with the seminal paper by [1] the incentive properties of tournaments have repeatedly been analyzed (e.g. [2]).

In our paper, we analyze the effect of idiosyncratic, *i.e.* contestant-specific, risk in a tournament where contestants are heterogeneous. While the literature has regarded the effects of both idiosyncratic risk and contestant heterogeneity in isolation, the interplay of the two has not received much attention yet.

Starting first with *contestant heterogeneity*, this refers to a situation where contestants in a tournament are not equally talented in doing their job. In a two-person tournament, e.g., where one of the two contestants is of much higher ability, both contestants will not be inclined to put in much effort in the tournament—knowing that the more talented one will win anyway. Consequently, tournament incentives are distorted in a situation where contestants are heterogeneous (see, e.g. [1]).

Concerning *risks*, it is important to distinguish between two different types of risk: common risks on the one hand and idiosyncratic risks on the other. While the former affect the output of all contestants alike (e.g. seasonal fluctuations or fluctuations over the business cycle), the latter are contestant-specific and are not leveled out by the tournament. From the literature it is clear that if contestants are homogenous (*symmetric tournament*), an increase in idiosyncratic risk will decrease tournament incentives as the expected marginal return of an increased effort level is reduced. However, if and how an increase in idiosyncratic risk will affect tournament incentives in an *asymmetric* tournament, *i.e.*, in a tournament that is characterized by contestant heterogeneity, is far less clear and has not been explored so far. This is despite the fact that in reality we will typically observe both, contestant heterogeneity *and* idiosyncratic risks, at the same time.

In the recent literature on asymmetric tournaments (e.g. [3]), only [4,5] are concerned with the role of idiosyncratic risk. However, other than in this paper, [4] as well as [5] are interested in agents' active risk-taking strategies and model risk as a second choice variable of contestants[1]. To the contrary, in our paper we are concerned with exogenously determined idiosyncratic risks which are inherent in almost any production or measurement technology. Further, and on a more technical note, our paper differs from the one by [4] in that [4] vary the degree of heterogeneity for two distinct levels of risk, whereas we vary the level of idiosyncratic risk—given the level of heterogeneity. While [4] as well as [5] find that in a situation with a low degree of contestant heterogeneity, an (endogenous) increase in idiosyncratic risk will generally reduce tournament incentives, in our framework this is no longer the case: An exogenous increase in the amount of idiosyncratic risk in an asymmetric tournament starting from an initially very low level of risk will rather at first increase tournament incentives and only later on (after a critical level of idiosyncratic risk has been reached) reduce these.

The intuition of this ambivalent effect is as follows: At very low levels of risk inherent in the production technology, even a small degree of (publicly known) contestant heterogeneity is apt to distort tournament incentives as the outcome of the tournament becomes more or less predictable: The more able contestant will know that even a low level of effort will make her win the tournament, and hence the best response of the less able contestant will be to choose a low level of effort as well. In such a situation, an increase in the amount of idiosyncratic risk will reduce the predictability of the outcome and will therefore make it more worthwhile for the two contestants to exert high effort levels. However, when a certain critical level of idiosyncratic risk has been reached, a further increase in risk will decrease incentives again—just as it is the case in symmetric tournaments, *i.e.*, as long as idiosyncratic risks do not fully compensate for contestant heterogeneity, adding more risk to the contest will increase incentives; as soon as idiosyncratic risks more than compensate for contestant heterogeneity, adding more risk will decrease incentives.

The level of idiosyncratic risk where the positive relation between risk and tournament incentives turns into a negative one depends on the degree of contestant heterogeneity: The smaller the degree of contestant heterogeneity, the lower the critical risk level, *i.e.*, the smaller the range of risk levels where the effect of an increase in risk on equilibrium effort is positive. Hence, provided that contestant heterogeneity is sufficiently low, an increase in idiosyncratic risk will decrease tournament incentives over wide ranges of the risk spectrum. For higher degrees of contestant heterogeneity, however, this is no longer true: Over a large range of the risk spectrum, an increase in idiosyncratic risk will rather increase tournament incentives.

The remainder of this paper is organized as follows: Section 2 starts with a reference model with two homogeneous contestants and then introduces heterogeneity on the part of contestants. Section 3 presents a short discussion and practical implications, Section 4 concludes.

2. The Model

In a first reference case, let there be two homogeneous employees i $(i=1,2)$ who compete in a rank-order tournament. Both employees independently choose an effort level e_i, which is not observable and only known to the respective employee. Individual output q_i is assumed to be observable and is a function of effort level e_i and an idiosyncratic error term x_i with $q_i = e_i + x_i$. The idiosyncratic error terms x_i are assumed to be identically and independently distributed with $x_i \sim \mathcal{N}(0,\sigma^2)$. The tournament foresees that employee i is awarded the tournament prize t if $q_i > q_{-i}$. When choosing his or her effort level, each of the risk-neutral employees i individually maximizes his or her expected utility:

$$E[U_i] = p_i(e_i,e_{-i})\cdot t - c(e_i) \quad (1)$$

where p_i denotes the probability of winning the tournament for employee i and where $c(e_i)$ denotes the costs of effort with $c(0)=0,\ c'(e_i)>0$ and $c''(e_i)>0$.

The probability p_i of winning the tournament is given by:

$$\begin{aligned} &p_i(e_i,e_{-i}) \\ &= \Pr\{q_i > q_{-i}\} = \Pr\{e_i + x_i > e_{-i} + x_{-i}\} \quad (2) \\ &= \Pr\{e_i - e_{-i} > \xi\} = G(e_i - e_{-i}), \end{aligned}$$

where ξ is the composed error term $\xi = x_{-i} - x_i$ and where $G(\cdot)$ denotes its cumulated distribution function. The composed error term ξ is normally distributed with $\xi \sim \mathcal{N}(0,2\sigma^2)$. Solving the maximization problem in Equation (1) and substituting for p_i according to Equation (2), one arrives at the following reaction function for employee i:

$$c'(e_i^*) = p_i'(e_i^*,e_{-i}^*)\cdot t = g(e_i^* - e_{-i}^*)\cdot t. \quad (3)$$

Hence, we arrive at the well-known result that each employee will choose an effort level such that his or her marginal costs of effort $c'(e_i)$ are equal to his or her marginal returns in form of an increased chance of winning the tournament $p_i'(e_i^*,e_{-i}^*)$ multiplied by the tournament prize t, where $p_i'(e_i^*,e_{-i}^*)$ may be written in terms of the density function of the composed error

[1]Similarly, [6] theoretically and experimentally studies active risk-taking in a field of heterogeneous contestants, but they regard risk-taking as the only choice variable (no effort choice). [7] again, analyzes both, risk-taking and effort choice, but in a symmetric tournament with homogeneous contestants.

term evaluated at $\xi = e_i^* - e_{-i}^*$. Symmetry of $g(\cdot)$ implies that, if a Nash-equilibrium in pure strategies exists[2], we have $e_i^* = e_{-i}^*$. Hence, Equation (3) can be re-written as:

$$c'(e_i^*) = g(0) \cdot t.$$

Concerning the impact of idiosyncratic risk on tournament incentives, a higher amount of risk (*i.e.*, a lower value of $g(0)$), will generally *decrease* effort levels in a symmetric tournament.

Example 2.1. *The following example—which will prove to be useful in the case of heterogeneous contestants—may illustrate this effect: Assuming quadratic effort costs with* $c(e_i) = 0.5 \cdot c \cdot e_i^2$, *the equilibrium effort level* e_i^* *is given by:*

$$e_i^* = \frac{t}{2\sqrt{\pi} \cdot \sigma \cdot c}.$$

Hence, an increase in idiosyncratic risk as indicated by a larger σ will decrease equilibrium effort.

In what follows, heterogeneity on the part of employees is introduced. In accordance with [1] and with e.g. [5,8,9], we do so by assuming that employees vary in their marginal costs of effort[3]. Again let e_i denote the effort level and $c_i(e_i)$ the costs of effort of contestant i. Let employee 1 be characterized by generally lower marginal costs of effort than employee 2, *i.e.* assume that $c_1'(e_i) < c_2'(e_i)$ holds for all effort levels $e_i \neq 0$. When no effort is displayed, there are zero costs $(c_i(0) = 0)$ and also marginal costs are set to zero $(c_i'(0) = 0)$. Furthermore and for technical reasons we assume that for the second derivatives we have $0 < c_1'' < c_2''$ and that $\left((c_2')^{-1}\right)' \leq \left((c_1')^{-1}\right)'$ holds. In a Nash-equilibrium, the reaction function of employee i will then take the following form:

$$c_i'(e_i^*) = g(e_i^* - e_{-i}^*) \cdot t = \frac{t}{\sqrt{4\pi}\sigma} \exp\left(-\frac{(e_i^* - e_{-i}^*)^2}{2\sigma^2}\right). \quad (4)$$

Since $g(\cdot)$ is symmetric, $g(e_i^* - e_{-i}^*) = g(e_{-i}^* - e_i^*)$ holds. Hence, with $c_1'(e_i) < c_2'(e_i)$ for all effort levels $e_i \neq 0$, in equilibrium employee 1 will choose a higher effort level than employee 2: $e_1^* > e_2^*$. As $g(\xi)$ displays a maximum at $\xi = 0$ (see **Figure 1**), we can further write:

$$g(e_i^* - e_{-i}^*) = g(e_{-i}^* - e_i^*) < g(0). \quad (5)$$

Thus, in an asymmetric tournament, for a given tournament prize t, both employees will choose lower effort levels than each of them would have chosen in a symmetric tournament. The intuition for this effect is straight forward: For each of the employees, the marginal revenue of choosing a higher effort level (as is being represented by an increase in the probability of winning the tournament multiplied by the tournament prize) is reduced in an asymmetric as compared to a symmetric tournament where the ex ante [and ex post] chances to win the tournament are identical for the two contestants. The larger the ability differentials, *i.e.*, the larger the degree of contestant heterogeneity, the lower the incentives to provide effort (for given levels of idiosyncratic risk).

Concerning the effect of idiosyncratic risk on effort levels, however, the picture is less clear: Tournament incentives may in fact either increase or decrease with the level of idiosyncratic risk—depending on the (endogenously to be determined) difference in equilibrium effort levels.

Example 2.2. *Recurring on the above example and assuming quadratic effort costs for both contestants with* $c_i(e_i) = 0.5 \cdot c_i \cdot e_i^2 \ (i = 1,2)$ *yields that we have* $c_i'(e_i) = c_i e_i$ *giving us* $c_i e_i^* = c_i'(e_i^*) = c_{-1}'(e_{-i}^*) = c_{-i} e_{-i}^*$, *and hence we obtain:*

$$e_i^* = \frac{t}{\sqrt{2\pi} \cdot \sqrt{2} \cdot \sigma \cdot c_i} \cdot \exp\left(-\frac{\left(e_i^* \cdot \left(1 - \frac{c_i}{c_{-i}}\right)\right)^2}{4\sigma^2}\right)$$

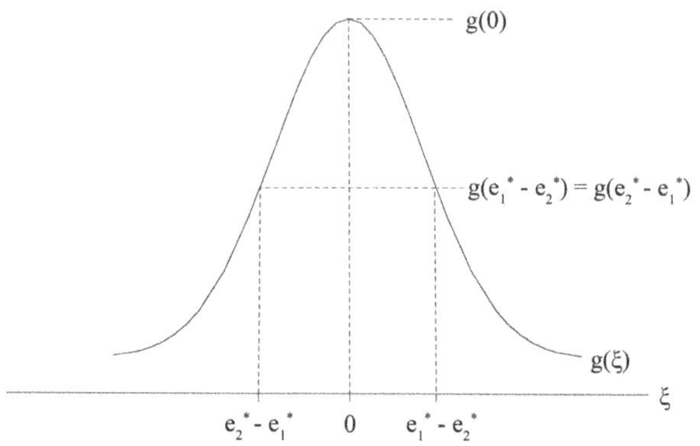

Figure 1. Idiosyncratic risk and equilibrium effort levels.

[2] The existence of a pure-strategy equilibrium in a tournament model is not automatically assured (see e.g. the discussion in [1:845] or in [4: 106]). Rather, it needs a minimum amount of idiosyncratic risk in the tournament. Otherwise contestants would deduce their opponents' effort levels from the publicly known cost functions and choose slightly higher effort levels than their opponents. As a result, there will only be mixed-strategy equilibria. In what follows, we assume that the idiosyncratic risk in the tournament is high enough to ensure the existence of a pure-strategy equilibrium.

[3] [4] takes a different road and model differing ability levels by introducing additive shift factors of different size into the production functions of the two contestants. [10] introduces contestant heterogeneity by modeling individual output as being the product of effort and ability level.

Figure 2 plots the equilibrium effort level of contestant i as a function of the level of idiosyncratic risk as measured by σ for the parameters $t = 100$, $c_i = 1$ and $c_{-i} = 0.5$.

As **Figure 2** shows, an increase in idiosyncratic risk will at first increase incentives and then reduce them. The intuition for this effect is as follows: At very low levels of idiosyncratic risk[4], contestant heterogeneity will adversely affect effort levels. Adding risk to the contest $(\sigma \uparrow)$ will reduce the predictability of the outcome, increase the marginal return of exerting higher effort levels for the two contestants and will hence make it more worthwhile for the contestants to exert positive effort levels. However, when a critical level of risk $\hat{\sigma}$ is reached, a further increase in risk will decrease incentives again—just as it is the case in symmetric contests, *i.e.*, as long as idiosyncratic risks do not fully compensate for contestant heterogeneity, adding more risk to the contest will increase incentives; as soon as idiosyncratic risks more than compensate for contestant heterogeneity, adding more risk will decrease incentives. This is equivalent to stating that the function for e_i^* displays a maximum in the idiosyncratic risks σ where $\sigma > 0$. This maximum is displayed at the critical risk level $\hat{\sigma}$. We obtain:

Theorem 2.3. *There is a unique risk level* $\hat{\sigma} \neq 0$ *for which* e_i^* *are simultaneously maximal and for this level the following equation holds*:

$$\hat{\sigma} = \left(c_1'\right)^{-1}\left(\frac{t}{\hat{\sigma}\sqrt{4\pi}}\mathrm{e}^{-0.5}\right) - \left(c_2'\right)^{-1}\left(\frac{t}{\hat{\sigma}\sqrt{4\pi}}\mathrm{e}^{-0.5}\right).$$

Proof. See Appendix.

The theorem gives us an equation for the level of risk in the tournament at which the effort of both contestants is at a maximum. This equation does not depend on the effort levels; unfortunately, however, it is an implicit formula. As we will see in the following Example 2.4, when choosing suitable cost functions we can compute an explicit value for the optimal risk level which only depends on contestant heterogeneity.

Example 2.4. *Assuming the same cost functions as in* 2.2 *Theorem* 2.3 *yields an explicit formula for the critical risk level* $\hat{\sigma}$:

$$\hat{\sigma} = \sqrt{\frac{c_2 - c_1}{c_1 c_2}} \cdot \sqrt{\frac{t}{\sqrt{4\pi}}\exp(-0.5)},$$

where the first factor can be interpreted as heterogeneity of the contestants.

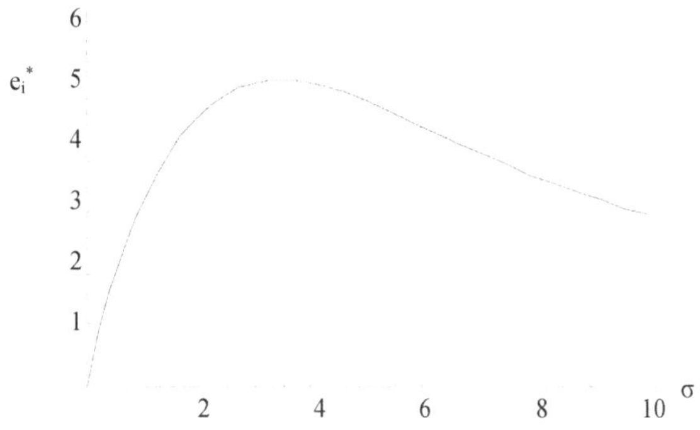

Figure 2. Idiosyncratic risk and equilibrium effort levels in an asymmetric tournament.

The critical risk level $\hat{\sigma}$ at which the positive effect of idiosyncratic risk on tournament incentives turns into a negative one, depends on the degree of contestant heterogeneity with a higher degree of contestant heterogeneity leading to a higher critical risk level.

Figure 3 plots the equilibrium effort level of contestant i as a function of the level of idiosyncratic risk as measured by σ for (a) a situation where contestants are almost homogeneous in their marginal effort costs and (b) a situation where the degree of contestant heterogeneity is rather large[5]. If the differential in marginal effort costs is low (**Figure 3(a)**), the critical risk value beyond which the positive effect on incentives turns into a negative one is reached at a lower risk level than if the differential in marginal effort costs is high (**Figure 3(b)**). Hence, for a low level of contestant heterogeneity an increase in risk will decrease incentives over a wide range of the risk spectrum (just as is the case in a symmetric tournament) while for a high level of contestant heterogeneity an increase in risk will increase incentives over a wide range of the risk spectrum.

3. Discussion

Unlike [4]—and, similarly, [5]—we find that when risk is not a choice variable, but rather inherent to the production process, introducing risk into an asymmetric tournament will always at first increase equilibrium effort levels and then decrease them—*irrespective* of the size of the ability differential.

Note, however, that the equilibrium effort levels chosen in a situation with a low degree of contestant heterogeneity are by far higher than those in a situation with a high degree of contestant heterogeneity. The results concerning a high degree of contestant heterogeneity are well in line with the suppositions of [11] and [12] who each postulate that increasing the risk in a contest

[4]Of course, we need to make sure that idiosyncratic risk is above the minimum level guaranteeing the existence of a pure-strategy equilibrium (see above). To argue our point the minimum level of risk required to obtain an equilibrium in pure strategies needs to be below the level of risk granting the highest effort level (see **Figure 2**). Even if this might not hold for a situation of very low contestant heterogeneity, this will clearly be the case for higher degrees of contestant heterogeneity (see **Figure 3(b)** vs. **Figure 3(a)**).

[5]The parameters for c_{-i} were chosen as follows: (a) $c_{-i} = 0.99$, (b) $c_{-i} = 0.01$. Again, $t = 100$ and $c_i = 1$.

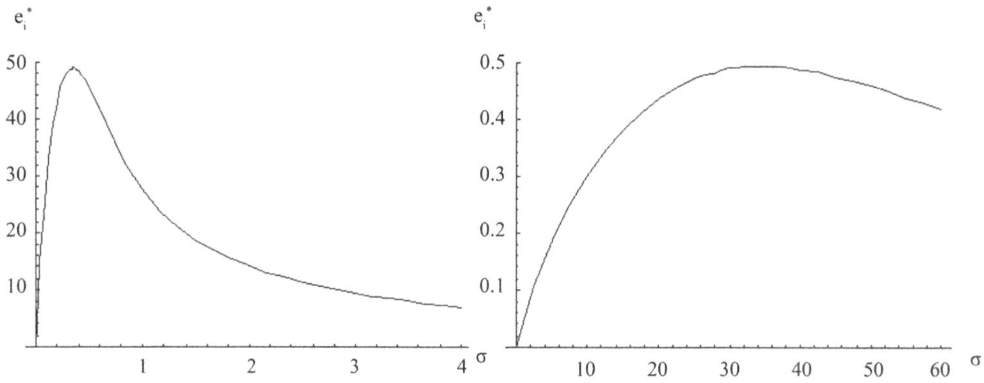

(a) (b)

Figure 3. Idiosyncratic risk and equilibrium effort levels in more or less uneven tournaments. (a) Low degree of contestant heterogeneity; (b) High degree of contestant heterogeneity.

(through less monitoring by the tournament sponsor) might in fact lead to higher effort levels by all contestants.

With respect to practical implications, our analysis shows that it is more important to invest in a decrease of idiosyncratic risk (e.g., by reducing measurement error) in tournament compensation systems when contestants are similar in their effort costs (low level of contestant heterogeneity). The more heterogeneous contestants are, the less beneficial (if not even costly) are these attempts. In light of the fact that equilibrium effort levels in tournaments with a low level of contestant heterogeneity are by far higher than those in tournaments with high levels of contestant heterogeneity, the practical advice would be to simultaneously reduce contestant heterogeneity (e.g., by league-building or handicapping) *and* idiosyncratic risk.

4. Conclusion

We show that an increasing amount of idiosyncratic risk does not generally decrease incentives when contestants are heterogeneous. Rather, an increase in idiosyncratic risk will first increase incentives in an asymmetric tournament and will only start to decrease incentives after some—critical—risk level has been reached. This critical risk level—in turn—depends on the degree of contestant heterogeneity: The lower contestant heterogeneity, the lower is the critical risk level: *i.e.*, for very low levels of contestant heterogeneity, an increase in idiosyncratic risk will *decrease* tournament incentives over a wide range of the risk spectrum while for high levels of contestant heterogeneity, increasing the amount of risk in the contest will *increase* tournament incentives over a wide range of the risk spectrum.

5. Acknowledgements

The authors would like to thank Matthias Kräkel and Dirk Sliwka for helpful comments and suggestions.

REFERENCES

[1] E. P. Lazear and S. Rosen, "Rank-Order Tournaments as Optimum Labor Contracts," *Journal of Political Economy*, Vol. 89, No. 5, 1981, pp. 841-864.

[2] B. E. Becker and M. A. Huselid, "The Incentive Effects of Tournament Compensation Systems," *Administrative Science Quarterly*, Vol. 37, No. 2, 1992, pp. 336-350.

[3] C. Harbring and G. K. Lünser, "On the Competition of Asymmetric Agents," *German Economic Review*, Vol. 9, No. 3, 2008, pp. 373-395.

[4] M. Kräkel and D. Sliwka, "Risk Taking in Asymmetric Tournaments," *German Economic Review*, Vol. 5, No. 1, 2004, pp. 103-116.

[5] M. Kräkel, "Optimal Risk Taking in an Uneven Tournament Game with Risk Averse Players," *Journal of Mathematical Economics*, Vol. 44, No. 11, 2008, pp. 1219-1231.

[6] P. Nieken and D. Sliwka, "Risk-Taking Tournaments: Theory and Experimental Evidence," *Journal of Economic Psychology*, Vol. 31, No. 3, 2010, pp. 254-268.

[7] P. Nieken, "On the Choice of Risk and Effort in Tournaments-Experimental Evidence," *Journal of Economics and Management Strategy*, Vol. 19, No. 3, 2010, pp. 811-840.

[8] C. Bull, A. Schotter and K. Weigelt, "Tournaments and Piece Rates: An Experimental Study," *Journal of Political Economy*, Vol. 95, No. 1, 1987, pp. 1-33.

[9] K. J. McLaughlin, "Aspects of Tournament Models: A Survey," *Research in Labor Economics*, Vol. 9, No. 1, 1988, pp. 225-256.

[10] M. O'Keefe, W. K. Viscusi and R. J. Zeckhauser, "Economic Contests: Comparative Reward Schemes," *Journal*

of Labor Economics, Vol. 2, No. 1, 1984, pp. 27-56.

[11] T. Cowen and A. Glazer, "More Monitoring Can Induce Less Effort," *Journal of Economic Behavior & Organisation*, Vol. 30, No. 1, 1996, pp. 113-123.

[12] P. Dubey and C. Wu, "Competitive prizes: When less Scrutiny Induces More Effort," *Journal of Mathematical Economics*, Vol. 36, No. 4, 2001, pp. 311-336.

Appendix: Proof of Theorem 2.3

Let us recall some of the notation used. By e_i we denote the effort level and by c_i the costs of effort of contestant i. In a Nash-equilibrium we then obtain

$$c_i'(e_i^*) = g(e_i^* - e_{-i}^*)\cdot t = \frac{t}{\sqrt{4\pi}\sigma}\exp\left(-\frac{(e_i^* - e_{-i}^*)^2}{2\sigma^2}\right), \quad (6)$$

where by e_i^* we denote the equilibrium effort levels. Symmetry of g yields

$$c_i'(e_i^*) = g(e_i^* - e_{-i}^*)\cdot t = g(e_{-i}^* - e_i^*)\cdot t = c_{-i}'(e_{-i}^*). \quad (7)$$

We now assume $c_i(0)$ and $c_i'(0)$ to vanish; contestant heterogeneity is modeled by $c_1(e_i) < c_2(e_i)$ for every level $e_i > 0$. Furthermore for the second derivatives $0 < c_1'' < c_2''$ shall hold. This means c_i' is strictly increasing, *i.e.* the inverse function $(c_i')^{-1}$ exists. Further, we assume that $\left((c_2')^{-1}\right)' \le \left((c_1')^{-1}\right)'$ holds.

For the sake of simplifying the calculation we fix some more notation and do some technical preparations. Let $\kappa_i(z) := (c_{-i}')^{-1}(c_i'(z))$ and

$$\delta_i(z) := \begin{cases} z - \kappa_1(z), \text{if } i = 1, \\ \kappa_2(z) - z, \text{if } i = 2. \end{cases}$$

Lemma 5.1. *For any* $z \ge 0$ *and the equilibria* e_i^* *the following equations hold*

1) $c_i'(z) = c_{-i}'(\kappa_i(z))$,
2) $\kappa_i(e_i^*) = e_{-i}^*$ and
3) $\delta_1(e_1^*) = e_1^* - e_2^* = \delta_2(e_2^*)$.

Proof. The first claim follows directly from the definition of κ_i. Using Formula (7) we see that

$$\kappa_i(e_i^*) = (c_{-i}')^{-1}(c_i'(e_i^*)) = (c_{-i}')^{-1}(c_{-i}'(e_{-i}^*)) = e_{-i}^*$$

holds. And the last assertion follows from

$$\delta_1(e_1^*) = e_1^* - \kappa_1(e_1^*) = e_1^* - e_2^* = \kappa_2(e_2^*) - e_2^* = \delta_2(e_2^*). \quad \square$$

Lemma 5.2. *For any* $z \ge 0$ *and* $i \in \{1,2\}$ *the expression* $\delta_i(z)\delta_i'(z)$ *is non-negative.*

Proof. We only prove the lemma for $i = 1$, the other case follows by an analogous argument. It suffices to show that $\delta_1'(z) = 1 - \kappa_1'(z) \ge 0$ holds, because $\delta_1(0) = 0$. By differentiating $c_1'(z) = c_2'(\kappa_1(z))$ with respect to z, we obtain $\kappa_1'(z) = c_1''(z)/c_2''(\kappa_1(z))$ and it remains to prove $c_2''(\kappa_1(z)) \ge c_1''(z)$. This, however, follows from

$$\frac{1}{c_2''(\kappa_1(z))} = \left((c_2')^{-1}\right)'(c_2'(\kappa_1(z)))$$

$$= \left((c_2')^{-1}\right)'(c_1'(z)) \le \left((c_1')^{-1}\right)'(c_1'(z)) = \frac{1}{c_1''(z)}. \quad \square$$

Lemma 5.3.

1) The derivative of e_i^* with respect to σ is given by

$$\frac{de_i^*}{d\sigma} = -\frac{\sigma^2 - \delta_i(e_i^*)^2}{\sigma^3 \frac{c_i''}{c_i'}(e_i^*) + \sigma\delta_i(e_i^*)\delta_i'(e_i^*)}.$$

2) The equation $\delta_i(e_i^*(\sigma)) = \sigma$ has a unique solution $\hat{\sigma}$. With $\hat{e}_i^* := e_i^*(\hat{\sigma})$ denoting the corresponding effort level the evaluation of the second derivative of e_i^* at $\hat{\sigma}$ is given by

$$\frac{d^2 e_i^*}{d\sigma^2}(\hat{\sigma}) = -2\frac{\hat{\sigma}^4 \frac{c_i''}{c_i'}(\hat{e}_i^*) + \hat{\sigma}^2\delta_i(\hat{e}_i^*)\delta_i'(\hat{e}_i^*)}{\left(\sigma^3 \frac{c_i''}{c_i'}(\hat{e}_i^*) + \sigma\delta_i(\hat{e}_i^*)\delta_i'(\hat{e}_i^*)\right)^2}.$$

Proof.

1) Applying the natural logarithm to Formula (6) and differentiating with respect to σ we get

$$\frac{c_i''(e_i^*)}{c_i'(e_i^*)}\frac{de_i^*}{d\sigma} = -\frac{1}{\sigma} - \frac{1}{\sigma^3}\left(\sigma\delta_i(e_i^*)\delta_i'(e_i^*)\frac{de_i^*}{d\sigma} - \delta_i(e_i^*)^2\right).$$

Redistributing the terms gives our claim.

2) The quotient rule yields the second derivative. For any solution $\hat{\sigma}$ of $\delta_i(e_i^*(\sigma)) = \sigma$ the following equations hold

$$\frac{de_i^*}{d\sigma}(\hat{\sigma}) = 0 \text{ and } \hat{\sigma} = \delta_i(\hat{e}_i^*).$$

By Lemma 5.2, it then follows that the second derivative is negative in all extremal points, *i.e.* there are only maxima. This yields uniqueness. $\square$

Proof of Theorem 2.3. From Lemma 5.3, it follows directly that the derivative of e_i^* with respect to σ vanishes independently of i if and only if $\sigma = \delta(e_i^*(\sigma))$ holds. Moreover this is a maximum because by the same lemma the second derivative is negative. Substituting this result into Formula (6) we obtain

$$c_1'(\hat{e}_1^*) = \frac{t}{\sqrt{4\pi}\hat{\sigma}}\exp(-0.5),$$

$$c_2'(\hat{e}_1^* - \hat{\sigma}) = c_2'(\hat{e}_2^*) = \frac{t}{\sqrt{4\pi}\hat{\sigma}}\exp(-0.5).$$

Taking the respective inverse functions and subtracting the two equations shows that

$$\hat{\sigma} = (c_1')^{-1}\left(\frac{t}{\hat{\sigma}\sqrt{4\pi}}e^{-0.5}\right) - (c_2')^{-1}\left(\frac{t}{\hat{\sigma}\sqrt{4\pi}}e^{-0.5}\right). \quad \square$$

6

On the Internal Consistency of the Black-Scholes Option Pricing Model

Jeremy Berkowitz
Department of Finance, Bauer College of Business, University of Houston, Houston, USA

ABSTRACT

We study the information structure implied by models in which the asset price is always risky and there are no arbitrage opportunities. Using the martingale representation of Harrison and Kreps [1], a claim takes its value from the stream of discounted expected payments. Equivalently, a pricing-kernel is sufficient to value the payment stream. If a price process is always risky, then either the payment or the discount factor must also be continually risky. This observation substantially complicates the valuation of contingent claims. Many classical option pricing formulas abstract from both risky dividends and risky discount rates. In order to value contingent claims, one of the assumptions must be abandoned.

Keywords: Diffusions; Binomial Model; Arbitrage

1. Introduction

The pioneering work of Black and Scholes [2] and Merton [3] and introduced continuous-time methods and, in particular, diffusion models into contingent claims valuation. Diffusion processes have become the standard specification of the underlying asset price in option pricing models (e.g., Melino and Turnbull [4], Heston [5] among many others) and of the term structure of interest rates (e.g., Cox, Ingersoll, Ross [6] and Heath, Jarrow and Morton [7]).

A diffusion process can be thought of as the continuous-time limit of a binomial tree. A shared feature among all these models is that at any time $t - 1$, we do not know the value of the asset at time t. The one-step ahead price is always risky. Equivalently, the one-step ahead variance of the price is always positive.

In the present paper, we study the information structure implied by models with continually risky prices when there is no arbitrage. We use the binomial tree to motivate the problem and provide intuition before providing the analysis in continuous time.

If an economy has no arbitrage, the martingale representation of Harrison and Kreps [1] and Harrison, Pliska [8] implies that an asset price p_t can be written

$$p_t = \mathrm{d}_t + \frac{1}{1+r} E p_{t+1} m_{t,t+1} \qquad (1)$$

where d_t are the cashflows and $m_{t,t+1}$ is a stochastic discount factor (SDF)[1]. This says that the value of a claim can be decomposed into the payments and a covariance term.

If the asset price is a binomial process (or diffusion), the one-step ahead conditional variance is

$$\mathrm{var}_{t-1}(p_t) > 0. \qquad (2)$$

Combining Equations (1) and (2), the conditional variance of the RHS of Equation (1) must also be positive. Thus under no arbitrage, either the payout d_t or the SDF $m_{t,t+1}$ (or both) must also be risky each period.

For the purposes valuing contingent claims, this complicates the interpretation and application of classical methods[2]. Black and Scholes [2] assume the underlying stock price is a diffusion process. It is continuously risky (the instantaneous variance is positive). This means the LHS of Equation (1) has a strictly positive variance. But

[1]We follow Cox and Rubinstein [9] in using the term "binomial process" to refer generally to two-state models in discrete time. This encompasses models in which the log of the stock price at any time period has a binomial distribution. The convergence of binomial models to diffusion limits is formally studied in Brennan and Schwartz [10], Cox, Ross and Rubinstein [11], Duffie and Protter [12] and He [13].

[2]Note that this problem cannot be illustrated in model with less than 3 periods, as Equation (1) is ill-defined if T < 3. In this sense, there is a strong loss-of-generality is describing the continuous-time framework with a 2-period model as is commonly done in textbook expositions of option-pricing.

they also assume that there are no risky payments and no risky discounting. This would imply the RHS of Equation (1) has identically zero variance.

The full set of assumptions made in Black and Scholes [2] can be made consistent by dropping the standard no arbitrage condition. Without a no arbitrage condition, the martingale representation (1) of Harrison and Kreps [1] and Harrison and Pliska [8] needs not hold. Changes in the asset price can be divorced from *both payments and discounting*. For example, price moves could be driven by incomplete information or by learning about distributions of random variables.

Unfortunately, such a solution then creates another problem. If the economy violates the no arbitrage condition, we cannot use it to value contingent claims. This does not mean that they cannot be valued-rather, they cannot be valued by arbitrage methods.

We could as an alternative solution insist on keeping the no arbitrage condition and drop the classical assumptions about either dividends or discount rates. No arbitrage can be maintained if the binomial asset price is driven by binomial dividends or a binomial discount rate.

For stocks, bonds and many other assets types, it would be empirically unreasonable to assume risky payments are made every period. This leaves as the only realistic possibility allowing the discount rate to be risky every period. In this case, the asset behaves like a perpetuity. All variations in the asset price come from changes in the discount rate.

The structure of the article is as follows: Section 2 outlines the main result in discrete time using the binomial model. Section 3 analyzes the implications for continuous-time option pricing models. Some solutions are discussed in Section 4 and Section 5 concludes.

2. Risky Asset Prices under No Arbitrage

Before turning to the analysis in continuous time, we discuss the Binomial model. The discrete time analog simplifies the mathematics somewhat without any loss in intuition. If there is no arbitrage, the value of a claim p_t can be written as an expectation

$$p_t = \mathrm{d}_t + \frac{1}{1+r} E\left[p_{t+1} m_{t,t+1} \right] \tag{3}$$

where d_t is the payout at time *t* and $m_{t,t+1}$ is the 1-step ahead stochastic discount factor (SDF) at time *t*.

Under the no arbitrage condition (as defined by Harrison and Kreps [1]), an asset price is equal to an observed payment d_t plus a covariance. To calculate the covariance term at any time *t*, all we need to know is the joint distribution of p_{t+1} and $m_{t,t+1}$.

The simplest binomial asset price model is the process

$$p_{t+1} = p_t + \varepsilon_{t+1} \tag{4}$$

where

$$\varepsilon_{t+1} = \begin{cases} u & \text{with probability } q \\ -u & \text{with probability } 1-q \end{cases}$$

and $u > 0$ is the step size[3]. Combining (3) with (4), the asset price equals

$$p_t = \mathrm{d}_t + \frac{1}{1+r} E_t^*\left[p_t + \varepsilon_{t+1} \right].$$

Rearranging and simplifying terms,

$$p_t \frac{r}{1+r} = \mathrm{d}_t + \frac{1}{1+r} E_t^*\left[\varepsilon_{t+1} \right].$$

Write out the expectation,

$$p_t \frac{r}{1+r} = \mathrm{d}_t + \frac{1}{1+r}\left[uq_t^* - u\left(1-q_t^*\right)\right] \tag{5}$$

where q_t^* is the Arrow-Debreu state price or martingale-equivalent probability of an up move. From Harrison and Pliska [8], these subjective probabilities are given by

$$q_t^* = qm_{t,t+1} \tag{6}$$

where q is the actual probability of an up-move and $m_{t,t+1}$ the SDF. Making this replacement in Equation (5),

$$p_t \frac{r}{1+r} = \mathrm{d}_t + \frac{1}{1+r}\left[uqm_{t,t+1} - u\left(1-qm_{t,t+1}\right)\right]$$

and simplifying

$$p_t \frac{r}{1+r} = \mathrm{d}_t + \frac{1}{1+r}\left[2uqm_{t,t+1} - u\right]. \tag{7}$$

We can explicitly calculate the variance of the LHS of this equation. The one-step ahead conditional variance at $t-1$,

$$\begin{aligned} &\mathrm{var}_{t-1}\left(p_t\right) \\ &= \mathrm{var}_{t-1}\left(p_{t-1} + \varepsilon_t\right) = \mathrm{var}_{t-1}\left(\varepsilon_t\right) = u^2\left(1-(2q-1)^2\right) \end{aligned}$$

which is strictly positive for any non-degenerate Binomial. This of course implies the conditional variance

$$\mathrm{var}_{t-1}\left(p_t \frac{r}{1+r} \right) > 0. \tag{8}$$

Turning to the RHS of Equation (7), the conditional variance equals

[3]This discussion is not sensitive to the particular functional form of the two-state Binomial model. The analysis would be virtually identical, for example, if the price was a geometric Brownian motion, $p_{t+1} = p_t\left(1+\varepsilon_{t+1}\right)$.

$$\begin{aligned}&\operatorname{var}_{t-1}\left(\mathrm{d}_t+\frac{1}{1+r}\left[2uqm_{t,t+1}-u\right]\right)\\&=\operatorname{var}_{t-1}\left(\mathrm{d}_t\right)+\left(\frac{2uq}{1+r}\right)^2\operatorname{var}_{t-1}\left(m_{t,t+1}\right)\\&+\frac{2uq}{1+r}\operatorname{cov}_{t-1}\left(\mathrm{d}_t,m_{t,t+1}\right).\end{aligned}\quad(9)$$

If for some t, the payments and SDF were known

$$\operatorname{var}_{t-1}\left(\mathrm{d}_t\right)=\operatorname{var}_{t-1}\left(m_{t,t+1}\right)=0\quad(10)$$

expression (9) would be identically zero. Since a Binomial asset price is always risky, Equation (10) cannot hold. At least one of the two variables must be random each period so that

$$\operatorname{var}_{t-1}\left(\mathrm{d}_t\right)>0\ \text{ or }\ \operatorname{var}_{t-1}\left(m_{t,t+1}\right)>0$$

for any t.

3. Implications for Option Pricing Models

The workhorse model of asset prices in continuous-time models is the generic diffusion process

$$\mathrm{d}P_t=\mu_t\left(P_t\right)\mathrm{d}t+\sigma_t\left(P_t\right)\mathrm{d}W_t\quad(11)$$

where $\mathrm{d}W_t$ is a standard Brownian motion. The variance is determined by the function $\sigma_t\left(P_t\right)$ which is defined as

$$\sigma_t^2\left(p\right)=\lim_{h\to 0}\frac{1}{h}E\left(P_{t+h}-P_t\middle|P_t=p\right)^2.$$

At any time t, $\sigma_t\left(P_t\right)$ is the instantaneous variance and $\mu_t\left(P_t\right)\mathrm{d}t$ the instantaneous drift.

For the diffusions typically used in Finance, including Black-Scholes [2], Cox, Ingersoll, Ross [6] and in the multivariate case, Heath, Jarrow, Morton [7] and Heston [5], the instantaneous variance is positive for all t and all P_t

$$\sigma_t\left(P_t\right)>0.\quad(12)$$

There is no state of the world in which changes in price are deterministic.

A leading example is the lognormal diffusion of Black-Scholes [2],

$$\mathrm{d}P_t=\mu P_t\mathrm{d}t+\sigma P_t\mathrm{d}W_t\quad(13)$$

where $\left(\mu,\sigma\right)$ are fixed constants. The volatility parameter σ must be strictly positive or the price process would be purely deterministic for all time periods. In this case, the instantaneous variance is simply

$$\sigma_t^2\left(P_t\right)=\sigma^2P_t>0\quad(14)$$

and is strictly positive.

The option pricing formula originally formulated in Black and Scholes [2] is derived under the conditions:

Assumption 1. The underlying stock price P_t is a Geometric Brownian Motion.

Assumption 2. The discount rate is not stochastic.

Assumption 3. The dividend payment D_t is not stochastic over $0\le t<T$.

Assumptions 1-3 cannot all hold simultaneously under the no arbitrage condition defined in Harrison and Kreps [1] and Harrison and Pliska [8]. The martingale representation which results from no arbitrage implies that the price is an expectation,

$$P_t=\int_0^T E_t^*D_{t+s}\mathrm{d}s+E_t^*P_T=\int_0^T E\left(D_{t+s}\Lambda_{t,t+s}\right)\mathrm{d}s+E\left(P_T\Lambda_{t,T}\right)\quad(15)$$

where T is any future date and $\Lambda_{t,t+s}$ is the stochastic discount factor. Rearranging Equation (15),

$$P_t=D_t+\left[\int_{\mathrm{d}t}^T E\left(D_{t+s}\Lambda_{t,t+s}\right)\mathrm{d}s+E\left(P_T\Lambda_{t,T}\right)\right]\quad(16)$$

for any $t<T$. The instantaneous variance of P_t is just

$$\operatorname{var}_t\left(P_t\right)=\operatorname{var}_t\left(D_t+\int_{\mathrm{d}t}^T E\left(D_{t+s}\Lambda_{t,s}\right)\mathrm{d}s+E\left(P_T\Lambda_{t,T}\right)\right).\quad(17)$$

Expanding the conditional variance,

$$\begin{aligned}&\operatorname{var}_t\left(D_t\right)+\operatorname{var}_t\left(\int_{\mathrm{d}t}^T E\left(D_{t+s}\Lambda_{t,s}\right)\mathrm{d}s\right)\\&+\operatorname{var}_t\left(E\left(P_T\Lambda_{t,T}\right)\right)+\sum\operatorname{cov}_t.\end{aligned}\quad(18)$$

Under the Black-Scholes Assumption 3, the variance of the payments D_{t+s} are zero for $t<T$. The first term in (18) is trivially zero.

Assumption 2 of Black-Scholes says the discount factors $\Lambda_{t,t+s}$ also have zero variance. This implies that

$$E\left(D_{t+s}\Lambda_{t,t+s}\right)=\Lambda_{t,t+s}E\left(D_{t+s}\right)$$

which is a known constant. The conditional variance

$$\begin{aligned}&\operatorname{var}_t\left(\int_{\mathrm{d}t}^T E\left(D_{t+s}\Lambda_{t,t+s}\right)\mathrm{d}s\right)=\int_{\mathrm{d}t}^T\operatorname{var}_t\left(E\left(D_{t+s}\Lambda_{t,t+s}\right)\right)\mathrm{d}s\\&=\int_{\mathrm{d}t}^T\Lambda_{t,t+s}^2\operatorname{var}_t\left(E\left(D_{t+s}\right)\right)\mathrm{d}s=0\end{aligned}$$

since the variance of a unconditional mean is zero. Similarly the third term in (18) is

$$\begin{aligned}&\operatorname{var}_t\left[E\left(P_T\Lambda_{t,T}\right)\right]=\operatorname{var}_t\left[\Lambda_{t,T}E\left(P_T\right)\right]\\&=\Lambda_{t,t+s}^2\operatorname{var}_t\left[E\left(P_T\right)\right]=0\end{aligned}\quad(19)$$

where $E\left(P_T\right)$ is an unconditional mean. The covariance terms also vanish so that each element in (18) is identically zero.

We conclude that the conditional variance would be

$\text{var}_t\left(P_t\right)=0$ under the standard no arbitrage condition. This contradicts Assumption 1, that the price is a diffusion process.

4. Possible Solutions

Under no arbitrage the price of an asset is driven by two fundamentals—the payments on which it is a claim and the discount rate. The Black-Scholes [2] Assumptions 1-3 can be made consistent but only by violating no arbitrage.

Intuitively, Black-Scholes [2] construct a stock price that is continuously risky but for no fundamental reason—not because of risky payments nor because of changes in discounting. We can imagine, for example, that unpredictable stock moves are driven by incomplete information or by learning about distributions of random variables. Learning allows the stock price to be de-coupled from the fundamentals, in the manner of Assumptions 1-3. But this comes at the cost of violating the no arbitrage condition.

This is an important consideration. If the economy violates no arbitrage, we can no longer use it to value derivatives. Without some additional restriction, it is not necessarily true that the value of a contingent claim will depend on its underlying.

Since the stock does not depend on *its* underlying (the dividends), it would seem unnatural to assume that an option or other contingent claim would depend on *its* underlying (the stock). Nevertheless, we could follow the original Black-Scholes [2] development and explicitly add a condition like:

Assumption 4. The value of an option depends on its underlying asset price $V_t=V\left(P_t,t\right)$ and not on any other random variables.

However, Assumption 4 *cannot be made consistent with a no arbitrage condition.* Rather it must *replace* the no arbitrage condition, since Assumptions 1-3 imply no arbitrage is violated.

We could also examine what would happen if we drop the assumptions about either dividends or discount rates. Continue to assume that the underlying asset price is a Geometric Brownian motion. First, make no assumption about the dividend payments, but suppose the discount rate is not stochastic.

From (16), the instantaneous variance of the underlying price is

$$\text{var}_t\left(D_t+\frac{1}{\Lambda_t}\int_{dt}^{T}E\left(D_s\Lambda_s\right)\text{d}s+\frac{1}{\Lambda_t}E\left(P_T\Lambda_T\right)\right)>0 \quad (20)$$

which is strictly positive for all $t<T$. The second and third terms in expression (17)

$$\frac{1}{\Lambda_t}\int_{dt}^{T}E\left(D_s\Lambda_s\right)\text{d}s+\frac{1}{\Lambda_t}E\left(P_T\Lambda_T\right) \quad (21)$$

contain only constants and unconditional moments. The variance of an unconditional moment is zero so that

$$\text{var}_t\left(\frac{1}{\Lambda_t}\int_{dt}^{T}E\left(D_s\Lambda_s\right)\text{d}s+\frac{1}{\Lambda_t}E\left(P_T\Lambda_T\right)\right)=0.$$

The only term that remains is D_t as the sole source of risk. It follows that

$$\text{var}_t\left(P_t\right)\equiv\text{var}_t\left(D_t\right)$$

all variance in the asset price is explained by the risky dividend.

This would hold, for example, with dividends that are proportional to the stock price, $D_t=kP_t$ where k is some constant. This implies D_t is linear in P_t and in particular that the dividend process D_t is also a lognormal diffusion (this follows immediately from Ito's Lemma).

Since the instantaneous variance of the dividend is positive, the discount rate must be constant if we want to use arbitrage pricing. The asset price would in this case equal

$$P_t=E\int_0^{\infty}D_{t+s}\text{e}^{-rs}\text{d}s$$

where r is the constant discount rate. Since

$$\frac{\text{d}D_t}{D_t}=\mu\text{d}t+\sigma\text{d}W_t$$

we can write the price

$$P_t=D_t\int_0^{\infty}\text{e}^{(\mu-r)s}\text{d}s=D_t\frac{1}{r-\mu}.$$

The stock is a linear derivative written on the dividend payment and obeys a form of the Gordon growth model for stock prices. This may be an unrealistic characterization of dividend payments at high frequency such as daily observations.

Risky Discounting

Suppose that instead of deriving the behavior of dividends, we assume dividends are deterministic

$$\text{var}_t\left(D_t\right)=0 \quad (22)$$

but we make no assumptions about discount rates.

The variance of the asset price is thus given by the last two terms in (18). The instantaneous variance is

$$\begin{aligned}&\text{var}_t\left[\frac{1}{\Lambda_t}\left(\int_{dt}^{T}E\left(D_s\Lambda_s\right)\text{d}s+E\left(P_T\Lambda_T\right)\right)\right]\\&=\text{var}_t\left(\Lambda_t^{-1}\right)\left(\int_{dt}^{T}E\left(D_s\Lambda_s\right)\text{d}s+E\left(P_T\Lambda_T\right)\right)^2\end{aligned} \quad (23)$$

where we have taken the unconditional moments out of the variance. Expression (20) is positive if and only if

$$\text{var}_t\left(\Lambda_t^{-1}\right) > 0 \qquad (24)$$

the discount rate is stochastic at any time t.

5. Conclusions

If an asset price is modeled using binomial trees or their continuous-time diffusion limits, it is risky each period. A standard no arbitrage condition implies that there must also be a risky dividend and/or risky discount rate each period.

In order to value derivatives on an asset by arbitrage, we cannot allow both to be risky simultaneously. This leaves two possibilities. We can treat the dividends as a diffusion and fix the discount rate. This would seem somewhat unrealistic for most asset types such as stocks whose dividends tend to be smooth and paid only intermittently. Alternatively, we can assume dividends are purely deterministic and let the discount rate be a diffusion.

Another possibility is to abandon arbitrage valuation of contingent claims in favor of other methods (e.g., Heston [5]) which can accommodate multiple risky shocks. This would permit modeling both the discount rate and the dividend payment as risky simultaneous.

6. Acknowledgements

I am grateful to Peter Christoffersen, Tom George and Larry Samuelson for their comments. Any errors or inaccuracies are mine.

REFERENCES

[1] J. M. Harrison and D. M. Kreps, "Martingales and Arbitrage in Multiperiod Securities Markets," *Journal of Economic Theory*, Vol. 20, No. 3, 1979, pp. 381-408.

[2] F. Black and M. Scholes, "The Pricing of Options and Corporate Liabilities," *Journal of Political Economy*, Vol. 81, No. 3, 1973, pp. 637-659.

[3] R. C. Merton, "The Theory of Rational Option Pricing," *Bell Journal of Economics and Management Science*, Vol. 4, No. 1, 1973, pp. 141-183.

[4] A. Melino and S. Turnbull, "Pricing Foreign Currency Options with Stochastic Volatility," *Journal of Econometrics*, Vol. 45, No. 1-2, 1990, pp. 239-265.

[5] S. Heston, "A Closed-Form Solution for Optoins with Stochastic Volatilityi with Applications to Bond and Currency Options," *Review of Financial Studies*, Vol. 6, No. 2, 1993, pp. 327-344.

[6] J. C. Cox, J. E. Ingersoll and S. A. Ross, "A Theory of the Term Structure of Interest Rates," *Econometrica*, Vol. 53, No. 2, 1985, pp. 385-408.

[7] D. Heath, R. Jarrow and A. Morton, "Bond Pricing and the Term Structure of Interest Rates: A New Methodology for Contingent Claims Valuation," *Econometrica*, Vol. 60, No. 1, 1992, pp. 77-106.

[8] J. M. Harrison and S. Pliska, "Martingales and Stochastic Integrals in the Theory of Continuous Trading," *Stochastic Processes and Their Applications*, Vol. 11, No. 3, 1981, pp. 215-260.

[9] J. C. Cox and M. Rubinstein, "Options Markets," Prentice-Hall, Upper Saddle River, 1985.

[10] M. J. Brennan and E. S. Schwartz, "Finite Difference Methods and Jump Processes Arising in the Pricing of Contingent Claims: A Synthesis," *Journal of Financial and Quantitative Analysis*, Vol. 13, No. 3, 1978, pp. 461-474.

[11] J. C. Cox, S. A. Ross and M. Rubinstein, "Options Pricing: A Simplified Approach," *Journal of Financial Economics*, Vol. 7, No. 3, 1979, pp. 229-263.

[12] J. D. Duffie and P. Protter, "From Discrete to Continuous Time Finance: Weak Convergence of the Financial Gain Process," Stanford University, Stanford, 1988.

[13] H. He, "Convergence from Discrete to Continuous Time Contingent Claim Prices," *Review of Financial Studies*, Vol. 3, No. 4, 1990, pp. 523-546.

7

Estimating Probability Distribution of Asset Value Based on Dual Effects of Deposit Insurance with the Minimum Cross-Entropy Principle

Xiaoning Lv[1], Xuezhi Qin[1], Tao Sun[2]
[1]Faculty of Management and Economics, Dalian University of Technology, Dalian, China
[2]School of Mathematics, Liaoning Normal University, Dalian, China

ABSTRACT

A model is proposed to estimate the probability distribution of asset value based on the benefit effects as well as the risk effects of deposit insurance with the minimum cross-entropy principle. Three scenarios are constructed to depict situations with different dual effects of deposit insurance. The corresponding assets distribution functions are obtained accordingly. The results show that it is positively correlated between the supervision level and the risk aversion effects of deposit insurance. The increase of the deposit insurance premium moves the bank's assets distribution to the right side although not significantly. The asset probability distributions estimated in this paper can be taken as a reference for banks to choose the proper credit investment projects.

Keywords: Probability Distribution; Deposit Insurance; Dual Effects; Cross-Entropy

1. Introduction

Deposit insurance is generally considered as an important institutional arrangement for the stability of the banking system. Currently more than 90 countries and regions around the world have established deposit insurance system. The recent crisis occurred in 2008 made 165 banks go bankrupt in the United States, which involves total deposits of 318.9 billion dollars. The federal deposit insurance corporation (FDIC) had played a positive role in a series of important crisis disposal process. To strengthen the depositors' confidence, many counties chose to increase the coverage of deposit insurance during the crisis period. On one hand, the financial institutions may benefit from deposit insurance for the reduction of operational risk, on the other hand, they have the motive to increase the credit risk after taking deposit insurance, which may bring more threats to the financial system (See [1,2]). Therefore, it is worth concerning with the above dual effects of deposit insurance.

Several researches are engaged in the area of the dual effects of deposit insurance. Reference [3] discusses the microeconomic effects of deposit insurance during financial crisis. The results suggest that the increase of deposit insurance coverage helped to prevent a more serious and dangerous meltdown of deposits. Reference [4] finds that deposit insurance is partially effective in preventing bank runs by using minute-by-minute depositor withdrawal data. In recent years, with the outbreak and spread of the financial crisis, the limitation of deposit insurance system is gradually highlighting. For example, the "moral hazard" problem induced by deposit insurance could further aggravate the risk of the financial system. Accordingly, more and more scholars pay close attention to the risk effects of deposit insurance. The conclusions, however, are inconsistent among different researches that use diverse samples and methods. The empirical results do not support the existence of the risk effects of deposit insurance for the sample given in [5]. While [6] gives the opposite conclusion that deposit insurance significantly increases the credit risk of financial institutions. In fact, the benefit effects and the risk effects of deposit insurance may exist in the same time. By empirically analyzing the dual effects of deposit insurance, reference [7] finds that deposit insurance can effectively improve the efficiency of financial system and has a significant risk effects too.

Most of the researches aim at the results analysis on the dual effects of deposit insurance. The fact is that deposit insurance influences the probability distribution of the insured institution's assets value at the first place and then engenders the dual effects. Therefore, it is important to properly estimate the assets distribution taking the deposit insurance into account. The minimum cross-entropy principle offers a method to implement distribution estimation considering some known information (See [8]). This paper tries to estimate the probability distribution of the insured institution's assets value based on the dual effects of deposit insurance with the minimum cross-entropy principle.

The rest of the paper proceeds as follows. Section 2 presents the main method and the related calculations. Section 3 analyzes the simulation results. Section 4 draws a conclusion.

2. Methodology

2.1. Minimum Cross-Entropy

Definition 2.1. *Two probability distributions F and G are defined on the probability space* (Ω, F, G). *The corresponding density functions are f and g, respectively. The cross-entropy,* $D(G,F)$, *between F and G is defined as follows*

$$D(G,F)=\int_{\Omega} g\ln(g/f)\mathrm{d}x. \quad (1)$$

The cross-entropy $D(G,F)$ measures the differences between the unknown distribution G and the given one F. The minimum cross-entropy principle that proposed by Kullback in 1956 (See [9]), provides a rule to estimate the probability distribution which is as close as possible to the prior distribution. The distribution obtained then is supposed to be the most appropriate one that can be estimated according to the known information. The minimum cross-entropy principle can be expressed as the following programming problem:

$$\begin{aligned} &\min D(G,F)=\int_{\Omega} g\ln(g/f)\mathrm{d}x \\ &s.t. \int_{\Omega} g\mathrm{d}x=1,\ g\ge 0 \\ &\int_{\Omega} gM_i(x)\mathrm{d}x=a_i, i=1,2,\cdots,n \end{aligned} \quad (2)$$

where $M_i(x)$ are the moment functions and a_i are the observed statistical moments. The first two constraints guarantee g to be a probability density function. The moment constraints make sure the distribution g has the same statistical moments as observed.

Proposition 2.2. *The solution of problem* (2) *is given as follows*:

$$g=\frac{\exp\left[\sum_{i=1}^{n}\lambda_i M_i(x)\right]}{\int_{\Omega}\exp\left[\sum_{i=1}^{n}\lambda_i M_i(x)\right]f\mathrm{d}x}f \quad (3)$$

Proof. The Lagrange function of problem (2) can be written as

$$\begin{aligned} L(g,f,\lambda)=&-\int_{\Omega} g\ln(g/f)\mathrm{d}x+(\lambda_0+1)\left(\int_{\Omega} g\mathrm{d}x-1\right) \\ &+\sum_{i=1}^{n}\lambda_i\left[\int_{\Omega} gM_i(x)\mathrm{d}x-a_i\right], \end{aligned}$$

where $\lambda_i (i=0,1,\cdots,n)$ are the Lagrange multipliers. The condition of optimization solution is

$$\ln(g/f)=\lambda_0+\sum_{i=1}^{n}\lambda_i M_i(x), \text{ or}$$

$$g=\mathrm{e}^{\lambda_0}\exp\left[\sum_{i=1}^{n}\lambda_i M_i(x)\right]f. \quad (4)$$

Integrating both sides of Equation (4), it infers

$$\mathrm{e}^{-\lambda_0}=\int_{\Omega}\exp\left[\sum_{i=1}^{n}\lambda_i M_i(x)\right]f\mathrm{d}x. \quad (5)$$

Substituting Equation (5) into Equation (4), Equation (3) holds.

2.2. Modeling

Assume that the representative bank's liabilities are all derived from deposit which is insured by the insurance company. Denote x_t as the value of the bank's assets at time t, and assume x_t follows a lognormal process

$$\mathrm{d}x_t=\mu x_t\mathrm{d}t+\sigma x_0\mathrm{d}w,$$

where w is a Brownian motion process, μ is the instantaneous expected rate of return of the bank's assets, and σ is the volatility of the rate of return. Denote the deposit insurance underwriting date as 0 and define x_0 as the bank's assets value before paying the total deposit insurance premium P at the beginning of the insurance period. The bank goes bankrupt if the bank's assets value is less than its liabilities value on the insurance expiry date T. The bank's assets value on date T satisfies

$$\ln x_T\sim\Phi\left[\ln(x_0-P)+\left(\mu-\frac{\sigma^2}{2}\right)T,\sigma^2 T\right],$$

from which the probability density function of x_T can be derived as follows:

$$f(x_T)=\mathrm{e}^{-\frac{1}{2}\left[\frac{\ln x_T-\ln(x_0-P)-(\mu-\sigma^2/2)T}{\sigma\sqrt{T}}\right]^2}\Big/\left(\sqrt{2\pi T}\sigma x_T\right). \quad (6)$$

The distribution of the bank's assets value can be obtained by integrating Equation (6), that is

$$F(x_T)=\int_0^{x_T}f(x_T)\mathrm{d}x_T. \quad (7)$$

Deposit insurance may induce more benefits to the bank by strengthening the depositors' confidence. However, after taking deposit insurance, the bank is more likely to issue riskier loans, which may increase the bank's default risk. Under both the benefit effect and the risk effect of deposit insurance, the bank's assets value may no longer subject to the prior lognormal distribution $F(x_T)$. Let $G(x_T)$ represent the distribution of the bank's assets value considering the dual effects of deposit insurance, and $g(x_T)$ is the density function accordingly. $G(x_T)$ is a proximate distribution to $F(x_T)$. And $g(x_T)$ can be obtained by minimizing the cross-entropy between $F(x_T)$ and $G(x_T)$ subject to some constraints, that is

$$\begin{aligned} &\min D(G,F)=\int_0^{+\infty} g(x_T)\ln\left[g(x_T)/f(x_T)\right]\mathrm{d}x_T \\ &s.t.\int_0^{+\infty} g(x_T)x_T\mathrm{d}x_T = c_1 E_{\bar{F}}(x_T) \\ &\int_0^{+\infty} g(x_T)\left[x_T - c_1 E_{\bar{F}}(x_T)\right]^2 \mathrm{d}x_T = c_2 \operatorname{Var}_{\bar{F}}(x_T) \\ &\int_0^{+\infty} g(x_T)\mathrm{d}x_T = 1, g(x_T)\ge 0, \end{aligned} \tag{8}$$

where $c_1 > 0, c_2 > 0$ are constants, and

$$\begin{aligned} &E_{\bar{F}}(x_T)=\int_0^{+\infty} \bar{f}(x_T)x_T\mathrm{d}x_T \\ &\operatorname{Var}_{\bar{F}}(x_T)=\int_0^{+\infty} \bar{f}(x_T)\left[x_T - E_{\bar{F}}(x_T)\right]^2 \mathrm{d}x_T \\ &\bar{f}(x_T)=\mathrm{e}^{-\frac{1}{2}\left[\frac{(\ln x_T-\ln x_0)-(\mu-\sigma^2/2)T}{\sigma\sqrt{T}}\right]^2}\Big/\left(\sqrt{2\pi T}\sigma x_T\right) \end{aligned} \tag{9}$$

Here $\bar{f}(x_T)$ is the probability density function of the bank's assets value before purchasing deposit insurance. It is the insurance premium P that makes $\bar{f}(x_T)$ differ from $f(x_T)$. The first constraint of problem (8) measures the benefit effect of deposit insurance, while the second constraint reflects the risk effect accordingly. The dual effects of deposit insurance are determined by various factors, which can be generally divided into the bank level and the regulation level. Banks pay more attention to the benefits they may get after taking deposit insurance, which means only when $c_1 \ge 1$ would they join the deposit insurance system, and the regulators on the other hand are also concerned with the bank's risk taking behaviors besides the benefit efficiency. With strict supervision, which means $0 < c_2 \le 1$, the bank is restricted to limit its assets variance no more than that without deposit insurance. However, it may not be possible to increase the bank's benefits while decrease the relevant risk. Sometimes the supervisors have to tolerate some extra risk so as to attain the benefit objects. Using a small positive constant, ε, as the maximal extent of tolerance, the forbearance supervision is described by $1 < c_2 \le 1+\varepsilon$. Also, in the extreme case where there is no supervision at all, the second constraint of problem (8) would be omitted.

According to proposition 2.2, the solution of problem (8) can be written as

$$g(x_T) = \frac{\exp\left\{\lambda_1 x_T + \lambda_2\left[x_T - c_1 E_{\bar{F}}(x_T)\right]^2\right\} f(x_T)}{\int_0^{+\infty} f(x_T)\exp\left\{\lambda_1 x_T + \lambda_2\left[x_T - c_1 E_{\bar{F}}(x_T)\right]^2\right\}\mathrm{d}x_T}. \tag{10}$$

2.3. Scenarios

Three scenarios are described to discuss the corresponding probability distributions of the bank's assets value under different benefit and regulatory constraints.

- Scenario I: Strong benefit motivation with no supervision.

The corresponding minimum cross-entropy problem can be written as

$$\begin{aligned} &\min D(G,F)=\int_0^{+\infty} g(x_T)\ln\left[g(x_T)/f(x_T)\right]\mathrm{d}x_T \\ &s.t.\int_0^{+\infty} g(x_T)x_T\mathrm{d}x_T = c_{1,1} E_{\bar{F}}(x_T) \\ &\int_0^{+\infty} g(x_T)\mathrm{d}x_T = 1, g(x_T)\ge 0 \end{aligned} \tag{11}$$

where $c_{1,1} \ge 1$. According to Equation (10), the density function $g_1(x_T)$ is

$$g_1(x_T)=\frac{\mathrm{e}^{\lambda_{1,1}x_T}}{\int_0^{+\infty} f(x_T)\mathrm{e}^{\lambda_{1,1}x_T}\mathrm{d}x_T} f(x_T). \tag{12}$$

- Scenario II: Strong benefit motivation with tolerant supervision.

The minimum cross-entropy problem is listed as

$$\begin{aligned} &\min D(G,F)=\int_0^{+\infty} g(x_T)\ln\left[g(x_T)/f(x_T)\right]\mathrm{d}x_T \\ &s.t.\int_0^{+\infty} g(x_T)x_T\mathrm{d}x_T = c_{2,1} E_{\bar{F}}(x_T) \\ &\int_0^{+\infty} g(x_T)\left[x_T - c_1 E_{\bar{F}}(x_T)\right]^2 \mathrm{d}x_T = c_{2,2} \operatorname{Var}_{\bar{F}}(x_T) \\ &\int_0^{+\infty} g(x_T)\mathrm{d}x_T = 1, g(x_T)\ge 0 \end{aligned} \tag{13}$$

where $c_{2,1} \ge 1, 1 < c_{2,2} \le 1+\varepsilon$. Also, the density function $g_2(x_T)$ is

$$g_2(x_T)=\frac{\mathrm{e}^{\lambda_{2,1}x_T+\lambda_{2,2}\left[x_T-c_{2,1}E_{\bar{F}}(x_T)\right]^2}}{\int_0^{+\infty} f(x_T)\mathrm{e}^{\lambda_{2,1}x_T+\lambda_{2,2}\left[x_T-c_{2,1}E_{\bar{F}}(x_T)\right]^2}\mathrm{d}x_T} f(x_T). \tag{14}$$

- Scenario III: Neutral benefit motivation with strict supervision.

The following minimum cross-entropy problem represents this situation.

$$\begin{aligned} &\min D(G,F)=\int_0^{+\infty} g(x_T)\ln\left[g(x_T)/f(x_T)\right]\mathrm{d}x_T \\ &s.t.\int_0^{+\infty} g(x_T)x_T\mathrm{d}x_T = E_{\bar{F}}(x_T) \\ &\int_0^{+\infty} g(x_T)\left[x_T - E_{\bar{F}}(x_T)\right]^2 \mathrm{d}x_T = c_{3,2} \operatorname{Var}_{\bar{F}}(x_T) \\ &\int_0^{+\infty} g(x_T)\mathrm{d}x_T = 1, g(x_T)\ge 0, \end{aligned} \tag{15}$$

where $c_{3,1} = 1,\ 0 < c_{3,2} < 1$. The density function $g_3(x_T)$ is

$$g_3(x_T) = \frac{e^{\lambda_{3,1}x_T + \lambda_{3,2}[x_T - E_{\bar{F}}(x_T)]^2}}{\int_0^{+\infty} f(x_T) e^{\lambda_{3,1}x_T + \lambda_{3,2}[x_T - E_{\bar{F}}(x_T)]^2} \mathrm{d}x_T} f(x_T). \quad (16)$$

2.4. Calculation Method

It should be noticed that Equations (12), (14) and (16) are not the final solutions of $g_j(x_T)(j=1,2,3)$ for the Lagrange multipliers are not determined. Here dual method is used to calculate the Lagrange multipliers. Substituting Equations (12), (14) and (16) into the Lagrange functions of problem (11), (13) and (15) respectively, the dual problems of the three minimum cross-entropy programmings given in the scenarios above are as follows:

$$\max D_j(\lambda) = \begin{cases} -\ln\left[\int_0^{+\infty} e^{\lambda_{j,1}x_T} f(x_T)\mathrm{d}x_T\right] + \lambda_{j,1}c_{j,1}E_{\bar{F}}(x_T), j=1 \\ -\ln\left\{e^{\lambda_{j,1}x_T + \lambda_{j,2}[x_T - c_{j,1}E_{\bar{F}}(x_T)]^2} f(x_T)\mathrm{d}x_T\right\} + \lambda_{j,1}c_{j,1}E_{\bar{F}}(x_T) \\ \qquad + \lambda_{j,2}c_{j,2}\operatorname{Var}_{\bar{F}}(x_T), j=2,3 \end{cases} \quad (17)$$

Suppose $\lambda_{j,1}^*(j=1,2,3), \lambda_{j,2}^*(j=2,3)$ are the optimal solutions to Equation (17). Substituting $\lambda_{j,1}^*$ and $\lambda_{j,2}^*$ into Equations (12), (14) and (16), the density function $g_j^*(x_T)$ can be obtained as

$$g_j^*(x_T) = \begin{cases} \dfrac{e^{\lambda_{j,1}^* x_T}}{\int_0^{+\infty} f(x_T) e^{\lambda_{j,1}^* x_T}\mathrm{d}x_T} f(x_T), & j=1 \\ \dfrac{e^{\lambda_{j,1}^* x_T + \lambda_{j,2}^*[x_T - c_{j,1}E_{\bar{F}}(x_T)]^2}}{\int_0^{+\infty} f(x_T) e^{\lambda_{j,1}^* x_T + \lambda_{j,2}^*[x_T - c_{j,1}E_{\bar{F}}(x_T)]^2}\mathrm{d}x_T} f(x_T), & j=2,3 \end{cases} \quad (18)$$

It can be seen from Equation (18) that the density function $g_j^*(x_T)$ is determined by $\lambda_{j,1}^*$ and $\lambda_{j,2}^*$ which are actually influenced by the bank's benefit motivation along with the supervision level. Thereby, the density function $g_j^*(x_T)$ are affected by $c_{j,1}$ and $c_{j,2}$.

The bank's expected assets value $E_{\bar{F}}(x_T)$ and the corresponding variance $\operatorname{Var}_{\bar{F}}(x_T)$ before purchasing deposit insurance should be calculated so as to clarify the constraints of the minimum cross-entropy problem. Both of the two variables can be calculated from Equation (9)[1].

$$\begin{aligned} E_{\bar{F}}(x_T) &= \int_0^{+\infty} \bar{f}(x_T)x_T\mathrm{d}x_T = x_0e^{\mu T} \\ \operatorname{Var}_{\bar{F}}(x_T) &= \int_0^{+\infty} \bar{f}(x_T)[x_T - E_{\bar{F}}(x_T)]^2\mathrm{d}x_T \\ &= x_0^2 e^{2\mu T}\left(e^{\sigma^2 T} - 1\right) \end{aligned} \quad (19)$$

Another factor implied in $g_j^*(x_T)$ is the deposit insurance premium P. The total premium consists of the net premium and the extra premium. The net premium is equal to the actuarial present value of the insurer's total

[1]From Equation (9):

$E_{\bar{F}}(x_T)$

$$= \int_0^{+\infty} \bar{f}(x_T)x_T\mathrm{d}x_T = \int_0^{+\infty} e^{-\frac{1}{2}\left[\frac{(\ln x_T - \ln x_0)-(\mu-\sigma^2/2)T}{\sigma\sqrt{T}}\right]^2} \Big/ \left(\sqrt{2\pi T}\sigma x_T\right)x_T\mathrm{d}x_T = x_0e^{(\mu-\sigma^2/2)T}\int_{-\infty}^{+\infty} e^{-\frac{1}{2}m^2+\sigma\sqrt{T}m}\Big/\left(\sqrt{2\pi}\right)\mathrm{d}m = x_0e^{(\mu-\sigma^2/2)T}\int_{-\infty}^{+\infty} e^{-\frac{1}{2}[m-\sigma\sqrt{T}]^2+\sigma^2T/2}\Big/\left(\sqrt{2\pi}\right)\mathrm{d}m = x_0e^{\mu T},$$

$$\operatorname{Var}_{\bar{F}}(x_T) = \int_0^{+\infty} \bar{f}(x_T)[x_T - E_{\bar{F}}(x_T)]^2\mathrm{d}x_T = \int_0^{+\infty} e^{-\frac{1}{2}\left[\frac{(\ln x_T - \ln x_0)-(\mu-\sigma^2/2)T}{\sigma\sqrt{T}}\right]^2}\Big/\left(\sqrt{2\pi T}\sigma x_T\right)x_T^2\mathrm{d}x_T - [E_{\bar{F}}(x_T)]^2 = x_0^2e^{(2\mu-\sigma^2)T}\int_{-\infty}^{+\infty} e^{-\frac{1}{2}m^2+2\sigma\sqrt{T}m}\Big/\left(\sqrt{2\pi}\right)m - [E_{\bar{F}}(x_T)]^2$$

$$= x_0^2e^{(2\mu-\sigma^2)T}\int_{-\infty}^{+\infty} e^{-\frac{1}{2}[m-2\sigma\sqrt{T}]^2+2\sigma^2T}\Big/\left(\sqrt{2\pi}\right)m - [E_{\bar{F}}(x_T)]^2 = x_0^2e^{2\mu T}\left(e^{\sigma^2T}-1\right)$$

where $m = \dfrac{(\ln x_T - \ln x_0)-(\mu-\sigma^2/2)T}{\sigma\sqrt{T}}$.

claim payments on date T and the extra premium is used to compensate the unexpected risk the insurer may encounter. The premium P can be calculated as[2]

$$\begin{aligned} P &= \mathrm{e}^{-rT}\int_0^{D_T}\left(D_T - x_T\right)\bar{f}\left(x_T\right)\mathrm{d}x_T + \theta\,\mathrm{Var}_{\bar{F}}\left(x_T\right) \\ &= D_0 N\left(k\right) - \mathrm{e}^{(\mu-r)T}x_0 N\left(k-\sigma\sqrt{T}\right) \\ &\quad + \theta x_0^2\mathrm{e}^{2\mu T}\left(\mathrm{e}^{\sigma^2 T}-1\right), \end{aligned} \tag{20}$$

where

$$k = \left[\left(\ln D_T - \ln x_0\right) - \left(\mu - \sigma^2/2\right)T\right] \Big/ \left(\sigma\sqrt{T}\right),$$

and r is the risk-free interest rate and $D_T = \mathrm{e}^{rT}D_0$ is the accumulated future value of the bank's deposit value on date T using the risk free interest rate. $N(\cdot)$ is the standard normal distribution function, and θ is defined as an additional safety factor.

Substituting Equations (19), (6) and (20) into problem (17), the Lagrange multipliers $\lambda_{j,1}^*$ and $\lambda_{j,2}^*$ can be obtained by solving the relevant dual problems in (17)[3]. Putting the estimated $\lambda_{j,1}^*$ and $\lambda_{j,2}^*$ along with Equations (7) and (19) into Equation (18), $g_j^*\left(x_T\right)$ can be derived then.

3. Simulation

3.1. Basic Simulation Results

Suppose the representative bank's assets value is 7 billion RMB on date 0, of which the deposit accounts for 90 percent. The term of the deposit is one year and so is the duration of the deposit insurance. The expected rate of return on bank assets is 0.225, and the volatility of the rate of return is 0.135. To compute the insurance premium, the additional safety factor θ should be assigned. There is no extra premium when θ equals zero. The assumption of $\theta = 0$ is used to calculate the basic simulation results here, and the consequence of other cases will be discussed in the next section. The risk-free interest rate is assumed to be 2.25%. The values of the parameters are given in **Table 1**.

Using the parameters given in **Table 1**, the expected assets value before purchasing deposit insurance and the corresponding variance can be calculated by Equation (19). The insurance premium is obtained via Equation (20). The calculating results are listed in **Table 2**.

For scenario I, 5% increase of the bank's expected assets value is assumed. Both the expectation and the variance of the bank's assets value are supposed to increase by 2.5% in scenario II. Scenario III describes the situation with no change of the bank's expected assets value and 5% decrease of assets variance. The corresponding value of $c_{j,1}$ and $c_{j,2}$ are listed in **Table 3**. Minimizing problem (17) can determine the optimal Lagrange multipliers. The results are given in **Table 3**.

The estimated probability density functions can be obtained using the values of $\lambda_{j,1}^*$ and $\lambda_{j,2}^*$ in **Table 3**. **Figure 1** shows the curves of the density functions. Compared with the original density function $f(x)$, the adjusted density functions reveal different features. The density functions $g_1^*\left(x_T\right)$ and $g_2^*\left(x_T\right)$ stand for the situations of no supervision and tolerant supervision respectively with the same benefit effects of deposit insurance. As can be seem from **Figure 1**, the distribution $G_2^*\left(x_T\right)$ is more concentrated than the distribution $G_1^*\left(x_T\right)$, which means the supervision level positively affects the risk aversion effects of deposit insurance under the same benefit effects. The same pattern also can be seen from the comparison of the density $f\left(x_T\right)$ and the density $g_3^*\left(x_T\right)$, which reflects the situation of the same benefit effects and two different supervision levels.

The density function $g_2^*\left(x_T\right)$ shows a positive change of the expected assets value compared with $g_3^*\left(x_T\right)$ and

Table 1. The value of the parameters.

x_0 (RMB)	D_0 (RMB)	T (year)	μ	σ	θ	r
7	6.3	1	0.225	0.135	0	0.0225

Table 2. The calculated results of the intermediate variables.

$E_F(x_T)$ (billion yuan)	$Var_F(x_T)$ (billion yuan^2)	P (billion yuan)
8.766	1.413	0.00384

Table 3. The Lagrange multipliers.

Scenario	$c_{j,1}$	$c_{j,2}$	$\lambda_{j,1}^*$	$\lambda_{j,2}^*$
1	1.025	-	0.153	-
2	1.025	1.025	0.185	−0.035
3	1	0.95	0.012	−0.018

[2]The insurer's total claim payments on date T can be described as $\begin{cases} 0, & x_T \ge D_T \\ D_T - x_T, & x_T < D_T \end{cases}$. Thus the net premium can be calculated as

$$\begin{aligned} P_{\text{net}} &= \mathrm{e}^{-rT}\int_0^{D_T}\left(D_T - x_T\right)\bar{f}\left(x_T\right)\mathrm{d}x_T \\ &= \mathrm{e}^{-rT}\int_0^{D_T}\left(D_T - x_T\right)\mathrm{e}^{-\frac{1}{2}\left[\frac{(\ln x_T - \ln x_0)-(\mu-\sigma^2/2)T}{\sigma\sqrt{T}}\right]^2} \Big/ \left(\sqrt{2\pi T}\sigma x_T\right)\mathrm{d}x_T, \\ &= D_T\mathrm{e}^{-rT}\int_{-\infty}^{k}\frac{\mathrm{e}^{-\frac{1}{2}m^2}}{\sqrt{2\pi}}\mathrm{d}m - x_0\mathrm{e}^{(\mu-\sigma^2/2)T-rT}\int_{-\infty}^{k}\frac{\mathrm{e}^{-\frac{1}{2}\left[m-\sigma\sqrt{T}\right]^2+\sigma^2T/2}}{\sqrt{2\pi}}\mathrm{d}m \\ &= D_0 N\left(k\right) - x_0\mathrm{e}^{(\mu-r)T}N\left(k-\sigma\sqrt{T}\right) \end{aligned}$$

where $k = \dfrac{\left(\ln D_T - \ln x_0\right) - \left(\mu - \sigma^2/2\right)T}{\sigma\sqrt{T}}$. Substituting equation (19) into Equation (20), the total premium P equals $P = D_0 N\left(k\right) - \mathrm{e}^{(\mu-r)T}x_0 N\left(k-\sigma\sqrt{T}\right) + \theta x_0^2\mathrm{e}^{2\mu T}\left(\mathrm{e}^{\sigma^2 T}-1\right)$.

[3]Here Matlab 7.0 is used to write a program to solve problem (17).

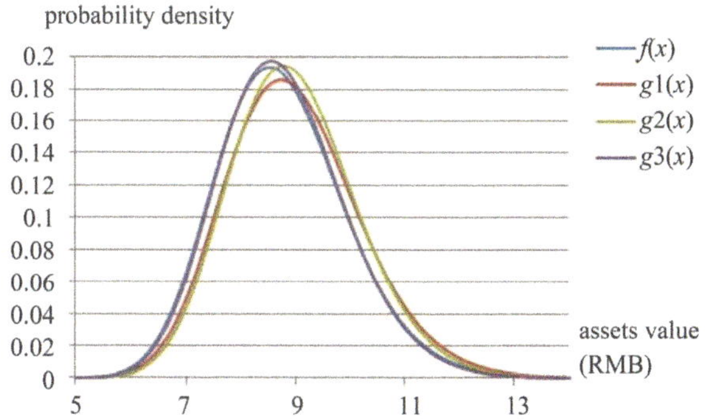

Figure 1. The estimated probability densities.

a negative difference with the assets variance of $g_1^*(x_T)$. To consider the benefit effect and the risk effect of deposit insurance at the same time, the distribution $G_2^*(x_T)$ may be an ideal one for it represents the case of an increase of benefit and an acceptable level of risk.

3.2. Effects of Safety Premium

In this section, the additional safety factor θ is set to be 0.001 and 0.01 so as to measure the effects of the safety premium. The values of $\lambda_{j,1}^*$ and $\lambda_{j,2}^*$ with different θ are given in **Table 4**. The shapes of the density functions accordingly are given in **Figure 2**. Compared with the bank's total assets, the premium of deposit insurance is relatively minor. For that reason, the effects of the additional premium to the assets density function are also limited. The blue curve in **Figure 2** represents the density function $g_2^*(x_T)$ with no additional premium while the red one stands for the same function but with additional premium. The red curve deviates from the blue one slightly to the right side.

4. Conclusions

Considering both the benefit effects and the risk effects of deposit insurance, this paper provides a method to estimate the probability distribution of the bank's assets value based on the minimum cross-entropy principle.

Three scenarios are given to describe situations with different dual effects of deposit insurance. The corresponding assets distribution functions are obtained respectively. The results show that the supervision level positively affects the risk aversion effects of deposit insurance under the same benefit effects. While the increase of the deposit insurance premium moves the bank's assets distribution slightly to the right side. The distributions, which are estimated under different benefit and risk objects, can be taken as a reference for banks to choose the proper credit projects.

The scenarios constructed in this paper are simple and limited. Taking into account some more complicated conditions, the model can be improved. Moreover, this paper aims only at estimating the assets distributions affected by deposit insurance. Other analysis such as the distortion level that may be measured by calculating the cross-entropy between the original and estimated assets distributions will be discussed in further research.

Table 4. Lagrange multipliers.

Scenario	$\lambda_{j,1}^*$		$\lambda_{j,2}^*$	
	$\theta=0.1\%$	$\theta=1\%$	$\theta=0.1\%$	$\theta=1\%$
1	0.154	0.165	-	-
2	0.187	0.198	−0.036	−0.034
3	0.013	0.024	−0.018	−0.018

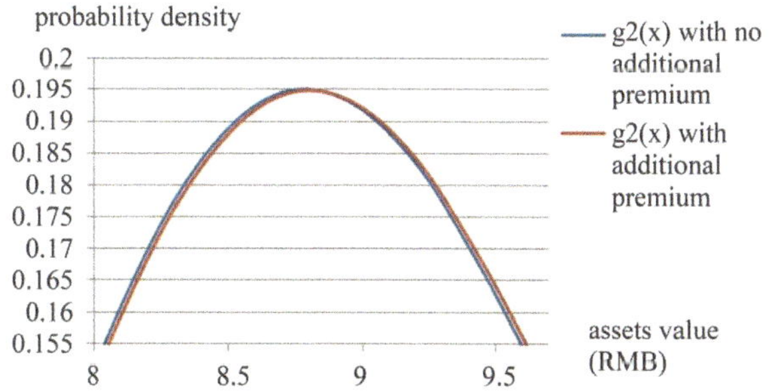

Figure 2. The top part of the density $g_2^*(x_T)$ with and without additional premium[4].

5. Acknowledgements

The research is supported by National Science Foundation of China (71171032), and the central university special funds for basic research business expenses (DUT11-RW202).

REFERENCES

[1] J. C. Du, A. F. Moreau and C. W. Sealey, "Fixed-Rate Deposit Insurance and Risk-Shifting Behavior at Commercial Banks," *Journal of Banking & Finance*, Vol. 16, No. 4, 1992, pp. 715-742.

[2] A. Hovakimian and E. Kane, "Effectiveness of Capital Regulation at U.S. Commercial Banks, 1985 to 1994," *Journal of Finance*, Vol. 55, No. 1, 2000, pp. 451-468.

[3] N. Prean and H. Stix, "The Effect of Raising Deposit Insurance Coverage in Times of Financial Crisis—Evidence from Croatian Microdata," *Economic Systems*, Vol. 35, No. 4, 2011, pp. 496-511.

[4] R. Iyer and M. Puri, "Understanding Bank Runs: The Importance of Depositor-Bank Relationships and Net-

[4]The differences between the two density functions can not be seen clearly if the whole figure, instead of the top parts, is given here for the reason discussed in the paper.

works," Working Paper, The National Bureau of Economic Research (NBER), Cambridge, 2008.

[5] L. Mbarek and D. M. Hmaied, "Deposit Insurance and Bank Risk-shifting Incentives: Evidence from the Tunisian Banking System," *Journal of Money, Investment & Banking*, Vol. 20, 2011, pp. 41-53.

[6] V. P. Ioannidou and M. F. Penas, "Deposit Insurance and Bank Risk-Taking: Evidence from Internal Loan Ratings," *Journal of Financial Intermediation*, Vol. 19, No. 1, 2010, pp. 95-115.

[7] L. Chernykh and R. A. Cole, "Does Deposit Insurance Improve Financial Intermediation? Evidence from the Russian Experiment," *Journal of Banking & Finance*, Vol. 35, No. 2, 2011, pp. 388-402.

[8] M. Monoyios, "The Minimal Entropy Measure and an Esscher Transform in an Incomplete Market Model," *Statistics and Probability Letters*, Vol. 77, No. 11, 2007, pp. 1070-1076.

[9] M. Avellanada, "Minimum Relative-Entropy Calibration of Asset-Pricing Models," *International Journal of Theoretical and Applied Finance*, Vol. 1, No. 4, 1998, pp. 447-472.

8

Why Are Children Impatient? Evolutionary Selection of Preferences

Junji Kageyama
Department of Economics, Meikai University, Urayasu, Japan

ABSTRACT

This study aims to explain why children are impatient. Using a biological framework called the life history theory, the study investigates the evolutionary root of time preference, paying particular attention to childhood. The results show that the biologically endowed rate of time preference is equal to the mortality rate not only in adulthood but also in childhood, reflecting the change in the biological value of survival. Mortality is the baseline for time preference through the entire course of life. These results are consistent with the findings in previous empirical and experimental studies that the discount rate is U-shaped in age, and account for why young children, in particular, are impatient. In addition, the difference in time preference between adults and children provides a biological explanation for the parent-offspring conflict, in which the higher discount rate among children causes parents and their children to disagree over intertemporal allocation of resources in collective decision-making particularly within the household.

Keywords: Time Preference; Value of Survival; Life History Theory; Mortality; Parent-Offspring Conflict

1. Introduction

The decision-making process within a household typically involves multiple individuals such as the wife, husband and children. As a result, collective decisions made in the household depend on preferences of household members. For example, Dauphin *et al.* [1] showed that children as well as parents influence household economic decisions[1].

Nevertheless, children, who sometimes make up the larger portion of the family, seldom receive much attention in the study of economics. Considering that even an infant is capable of tilting household decisions toward his/her preferred choices using his/her limited but powerful strategies, this gap needs to be addressed.

As a step toward this objective, this study investigates the intertemporal choice of children, focusing on the cause of their impatience. As found in Bettingera and Slonim [4] and Steinberg *et al.* [5], patience increases with age during childhood, suggesting that young children are particularly impatient[2].

[1]To justify the unitary model in which the unitary decision maker maximizes household utility, we often require restrictive assumptions. The rotten kid theorem (Becker [2]) is such an example. See Bergstrom [3] for details.

[2]For other psychological studies, see Teuscher and Mitchell [6] for a review.

To be more specific, this study searches for the evolutionary root of impatience of children, employing a biological framework. An increasing body of literature uses this method to search for the biological basis of preferences.

The basic idea of this literature comes from the biological finding that preferences or, more broadly, genotypes and associated phenotypes (strategies), are the end-products of natural selection. Since preferences that are successful in reproduction spread over the population in the evolutionary time scale, preferences in the current human population can be deduced from the preferences that maximized fitness in the environment where we evolved. Such environment is considered to be the African savannah where our genus *Homo* appeared two million years ago and stayed for most of our history as hunter-gatherers. Human-specific characteristics are considered to have evolved in this ancestral environment.

Time preference is a leading topic in this literature. Hansson and Stuart [7] showed that the marginal rate of substitution in utility is equal to the marginal rate of substitution in fitness, suggesting that resource allocation maximizing utility corresponds to allocation maximizing fitness. Later, Rogers [8] applied this idea to the intertemporal allocation of resources, and explained the evolutionary origin of time preference. More recently, technical similarities for studying aging in bio-demography and the intertemporal allocation in economics have allowed biologists, demographers and economists to enter this hybrid field, leading to the examination of how the time-discounting behavior relates to senescence (Sozou and Seymour [9]) and to intergenerational transfers (Chu *et al.* [10]), why it is hyperbolic (Robson and Samuelson [11]), the rationale for social discounting (Sozou [12]), how it depends on age (Kageyama [13]), and how it relates to extrinsic mortality (Chowdhry [14])[3].

To investigate the impatience of children, the present study follows this literature and extends Kageyama [13] by incorporating childhood, *i.e.*, the growth period to maturity. In previous studies, Chu *et al.* [10] built a biological model incorporating the growth period and showed that the impatience relates to the productivity growth in childhood. Similarly, Robson *et al.* [16] examined the impatience of children, but paid more attention to adulthood and did not explicitly consider the role of the growth period.

Despite these differences, both of these previous studies concluded that the impatience of children does not relate to the absolute level of mortality. This presents a sharp contrast to the result that mortality is a major factor associated with time preference in adulthood.

The present study, on the other hand, finds that the impatience of children relates to the mortality rate, as does time preference in adulthood. The same logic applies in both childhood and adulthood.

Explaining time preference with evolutionary biology, however, does not negate the relationship between time-discounting behavior and non-biological factors. As Becker and Mulligan [17] argue, social factors such as culture and education affect time discounting. This paper aims to assess the biological basis of time preference, referred to as the "endowed discount factor" in the above study.

The rest of the paper is organized as follows. Section 2 examines the evolutionary optimal strategies using a biological framework. Based on the results in Section 2, Section 3 provides a biological explanation for time preference, and shows that the optimal rate of time preference is equal to the mortality rate in the entire life course. This implies that the biologically endowed rate of time preference is U-shaped in age, as is the mortality rate, and that children and old adults are, by nature, less patient than young adults. Section 4 concludes.

2. The Model

2.1. The Basic Structure

The model in this study is based on life history theory, *i.e.*, an analytical framework in biology to study species-specific life-history strategies such as the age-trajectories of fertility and mortality, presuming that life-history traits are the end-products of natural selection. Technically, it solves for the fitness-maximizing strategies under given constraints to deduce species-specific life-history traits[4].

In particular, as in a standard life-history model, I consider a model with the following properties. First, the population is stationary at the upper limit of the carrying capacity. This is to follow the carrying-capacity argument that human population in our evolutionary past was confined by the environmental capacity[5]. Second, reproduction is asexual. This is simply to avoid complexities related to matching between females and males.

With these specifications, the measure of fitness is given by the expected number of offspring at the beginning of life, which is expressed as

$$R(0)=\int_0^{\infty} l(x)m(x)\,\mathrm{d}x \tag{1}$$

where $l(x)$ is the survival probability to age x and $m(x)$ is the reproductive output at age x[6]. With the pressure of natural selection, genotypes and associated phenotypes that generate a higher value of $R(0)$ spread over and fix in the population. Note that, in a stationary population where the population growth rate converges to zero, $R(0)$ is equivalent to the reproductive value at birth and converges to one. The lifetime expected number of offspring is, *ex post*, just sufficient to replace the current individual.

Survival and reproduction depend on age and the amount of energetic resources respectively invested in. Once consumed, resources are physiologically allocated to either survival investment or reproductive investment. Therefore, given that

$$l(x)=\exp\left[-\int_0^x \mu(\hat{x})\,\mathrm{d}\hat{x}\right] \tag{2}$$

where $\mu(x)$ is the mortality rate at age x, the dependence of survival and reproduction on resources can be expressed as $\mu(x)=\mu\left[w(x),x\right]$ and $m(x)=m\left[v(x),x\right]$ where $w(x)$ and $v(x)$ are respectively survival and reproductive investments. To avoid unnecessary technical complexity, I assume that both

[3]Acharya and Balvers [15] examined time preference in an economic framework, assuming that utility captures the effect of consumption on mortality. Their model can also be interpreted as a biological model that assumes that reproductive success solely depends on the length of life.

[4]See Stearns [18] for the general introduction of life history theory, and Perrin and Sibly [19] for the technical introduction.

[5]It is technically possible to examine the case that the population growth rate takes non-zero constant values. See Taylor *et al.* [20].

[6]Equation (1) does not imply that lifespan is infinite.

investments exhibit diminishing marginal returns, satisfying $\mu_w[w(x),x]<0$, $\mu_{ww}[w(x),x]>0$, $m_v[v(x),x]>0$, and $m_{vv}[v(x),x]<0$ where the subscript indicates a partial derivative, and also that the individual will certainly die without survival investment and will not have any reproductive output without reproductive investment.

In addition, reproduction depends on growth investment, $z(x)$, in the earlier stages of life. Investing in growth enhances the reproductive capacity and increases the reproductive efficiency in the later stages.

To incorporate this relationship, I focus on determinate growers, *i.e.*, organisms that stop growing at maturity, as in the case of humans[7]. Thus, denoting the age of maturity by α, we have $v(x)=0$ for all $x<\alpha$ and $z(x)=0$ for all $x\geq\alpha$.

Besides, I assume that $m[v(x),x]$ can be separated into the age-dependent reproductive capacity, $A(x)$, and the contribution of resources, $f[v(x)]$, such that

$$m[v(x),x]=A(x)f[v(x)]. \quad (3)$$

Note that $f[v(x)]$ is concave in $v(x)$ as is $m[v(x),x]$. In this setting, the development of the reproductive capacity during the growth period can be expressed as

$$A(x)=A(0)+\int_0^x B(\hat{x})f[z(\hat{x})]\mathrm{d}\hat{x} \quad (4)$$

where $A(0)$ is the innate reproductive capacity and $B(x)$ is the age-dependent growth efficiency. Here, the contribution of resources to growth follows the same law as the one to reproduction, and, thus, both reproductive and growth investments share the same $f(\cdot)$.

Turning to the budget constraint, the model incorporates resource transfers. The extensive use of resource transfers, such as intergenerational transfers between parents and children and food sharing between households, is one of the most distinctive human characteristics[8]. In this case, the budget constraint does not necessarily hold at each point in time, and is given by the lifetime budget constraint,

$$\int_0^\infty l(x)y(x)\mathrm{d}x\geq\int_0^\infty l(x)[v(x)+z(x)+w(x)]\mathrm{d}x \quad (5)$$

where $y(x)$ is the amount of resources that the individual obtains at age x. Note that $y(x)$ is exogenous, and that the interest rate is equal to zero since keeping resources does not generate any return.

With these conditions, we can solve for the optimal allocation of resources, expressed by $v(x)$, $z(x)$, $w(x)$, and α, using the Lagrangian method. Given the objective function (1), the budget constraint (5), and the Lagrangian multiplier, λ, the Lagrangian is defined as

$$L=\int_0^\infty l(x)m(x)\mathrm{d}x+\lambda\int_0^\infty l(x)[y(x)-v(x)-z(x)-w(x)]\mathrm{d}x \quad (6)$$

where $l(x)$, $m(x)$, and $A(x)$ are respectively specified by Equations (2), (3), and (4). Using the Volterra derivative (see Ryder and Heal [24]) to examine the effect of changes in the investments around a particular age x, we obtain the first-order conditions:

$$\frac{\partial L}{\partial v(x)}=l(x)A(x)f_v[v(x)]-\lambda l(x)=0 \text{ for } x\geq\alpha, \quad (7)$$

$$\frac{\partial L}{\partial z(x)}=B(x)f_z[z(x)]\eta(\alpha)-\lambda l(x)=0 \text{ for } x<\alpha, \quad (8)$$

$$\frac{\partial L}{\partial w(x)}=-\mu_w[w(x),x][R(x)+\lambda k(x)]-\lambda l(x)=0, \quad (9)$$

and

$$\frac{\partial L}{\partial \lambda}=\int_0^\infty l(x)[y(x)-v(x)-z(x)-w(x)]\mathrm{d}x=0 \quad (10)$$

where

$$\eta(\alpha)=\int_\alpha^\infty l(\hat{x})f[v(\hat{x})]\mathrm{d}\hat{x}, \quad (11)$$

$$R(x)=\int_x^\infty l(\hat{x})A(\hat{x})f[v(\hat{x})]\mathrm{d}\hat{x}, \quad (12)$$

and

$$k(x)=\int_x^\infty l(\hat{x})[y(\hat{x})-v(\hat{x})-z(\hat{x})-w(\hat{x})]\mathrm{d}\hat{x}. \quad (13)$$

Here, $\eta(\alpha)$ represents the benefit of an increment in the reproductive capacity, and $R(x)$ and $k(x)$ express the benefits of an increase in survival at age x respectively for reproduction and production.

At the same time, the age of maturity is determined by the returns of growth and reproductive investments. These returns are given by $B(x)f[z(x)]\eta(x)$ and $l(x)A(x)f[v(x)]$, which respectively represent the increase in the future reproduction due to a greater reproductive capacity and the increase in immediate reproduction. The individual switches from the growth phase to the reproductive phase when the return for reproduction overtakes the one for growth. Therefore, the age of maturity is implicitly given by

$$B(\alpha)\eta(\alpha)=l(\alpha)A(\alpha). \quad (14)$$

[7]To account for determinate growth, we can, for example, assume that the transition from the growth phase to the reproductive phase, or the other way around, incurs significant costs. This is consistent with the fact that determinate growers go through some sort of metamorphosis at maturity.

[8]See, e.g., Wiessner [21,22] and Gurven *et al.* [23] for the importance of food sharing in modern foraging populations.

2.2. Optimal Life-History Strategies

These conditions can be interpreted as follows. From here on, I will suppress the age notation when no confusion arises.

First, Equation (7) indicates that the marginal productivity of reproductive investment, $Af_v(v)$, is equal to the shadow price of resources and is constant across ages. For example, if A depreciates after maturity, $f_v(v)$ increases and, thus, reproductive investment decreases with age. The decline in the reproductive efficiency is offset by the decline in reproductive investment.

Second, by rewriting Equation (8) as

$$Bf_z(z)\frac{\eta(\alpha)}{l(x)}=\lambda, \tag{15}$$

Equation (15) shows that the marginal return of growth investment conditional on survival to age x is equal to the shadow price and is constant across ages. It is conditional on survival because, while the timing of starting to reap the return on growth investment is fixed by the age of maturity that is endogenously determined, the chance of reaching maturity changes with age. This asymmetry makes the return of growth investment age-dependent. As maturity approaches, the expected return, $\eta(\alpha)/l(x)$, increases, and, to take advantage of the higher return, the marginal productivity, $Bf_z(z)$, decreases. For example, if B is constant across ages, $f_z(z)$ decreases and growth investment increases toward maturity.

Third, by letting

$$\bar{R}(x)=\int_x^\infty \frac{l(\hat{x})}{l(x)}A(\hat{x})f\left[v(\hat{x})\right]d\hat{x}, \tag{16}$$

and

$$\bar{k}(x)=\int_x^\infty \frac{l(\hat{x})}{l(x)}\left[y(\hat{x})-v(\hat{x})-z(\hat{x})-w(\hat{x})\right]d\hat{x}, \tag{17}$$

Equation (9) can be rewritten as

$$-\mu_w\left[w(x),x\right]\left[\bar{R}(x)+\lambda\bar{k}(x)\right]=\lambda. \tag{18}$$

The upper bar indicates that the value is adjusted by the survival probability at the corresponding age. Thus, $\bar{R}(x)$ represents the expected reproductive output in the remaining lifetime for the individual survived to age x, and $\bar{k}(x)$ expresses the expected productive surplus in the remaining lifetime for the same individual. Therefore, given that λ is the value converter of productive surplus to reproductive contribution, the terms in the brackets in Equation (18), $\bar{R}(x)+\lambda\bar{k}(x)$, represents the value of survival that includes both reproductive and productive contributions. With resource transfers, the value of survival consists of not only reproductive contribution but also productive contribution.

With these results, Equation (18) shows that the marginal benefit of survival investment is equal to the shadow price and is constant across ages. This implies that the marginal productivity of survival investment, $-\mu_w(w)$, depends on the change in the value of survival, and reaches its lowest level at the prime of life at which the value of survival is the highest. Assuming, for example, that $\mu\left[w(x),x\right]$ is independent of age, we can expect that the mortality rate reaches its lowest level at the prime of life.

An example of such a mortality curve is presented in **Figure 1**. It shows that the mortality rate reaches its lowest level in age-class two and increases thereafter, corresponding to the result that the value of survival hits its highest level in age-class three.

3. Implications on Intertemporal Allocation

3.1. Intertemporal Marginal Rate of Substitution

The intertemporal marginal rate of substitution (MRS) measures the importance of resources at one point in time over another. Specifically, it is defined as the rate to compensate for a loss of resources at one point in time in exchange for resources at another point in time while keeping $R(0)$ constant. In a continuous-time setting, MRS at age x can be calculated as

$$\frac{-\partial \log R_v(0)}{\partial x}=-\frac{l_x}{l}-\frac{A_x}{A}-\frac{f_{vx}(v)}{f_v(v)}, \tag{19}$$

$$\frac{-\partial \log R_z(0)}{\partial x}=-\frac{B_x}{B}-\frac{f_{zx}(z)}{f_z(z)}, \tag{20}$$

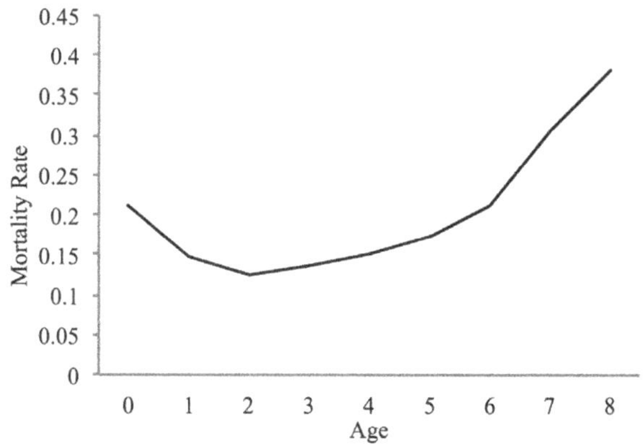

Figure 1. Age-trajectory of Mortality. The maximum age-class to which the individual can possibly survive is set to nine, and the functional forms and parameter values are given as follows: $\mu\left[w(x),x\right]=e^{-qw(x)}$, $A(x)f\left[v(x)\right]=A(\alpha)v(x)^\gamma$, $B(x)f\left[z(x)\right]=Bz(x)^\gamma$, **$\gamma = 0.25$, $q = 0.5$, $B = 0.15$, $A(0) = 0.18$, $y(0) = 0$, $y(1) = 2$, $y(2) = 4$, $y(3) = 6$, $y(4) = 6$, $y(5) = 6$, $y(6) = 6$, $y(7) = 6$, $y(8) = 4$, and $y(9) = 4$.**

and

$$\frac{-\partial \log R_w(0)}{\partial x} = -\frac{\mu_{wx}(w)}{\mu_w(w)} - \frac{\bar{R}_x + \lambda \bar{k}_x}{\bar{R} + \lambda \bar{k}} - \frac{l_x}{l} \quad (21)$$

where $R_v(0)$, $R_z(0)$, and $R_w(0)$ are respectively the marginal effects of reproductive, growth, and survival investments on $R(0)$. Note that, with respect to survival investment, the change in resource surplus must be taken into account.

These equations show that MRS depends on various factors. Equation (19) illustrates that, in adulthood, MRS consists of three components; the mortality rate, the change in the reproductive efficiency, and the change in the marginal contribution of resources. This result is consistent with Sozou and Seymour [9], Chu *et al.* [10], and Kageyama [13].

In childhood, on the other hand, Equation (20) shows that MRS consists of two components; the change in the growth efficiency and the change in the marginal contribution of resources. As in Chu *et al.* [10], the mortality rate does not appear in MRS in childhood.

Furthermore, Equation (21) shows that, throughout the life course, MRS can be calculated as the sum of three components; the change in the marginal contribution of resources, the change in the value of survival, and the mortality rate.

Despite these variations, however, the values of MRS derived in Equations (19)-(21) are all equal to the mortality rate when resources are optimally allocated. In Equation (19), the second and the third terms cancel out on the optimal path as indicated in Equation (7), and MRS is reduced to the mortality rate. Similarly, as in Equation (8), the two terms in Equation (20) sum up to the mortality rate. Turning to Equation (21), it is also reduced to the mortality rate since, as indicated in Equation (18), the first two terms cancel out.

This result is intuitive in the reproductive period. The change in the reproductive efficiency is neutralized by the change in reproductive investment on the optimal path. However, giving up a unit of current reproductive investment for future investment still accompanies the mortality risk. Thus, to keep $R(0)$ constant, the mortality risk needs to be compensated.

By contrast, the result that MRS is equal to the mortality rate during the growth period might be counter-intuitive. As children do not yet reproduce, the timing of growth investment seems irrelevant as long as they build up the same level of reproductive capacity at maturity.

The reason for this result is that the marginal productivity, $Bf_z(z)$, changes with age. As shown in Subsection 2.2, the marginal productivity decreases as the chance of reaching maturity increases, and its changing rate is exactly equal to the mortality rate. This is intuitive considering that the change in the marginal productivity is originated by the change in the survival probability to maturity. For example, if B is constant across ages, the marginal productivity decreases with age to satisfy $-f_{zx}(z)/f_z(z) = -l_x/l$. To give up a unit of current growth investment for future investment, the reduction in the marginal productivity must be compensated, and this compensation rate is given by the mortality rate. For this reason, MRS in childhood is, as in adulthood, equal to the mortality rate.

3.2. Growth Process, Mortality, and MRS

The result that MRS in childhood on the optimal path is equal to the mortality rate does not depend on the type of growth process. For example, consider as in Chu *et al.* [10] that the amount of resources, $y(x)$, is determined by body size, which in turn depends on growth investment up to age x. I assume, for simplicity, that $y(x)$ is equal to body size at age x.

In this case, the growth process can be described as

$$y(x) = y(0) + \int_0^x g\left[s(\hat{x}), \hat{x}\right] d\hat{x} \quad (22)$$

where $s(x)$ is growth investment allocated for increasing body size and $g\left[s(x), x\right]$ is the contribution of the investment at each point in time. Here, I assume that $g\left[s(x), x\right]$ is sufficiently concave in $s(x)$ to have an interior solution[9].

Incorporating this size effect into the lifetime budget constraint in Equation (5), we obtain the first-order conditions:

$$g_s\left[s(x), x\right] \bar{L}(x) = 1 \quad (23)$$

for all x where $\bar{L}(x) = \int_x^\infty l(\hat{x})/l(x) d\hat{x}$, *i.e.*, the remaining life expectancy at age x. This shows that the marginal return of investing in body size is equal to its cost. The return is measured by the amount of resources that the individual is expected to accrue in the future, and the cost is equal to one, representing a unit of resource necessary for the investment.

Equation (23) further illustrates that the change in the marginal productivity, $g_s(s)$, depends on the change in the remaining life expectancy. While the remaining life expectancy is high, the marginal productivity is low so as to take advantage of the higher expected return. Therefore, if the growth efficiency is independent of age, $g_s(s)$ increases and s decreases with age[10]. This is consistent with Chu *et al.* [10].

The next step is to calculate MRS. By applying the same method as before, it is given by

[9] We can also assume that $y(x)$ depends on knowledge learned in the past and interpret $g\left[s(x), x\right]$ as the increment of knowledge. See Ng [25] for how knowledge affects fitness.

[10] The results that the two types of growth investment, s and z, change in the opposite direction suggests that the age-trajectory of whole growth investment is indeterminate.

$$\frac{-\partial \log R_s(0)}{\partial x} = -\frac{g_{sx}(s)}{g_s(s)} - \frac{\bar{L}_x}{\bar{L}} - \frac{l_x}{l}. \quad (24)$$

The first term represents the change in the marginal productivity, the second term expresses the change in the remaining life expectancy, and the third term is the mortality rate. As indicated in Equation (23), the first two terms cancel out on the optimal path. As a result, MRS in childhood is again given by the mortality rate.

3.3. Time Preference

While the intratemporal allocation of resources is involuntary depending mostly on physiology, the intertemporal allocation is voluntary. It primarily depends on behavior since we can deliberately control the allocation by deciding how much to consume at present.

This implies that, to further analyze the intertemporal allocation, we need to move on to the economic framework that allows us to study voluntary behavior. We need to remember that humans do not intend to maximize fitness but rather behave in a utility-maximizing manner, and that those who had preferences that coincided with the fitness-maximizing behavior spread over and fixed in the population.

To do this, I employ a standard economic model in which the objective function is given by lifetime utility,

$$U = \int_0^\infty \beta(x) u[c(x), x] \mathrm{d}x, \quad (25)$$

where $\beta(x)$ is the discount factor for future utility, $u[c(x), x]$ is a strictly concave instantaneous utility function, and $c(x)$ is consumption, which can be regarded as the sum of growth, reproductive, and survival investments. Note that the lifetime budget constraint presented in Equation (5) is still relevant.

Here, the instantaneous utility directly depends on age. Given that preferences were shaped by natural selection, the instantaneous utility should reflect the effect of consumption on reproductive success at the corresponding age. To incorporate this aspect into the model, I assume that the marginal utility on the fitness-maximizing consumption path is constant across ages. This type of utility induces the individual to consume more while its marginal effect on fitness is high.

In this setting, MRS in utility is given by

$$-\frac{\beta_x(x)}{\beta(x)} - \frac{u_{cx}[c(x), x]}{u_c[c(x), x]}. \quad (26)$$

The individual applies this rate to evaluate future consumption and determines the intertemporal allocation. Thus, for the voluntary allocation to match the fitness-maximizing allocation, this rate must be consistent with MRS in fitness obtained in Subsection 3.1, and must be equal to the mortality rate when it is evaluated on the fitness maximizing consumption path. In particular, when the instantaneous utility depends on age as described above, $u_{cx}[c(x), x]$ is equal to zero on the fitness-maximizing path, and, thus, $-\beta_x(x)/\beta(x)$, *i.e.*, the *pure* rate of time preference, is equal to the mortality rate[11].

These results further imply that, considering that time preference is psychologically embedded, the endowed rate of time preference is equal to the mortality rate in our evolutionary past when we existed as hunter-gatherers. As a result, presuming that the age-trajectory of mortality in our evolutionary past is similar to the one in modern hunter-gatherer populations, we can predict that the endowed rate of time preference is U-shaped in age, reaching its lowest level in early adulthood, as is the age-trajectory of the mortality rate in modern hunter-gatherer populations (e.g., Hill and Hurtado [26]; Hill *et al.* [27]).

This is consistent with empirical findings. As discussed in Section 1, the discount rate decreases in childhood. In adulthood, on the other hand, while still empirically inconclusive, Trostel and Taylor [28] and Read and Read [29] found that the discount rate increases with senescence[12]. The present study focuses on the biological discount rate ignoring the effect of social factors such as education, and may overestimate the discount rate in adulthood in modern human populations. Nevertheless, the age-trajectory of time preference predicted in the present analysis is still in line with the empirical findings.

4. Concluding Remarks

This paper aims to understand the mechanism that coordinates intertemporal choice, paying particular attention to the impatience of children. To do this, it examines human life-history strategies, incorporating the growth period to maturity. The results show that the endowed rate of time preference is equal to the mortality rate in the entire life course and, thus, is U-shaped in age, indicating that it is higher for children than for young adults.

At the behavioral level, this provides a biological explanation as to why parents and children often have conflicts in the allocation of resources when they make collective decisions. Due to the difference in the discount rate, parents, who follow their own time preference, would allocate less to the present than their children would. Namely, the difference in time preference gener-

[11] If we correctly perceive the survival probability and discount future utilities accordingly, the pure rate of time preference would be equal to zero. However, there is no biological basis to suppose that we are able to correctly perceive the survival probability. Given that time discounting is not limited to humans, it makes more sense to consider that time preference is psychologically embedded.

[12] These studies, however, differ in the age at which the discount rate reaches the lowest level. While Trostel and Taylor [28] found that the discount rate is lowest among individuals in their twenties, Read and Read [29] argued that it is lowest in their forties. Thus, the age at which time preference reaches its lowest level is still an open question.

ates parent-offspring conflict over the intertemporal allocation of resources, affecting the decision-making process particularly within the household[13].

One limitation of this study, however, is that it treats the growth period as one state and compresses the reproductive capacity into one parameter. This is equivalent to assuming that a unit of growth investment is exchangeable between any points in time within the growth period although such a transaction may incur additional costs.

In reality, it is often not the case. A deficiency in a particular type of growth investment at a certain age, for example, may not be compensated by the same kind of investment at a later age, and may have a permanent effect. In such cases, intertemporal choice would not be as simple as the present analysis suggests, and the impatience of children, in particular, would be underestimated.

Nevertheless, as the first-order approximation, this study provides an explanation for the age-trajectory of time preference, connecting it to mortality in both childhood and adulthood. The future is discounted because survival is uncertain (Yaari [31]), and survival is uncertain because the future is discounted (Kirkwood [32]; Kirkwood and Rose [33]). Both propositions hold in the entire life course because time discounting and survival uncertainty are two sides of the same coin, reflecting the change in the value of survival. There are other factors, including the variability of the environment, sexual reproduction and genetic relatedness, that can possibly affect time preference, but mortality is the baseline for time preference through the entire course of life.

This study also suggests that the traditional view that time discounting is something unfavorable is not entirely accurate. Time discounting generally carries negative connotations and has been described as cognitive deficiency, impatience, shortsightedness, myopia, irrationality, and so forth. For example, Ramsey [34] regarded time-discounting behavior as "a practice which is ethically indefensible and arises merely from the weakness of the imagination (p. 543)". However, as discussed in this paper, being impatient is not a deficiency, but an optimal trait in the biological sense that was acquired in the course of evolution. Our surrounding environment has changed since our evolutionary past, and the endowed rate of time preference is no longer optimal in the economic sense. Nevertheless, being too patient is not necessarily favorable either as it would cause other problems such as dynamic inefficiency in macroeconomics and the postponement of reproduction that, together with the decline in reproductive efficiency, results in below-replacement fertility. Given our human nature, an appropriate level of impatience may in fact be beneficial to our well-being.

[13]The parent-offspring conflict in the present study differs from the original parent-offspring conflict in Trivers [30]. While the ultimate cause of the original parent-offspring conflict is the difference in relatedness, the ultimate cause in the present study is the difference in life-history phase.

5. Acknowledgements

I thank Akihiko Matsui and Takashi Shimizu for their helpful suggestions in developing ideas for this paper, and Kazuhiko Kato for his helpful comments on the earlier draft of this paper. Any remaining errors are my own. This study is supported by Grant-in-Aid for Challenging Exploratory Research from the Ministry of Education, Culture, Sports, Science and Technology in Japan (No. 23653055).

REFERENCES

[1] A. Dauphin, A. R. El Lahga, B. Fortin and G. Lacroix, "Are Children Decision-Makers within the Household?" *Economic Journal*, Vol. 121, No. 553, 2011, pp. 871-903.

[2] G. S. Becker, "A Theory of Social Interactions," *Journal of Political Economy*, Vol. 82, No. 6, 1974, pp. 1063-1093.

[3] T. C. Bergstrom, "A Fresh Look at the Rotten Kid Theorem—And Other Household Mysteries," *Journal of Political Economy*, Vol. 97, No. 5, 1989, pp. 1138-1159.

[4] E. Bettinger and R. Slonim, "Patience among Children," *Journal of Public Economics*, Vol. 91, No. 1-2, 2007, pp. 343-363.

[5] L. Steinberg, S. Graham, L. O'Brien, J. Woolard, E. Cauffman and M. Banich, "Age Differences in Future Orientation and Delay Discounting," *Child Development*, Vol. 80, No. 1, 2009, pp. 28-44.

[6] U. Teuscher and S. H. Mitchell, "Relation between Time Perspective and Delay Discounting: A Literature Review," *Psychological Record*, Vol. 61, No. 4, 2011, pp. 613-632.

[7] I. Hansson and C. Stuart, "Malthusian Selection of Preferences," *American Economic Review*, Vol. 80, No. 3, 1990, pp. 529-544.

[8] A. R. Rogers, "Evolution of Time Preference by Natural Selection," *American Economic Review*, Vol. 84, No. 3, 1994, pp. 460-481.

[9] P. D. Sozou and R. M. Seymour, "Augmented Discounting: Interaction between Ageing and Time-Preference Behaviour," *Proceedings of the Royal Society B*, Vol. 270, No. 1519, 2003, pp. 1047-1053.

[10] C. Y. C. Chu, H. K. Chien and R. D. Lee, "The Evolutionary Theory of Time Preference and Intergenerational Transfers," *Journal of Economic Behavior and Organization*, Vol. 76, No. 3, 2010, pp. 451-464.

[11] A. J. Robson and L. Samuelson, "The Evolution of Time Preference with Aggregate Uncertainty," *American Economic Review*, Vol. 99, No. 5, 2009, pp. 1925-1953.

[12] P. D. Sozou, "Individual and Social Discounting in a Viscous Population," *Proceedings of the Royal Society B*, Vol. 276, 1669, 2009, pp. 2955-2962.

[13] J. Kageyama, "The Intertemporal Allocation of Consumption, Time Preference, and Life-History Strategies," *Journal of Bioeconomics*, Vol. 13, No. 2, 2011, pp. 79-95.

[14] B. Chowdhry, "Possibility of Dying as a Unified Explanation of Why We Discount the Future, Get Weaker with Age, and Display Risk-Aversion," *Economic Inquiry*, Vol. 49, No. 4, 2011, pp. 1098-1103.

[15] A. K. Acharya and R. J. Balvers, "Time Preference and Life Cycle Consumption with Endogenous Survival," *Economic Inquiry*, Vol. 42, No. 4, 2004, pp. 667-678.

[16] A. J. Robson, B. Szentes and E. Iantchev, "The Evolutionary Basis of Time Preference: Intergenerational Transfers and Sex," *American Economic Journal: Microeconomics*, Vol. 4, No. 4, 2012, pp. 172-201.

[17] G. S. Becker and C. B. Mulligan, "The Endogenous Determination of Time Preference," *Quarterly Journal of Economics*, Vol. 112, No. 3, 1997, pp. 729-758.

[18] S. C. Stearns, "The Evolution of Life Histories," Oxford University Press, Oxford, 1992.

[19] N. Perrin and R. M. Sibly, "Dynamic Models of Energy Allocation and Investment," *Annual Review of Ecology and Systematics*, Vol. 24, 1993, pp. 379-410.

[20] H. M. Taylor, R. S. Gourley, C. E. Lawrence and R. S. Kaplan, "Natural Selection of Life History Attributes: An Analytical Approach," *Theoretical Population Biology*, Vol. 5, No. 1, 1974, pp. 104-122.

[21] P. Wiessner, "Leveling the Hunter: Constraints on the Status Quest in Foraging Societies," In: P. Wiessner and W. Schiefenhövel, Eds., *Food and the Status Quest: An Interdisciplinary Perspective*, Berghahn Books, Oxford, 1996, pp. 171-191.

[22] P. Wiessner, "Hunting, Healing, and *hxaro* Exchange: A Long-Term Perspective on! Kung (ju/'hoansi) Large-Game Hunting," *Evolution and Human Behavior*, Vol. 23, No. 6, 2002, pp. 407-436.

[23] M. Gurven, W. Allen-Arave, K. Hill and M. Hurtado, "'It's a Wonderful Life': Signaling Generosity among the Ache of Paraguay," *Evolution and Human Behavior*, Vol. 21, No. 4, 2000, pp. 263-282.

[24] H. E. Ryder and G. M. Heal, "Optimal Growth with Intertemporally Dependent Preferences," *Review of Economic Studies*, Vol. 40, No. 1, 1973, pp. 1-33.

[25] Y. K. Ng, "The Paradox of the Adventurous Young and the Cautious Old: Natural Selection vs. Rational Calculation," *Journal of Theoretical Biology*, Vol. 153, No. 3, 1991, pp. 339-352.

[26] K. Hill and A. M. Hurtado, "Ache Life History," Aldine De Gruyter, New York, 1996.

[27] K. Hill, A. M. Hurtado and R. S. Walker, "High Adult Mortality among Hiwi Hunter-Gatherers: Implications for Human Evolution," *Journal of Human Evolution*, Vol. 52, No. 4, 2007, pp. 443-454.

[28] P. A. Trostel and G. A. Taylor, "A Theory of Time Preference," *Economic Inquiry*, Vol. 39, No. 3, 2001, pp. 379-395.

[29] D. Read and N. L. Read, "Time Discounting over the Lifespan," *Organizational Behavior and Human Decision Processes*, Vol. 94, No. 1, 2004, pp. 22-32.

[30] R. L. Trivers, "Parent-Offspring Conflict," *American Zoologist*, Vol. 14, No. 1, 1974, pp. 249-264.

[31] M. E. Yaari, "Uncertain Lifetime, Life Insurance, and the Theory of the Consumer," *Review of Economic Studies*, Vol. 32, No. 2, 1965, pp. 137-150.

[32] T. B. L. Kirkwood, "Evolution of Ageing," *Nature*, Vol. 270, No. 5635, 1977, pp. 301-304.

[33] T. B. L. Kirkwood and M. R. Rose, "Evolution of Senescence: Late Survival Sacrificed for Reproduction," *Philosophical Transactions of the Royal Society B*, Vol. 332, No. 1262, 1991, pp. 15-24.

[34] F. P. Ramsey, "A Mathematical Theory of Saving," *Economic Journal*, Vol. 38, No. 152, 1928, pp. 543-559.

Modelling Consumer Behavior by Inverse Demand Functions

Susanne Fuchs-Seliger
Institut für Volkswirtschaftslehre Karlsruher Institut für Technologie, Karlsruher, Deutschland

ABSTRACT

In this article a model of consumer behavior will be developed, based on preferences on the price space reflecting the individual's willingness to pay for certain quantities of commodities under the supposition that the individual is restricted to his or her income. Firms offer certain amounts of commodities at the market and consumers react to these offers by their willingness to pay. Existence and continuity of the inverse demand function describing consumer's behavior under appropriate conditions will be shown. Furthermore, differences between a model of consumer behavior based on preferences on the commodity space and that which is based on preferences on the price space will be pointed out.

Keywords: Consumer Theory; Preference Relation; Inverse Demand Functions; Duality Theory

1. Introduction

We will consider inverse demand functions which assign, to every commodity bundle x, those market price combinations p the individual is willing to pay for x at most when income M prevails. The demand function, defined on prices and income, and the related inverse demand function, defined on commodities offered at the market and on the individual's income, are dual concepts describing consumer behavior. According to its definition, a demand function associates with every budget set $B(p,M)=\{x\in X \mid px\le M\}$, that commodity bundle which according to the preferences of the individual is the one he or she prefers to the other ones available in the given budget set. From the point of duality, according to the individual's preferences with regard to prices, the inverse demand function points out that price combination the individual would spend for x at most, given income M. As an example we may consider the following one: the individual is not willing to pay more than two Euro for one pound of bred. Then he can afford to buy cheese for not more than three Euro and ham for two Euro. In total the individual cannot spend more than seven Euro for these goods. Evidently, he would be happy if these commodities were cheaper. As another example we can fancy a market where carpets are sold and the agent is not willing to pay more than a certain amount of money for a special carpet.

Inverse demand functions often are a convenient tool for modelling market behavior in the presence of monopolistic firms ([1], p. 326). If the firms have information about the individual's preferences on prices, then they will know that he or she cannot accept prices higher than a certain limit.

The analysis in this article will be based on preference relations on prices instead of indirect utility functions. Therefore, a more general framework for inverse demand will be established. We will introduce axioms concerning consumer's preferences on the price space IR^n_{++}. Based on these axioms properties of the inverse demand function will be deduced. For comparison, we will also point out the difference between a model of consumer behavior based on preferences on the commodity space and that which is based on the price space.

2. Hypotheses on Consumer's Preferences

Modelling consumer's behavior we will assume the following hypotheses:

(P1) $\succeq$ is a relation on the strictly positive n-dimensional vector space IR^n_{++}. Every $p\in \mathrm{IR}^n_{++}$ represents an income-normalized price vector, *i.e.* $p=\frac{P}{M}$, where $P\in \mathrm{IR}^n_{++}$ are the market prices, P_i is the price of one unit of the good x_i, and M is the income of the individual, where $M>0$.

(P2) $\succeq$ is transitive and complete[1].

(P3) $\succeq$ is continuous, *i.e.*

(P3.1) $\{p \in \mathrm{IR}^n_{++} | p^0 \succeq p\}$ is closed in IR^n_{++} for every $p^0 \in \mathrm{IR}^n_{++}$ (lower semicontinuity),

(P3.2) $\{p \in \mathrm{IR}^n_{++} | p \succeq p^0\}$ is closed in IR^n_{++} for every $p^0 \in \mathrm{IR}^n_{++}$ (upper semicontinuity).

(P4) $p^1 < p^2 \Rightarrow p^1 \succ p^2$, where $\succ$ is the asymmetric part of $\succeq$ [2].

(P5) Let $\langle p^k \rangle, p^k \in \mathrm{IR}^n_{++}$, be a sequence such that $\lim_{k\to\infty} p^k = p^0 \not> 0$, where $0 \in \mathrm{IR}^n_{+}$, and $p \in \mathrm{IR}^n_{++}$. Then there exists a positive integer N such that $p^k \succ p$ for all $k > N$.

The term $p \succeq p'$ means: the consumer either prefers the price vector p to p' or he is indifferent between them. (P4) should be interpreted as follows: if the individual can achieve a commodity bundle x in the price situation p^1 at which all of the commodity prices are lower than those in the price situation p^2, then the individual prefers p^1 to p^2.

(P5) can be interpreted as: if the prices of some goods turn to 0, then the value of the whole price systems increases and becomes greater than any given positive price system p. However, the value may not converge to infinity, but to a point of saturation. (P5) is a regularity condition for proving Theorem 1 and 3. In reality no market price turns to 0.

3. Inverse Demand Functions

Let us consider a commodity space $X \subseteq \mathrm{IR}^n_{+}$ and the price space IR^n_{++}. Then the mapping $b: X \to 2^{\mathrm{IR}^n_{++}}, b(x) \neq \varnothing$, is called an "inverse demand correspondence". If $b(x)$ is single-valued, then b is called an inverse demand function. $2^{\mathrm{IR}^n_{++}}$ denotes the power set of IR^n_{++}.

By $B(x)$ we will denote all those income-normalized price vectors at which x is available, *i.e.* $B(x) = \{p \in \mathrm{IR}^n_{++} | px \leq 1\}$. It has been shown (see [2], Theorem 1, pp. 241-242), that the correspondence $B: \mathrm{IR}^n_{+} \to 2^{\mathrm{IR}^n_{++}}, B(x) = \{p \in \mathrm{IR}^n_{++} | px \leq 1\}$, is lower hemicontinuous.

The inverse demand function corresponds to the indirect utility function being the dual counterpart to the (direct) utility function to which the demand function corresponds [3]. Given an indirect utility function v or, more generally, a preference relation $\succeq$ on the (income-normalized) price space IR^n_{++}, we will ask when the equality

$$\{p \in \mathrm{IR}^n_{++} | p \in B(x) \wedge \forall p' \in B(x) : p' \succeq p\} \neq \varnothing, \qquad (1)$$

holds. Then we can define an inverse demand correspondence $b: X \to 2^{\mathrm{IR}^n_{++}}$ such that $b(x) = \{p \in \mathrm{IR}^n_{++} | p \in B(x) \wedge \forall p' \in B(x) : p' \succeq p\}$. Thus, $b(x)$ points out special real price vectors $P \in \mathrm{IR}^n_{++}$ at income M of those price vectors, which are at the individual's disposal so that $Px \leq M$, *i.e.* $px = \frac{P}{M}x \leq 1$, holds (for $M > 0$) when commodity bundle x is available at the market.

By interpretation, $b(x)$ represents the set of all those income-normalized price vectors which are most unfavourable in the budget set $B(x)$ according to the individual's opinion. Therefore, producers of the commodity bundle x should know that the individual will not accept prices still worse than those indicated by $b(x)$. In case the profit maximizing firms are content with those prices, a market equilibrium can be attained. In view of (P4) $b(x)$ consists of the highest prices the individual is willing to pay at most for x under the restriction that he or she is limited by his or her income.

If $b(x)$ satisfies equality (1), then we will also call $b: X \to 2^{\mathrm{IR}^n_{++}}$ as to be "consistent with $\succeq$". The above definition of consistency can be considered as the dual counterpart to rationality of demand correspondences with respect to a given relation R on the commodity space $X \subseteq \mathrm{IR}^n_{+}$, *i.e.*:

$$h(p) = \{x \in X | x \in B'(p) \wedge \forall y \in B'(p) : xRy\},$$

where

$$B'(p) = \{z \in X | pz \leq 1\}, \forall p \in \mathrm{IR}^n_{++}.$$

For comparison, if we start describing consumer behavior based on preferences on the commodity space, then one can impose the following hypotheses (A1) to (A4) on the commodity space X, and on the relation R on X:

(A1) $X \subseteq \mathrm{IR}^n_{+}, X \neq \varnothing$, is supposed to be a closed set of alternatives.

(A2) R is a reflexive relation on X.

(A3) R is upper semicontinuous on X, *i.e.* $R(x) = \{y | y \in X \wedge yRx\}$ is closed in X for all $x \in X$.

(A4) For all $z \in X, \tilde{P}(z) = \{y | y \in X \wedge \neg(zRy)\}$ is supposed to be convex and non-empty.

Then $h(p) = \{x | x \in B'(p) \wedge \forall y \in B'(p) : xRy\} \neq \varnothing$ (see [4], p. 303).

We can realize that these hypotheses are quite mild. Even transitivity and completeness of the individual's preferences on the commodity space are not assumed. The proof has been done by the help of the finite intersection property since the budget sets $B'(p) = \{x \in X | px \leq 1\}, \forall p \in \mathrm{IR}^n_{++}$, are compact. How-

---

[1] $\forall p, p' \in \mathrm{IR}^n_{++} : p \succeq p' \vee p' \succeq p$.

[2] $p^1 < p^2$ means, $p^1_i < p^2_i \;\; \forall i \leq n$.

ever, since $B(x)=\{p\in IR^n_{++} | px\le 1\}$ is not compact, the finite intersection property cannot be applied for showing $b(x)\neq\emptyset$, and we therefore need different assumptions.

If we assume (P1) to (P5), then $b(x)\neq\emptyset$ follows. This will be shown by the next theorem.

Theorem 1 *Let the commodity space be the* IR^n_{++} *and assume* (P1) *to* (P5). *Then for all* $x\in IR^n_{++}$,

$$b(x)=\{p\in IR^n_{++} | p\in B(x)\wedge\forall p'\in B(x): p'\succeq p\}\neq\emptyset.$$

Proof.

By assumption $\succeq$ is a complete, transitive and continuous relation on IR^n_{++}. Therefore, by Debreu's representation theorem [5], it can be represented by a continuous function $v: IR^n_{++}\to IR_+$ such that $p\succeq p'\Leftrightarrow v(p)\ge v(p'), \forall p,p'\in IR^n_{++}$. The function v will be interpreted as an indirect utility function. In view of (P4) v is decreasing[3]. It suffices to show now, that for all $x\in IR^n_{++}$,

$$b(x) =\{p\in IR^n_{++} | p\in B(x)\wedge\forall p'\in B(x): v(p')\ge v(p)\} \neq\emptyset.$$

Since $v(p)$ is decreasing

$$\inf\{v(p) | px=1, p\in IR^n_{++}\} =\inf\{v(p) | px\le 1, p\in IR^n_{++}\} \equiv\inf M(x).$$

We will now continue strictly according to the proof of Theorem 3 in [2], pp. 242-243. For abbreviation set $s=\inf M(x)$. One can show that in view of the continuity of $v(p)$ and of (P4) there exists $\tilde{p}\in IR^n_{++}$ such that $v(\tilde{p})=s$. Constructing a sequence $s^k=s+\frac{1}{k}, \forall k\ge 1$, it follows that for every s^k there exists p^k such that $p^kx=1$ and $s\le v(p^k)<s^k$. Since $\langle p^k\rangle$ is bounded there exists a convergent subsequence of $\langle p^k\rangle$, denoted by $\langle p^{k_j}\rangle$ such that $\lim_{j\to\infty} p^{k_j}=p^0$, and $s\le\lim_{j\to\infty} v(p^{k_j})\le\lim_{j\to\infty} s^{k_j}=s<v\left(\frac{\tilde{p}}{2}\right)$. Hence, there does not exist a positive integer N such that $p^{k_j}\succ\frac{\tilde{p}}{2}$ for all $j\ge N$. Application of (P5) to this result implies $p^0>0$. In view of the continuity of v we obtain $\lim_{j\to\infty} v(p^{k_j})=v(p^0)$, and therefore $v(p^0)=s$. Since $s=\inf M(x)$ and since $p^0x=1$, we have $p^0\preceq p', \forall p'\in IR^n_{++}$ such that $p'x=1$. Therefore

$$p^0\in\{p\in IR^n_{++} | p\in B(x)\wedge\forall p'\in B(x): v(p')\ge v(p)\}.$$

Hence, $b(x)\neq\emptyset$ and thus b can be well defined for all $x\in IR^n_{++}$.

This concludes our proof.

If the inverse demand function is based on an indirect utility function satisfying the following condition ([2], p. 240):

(γ) for every sequence $\langle p^k\rangle$, $p^k\in IR^n_{++}$, $[p^k\to p^0\not>0]\Rightarrow[v(p^k)\to\infty]$, then (P5) follows. Hence, (γ) is stronger than (P5).

Lemma 2 *Consider a continuous indirect utility function* v: $IR^n_{++}\to IR_+$ *satisfying condition* (γ). *Then the corresponding preference relation* $\succeq$ *defined by* $p\succeq p' :\Leftrightarrow v(p)\ge v(p')$, satisfies (P5).

Proof.

Given a sequence of price vectors $\langle p^k\rangle$, $p^k\in IR^n_{++}$, such that $\lim_{k\to\infty} p^k=p^0\not>0$, and a $p\in IR^n_{++}$. By (γ) it follows $v(p^k)\to\infty$. Since $v(p)\in IR_+$ and since $v(p^k)\to\infty$, there exsists a positive integer N such that for all $k>N$, $v(p^k)>v(p)$, and hence $p^k\succ p$, concluding our proof.

According to (P5) the indirect utility function v may converge to a finite value when $p^k\to p^0\not>0$. Therefore, condition (P5) is weaker than (γ).

4. Some Properties of the Inverse Demand Correspondence

It will now be shown that $b: IR^n_{++}\to 2^{R^n_{++}}$ is upper hemicontinuous. We will characterize upper hemicontinuity by sequences ([6], pp. 262-263, Theorem A III. 1, part (b) of the proof, where compact-valuedness of the correspondence is not needed, see also [7], p. 532, Theorem 16.17):

Let $F: S\to 2^T$, where $S,T\subseteq IR^n$, then F is called "upper hemicontinuous" at $x^0\in S$, if for every sequence $\langle x^k\rangle$ with $\lim_{k\to\infty} x^k=x^0$ and for every sequence $\langle y^k\rangle$ with $y^k\in F(x^k)$, there exists a convergent subsequence of $\langle y^k\rangle, \langle y^{kj}\rangle$, such that $\lim_{j\to\infty} y^{kj}=y\in F(x^0)$. F is called upper hemicontinuous if it is upper hemicontinuous at every $x\in S$.

Theorem 3 *If the relation* $\succeq$ *satisfies* (P1) *to* (P5) *and if* $b: IR^n_{++}\to 2^{R^n_{++}}$ *is consistent with* $\succeq$, *then* b *is upper hemicontinuous.*

Proof.

Let $\langle x^k\rangle, x^k\in IR^n_{++}$, be a sequence such that $\lim_{k\to\infty} x^k=\tilde{x}\in IR^n_{++}$. Thus, for any k and for all $p'\in IR^n_{++}$ such that $p'x^k\le 1$ it follows, $p'\succeq p^k$, where

[3]The (income normalized) indirect utility function v is called decreasing if $p>p'\Rightarrow v(p)<v(p')$, for all $p,p'\in IR^n_{++}$.

$p^k \in b(x^k)$ and $p^k = (p_1^k, \cdots, p_n^k)$. If $\langle p^k \rangle$ is not bounded, then there must exist a positive integer $j \leq n$ and a sequence $\langle p_j^k \rangle$ such that $\lim_{j\to\infty} p_j^k = \infty$. Since $\lim_{k\to\infty} x_j^k = \tilde{x}_j > 0$, we obtain $p_l^k x_l^k > 1$ for some $m \in \mathrm{IN}$ and for all $l > m$, contradicting $p^k x^k \leq 1$. Hence $\langle p^k \rangle$ is bounded, and therefore, taking a subsequence if necessary, $\lim_{k\to\infty} p^k = \tilde{p}$. In order to obtain a contradiction, suppose $\tilde{p} \not> 0$. Obviously, there exists $\overline{p} \in \mathrm{IR}^n_{++}$ such that $\overline{p} \cdot \tilde{x} < 1$. Since $\lim_{k\to\infty} x^k = \tilde{x}$ there also exists an integer $N^1 > 0$ such that for all $k > N^1 : \overline{p} \cdot x^k < 1$. Hence, by consistency, $p^k \preceq \overline{p}$. On the other side, (P5) yields the existence of an integer $N^2 > 0$ such that for all $k > N^2$, $p^k \succ \overline{p}$. Take $\tilde{N} = \max\{N^1, N^2\}$, then for all $k > \tilde{N}$, $p^k \succ \overline{p}$ and $p^k \preceq \overline{p}$, a contradiction. Hence, $\tilde{p} > 0$.

Now, it will be shown that $\tilde{p} \in b(\tilde{x})$. Therefore, let us consider $\hat{p} \in \mathrm{IR}^n_{++}$ such that $\hat{p}\tilde{x} \leq 1$. In order to obtain that $\tilde{p} \preceq \hat{p}$, we have to consider two cases.

1) $\hat{p}\tilde{x} < 1$.

Hence, there exists a positive integer N such that $\hat{p}x^k < 1$ for all $k > N$, and therefore $p^k \preceq \hat{p}$, for all $k > N$. In view of lower semicontinuity of $\preceq$, $\lim_{k\to\infty} p^k = \tilde{p} \preceq \hat{p}$.

2) $\hat{p}\tilde{x} = 1$.

Let $\langle q^l \rangle, q^l \in \mathrm{IR}^n_{++}$, be a sequence such that $\lim_{k\to\infty} q^l = \hat{p}$ and $q^l \tilde{x} < 1$. Obviously, such a sequence does exist. Since we have $q^l x^k < 1$ for some positive integer $\hat{N}$ and for all $k > \hat{N}$, we obtain $p^k \preceq q^l$. By lower semicontinuity this implies, $\lim_{k\to\infty} p^k = \tilde{p} \preceq q^l$. In view of upper semicontinuity of $\preceq$, we thus obtain $\tilde{p} \preceq \hat{p}$. Hence $\tilde{p} \in b(\tilde{x})$. This concludes our proof

Corollary: In the light of Lemma 2 and the previous remarks it follows: given a continuous and decreasing indirect utility function v: $\mathrm{IR}^n_{++} \to \mathrm{IR}_+$ satisfying condition (γ), then the inverse demand correspondence b: $\mathrm{IR}^n_{++} \to 2^{\mathrm{IR}^n_{++}}$, defined by $b(x) = \{p \in B(x) | v(p) \leq v(p'), \text{ for all } p' \in B(x)\}$ is upper hemicontinuous.

Finally, since strict concavity of $\succeq$ implies single-valuedness of the inverse demand correspondence we immediately obtain the following theorem. Preliminarily, remember that strict concavity is defined as follows: let Y be a convex set, and let $p, p' \in Y$ with $p \neq p'$, then:

$$p \succeq p' \Rightarrow p \succ \lambda p + (1-\lambda) p', \forall \lambda \in (0,1).$$

Theorem 4 *Let* $\succeq$ *satisfy* (P1) *to* (P5) *and let it be strictly concave, then*

a) $b(x)$ is single-valued if b is consistent with $\succeq$, and b: $\mathrm{IR}^n_{++} \to \mathrm{IR}^n_{++}$ is a continuous function,

b) if $\succeq$ is homothetic[4], then b is homogeneous of degree -1.

Note, that upper hemicontinuity and continuity are identical, when b is a function ([6], p. 262).

5. Summary

In the previous analysis, a formal frame for modelling consumer behavior has been presented when firms offer certain amounts of commodities at the market and consumers react to these offers by their willingness to pay. This willingness to pay can be described by the inverse demand correspondence. When the plans of consumers and firms coincide then the deal will take place, and the consumers will achieve the goods.

REFERENCES

[1] A. Mas-Colell, M. D. Whinston and J. R. Green, "Microeconomic Theory, Volume 1," Oxford University Press, New York, 1995.

[2] G. Debreu, "Theory of Value: An Axiomatic Analysis of Economic Equilibrium," Yale University Press, New Haven, 1959.

[3] S. Fuchs-Seliger, "A Note on Duality in Consumer Theory," *Economic Theory*, Vol. 13, No. 1, 1999, pp. 239-246.

[4] W. Erwin Diewert, "Applications of Duality Theory," In: M. D. Intriligator and D. A. Kendrick, Eds., *Frontiers of Quantitative Economics*, Vol. II, North-Holland, Amsterdam, 1974, pp. 106-176.

[5] S. Fuchs-Seliger, "Compensated and Direct Demand without Transitive and Complete Preferences," *Annals of Operations Research*, Vol. 23, No. 1, 1990, pp. 299-310.

[6] C. D. Aliprantis and C. Kim, "Infinite Dimensional Analysis: Hitchhikers Guide," Springer-Verlag, New York, 1986.

[7] W. Hildenbrand and A. P Kirman, "Equilibrium Analysis," North-Holland Publishing Company, Amsterdam, 1988.

[4] $\succeq$ is called "homothetic", if $x \succeq y \to \lambda x \succeq \lambda y, \forall \lambda > 0$.

Cycles and Rationalization

Patrick de Lamirande
Financial and Information Management, Cape Breton University, Sydney, Canada

ABSTRACT

This paper studies the composition of the Paretian allocation set in the context of a finite number of agents and a finite number of indivisible goods. Each agent receives at most one good and no monetary compensation is possible (typically called the house allocation problem). I introduce the concept of a cycle which is a sequence of allocations where each allocation is linked to the following allocation in the sequence by the same switch of goods between a subset of agents. I characterize the profiles of agent preferences when the Paretian set has cycles.

Keywords: Indivisible Goods; Cycle; Rationalizability; Pareto Allocations

1. Introduction

The house allocation problem consists of the assignment of indivisible goods to a set of agents who can receive only one object in the final allocation. Such problems are very common: allocation of rooms between roommates, lectures between professors, offices between colleagues, etc.

This class of problems was introduced by [1]. For this paper, agents own all goods collectively. While authors prove the existence of a competitive equilibrium, [2] shows that this competitive equilibrium is unique when preferences are strict over the set of goods. Reference [3] proves that this unique solution can be implemented by a strategy-proof allocation mechanism. Furthermore, there is a unique strategy-proof, individually rational and Pareto optimal allocation mechanism leading to the unique core allocation [4]. Reference [5] shows the equivalence between the competitive allocation from random endowments and the random serial dictatorship while [6] proves that all mechanisms that are strategy-proof, non-bossy and neutral must be serially dictatorial. Reference [7] models the case where there exists at the same time tenants and new comers on the same market. They introduce the top trading cycles mechanism in this set-up and show that it is Pareto efficient, individually rational and strategy-proof. Reference [8] introduces the possibility of having weak preferences over the set of goods and shows some restrictions on agent preferences for which efficiency and coalitional strategy-proofness are compatible[1].

The purpose of this paper is to look at rationalizability in the context of the house allocation problem. In other words, I am interested in answering the following questions: is it possible to say if, for a given set of allocations, there is a preference profile which supports this set as a Paretian allocation set? An example is students' seats in class. For every lecture, there is an allocation of seats. Considering the set of allocations, it is possible to test the rationality of students' preferences over seats by studying observed allocations.

In existing papers on the house allocation problem, only the [9] mentions explicitly the composition of the Paretian allocation set. They show that for any two allocations in the Paretian set, there exists a sequence of allocations belonging to the Paretian set such that they are pairwise connected, *i.e.* there are only two agents switching their goods and all others stay with the same good. This means that a set with two allocations that are not pairwise connected cannot be rationalized.

The main difficulty of using direct inference, *i.e.* testing each possible preference profile if it supports the allocation set as a Paretian allocation set, is linked to number of such preference profiles. As an example, if the number of goods is 5, then the number of possible allo-

[1]This list of papers treating of the house allocation problem is not exhaustive.

cations is 120 but the number of preference profiles is close to 25 billion[2]. Consequently, it seems reasonable to find a quickest method to study rationalizability.

In this paper, I introduce the concept of a cycle. A cycle is a subset of allocations in which a subset of agents switches their goods according to a specific scheme. The presence of cycles in a given set of allocations which is presumingly a Paretian set gives us information on the potential preference profiles which would support this set as a Paretian allocation set. With the concept of a cycle, I derive some conditions regarding the number of allocations that have to belong to an allocation set in order for it to be a Paretian allocation set.

The paper is organized as follows. In Section 2, I present the house allocation problem and I define the concept of a cycle. Section 4 talks about the properties of the cycle and Section 5 presents the implication of the presence of cycles in the Paretian allocation set. Section 6 concludes.

2. Definitions and Notations

Let $N=\{1,2,\cdots,\eta\}$ denote the set of agents with $\eta \geq 2$. The set of goods is $X=\{x_1,x_2,\cdots,x_\eta\}$ where all goods are different. I define an allocation $a=(a_1,a_2,\cdots,a_\eta)$ where $a_i \in X$ is the good allocated to agent i with $a_i \neq a_j$ for $i \neq j$. For any set of agents $\tilde{N} \subseteq N$ and for any set of goods $\tilde{X} \subseteq X$ with $|\tilde{N}|=|\tilde{X}|$, $A(\tilde{N},\tilde{X})$ denotes the set of all possible allocations of goods in $\tilde{X}$ to agents in $\tilde{N}$.

Agent i's preferences are represented by a binary relation P_i which is complete, transitive and antisymmetric (strict preference). Given $x_1,x_2 \in X$, $x_1 P_i x_2$ means that agent i strictly prefers x_1 to x_2. Also, $P_i|_Y = P_j|_Y$ means agents i and j have the same preferences over the set of goods Y. I define a profile as $P=(P_1,\cdots,P_\eta)$ and the domain of all possible profiles is denoted by $\mathbb{P}(N,X)$.

Definition 1: An allocation a is Pareto optimal for a given profile P if $\nexists \hat{a} \in A(N,X)$ such that

$$\hat{a}_i P_i a_i \quad \text{for at least one } i \in N$$
$$\hat{a}_j P_j a_j \ \text{ or } \hat{a}_j = a_j \quad \forall j=1,2,\cdots,\eta$$

$PO(P)$ denotes the set of all Paretian allocations when the profile is P. Then, $PO(P)$ must be an element of $\mathbb{A}(N,X)$ which is the set of all non-empty subsets of $A(N,X)$. It is important to note here that, for all preference profiles P, the set $PO(P)$ is never empty. This means that, for every preference profile P, there is at least one allocation which is not Pareto dominated by another allocation.

Definition 2: A set S is rationalizable if there is preference profile P such that the Paretian allocation set for P is S, *i.e.* $S=PO(P)$.

3. Cycles

Since direct inference is at least difficult, it seems natural to look at the structure of the Paretian set to identify some patterns that can be used to find one associated preference profile. Two groups of Paretian sets are trivially easy to rationalize. First, consider a Paretian set with only one allocation. Any preference profile where every agent has the allocated good as his most preferred good rationalizes this Paretian set. The second case is the other extreme case where the Paretian set is composed be all possible allocations. In such case, any preference profile where agents have the same preferences rationalizes this set.

However, intermediate cases are more difficult to infer directly. To solve this problem, I propose the concept of cycle.

Definition 3: Let the set $\tilde{N} \subseteq N$ and $\tilde{X} \subseteq X$ with $|\tilde{N}|=|\tilde{X}|=\tilde{\eta}$. Let $\tilde{n}=(\tilde{n}_1,\tilde{n}_2,\cdots,\tilde{n}_{\tilde{\eta}})$ with $\tilde{n}_1,\tilde{n}_2,\cdots,\tilde{n}_{\tilde{\eta}} \in \tilde{N}$ and $\tilde{x}=(\tilde{x}_1,\tilde{x}_2,\cdots,\tilde{x}_{e\eta})$ with $\tilde{x}_1,\tilde{x}_2,\cdots,\tilde{x}_{\tilde{\eta}} \in \tilde{X}$. A set $S \subseteq A(N,X)$ has a cycle $C(\tilde{n},\tilde{x})$ if $\exists S_s=\{a^1,a^2,\cdots,a^{\tilde{\eta}}\} \subseteq S$ such that

$$a^1_{\tilde{n}_1}=\tilde{x}_1, a^1_{\tilde{n}_2}=\tilde{x}_2,\cdots,a^1_{\tilde{n}_{\tilde{\eta}}}=\tilde{x}_{\tilde{\eta}}$$
$$a^2_{\tilde{n}_1}=\tilde{x}_2, a^2_{\tilde{n}_2}=\tilde{x}_3,\cdots,a^2_{\tilde{n}_{\tilde{\eta}}}=\tilde{x}_1$$
$$\vdots$$
$$a^{\tilde{\eta}-1}_{\tilde{n}_1}=\tilde{x}_{\tilde{\eta}-1}, a^{\tilde{\eta}-1}_{\tilde{n}_2}=\tilde{x}_{\tilde{\eta}},\cdots,a^{\tilde{\eta}-1}_{\tilde{n}_{\tilde{\eta}}}=\tilde{x}_{\tilde{\eta}-2}$$
$$a^{\tilde{\eta}}_{\tilde{n}_1}=\tilde{x}_{\tilde{\eta}}, a^{\tilde{\eta}}_{\tilde{n}_2}=\tilde{x}_1,\cdots,a^{\tilde{\eta}}_{\tilde{n}_{\tilde{\eta}}}=\tilde{x}_{\tilde{\eta}-1}$$

For example, if the set S has the cycle $C((1,2,3),(x_1,x_2,x_3))$, this means there are three allocations a^1, a^2 and a^3 belonging to S such that

$$a^1_1=x_1,\quad a^1_2=x_2,\quad a^1_3=x_3$$
$$a^2_1=x_2,\quad a^2_2=x_3,\quad a^2_3=x_1$$
$$a^3_1=x_3,\quad a^3_2=x_1,\quad a^3_3=x_2$$

It is important to underline that $\tilde{n}$ and $\tilde{x}$ are vectors and not subsets of N and X respectively. The reason is that the order of appearance within the vector is important to the definition of the cycle. To illustrate the importance of this distinction, consider the two following sets:

$$S_1=\{(x_1,x_2,x_3),(x_2,x_3,x_1),(x_3,x_1,x_2)\}$$
$$S_2=\{(x_2,x_1,x_3),(x_1,x_3,x_2),(x_3,x_2,x_1)\}$$

The set S_1 has the cycle $C((1,2,3),(x_1,x_2,x_3))$ and S_2 the cycle $C((1,2,3),(x_1,x_3,x_2))$. But those two cycles are different. For this reason, vectors must be used to define a cycle.

[2]The number of possible allocation is given by $n!$ while the number of possible preference profiles is $(n!)^n$.

Also, it should be noted that it is possible to write the same cycle in many ways. Lemma 1 gives the number of ways to write the same cycle[3].

Lemma 1: Any cycle of γ elements can be written in $card(R_\gamma)\cdot\gamma^2$ ways where

$$R_\gamma = \{\alpha \in \{1,2,\cdots,\gamma-1\} \mid \nexists \beta < \gamma \text{ with } mod_\gamma(\alpha\beta) = 0\}$$

where mod is the modulo operator and $card(R_\gamma)$ returns the number of elements in R_γ (cardinality of R_γ)[4].

The following example illustrates the lemma.

Example 1: Suppose I have the set $S = \{(x_1,x_2,x_3),(x_2,x_3,x_1),(x_3,x_1,x_2)\}$. Then, by Lemma 1, there are $(3-card(R_3))3^2 = 18$ ways to write the cycle:

$$C((1,2,3),(x_1,x_2,x_3)) \quad C((1,2,3),(x_2,x_3,x_1))$$
$$C((1,2,3),(x_3,x_1,x_2)) \quad C((2,3,1),(x_1,x_2,x_3))$$
$$C((2,3,1),(x_2,x_3,x_1)) \quad C((2,3,1),(x_3,x_1,x_2))$$
$$C((3,1,2),(x_1,x_2,x_3)) \quad C((3,1,2),(x_2,x_3,x_1))$$
$$C((3,1,2),(x_3,x_1,x_2)) \quad C((3,2,1),(x_3,x_2,x_1))$$
$$C((3,2,1),(x_2,x_1,x_3)) \quad C((3,2,1),(x_1,x_3,x_2))$$
$$C((2,1,3),(x_3,x_2,x_1)) \quad C((2,1,3),(x_2,x_1,x_3))$$
$$C((2,1,3),(x_1,x_3,x_2)) \quad C((1,3,2),(x_3,x_2,x_1))$$
$$C((1,3,2),(x_2,x_1,x_3)) \quad C((1,3,2),(x_1,x_3,x_2))$$

It must be noted that $card(R_\gamma)$ is always higher or equal to 2 when γ is higher or equal to 3. The number 1 and $\gamma-1$ always belong to R_γ.

Since the number of ways to write the same cycle can be large[5], I propose using the lexicographic ordering to have a unique notation for a given cycle.

Definition 4: For two vectors v and w of l components, v is lexicographically dominated by w if

$$w_1 > v_1 \text{ or}$$
$$w_1 = v_1, w_2 > v_2 \text{ or}$$
$$\vdots$$
$$w_1 = v_1, w_2 = v_2, \cdots, w_l > v_l$$

The first step is to choose from all possibilities of writing a given cycle the ways for which the vector $\tilde{n}$ is lexicographically dominated by (or equal to) the others. Secondly, from those variants, I choose the one for which the component subscripts of $\tilde{x}$ are lexicographically dominated by the other vector $\tilde{x}$.

Let's apply this process to the cycle in Example 1. The first step tells us to select the vector $\tilde{n}$ which is lexicographically dominated by the others. This vector is $(1,2,3)$. Then, from the different ways to write the cycle with $\tilde{n} = (1,2,3)$, which are $C((1,2,3),(x_1,x_2,x_3))$, $C((1,2,3),(x_2,x_3,x_1))$ and $C((1,2,3),(x_3,x_1,x_2))$, we select the one which has the vector $\tilde{x}$ whose component subscripts are lexicographically dominated by the component subscripts of the other $\tilde{x}$'s. I find that the unique solution is $C((1,2,3),(x_1,x_2,x_3))$.

I most emphasize that the definition of a cycle is independent of what other agents get. For example, consider the two following sets:

$S_1 =$

$\{(x_1,x_2,x_3,x_4,x_5),(x_1,x_2,x_4,x_5,x_3),(x_1,x_2,x_5,x_3,x_4)\}$

$S_2 =$

$\{(x_2,x_1,x_3,x_4,x_5),(x_2,x_1,x_4,x_5,x_3),(x_1,x_2,x_5,x_3,x_4)\}$

These sets have the same cycle $C((3,4,5),(x_3,x_4,x_5))$ even if they do not have the same allocations.

An interesting question is how many different cycles could the set S have for set of agents $\tilde{N}$ and a given subset of goods $\tilde{X}$? There are $\tilde{\eta}!$ different vectors $\tilde{n}$ and $\tilde{\eta}!$ different possible vectors $\tilde{x}$. There are $(\tilde{\eta}!)^2$ possibilities. But, I have already shown that there are $(card(R_{\tilde{\eta}}))\tilde{\eta}^2$ ways to write the same cycle. So there are $\dfrac{(\tilde{\eta}-1)!^2}{card(R_{\tilde{\eta}})}$ different cycles for a given subset of agents $\tilde{N}$ and a subset of goods $\tilde{X}$.

Also, it is possible that a Paretian set contains more than one cycle. In particular, it could happen that the Paretian set $PO(P)$ has two cycles: $C(\tilde{n},\tilde{x})$ and $C(\bar{n},\bar{x})$ with $\bar{N} \subset \tilde{N}$ and $\bar{X} \subset \tilde{X}$. To examine this case, I define the concept of subcycle.

Definition 5: Suppose that the set $S \subseteq A(X,N)$ has a cycle $C(\tilde{n},\tilde{x})$. The cycle $C(\bar{n},\bar{x})$ is a subcycle of $C(\tilde{n},\tilde{x})$ if $\bar{N} \subset \tilde{N}$ and $\bar{X} \subset \tilde{X}$.

Example 2 illustrates the concept of subcycle.

Example 2: Suppose that the set S has a cycle $C((1,2,3,4),(x_1,x_2,x_3,x_4))$. Let $S_s \subset S$ is the set of allocations a^s belonging to S such that

$$a_1^s = x_1,\ a_2^s = x_2,\ a_3^s = x_3,\ a_4^s = x_4 \text{ or}$$
$$a_1^s = x_2,\ a_2^s = x_3,\ a_3^s = x_4,\ a_4^s = x_1 \text{ or}$$
$$a_1^s = x_3,\ a_2^s = x_4,\ a_3^s = x_1,\ a_4^s = x_2 \text{ or}$$
$$a_1^s = x_4,\ a_2^s = x_1,\ a_3^s = x_2,\ a_4^s = x_3$$

Then, this cycle contains 4 different subcycles: $C((1,3),(x_1,x_3))$, $C((1,3),(x_2,x_4))$, $C((2,4),(x_1,x_3))$ and $C((2,4),(x_2,x_4))$

[3]All proofs are in Appendix.

[4]For $\alpha,\beta \in \mathbb{N}$, $mod_\alpha\beta$ is the remainder of the division of β by α.

[5]For example, if $m = 5$, then we can write the same cycle in 200 different ways.

To know if the cycle $C(\tilde{n},\tilde{x})$ has subcycles, I study the set $R_{\tilde{\eta}}$. The next lemma tells us the condition necessary for $C(\tilde{n},\tilde{x})$ to have subcycles.

Lemma 2: If $card(R_{\tilde{\eta}}) \neq \tilde{\eta}-1$, then $C(\tilde{n},\tilde{x})$ has subcycles.

Example 3: Suppose a set S has the cycle $C(\tilde{n},\tilde{x})$ with $\tilde{n}=(1,2,3,4,5,6)$ and $\tilde{x}=(x_1,x_2,x_3,x_4,x_5,x_6)$. This means there are 6 allocations $a^1,\cdots,a^6$ belonging to S such that:

$$a_1^1 = x_1,\ a_2^1 = x_2,\ a_3^1 = x_3,\ a_4^1 = x_4,\ a_5^1 = x_5,\ a_6^1 = x_6$$

$$a_1^2 = x_2,\ a_2^2 = x_3,\ a_3^2 = x_4,\ a_4^2 = x_5,\ a_5^2 = x_6,\ a_6^2 = x_1$$

$$\vdots$$

$$a_1^6 = x_6,\ a_2^6 = x_1,\ a_3^6 = x_2,\ a_4^6 = x_3,\ a_5^6 = x_4,\ a_6^6 = x_5$$

Set $R_6=\{2,3,4,6\}$. Then, cycle $C(\overline{n},\overline{x})$ with $\overline{n}=(1,4)$ and $\overline{x}=(x_1,x_4)$ is a subcyle of $C(\overline{n},\overline{x})$.

The last definition about cycles is the following:

Definition 6: The set $S \subseteq A(X,N)$ has a complete cycle $C_c(\tilde{N},\tilde{X})$ with $\tilde{N}\subseteq N$ and $\tilde{X}\subseteq X$ where $card(\tilde{N}) = card(\tilde{X})$ if for all $\tilde{n}=(\tilde{n}_1,\tilde{n}_2,\cdots,\tilde{n}_\eta)$ with $\tilde{n}_1,\tilde{n}_2,\cdots,\tilde{n}_{\tilde{\eta}}\in\tilde{N}$ and $\tilde{x}=(\tilde{x}_1,\tilde{x}_2,\cdots,\tilde{x}_{\tilde{\eta}})$ with $\tilde{x}_1,\tilde{x}_2,\cdots,\tilde{x}_{\tilde{\eta}}\in\tilde{X}$, S contains the cycle $C(\tilde{n},\tilde{x})$.

In other words, the set T has a complete cycle $C_c(\tilde{N},\tilde{X})$ if there is at least one allocation that belongs to A for all possible permutations of goods belonging to $\tilde{X}$ between agents belonging to $\tilde{N}$.

4. Properties of Cycles and Complete Cycles

The presence of a cycle $C(\tilde{n},\tilde{x})$ in a Paretian set $PO(P)$ gives information about the preferences of agents. The first insight given by a cycle is about pairs of goods which are neighbors in the vector $\tilde{x}$.

Proposition 1: If $PO(P)$ has a cycle $C(\tilde{n},\tilde{x})$, then $\forall i,j\in\tilde{N}$

$$P_i\big|_{x_1,x_{\tilde{\eta}}} = P_j\big|_{x_1,x_{\tilde{\eta}}}$$

$$\text{and } P_i\big|_{x_k,x_{k+1}} = P_j\big|_{x_k,x_{k+1}}$$

$\forall k=1,2,3,\cdots,\tilde{\eta}-1$.

Consequently, if the Paretian set has a cycle, then all agents belonging to the cycle have same preferences over any pairs of neighbor goods in that cycle. With this proposition, some information on the associated profile P is provided by the presence of a cycle in the Paretian set. However, information on preferences is only over each pair (x_k,x_{k+1}) and the pair $(x_1,x_{\tilde{\eta}})$. No information about the preferences over all pairs of goods belonging to the set $\tilde{X}$ can be extracted from the cycle. The following example demonstrates the problem.

Example 4: Suppose the cycle $C((1,2,3,4),(x_1,x_2,x_3,x_4))$ belongs to the Paretian set $PO(P)$. Then the following profile supports the cycle.

P_1	P_2	P_3	P_4
x_1	x_3	x_1	x_3
x_3	x_1	x_3	x_1
x_2	x_2	x_2	x_2
x_4	x_4	x_4	x_4

Then when the good x_3 is allocated to someone who belongs to $\{1,3\}$, the good x_1 is allocated to the other agent in that set. The cycle does not contain an allocation where the good x_1 is allocated to someone in $\{1,3\}$ and the good x_3 to someone in $\{2,4\}$. This means that agents in $\{1,3\}$ could have different preferences over the set $\{x_1,x_3\}$ than agents in $\{2,4\}$. The same is true for the set of goods $\{x_2,x_4\}$.

To analyze preferences over a pair of goods which are not neighbors to each other in the vector $\tilde{x}$, I use the concept of subcycle. In Section 2, I showed that a subcycle is a cycle. So, if a cycle has subcycles, Proposition 1 can be used to infer agents' preferences.

Proposition 2: Suppose $PO(P)$ has a cycle $C(\tilde{n},\tilde{x})$. For $\alpha\notin R_{\tilde{\eta}}$,

$$P_{\tilde{n}_i}\big|_{\{\tilde{x}_y,\tilde{x}_{y+\alpha}\}} = P_{\tilde{n}_{i+\alpha}}\big|_{\{\tilde{x}_y,\tilde{x}_{y+\alpha}\}}$$

$$\forall i=1,2,\cdots,\tilde{\eta}-\alpha,\ \forall y=1,2,\cdots,\tilde{\eta}-\alpha$$

Let's apply this proposition to the following example.

Example 5: Suppose $PO(P)$ has a cycle $C(\tilde{n},\tilde{x})$ with $\tilde{n}=(1,2,3,4,5,6)$ and $\tilde{x}=(x_1,x_2,x_3,x_4,x_5,x_6)$. Then, this means there are six allocations $a^1,a^2,a^3,a^4,a^5,a^6\in PO(P)$ such that

$$a_1^1 = x_1, a_2^1 = x_2,\cdots,a_6^1 = x_6$$

$$a_1^2 = x_2, a_2^2 = x_3,\cdots,a_6^2 = x_1$$

$$a_1^3 = x_3, a_2^3 = x_4,\cdots,a_6^3 = x_2$$

$$a_1^4 = x_4, a_2^4 = x_5,\cdots,a_6^4 = x_3$$

$$a_1^5 = x_5, a_2^5 = x_6,\cdots,a_6^5 = x_4$$

$$a_1^6 = x_6, a_2^6 = x_1,\cdots,a_6^6 = x_5$$

Consider goods x_1 and x_4. Then,

$$a_1^1 = x_1,\quad a_4^1 = x_4$$

$$a_1^4 = x_4,\quad a_4^4 = x_1$$

Then agents 1 and 4 have same preferences over the $\{x_1,x_4\}$. If we continue, we find that

1) Agents in $\{1,2,3,4,5,6\}$ have the same preferences over sets $\{x_1,x_2\}$, $\{x_2,x_3\}$, $\{x_3,x_4\}$, $\{x_4,x_5\}$, $\{x_5,x_6\}$ and $\{x_1,x_6\}$.

2) Agents in $\{1,3,5\}$ have the same preferences over sets $\{x_1,x_3\}$, $\{x_2,x_4\}$, $\{x_3,x_5\}$, $\{x_4,x_6\}$, $\{x_1,x_5\}$ and $\{x_2,x_6\}$.

3) Agents in $\{2,4,6\}$ have the same preferences over sets $\{x_1,x_3\}$, $\{x_2,x_4\}$, $\{x_3,x_5\}$, $\{x_4,x_6\}$, $\{x_1,x_5\}$

and $\{x_2, x_6\}$.

4) Agents in $\{1,4\}$ have the same preferences over sets $\{x_1, x_4\}$, $\{x_2, x_5\}$ and $\{x_3, x_6\}$.

5) Agents in $\{2,5\}$ have the same preferences over sets $\{x_1, x_4\}$, $\{x_2, x_5\}$ and $\{x_3, x_6\}$.

6) Agents in $\{3,6\}$ have the same preferences over sets $\{x_1, x_4\}$, $\{x_2, x_5\}$ and $\{x_3, x_6\}$.

This result gives additional information about the profile P since it provides information on preferences over pairs of goods which are not neighbors in the cycle. Subcycles can be analyzed on their own since they are themselves distinct cycles, but they could be supported by different preference profiles across agents than the larger cycle. However, by using subcycles, it is only possible to show that agents which are neighbors in a subcycle have the same preferences over all pairs of goods which are neighbor in this subcycle and it is possible that two distinct subsets of agents in the cycle hold different preferences over the same subset of goods.

While Proposition 2 gives us information about preferences over pairs of goods that are neighbors in a subcycle, Proposition 3 deals with the other pairs.

Proposition 3: Suppose that $PO(P)$ has a cycle $C(\tilde{n},\tilde{x})$. For all pairs of goods $\tilde{x}_\alpha, \tilde{x}_\beta \in \tilde{X}$ with $\beta > \alpha$ such that $(\beta - \alpha)$ belongs to $R_{\tilde{\eta}}$,

$$P_i\big|_{\{\tilde{x}_\alpha,\tilde{x}_\beta\}} = P_j\big|_{\{\tilde{x}_\alpha,\tilde{x}_\beta\}} \qquad \forall i,j \in \tilde{N}$$

It must be noted that if $\tilde{\eta}$ is a prime number, all pairs of goods are treated by Proposition 3 since $|R_{\tilde{\eta}}| = \{\tilde{\eta}-1\}$. In this case, all agents in $\tilde{N}$ have the same preferences over the set $\tilde{X}$.

Corollary 1: If $PO(P)$ has a cycle $C(\tilde{n},\tilde{x})$ and $\tilde{\eta}$ is a prime number, then $\forall i,j \in \tilde{N}$,

$$P_i\big|_Y = P_j\big|_Y$$

This result is very strong. Only one cycle is enough to conclude that a subset of agents have the same preferences over a subset of goods. Unfortunately, as showed above, this result cannot be extended to any number of individuals in $\tilde{N}$.

Another case can lead to the conclusion that agents in a subset of N have the same preferences over a subset of goods.

Proposition 4: If $PO(P)$ has a complete cycle $C_c(\tilde{N},\tilde{X})$, the agents in $\tilde{N}$ have the same preferences over $\tilde{X}$.

The presence of a complete cycle gives us more information about agent preferences. In fact, a cycle could give the same information if the number of elements in that cycle is a prime number. Unless it has this characteristic, a cycle by itself does not give information on preferences over all goods. But, if a single cycle cannot give the same information than a complete cycle, many cycles can provide it.

Proposition 5: Let the set $\tilde{N}$ be a subset of N and $\tilde{X}$ a subset of X with $card(\tilde{N}) = card.(\tilde{X}) = \tilde{\eta}$. Let α be the lowest prime number such that $mod_\alpha \tilde{\eta} = 0$. If $PO(P)$ has $\left[\left(\frac{\tilde{\eta}}{\alpha}-1\right)*(\tilde{\eta}-2)!+1\right]$ cycles with same $\tilde{n}$ and same $\tilde{X}$, then the agents in $\tilde{N}$ have the same preferences over $\tilde{X}$.

To illustrate the idea of this proof, consider the following example. Suppose $card(X) = 6$ and suppose S has the following cycles :

- the 6 cycles given by $C((1,2,3,4,5,6),(x_1,\cdot,x_2,\cdot,x_3,\cdot))$
- the 6 cycles given by $C((1,2,3,4,5,6),(x_1,\cdot,x_2,\cdot,x_4,\cdot))$
- the 6 cycles given by $C((1,2,3,4,5,6),(x_1,\cdot,x_2,\cdot,x_5,\cdot))$
- the 6 cycles given by $C((1,2,3,4,5,6),(x_1,\cdot,x_2,\cdot,x_6,\cdot))$
- the 6 cycles given by $C((1,2,3,4,5,6),(x_1,\cdot,x_3,\cdot,x_2,\cdot))$
- the 6 cycles given by $C((1,2,3,4,5,6),(x_1,\cdot,x_4,\cdot,x_2,\cdot))$
- the 6 cycles given by $C((1,2,3,4,5,6),(x_1,\cdot,x_5,\cdot,x_2,\cdot))$
- the 6 cycles given by $C((1,2,3,4,5,6),(x_1,\cdot,x_6,\cdot,x_2,\cdot))$

If S has only these cycles, this means agents 1, 3 and 5 could have different preferences over x_1, x_2 than agents 2, 4 and 6. To have all agents with the same preferences, I must add at least one more cycle.

An interesting question concerning the composition of the Paretian set is what happens to the remaining agents. If the Paretian set has a cycle $C(\tilde{n},\tilde{x})$, it is interesting to know if there is an allocation in $A(N\tilde{N}, X\tilde{X})$ such that agents outside the cycle get the same goods in all allocations which can constitute the cycle. In other words, if I define $\tilde{X}^c = X\tilde{X}$, $\tilde{N}^c = N\tilde{N}$, the question is: "Is there a $z \in A(\tilde{N}^c, \tilde{X}^c)$ such that the set S^c composed by all allocations belonging to $PO(P)$ where agents in $\tilde{N}^c$ get z has a cycle $C(\tilde{n},\tilde{x})$?" The answer is: there is no guarantee that the existence of such an element. Take the following example:

Example 6: Suppose the preferences for 6 agents are given by

P_1	P_2	P_3	P_4	P_5	P_6
x_1	x_1	x_1	x_1	x_6	x_6
x_3	x_3	x_3	x_3	x_2	x_4
x_2	x_4	x_2	x_4	x_5	x_5
x_4	x_2	x_5	x_5	x_1	x_1
x_5	x_5	x_4	x_2	x_3	x_3
x_6	x_6	x_6	x_6	x_4	y_2

Then

$$(x_1,x_2,x_3,x_4,x_5,x_6) \in PO(P)$$
$$(x_1,x_2,x_3,x_4,x_6,x_5) \in PO(P)$$
$$(x_2,x_3,x_4,x_1,x_5,x_6) \notin PO(P)$$
$$(x_2,x_3,x_4,x_1,x_6,x_5) \in PO(P)$$
$$(x_3,x_4,x_1,x_2,x_5,x_6) \in PO(P)$$
$$(x_3,x_4,x_1,x_2,x_6,x_5) \notin PO(P)$$
$$(x_4,x_1,x_2,x_3,x_5,x_6) \in PO(P)$$
$$(x_4,x_1,x_2,x_3,x_6,x_5) \in PO(P)$$

I obtain a cycle $C(\tilde{n},\tilde{x})$ with $\tilde{n}=(1,2,3,4)$ and $\tilde{x}=(x_1,x_2,x_3,x_4)$. But the subset of $PO(P)$ in which allocations give x_5 to agent 5 and x_6 to agent 6 does not contain the cycle $C(\tilde{n},\tilde{x})$. This is also true for the subset of $PO(P)$ in which allocations give x_6 to agent 5 and x_5 to agent 6.

Example 6 shows that the existence of such an elements is not guaranteed. Nevertheless if such element exists and the agents in $\tilde{N}$ have the same preferences over the set Y, then the Paretian set contains a complete cycle $C_c(\tilde{N},\tilde{X})$.

Proposition 6: Let the set $\tilde{N}$ be a subset of N and $\tilde{X}$ a subset of X with $card(\tilde{N})=card(\tilde{X})$. Suppose that all agents in $\tilde{N}$ have the same preferences over the set $\tilde{X}$. If the subset of $PO(P)$ composed of allocations in which agents belonging to $\tilde{N}^c$ get $z \in A(\tilde{N}^c,\tilde{X}^c)$ has the cycle $C(\tilde{n},\tilde{x})$, then $PO(P)$ has a complete cycle $C_c(\tilde{N},\tilde{X})$ in which $\tilde{N}^c$ get z.

To illustrate this proposition, consider the case where the Paretian set $PO(P)$ contains the allocations (x_1,x_2,x_3,x_4,x_5), (x_2,x_3,x_1,x_4,x_5) and (x_3,x_1,x_2,x_4,x_5). Then, $PO(P)$ has the cycle $C((1,2,3),(x_1,x_2,x_3))$. By Proposition 6, the allocations (x_1,x_2,x_3,x_4,x_5), (x_2,x_1,x_3,x_4,x_5) and (x_3,x_2,x_1,x_4,x_5) must also belong to $PO(P)$. Then, $PO(P)$ has a complete cycle $C_c(\{1,2,3\},\{x_1,x_2,x_3\})$.

5. Cycles and Paretian Sets

Finding a preference profile that rationalizes a set S is easy in some cases. When $S=A(N,X)$, then any preference profile such that agents have same preferences rationalizes the set S has a Paretian set. Also, if the set S has only one allocation a, this set can be rationalized by any preference profile in which each agent gets his most preferred good. Even in the case where S has two allocations, this set can be rationalized if the two allocations are pairwise connected. However, it is not possible to go further. At the first look, it is impossible to say if a set S can be rationalized even if all allocations are pairwise connected[6].

Fortunately, it is possible to find some necessary conditions on rationalizable sets. Before presenting some conditions on rationalizable sets, I need the following proposition.

Proposition 7: Suppose $PO(P)$ has a cycle $C(i,y)$. Let i be an agent belonging to $\tilde{N}$ and x_l an element of $\tilde{X}$. If all agents belonging to $\tilde{N}\{i\}$ have the same preferences over the set $\tilde{X}\{x_l\}$, then agents belonging to $\tilde{N}$ have same preferences over $\tilde{X}\{x_l\}$.

The next proposition describes the restrictions on the number of allocations $PO(P)$ must contain.

Proposition 8: If $n \geq 3$ and $PO(P) \neq A(N,X)$, then $card(PO(P)) \leq (n-1)*(n-1)!$ $\forall P$. If $|PO(P)|=(n-1)*(n-1)!$, then there exist an agent i and a good x_l belonging to X such that there is no allocation a^h belonging to $PO(P)$ with $a_i^h = x_l$ and the preference profile is given by

1) $P_g|_Y = P_h|_Y \quad \forall g,h \in N \quad Y = X \setminus \{x_l\}$
2) $P_g|_X = P_h|_X \quad \forall g,h \in N \setminus \{i\}$
3) $P_g|_{\{x_l,x_k\}} \neq P_i|_{\{x_l,x_k\}} \quad \forall g\ N \setminus \{i\}$ for some $x_k \in X \setminus \{x_l\}$

Using Proposition 8, it is possible to know if a set cannot be rationalized just by looking to the number of allocations belonging to this set. If $card(S) \in [(n-1)*(n-1)!+1, n!-1]$, then there exists no preference profile P such that $S=PO(P)$. But, the reverse is not true. This is a necessary condition. Furthermore, it is possible to use cycles to find other intervals such that, if the number of allocations of a set belongs to those intervals, then this set cannot be rationalized. However, it is not possible to find a general form for all of those intervals.

6. Conclusions

The rationalizability in the context of house allocation is hard to provide. Except in cases where there are only a few allocations (1, 2 or 3) or for extreme cases (the set of all possible allocations or for singleton), it is very difficult to conclude. The use of cycles can help to analyze the rationalizability of an allocation set.

While Proposition 8 studies the number of elements necessary for an allocation set to be rationalizable, Proposition 6 presents a case where the fact that a set contains a cycle implies that it must contain some specific allocations too. Proposition 8 could be extended to include more conditions, but to devise a complete statement of all cases promises to be very long and complicated. From my point of view, the most interesting ave-

[6]For example, consider the set $T=(x_1,x_2,x_3,x_4),(x_2,x_1,x_3,x_4),(x_1,x_2,x_4,x_3)$. All allocations are pairwise connected but this set cannot be rationalized.

nue for the use of cycles is to employ them like I do in Proposition 6. In short, cycles can be useful to study directly the rationalizability of an allocation set, since by using cycles, it is possible to say if a given allocation set is missing some allocations to be rationalizable.

7. Acknowledgements

I would like to acknowledge Mathieu Dufour, Walter Bossert, Lars Ehlers, Yves Sprumont and Yves Richelle for their helpful comments. Of course, all remanning errors are mine.

REFERENCES

[1] L. Shapley and H. Scarf, "On Cores and Indivisibility," *Journal of Mathematical Economics*, Vol. 1, No. 1, 1974, pp. 23-37.

[2] A. E. Roth and A. Postlewaite, "Weak versus Strong Domination in a Market with Indivisible Goods," *Journal of Mathematical Economics*, Vol. 4, 1977, pp. 131-137.

[3] A. Roth, "Incentive Compatibility in a Market with Indivisibilities," *Economic Letters*, Vol. 9, 1982, pp. 127-132.

[4] J. Ma, "Strategy-Proofness and the Strict Core in a Market with Indivisibilities," *International Journal of Game Theory*, Vol. 23, 1994, pp. 75-83.

[5] A. Abdulkadiroğlu and T. Sönmez, "Random Serial Dictatorship and the Core from Random Endowments in House Allocation Problems," *Econometrica*, Vol. 66, No. 3, 1998, pp. 689-701.

[6] L.-G. Svensson, "Strategy-Proof Allocation of Indivisible Goods," *Social Choice and Welfare*, Vol. 16, 1999, pp 557-567.

[7] A. Abdulkadiroğlu and T. Sönmez, "House Allocation with Existing Tenants," *Journal of Economic Theory*, Vol. 88, 1999, pp. 233-260.

[8] L. Ehlers, "Coalitional Strategy-Proofness House Allocation," *Journal of Economic Theory*, Vol. 105, 2002, pp. 298-317.

[9] A. Ben-Shoham, R. Serrano and O. Volij, "The Evolution of Exchange," *Journal of Economic Theory*, Vol. 114, 2004, pp. 310-328.

Appendix

Proof of Lemma 1: Suppose the set S has a cycle $C(\tilde{n},\tilde{x})$. Then, the set S contains $\tilde{\eta}$ allocations such that:

$$a_1^1 = x_1, a_2^1 = x_2, \cdots, a_{\tilde{\eta}}^1 = x_{\tilde{\eta}}$$
$$a_1^2 = x_2, a_2^2 = x_3, \cdots, a_{\tilde{\eta}}^2 = x_1$$
$$\vdots$$
$$a_1^{\tilde{\eta}} = x_{\tilde{\eta}}, a_2^{\tilde{\eta}} = x_1, \cdots, a_{\tilde{\eta}}^{\tilde{\eta}} = x_{\tilde{\eta}-1}$$

I can write this cycle by using $x' = (x_2, x_3, \cdots, x_{\tilde{\eta}}, x_1)$. Then, all cycles $C(\tilde{n},x')$ with x' which has its components switching neighbor to neighbor relative to $\tilde{x}$ give the same cycle. This gives $\tilde{\eta}$ different ways to write the same cycle. I can do the same thing by switching elements of $\tilde{n}$ and I find also $\tilde{\eta}$ ways to write the cycle. Now, consider the number r which is a positive integer strictly lower than $\tilde{\eta}$. Suppose that there exists no positive integer q strictly lower than $\tilde{\eta}$ such that $mod_{\tilde{\eta}} rq = 0$. Let

$$n'' = \left(1, r+1, mod_{\tilde{\eta}}(2r)+1, \cdots, mod_{\tilde{\eta}}((\tilde{\eta}-1)r)+1\right)$$
$$x'' = \left(x_1, x_{r+1}, x_{mod_{\tilde{\eta}}(2r)+1}, \cdots, x_{mod_{\tilde{\eta}}((\tilde{\eta}-1)r+1)}\right)$$

and consider the cycle $C(n'',x'')$. Since r does not belong to $R_{\tilde{\eta}}$, this means all components of n'' and x'' are different. So, the cycle $C(n'',x'')$ is the same than $C(\tilde{n},\tilde{x})$. This is true for all r which are positive integers strictly lower than $\tilde{\eta}$ and do not belong to $R_{\tilde{\eta}}$.

Finally, I obtain $card(R_{\tilde{\eta}})\tilde{\eta}^2$.

Proof of Lemma 2: Without lost of generality (WLOG), let's take the cycle $C(\tilde{n},\tilde{x})$ with $\tilde{n} = (1,2,\cdots,\tilde{\eta})$ and $\tilde{x} = (x_1, x_2, \cdots, x_{\tilde{\eta}})$. If $card(R_{\tilde{\eta}}) \neq \tilde{\eta}-1$, it means that there is atleast one $r < \tilde{\eta}$ which does not belong to $R_{\tilde{\eta}}$. If r does not belongs to $R_{\tilde{\eta}}$, this means there is a positive integer q strictly lower than $\tilde{\eta}$ such that $mod_{\tilde{\eta}} rq = 0$.

Now, consider the vector of agents $n' = \left(1, \rho+1, mod_{|I|}(2\rho)+1, \cdots, mod_{|I|}((q-1)\rho)+1\right)$ and the vector of goods

$$x' = \left(x_1, x_{\rho+1}, x_{mod_{|I|}(2\rho)+1}, \cdots, x_{mod_{|I|}((q-1)\rho)+1}\right)$$

Since r is not equal to $\tilde{\eta}$ and q is strictly lower then $\tilde{\eta}$, the set N' is not equal to $\tilde{N}$. I obtain the cycle $C(n',x')$ which is a subcycle of $C(\tilde{n},\tilde{x})$.

Proof of Proposition 1: WLOG, suppose that $\tilde{n} = (1,2,\cdots,\tilde{\eta})$ and $\tilde{x} = (x_1, x_2, \cdots, x_{\tilde{\eta}})$. Consider x_h, x_{h+1} where $h = 1,2,\cdots,\tilde{n}-1$. Suppose that agent 1 prefers x_{h+1} over x_h. Because $PO(P)$ has the cycle $C(\tilde{n},\tilde{x})$, there is an allocation belonging to $PO(P)$ such that x_{h+1} is allocated to agent 2 and x_h to agent 1. Since this allocation belongs to $PO(P)$, then agent 2 must also prefer x_{h+1} to x_h. Again, because $PO(P)$ has the cycle $C(\tilde{n},\tilde{x})$, there is an allocation belonging to $PO(P)$ such that x_{h+1} is allocated to agent 3 and x_h to agent 2. Since this allocation belongs to $PO(P)$, then agent 3 must prefer x_{h+1} to x_h. If I continue for all agents belonging to I, I find that all agents belonging to $\tilde{N}$ must have similar preferences for all pairs x_h, x_{h+1} with $h = 1,2,\cdots,\tilde{\eta}-1$ and for the pair $x_1, x_{\tilde{\eta}}$.

Proof of Proposition 2: WLOG, suppose that $\tilde{n} = (1,2,\cdots,\tilde{\eta})$ and $\tilde{x} = (x_1, x_2, \cdots, x_{\tilde{\eta}})$. Let $q(r)$ be the smallest integer such that, for $r < \tilde{\eta}$ and r not belonging to $R_{\tilde{\eta}}$, $mod_{\tilde{\eta}}(q(r)r) = 0$. If r does not belong to $R_{\tilde{\eta}}$, then for every $\gamma = 1,2,\cdots,r$ and every $\beta = 1,2,\cdots,q(r)-1$, the cycle $C(n^s,x^s)$ with

$$n^s = \left(\gamma, \gamma+r, \gamma+mod_{|I|}(2r), \cdots, \gamma+mod_{|I|}((q-1)r)\right)$$
$$x^s = \left(x_\beta, x_{\beta+r}, x_{\beta+mod_{|I|}(2r)}, \cdots, x_{\beta+mod_{|I|}((q-1)r)}\right)$$

is a subcyle of $C(\tilde{n},\tilde{x})$. Because $C(n^s,x^s)$ is a subcycle of $C(\tilde{n},\tilde{x})$, $PO(P)$ must have the cycle $C(n^s,x^s)$. I can then apply Proposition 1.

Proof of Proposition 3: WLOG, suppose that $\tilde{n} = (1,2,\cdots,\tilde{\eta})$ and $\tilde{x} = (x_1, x_2, \cdots, x_{\tilde{x}})$. Now, take x_α and x_β with $\alpha = 1,2,\cdots,\tilde{\eta}-1$ and $\beta = \alpha+1,\cdots,\tilde{e}ta$ and let $\delta = \beta - \alpha$. By assumption, δ belongs to the set $R_{\tilde{\eta}}$.

Suppose that $x_\alpha \ P_1 \ x_\beta$. Because $PO(P)$ has the cycle $C(\tilde{n},\tilde{x})$, there is an allocation belonging to $PO(P)$ such that x_α is allocated to agent $\delta+1$ and x_β to agent 1. Since this allocation belongs to $PO(P)$, then agent $\delta+1$ must prefer x_α to x_β. Again, because $PO(P)$ has the cycle $C(\tilde{n},\tilde{x})$, there is an allocation belonging to $PO(P)$ such that x_α is allocated to agent $mod_{\tilde{\eta}}(2\delta)+1$ and x_β to agent $\delta+1$. Since this allocation belongs to $PO(P)$, then agent $mod_{\tilde{\eta}}(2\delta)+1$ must prefer x_α to x_β.

I can continue until I show that

$$x_\alpha \quad P_\gamma \quad x_\beta$$

with

$$\gamma = 1, \delta+1, mod_{\tilde{\eta}}(2\delta)+1, \cdots, mod_{\tilde{\eta}}((\tilde{\eta}-1)\delta)+1$$

Since there is no positive integer $q < \tilde{\eta}$ such that $mod_{\tilde{\eta}}(\delta q) = 0$, then the set $\{1, \delta+1, mod_{\tilde{\eta}}(2\delta)+1, \cdots, mod_{\tilde{\eta}}((\tilde{\eta}-1)\delta)+1\}$ has $\tilde{\eta}$ elements. So all agents belonging to $\tilde{N}$ have the same preferences over the set $\{x_\alpha, x_\beta\}$.

Proof of Proposition 4: Suppose the opposite is true, *i.e.* there exists $i, j \in \tilde{N}$ and $x', x'' \in \tilde{X}$ such that

$$x' \ P_i \ x''$$
$$x'' \ P_j \ x'$$

This means the good x' will never be allocated to j

when the good x'' is allocated to i. That contradicts the existence of a complete cycle.

Proof of Proposition 5: Suppose $\tilde{\eta}$ is prime. By Corollary 1, if $PO(P)$ has a cycle $C(\tilde{n},\tilde{x})$, then all agents belonging to $\tilde{N}$ have the same preferences over the set $\tilde{X}$.

Now, suppose $\tilde{\eta}$ is not a prime number and let α be the smallest prime number higher than 1 such that $mod_{\alpha}(\tilde{\eta})=0$.

Suppose $x_1,x_2 \in \tilde{X}$. Let N^1 and N^2 be two non-empty subsets of $\tilde{N}$ such that all agents belonging to N^1 prefer goods x_1 to x_2 and all agents belonging to N^2 prefer goods x_2 to x_1.

Suppose $PO(P)$ has τ cycles $C(\tilde{n},\tilde{x}^t)$ for $t=1,2,\cdots,\tau$. By convention, $\tilde{x}_1^t = x_1$ for all t. For all cycles $C(\tilde{n},\tilde{x}^t)$, I define β^t the positions of x_2 in the vector $\tilde{v}^t$ so that $\tilde{x}_{\beta}^t = x_2$, and let $\delta^t = \beta^t - 1$.

By Proposition 3, if there is a t such that δ^t does not belong to $R_{\tilde{\eta}}$, then all agents must have the same preferences. Suppose δ^t belongs to $R_{\tilde{\eta}}$ for all t. Let the set Π be equal to $\{\alpha,2\alpha,\cdots,\tilde{\eta}-\alpha\}$ which is a subset of $R_{\tilde{\eta}}$.

The maximum number such that all δ^t belong to Π is $\left(\frac{\tilde{\eta}}{\alpha}-1\right)(\tilde{\eta}-2)!$. If $\tau=\left(\frac{\tilde{\eta}}{\alpha}-1\right)(\tilde{\eta}-2)!$, then there is at least one cycle $C(\tilde{n},\tilde{x}^t)$ with $\delta^t=\alpha$. By Proposition 2, then agents belonging to the same set $j,j+\alpha,1+2\alpha,\cdots,j+(\tilde{\eta}-\alpha)$ for $j=1,2,\cdots,\alpha$ have the same preferences. But, agents in different subsets could have different preferences.

If I add another cycle $C(\tilde{n},\tilde{x}^{\theta})$, then δ^{θ} does not belong to Π. If δ^{θ} does not belong to $R_{\tilde{\eta}}$, by Proposition 3, all agents must have the same preferences over $\{x_1,x_2\}$. If δ^{θ} belongs to $R_{\tilde{\eta}}$, by Proposition 1, for $h=1,2,\cdots,\delta^{\theta}$, agents belonging to $h,h+\delta^{\theta},1+mod_{\tilde{\eta}}(2\delta^{\theta}),\cdots,h+(\tilde{\eta}-\delta^{\theta})$ have the same preferences. Since δ^{θ} does not belong to Π, then h and $h+\delta^{\theta}$ does not belong to the same set $j,j+\alpha,1+2\alpha,\cdots,j+(\tilde{\eta}-\alpha)$ for $j=1,2,\cdots,\alpha$. So the two sets which contain agent h and $h+\delta^{\theta}$ must have the same preferences. I can continue to conclude that all agents must have the same preferences.

Proof of Proposition 6: WLOG, suppose that $\tilde{X}=\{x_1,x_2,\cdots,x_{\tilde{\eta}}\}$ and $\tilde{N}=\{1,2,\cdots,\tilde{\eta}\}$. Let the set X^c be equal to $X\tilde{X}$ and $N^c = N\tilde{N}$.

Now suppose that $a \notin PO(P)$ where agents belonging to $\tilde{N}$ get goods belonging to $\tilde{X}$. This means there exists an allocation $b \in A(X,I)$ such that

$$b_i P_i a_i \quad \text{for at least one } i$$

$$b_j P_j a_j \quad \text{or } b_j = a_j \qquad j=1,2,\cdots,|N|$$

There are three possible cases for the allocation b. The first case consists of a reallocation between agents in N^c..

But this kind of reallocation cannot Pareto dominate the allocation a because there exists an allocation $\tilde{a}$ belonging to the Paretian set in which agents belonging to N^c get z. If a reallocation between agents in N^c dominates a, then the allocation $\tilde{a}$ should not belong to $PO(P)$.

The second case is a reallocation between agents in N. Again, it is not possible for this new allocation to dominate the allocation a. I assume that all agents in N have the same preferences over goods in X. Then no reallocation between agents in N could Pareto dominate the allocation a.

Finally, the last possibility is a reallocation between agents in both sets Because the agents in N have the same preferences, y_1 is preferred to y_k by all agents in N.

Suppose the agent who gets y_1 in the new allocation is agent α. Because of the cycle, there is an allocation in this cycle such that α gets good y_k. Then this allocation could not be in the Paretian set because this allocation will be dominated.

This means that the allocation where α gets y_k is Pareto dominated and contradicts the existence of a cycle $C(\tilde{n},\tilde{x})$ in the set S.

Proof of Proposition 7: For all pairs of goods belonging to $\tilde{X}\{x_{\gamma}\}$, I can apply Proposition 2 or Proposition 3 to find that there is at least one agent belonging to $\tilde{N}\{\delta\}$ with the same preferences as δ. Because all agents belonging to $\tilde{N}\{\delta\}$ have the same preferences over $\tilde{X}\{x_{\gamma}\}$, then all agents belonging to $\tilde{N}$ have the same preferences over $\tilde{X}\{x_{\gamma}\}$.

Proof of Proposition 8: Let $\Psi = A(N,X)PO(P)$. By assumption, $|\Psi| \le (n-1)!$.

Step 1: Consider the good x_1. Suppose that agent 1 gets good x_1 the least often in the allocations belonging to Ψ. Then, the number of allocations in Ψ where agent 1 gets x_1 is less than

$$\frac{(\eta-1)!}{\eta}$$

which is strictly lower than $(\eta-2)!$. This means there is at least one cycle $C(n^1,x^1)$ with $n^1=(2,3,\cdots,\eta)$ and $X^1=\{x_2,x_3,\cdots,x_{\eta}\}$ since there are exactly $(\eta-2)!$ of such cycles.

Now take x_2. Again WLOG, suppose that x_2 is the good which is the least assigned to agent 2 in the set Ψ when good x_1 is assigned to agent 1. The number of allocations in this case is less than

$$\frac{(\eta-2)!}{(\eta-1)}$$

which is strictly lower than $(\eta-3)!$. This means there is at least one cycle $C(n^2,x^2)$ with $n^2=(3,\cdots,\eta)$ and

$x^2 = \{x_3, \cdots, x_{n^2}\}$ since there are exactly $(\eta - 3)!$ of such cycles.

I can continue until $\eta - t - 1$ is a prime number. Let x_α belong to $\{x_t, x_{t+1}, \cdots, x\eta\}$ and suppose that agent α gets good x_α the most often in the allocations belonging to $PO(P)$ when x_1 is allocated to agent 1, x_2 to agent $2, \cdots, x_{t-1}$ to agent $t-1$. Then, by Corollary 1, all agents who belong to $\{t, t+1, \cdots, \eta\}\{\alpha\}$ have the same preferences over the set $\{x_t, x_{t+1}, \cdots, x_\eta\}\{x_\alpha\}$.

Step 2: Now, consider the general case where agents in $\{s, s+1, \cdots, \eta\}\beta$ have the same preferences over the set $\{x_s, x_{s+1}, x_{s+2}, \cdots, x_\eta\}\{x_\beta\}$. But there is at least one cycle $C(\tilde{n}, \tilde{x})$ with $\tilde{n} = (s, s+1, \cdots, \eta)$ and $\tilde{x} = \{x_s, x_{s+1}, x_{s+2}, \cdots, x_\eta\}$. By Proposition 7, all agents belonging to $\tilde{N}$ must have the same preferences over the set $\{x_s, x_{s+1}, x_{s+2}, \cdots, x_\eta\}\{x_\beta\}$.

Step 3: I can use the same approach with the two remaining x_α. Doing so, I find that all agents belonging to $\{s, s+1, \cdots, \eta\}$ have the same preferences over the set $\{x_s, x_{s+1}, x_{s+2}, \cdots, x_\eta\}$.

I use this approach until I find that all agents belonging to $\{2, 3, \cdots, \eta\}$ have the same preferences over the set $\{x_2, x_3, \cdots, x_\eta\}$.

Step 4: If $|\Psi|$ is strictly lower than $(n-1)!$, this means there is at least one cycle $C(n, x)$, Then, by Proposition 7, all agents have the same preferences over the set $\{x_2, x_3, \cdots, x_\eta\}$. Now, if steps 1 to 3 are done once again with x_2 and x_3 instead of x_1, it can be seen that all agents must have the same preferences over the set $\{x_1, x_2, x_3, \cdots, x_\eta\}$.

Step 5: Now suppose that $|\Psi|$ is equal to $(\eta - 1)!$. Suppose that there are two allocations a^1 and a^2 belonging to Ψ such that all agents get different goods, there is no $\alpha \in \{1, 2, \cdots, \eta\}$ such that $a^1_\alpha = a^2_\alpha$.

Let the vector i be the cycle of goods from a^1 to a^2. In other words, the good allocated to agent i_α in the allocation a^1 goes to agent $i_{\alpha+1}$. Since there are two allocations composing the same cycle $C(n, x)$ and there are $(\eta - 1)!$ allocations, this means there is at least one cycle and I obtain that all agents must have the same preferences.

The only way to avoid the possibility of having a cycle of η elements in the set $PO(P)$ is for all allocations belonging to Ψ, there is a good which is never allocated to an agent.

Suppose this good is x_γ and the agent never getting x_γ in $PO(P)$ is δ. Since all allocations belong to $PO(P)$, all agents have the same preferences over the set $X\{x_\gamma\}$ and all agents belonging to $I\{\delta\}$ have the same preferences over the set X.

If all agents have the same preferences, then $PO(P)$ must contain all allocations. So, this means there is at least one good belonging to $X\{x_\gamma\}$ for which agent δ and other agents must have different preferences.

11

On the Endogenous Sustainability of Economic Growth: Why Is the Scale of Government Enlarged?

Masayuki Otaki
Institute of Social Science, University of Tokyo, Tokyo, Japan

ABSTRACT

Almost every developed country experiences serious enlargement of the scale of government, specifically the expansion of fiscal deficits. We inquire why such a phenomenon is so prominent based on a Keynesian growth model entirely compatible with a standard neoclassical microeconomics. The cost-minimizing investment plays a key role. Whenever the demand that each firm faces is constrained by the effective demand (such case includes the situation of monopolistic competition), a firm strives to raise the productivity of labor and save its production cost. Such a process incessantly continues even if the effective demand is kept intact. It also implies that the unemployment would tend to be unbounded because the labor productivity improves under the constant effective demand. As such, a ceaseless expansionary aggregate demand policy is inevitably required for sustaining explosive potentials of production.

Keywords: Endogenous Sustainability of Economic Growth; Accumulation of Fiscal Deficits; Cost-Reduction Investment; Principle of Effective Demand

1. Introduction

Almost every developed economy is bothered by the huge amount of fiscal deficit and/or accumulation of public debts. Where do such, at least seemingly, serious economic difficulties stem from? The article approaches this political economic issue by applying a new type of a Keynesian economic-growth theory which is completely consistent with standard neoclassical microeconomics postulates.

The crucial factor is the potential excess production capacity that is delivered by the labor-productivity enhancing, thereby, cost reduction investment. Whenever each employer faces his downward sloping demand curve the location of which is determined by the effective demand in monopolistic competition, it implies that his business opportunity is ultimately limited by the effective demand economy as a whole. Thus, it is urgently necessary for each employer to improve the labor productivity via effective wage-cost reduction. Since such an economic motive ceaselessly works independent of the level of effective demand, even if it is not a conscious consequence, it enlarges the potential production capacity economy as whole relatively to the effective demand. It immediately cases the serious unemployment problem unless some legitimate aggregate-demand management policies are adopted.

For expanding the effective demand that matches the explosive aggregate production potential, the enlargement of fiscal expenditure with non-negligible budget deficit is unavoidable. That is, the role of government is forced to be more active to secure stable jobs evenly to employees who are threatened by the mass unemployment under the incessant labor-productivity growth. Succinctly, economic growth in the monetary market economy is unsustainable per se, and it becomes to heavily rely on the governmental economic activities.

It is also noteworthy that Buchanan and Wagner [1], although it is a superficial and journalistic book, criticized that Keynes and his successors, including voters, underestimate the true social cost of fiscal expenditure, and such tendency exacerbates budget deficits. However, according to our view, the enlargement of government is inevitable owing to generic properties of the monetary market economy, not to the irrational recognitions and/or greedy political rent seeking.

In the standard neoclassical economic-growth theory (e.g. Solow [2], Swan [3], Romer [4]), such a tragedy never occurs. This is because there never exists the concept of effective demand in the theory. Incomes are determined by the amount of existing production resources, and all savings are automatically absorbed by the capital investment independent of income level. However, as developed by Otaki [5,6], these optimistic properties of the model never preserved in the monetary economy where money possesses its intrinsic value.

The reason why money circulates beyond generations is the *faith* to its intrinsic value. That is, the function of the monetary economy decisively depends on the people's belief that the future purchasing power of money kept stable. Since the future price level (the inverse of the purchasing power of money) affects the current price via current wage-price setting, the *faith* to the intrinsic value of money quite naturally leads us to *endogenous* current price inflexibility.

As such, it is a rather rare case in which the full-employment equilibrium is attained within a monetary economy. Unless ample money is provided via fiscal-monetary policy, the principle of effective demand works and incomes and savings are subject to the volume of the capital investment. To summarize, our growth theory deals with the economic phenomena in a monetary economy, and the scope of the neoclassical growth-theory is limited to a barter economy.

The article consists of the rest three sections. In Section 2, using a standard overlapping generations model in production economy, we construct a Keynesian growth model with money and tangible/intangible assets improving the labor productivity. Section 3 deals with some comparative statics and induces some important policy implications. Section 4 provides brief concluding remarks.

2. The Model

2.1. Structure of the Model

The deployed model basically depends on Otaki [7]. We consider a two period overlapping-generations model with infinite time horizon. In our economy, there are two social strata; employers and employees. Each employer consists of a kind of dynasty and specializes in producing some differentiated good z. He maximizes his own lifetime utility comparing with benefits of his descendants that are delivered by the accumulation of tangible/intangible assets that promote the labor productivity γ_t [1]. His income is the profits of his firm when he is young.

An employee also maximizes his lifetime utility. He can provide unit labor only when he is young and prepares for his retirement by hoarding money. We assume that the disutility of labor is β.

There are three kinds of market in this economy: the goods markets, labor markets, and money market. By Walras' law, we can skip the equilibrium condition for the money market. In addition, we assume that the real government expenditure is not enough, and imperfect employment equilibrium prevails. And thus, labor market is in equilibrium when the real reservation wage, which will be defined below, is equalized to the disutility of labor.

Goods are differentiated within the interval $Z \equiv [0,1]$. The lifetime utility function from consumption is identical between strata and is defined as

$$U_t \equiv [c_{1t}]^{1-s}[c_{2t+1}]^s, c_{it} \equiv \left[\int_0^1 [c_{it}(z)]^{1-\eta^{-1}} \mathrm{d}z\right]^{\frac{1}{1-\eta^{-1}}}, \quad (1)$$

$$0 < s < 1, \eta > 1$$

where c_{it} is the aggregate consumption level of an individual who belongs to the ith generation during period t [2].

The demand function $D_t(z)$ for good $z \in Z$ becomes

$$D_t(z) = \left[\frac{p_t(z)}{P_t}\right]^{-\eta} y_t, P_t \equiv \left[\int_0^1 [p_t(z)]^{1-\eta} \mathrm{d}z\right]^{\frac{1}{1-\eta}} \quad (2)$$

where $p_t(z)$ denotes the price of good z during period t, and P_t is the price index derived from instantaneous utility maximization. y_t is the real effective demand deflated by P_t. Furthermore, since the lifetime utility function is the Cobb-Douglas type, the aggregate saving function S_t becomes

$$S_t = s y_t. \quad (3)$$

All above discussions are concerning common properties across strata. Next, we shall depict the peculiar decision process of each stratum.

2.2. Employees

An employee faces the decision problem whether he participates or not. As above discussed, in any imperfect employment equilibrium, the real reservation wage is equalized to the disutility of labor, and thus any employee is indifferent whether to work or not. Since the indirect lifetime utility IU_t derived from consumption is expressed by

$$IU_t = \frac{W_t}{A[P_t]^{1-s}[P_{t+1}]^s}, A \equiv s^s[1-s]^{1-s} \quad (4)$$

[1] This assumption is based on *impure* altruism (Acemoglu [8]). See, for example, Andreoni [9], Banerjee and Newman [10,11], Galor and Zeira [12] and Aghion and Bolton [13], concerning the neoclassical model based on *impure* altruism. However, the policy implications are entirely different between preceding research and this article.

[2] The Cobb-Douglas form of the lifetime utility function is deployed mainly because of excluding the effect of inflation to consumption/saving decision that seems not only less important for analyzing a long-run economic problem such as economic growth but also consistent with empirical analyses.

the nominal reservation wage W_t^R satisfies the following equation:

$$\frac{W_t^R}{A[P_t]^{1-s}[P_{t+1}]^s} = \beta \Rightarrow W_t^R = A[P_t]^{1-s}[P_{t+1}]^s \beta. \quad (5)$$

2.3. Employers

We assume that the gain obtained from the progress of the labor productivity is equivalent to the same amount of future consumption, although the former is attributed to the next generation. In addition, savings per an employer are so abundant that there is no necessity of external borrowing.

Under these two assumptions, we can separate employer's saving decision from that for the capital investment because there is not substantive difference between money hoarding and capital investment. An employer's decision becomes 1) he decides how much he should save for maximizing the lifetime utility; 2) given the optimal saving, he should decide how much savings are alloted to the capital investment.

We have already solved the first-step optimization problem that is expressed in (3). Since, by assumption, the second-step optimization does not affect the first-step problem, what is left for us is to solve the optimal capital investment decision. The problem is formatted as

$$\max_{\gamma_t}\left[-P_t\left[\frac{\gamma_t}{\gamma_{t-1}}\right]^\alpha - \frac{1}{1+\tau}\frac{W^R(P_{t+1},P_{t+2})y_{t+1}}{\gamma_t}\right], \quad (6)$$
$$\alpha > 1$$

where $\left[\frac{\gamma_t}{\gamma_{t-1}}\right]^\alpha$ is the adjustment cost function for the capital investment. τ denotes the heritage tax rate incurred on the gain from the cost-reduction capital investment. We assume that the tax rate is proportionate to the inflation rate, and thus $\tau = \frac{p_{t+1}}{p_t} - 1$ holds. The first term of (6) is the cost of capital investment which enhances the labor productivity γ. The second term denotes the total wage cost which will be economized by the capital investment.

From the linear homogeneity of $W^R(\cdot)$,

$$W^R(P_{t+1},P_{t+2}) = P_{t+1}W^R\left(1,\frac{P_{t+2}}{P_{t+1}}\right). \quad (7)$$

Substituting (7) into (6), (6) is transformed into

$$\max_{\gamma_t}\left[-\left[\frac{\gamma_t}{\gamma_{t-1}}\right]^\alpha - \frac{W^R\left(1,\frac{P_{t+2}}{P_{t+1}}\right)y_{t+1}}{\gamma_t}\right], \quad (8)$$

The first-order condition for (8) is

$$\alpha\left[\frac{\gamma_t}{\gamma_{t-1}}\right]^\alpha = \frac{W^R\left(1,\frac{P_{t+2}}{P_{t+1}}\right)y_{t+1}}{\gamma_t}. \quad (9)$$

The profit-maximization condition requires

$$p_{t+1}(z) = \frac{W^R(P_{t+1},P_{t+2})}{\gamma_t\left[1-\eta^{-1}\right]} \Rightarrow 1-\eta^{-1} = \frac{W^R\left(1,\frac{P_{t+2}}{P_{t+1}}\right)}{\gamma_t}. \quad (10)$$

Combining (9) and (10), finally we obtain the investment cost function as

$$\left[\frac{\gamma_t}{\gamma_{t-1}}\right]^\alpha = \frac{1-\eta^{-1}}{\alpha}y_{t+1}. \quad (11)$$

2.4. The Government

The government issues fiat money to finance its real expenditure g_t. For simplicity, such expenditure is entirely wasteful and contributes to neither individual's utility nor the progress of the labor productivity. The budget constraint can be written as

$$m_t = [1+\theta]m_{t-1}, g_t = \theta m_{t-1} + \left[1-\frac{P_{t-1}}{P_t}\right]m_{t-1} \quad (12)$$

where m_t is the real cash balance during period t, which is defined by $m_t \equiv \frac{M_t}{P_t}$. The first term of the right-hand side of (12) is the newly issued money that is equal to the budget deficit. The second term represents the seignorage of money obtained via inflation.

2.5. Equilibrium Condition for Aggregate Goods Market

From (3), (11) and (12), the equilibrium condition for the aggregate goods market is

$$\begin{aligned} sy_t &= \frac{1-\eta^{-1}}{\alpha}y_{t+1} + g_t + \frac{P_{t-1}}{P_t}m_{t-1} \\ &= \frac{1-\eta^{-1}}{\alpha}y_{t+1} + [1+\theta]m_{t-1} \end{aligned} \quad (13)$$

where the third term of the right-hand side of (13) is the aggregate consumption of old generation. Solving (13) on y_t, we obtain the equilibrium GDP as

$$y_t^* = \frac{1+\theta}{1-\frac{1-\eta^{-1}}{\alpha s}}\frac{m_{t-1}}{s}. \quad (14)$$

Using (12) and (14), the equilibrium economic growth

rate becomes

$$\frac{y_{t+1}^*}{y_t^*} = 1 + \theta. \tag{15}$$

Thus, we obtain the following theorem.

Theorem 1. *The monetary market economy cannot attain economic growth without fiscal deficits.*

Proof.

It is clear from setting $\theta = 0$ in (15).

3. The Sustainability of Economic Growth and Fiscal Deficits

In this section, we discuss the sustainability of economic growth in our monetary market economy. To begin with, we shall define the *sustainability*.

Definition 1. *We call economic growth is sustainable only when it never reduces the level of employment.*

Although unemployment is voluntary in this model, it is not difficult to turn it involuntary if we use the method developed by Otaki [6]. Hence, at least for employees, economic growth is harmful unless the economy is sustainable.

Since the equilibrium employment level L_t^* satisfies $L_t^* \equiv \frac{y_t^*}{\gamma_{t-1}^*}$, whether or not economic growth in our monetary market economy is sustainable can be judged from the following inequality.

$$\Delta L \equiv \frac{\frac{y_{t+1}}{y_t}}{\frac{\gamma_t}{\gamma_{t-1}}} > 1. \tag{16}$$

When above inequality holds, economic growth is sustainable, otherwise unsustainable.

From (15), $\frac{y_{t+1}}{y_t} = 1 + \theta$. Solving (11) on $\frac{\gamma_t}{\gamma_{t-1}}$, we obtain

$$\frac{\gamma_t}{\gamma_{t-1}} = \sqrt[\alpha]{\frac{1-\eta^{-1}}{\alpha} y_{t+1}}.$$

Accordingly, (16) becomes

$$\Delta L = \frac{1+\theta}{\sqrt[\alpha]{\frac{1-\eta^{-1}}{\alpha} y_{t+1}}}. \tag{17}$$

Since y_{t+1} grows at the velocity $1+\theta$, ΔL eventually decreases on sufficient large t for any given θ. Such a property of our monetary market economy is summarized by the following theorem, that is,

Theorem 2. *Economic growth in the monetary market economy is unsustainable at least in the long run. Even if expansionary fiscal policy that is financed by budget deficit can temporarily stimulate the economy and boosts the employment in the short run, it will be surpassed by the cost-reduction behavior of capital accumulation and the growth ultimately becomes unsustainable in the long run.*

This dismal theory explains why the scale of a government is enlarged. Since the improvement of employment brought about by some fiscal expansion become ineffective with the advance of labor-productivity enhancing capital accumulation, more stimulative and more expensive policies are required for sustaining employment level. Such policies inevitably accumulate huge fiscal deficits, and thus the scale of government is enlarged.

4. Concluding Remarks

In this article, we have analyzed the properties of economic growth in a monetary market economy by a Keynesian growth model with a rigorous neoclassical microeconomic foundation. The obtained results are as follows.

First, although capital investment stimulates the effective demand, such an expansionary effect is not strong enough to promote economic growth. Hence, the monetary market economy cannot grow without some exogenous stimuli such as fiscal policies. However, such policies possibly incurs non-negligible fiscal deficits.

Second, since the labor productivity steadily grows by the capital investment even if the economy records no growth, it provokes the serious unemployment problem. To dissolve such a difficulty, artificial growth promoting policies seem to be desirable. However, not only these policies enlarge budget deficits but also the accelerated growth rate will be exceeded by the progress of the labor productivity, at least, in the long run, thereby emerging the unemployment problem once again. In this sense, expansionary fiscal policy is not an ultimate cure for the problem, and thus economic growth in the monetary market economy is not *sustainable*.

REFERENCES

[1] J. M. Buchanan and R. E. Wagner, "Democracy in Deficit: The Political Legacy of Lord Keynes," Reprinted by Liberty Fund, INC., Indianapolis, 1977.

[2] R. M. Solow, "A Contribution to the Theory of Economic Growth," *Quarterly Journal of Economics*, Vol. 70, No. 1, 1956, pp. 65-94.

[3] T. W. Swan, "Economic Growth and Capital Accumulation," *Economic Record*, Vol. 32, No. 2, 1956, pp. 334-361.

[4] P. M. Romer, "Increasing Returns and Long-Run Growth," *Journal of Political Economy*, Vol. 94, No. 5, 1986, pp. 1002-1037.

[5] M. Otaki, "The Dynamically Extended Keynesian Cross

and the Welfare-Improving Fiscal Policy," *Economics Letters*, Vol. 96, No. 1, 2007, pp. 23-29.

[6] M. Otaki, "A Welfare Economics Foundation for the Full-Employment Policy," *Economics Letters*, Vol. 102, No. 1, 2009, pp. 1-3.

[7] M. Otaki, "A Keynesian Endogenous Growth Theory with a Rigorous Microeconomic Foundation," *Theoretical Economics Letters*, Vol. 2, No. 4, 2012, pp. 369-372.

[8] D. Acemoglu, "Introduction to Modern Economic Growth," Princeton University Press, Princeton, 2009.

[9] J. Andreoni, "Giving with Impure Altruism: Applications to Charity and Ricardian Equivalence," *Journal of Political Economy*, Vol. 97, No. 6, 1989, pp. 1447-1458.

[10] A. V. Banerjee and A. Newman, "Risk Bearing and the Theory of Income Distribution," *Review of Economic Studies*, Vol. 58, No. 2, 1991, pp. 211-235.

[11] A. V. Banerjee and A. Newman, "Occupational Choice and the Process of Development," *Journal of Political Economy*, Vol. 101, No. 2, 1993, pp. 274-298.

[12] O. Galor and J. Zeira, "Income Distribution and Macroeconomics," *Review of Economic Studies*, Vol. 60, No. 1, 1993, pp. 35-52.

[13] P. Aghion and P. Bolton, "A Theory of Trickle-Down Growth and Development," *Review of Economic Studies*, Vol. 64, No. 2, 1997, pp. 151-172.

12

Evolutionarily Stable Conjectures and Social Optimality in Oligopolies

Swapnika Reddy Rachapalli, Praveen Kulshreshtha
Department of Humanities and Social Sciences, Indian Institute of Technology Kanpur, Kanpur, India

ABSTRACT

Following the evolutionary game-theoretic approach to analyze Conjectural Variations (CV) in oligopolies, a model is developed to derive the Evolutionarily Stable Strategies (ESS) for quantity-setting and price-setting oligopolies with CV, producing heterogeneous goods. It is shown that ESS coincides with the Consistent CV in the oligopoly model. Earlier studies have demonstrated the above result only for duopolies. It is also shown that the market outcome induced by ESS is socially suboptimal if firms produce heterogeneous products, but can be socially optimal if firms produce homogeneous goods. In general, the market outcome approaches the socially optimal outcome, as the number of firms increases to infinity.

Keywords: Conjectural Variations (CV); Consistent Conjectural Variations (CCV); Evolutionarily Stable Strategies (ESS); Quantity Competition; Price Competition; Social Optimality

1. Introduction

The theory of Conjectural Variations (CV) has witnessed several important developments since its origins in the industrial organization literature approximately a century ago (Bowley (1924) [1] and Frisch (1933) [2]). The CV of a firm in an oligopoly market is defined as the firm's perception or belief regarding the reaction of its rival firms to changes in its quantity (or output) decision[1]. CV was initially conceptualized in static games with complete information and rational players (Bresnahan (1981) [3]), and thereafter in dynamic games with complete information and rational players (Dockner (1992) [4]).

Bresnahan (1981) [3] introduced the notion of Consistent Conjectural Equilibrium (CCE) in static games, where the reaction functions of firms and their conjectures coincide (in equilibrium), thus "endogenising" the concept of CV[2]. Breshnahan showed that under the assumptions of constant marginal costs, linear demand and perfect substitutability in oligopolies, the Bertrand equilibrium is a CCE, but the Cournot equilibrium is not.

While the idea of consistent conjectures in static games brought in notions of rationality, the concept of reactions of a firm to the actions of the rival firm is dynamic in nature. Dockner (1992) [4] attempted to understand the relationship between dynamic oligopolistic competition and static conjectural variations equilibria, by comparing the long-run equilibrium of a dynamic oligopoly game to the conjectural variations equilibrium of the corresponding static game.

Dockner showed that the long-run "open-loop" equilibrium of the dynamic game coincides with the Cournot equilibrium of the corresponding static game, while the long-run 'closed-loop' equilibrium of the dynamic game coincides with the conjectural variations equilibrium of the corresponding static game[3]. Thus, the static conjectural variations approach can be viewed as the limit of dynamic strategic interactions in oligopolies.

Despite the attempts to rationalize the inclusion of CV in oligopoly models with the aid of dynamic games, many controversies still exist. The theoretical foundation based on complete information and full rationality is considered weak. Thus, during the last two decades, CV has been examined in dynamic games with incomplete information and boundedly rational players.

For instance, Itaya and Dasgupta (1995) [5] developed the first learning model of CV, where players can revise

[1]Various methods have been developed to incorporate the idea of beliefs in the existing game-theoretic literature and CV has provided a way to systematically analyze the beliefs of players in a game.

[2]Prior to this, significant research had been carried out on CV in the static framework, where CV is regarded as an "exogenous" variable. A major criticism of this static CV approach is that almost any outcome observed in oligopoly markets can be explained as an equilibrium outcome, with suitable choice of conjectures.

[3]Two types of strategies are available to firms in a dynamic game: "Open-loop" and "Closed-loop". The former refers to the set of strategies which are independent of the present state of the system and thus depend only on its initial state. The latter refers to strategies which are designed taking into consideration the information available regarding the system in its present state.

their conjectures based on past observations in a dynamic game. Similarly, Friedman and Mezzetti (2002) [6] developed an incomplete information game with boundedly rational players. Based on the above two analyses, Jean-Marie and Tidball (2002) [7] modeled a learning process where each player has a linear conjecture of the other player's behavior.

Dixon and Somma (2003) [8], Muller and Norman (2005) [9] and Possajennikov (2009) [10] employed an evolutionary game-theoretic framework to characterize CV using the notion of Evolutionarily Stable Strategies (ESS), first introduced by Maynard Smith (1982) [11]. ESS is defined as the Nash equilibrium strategy in an evolutionary game, which is stable in the sense that (a) it is the best response against itself in the population and (b) once it is fixed, no alternative strategy can invade the population successfully.

The above authors independently derive ESS for an evolutionary game involving a duopoly. They show that ESS coincides with the consistent CV of the static duopoly game, as defined by Bresnahan (1981) [3]. This coincidence between the outcomes of a game played by rational players (*i.e.* the static duopoly game) and irrational players (*i.e.* the evolutionary game) can be understood intuitively: only those players which maximize their payoff functions taking into consideration the *right* conjectures about the rival firm's behavior will be more successful in the market and these conjectures are the ones that remain in an evolutionary game too.

The purpose of this paper is two-fold: First, following the evolutionary duopoly model proposed by Muller and Norman (2005) [9], we derive the ESS for quantity-setting and price-setting oligopolies with conjectural variations, producing heterogeneous goods. We demonstrate that ESS coincides with the Consistent CV in the above oligopoly model. The existing evolutionary studies on CV (referred above) have only shown that the above result holds for duopolies.

Second, we analyze whether the market outcome associated with ESS in the above oligopoly model can be socially optimal. The social optimality of oligopoly market outcomes is an important issue in economic theory and welfare economics. However, not many studies of CV have addressed this issue explicitly. One exception is Jean-Marie and Tidball (2002) [7], who have examined the social optimality of the stable state equilibrium in a learning model[4].

We show that the market output and price induced by ESS can be socially optimal only if the firms produce homogeneous products. Moreover, if firms produce heterogeneous goods, the market output under ESS is less than socially optimal ("underproduction"), while the price exceeds the socially optimal price. Interestingly, as the number of firms in the market increases to infinity, the market outcome (output and price) approaches the socially optimal outcome. The above results hold true for quantity competition as well as price competition. The remaining paper is organized as follows:

Section 2 elucidates the general framework and model of our study. In Section 3, we derive the socially optimal outcome of our model, which is used as a benchmark for comparison later on. In Section 4, we derive the Nash equilibrium, Consistent CV and ESS for a quantity game, and obtain conditions for social optimality in the game. Section 5 explains the results of a similar analysis carried out for a price game. We conclude our discussion in Section 6.

2. The Model

We consider an economy populated with a large number of firms which are randomly grouped into n firm oligopolies. Now, let us consider n firms $(i = 1, 2, \cdots, n)$ in a differentiated goods oligopoly market. Inverse demand function for each firm i is linear, given as,

$$p_i(q_i, q_{-i}) = a - q_i - \theta q_{-i} \quad (1)$$

where, $a > 0$ (constant), p_i is the price faced by firm i, q_i is the quantity produced by firm i and q_{-i} is the aggregate quantity produced by all firms other than firm i. The parameter θ captures the extent of product differentiation in the market, with $\theta = 1$ denoting homogeneous goods and $\theta = 0$ corresponding to completely differentiated products.

Assuming symmetry between $(n-1)$ firms other than firm i, (explained in Section 4) *i.e.* $q_l = q_m = \frac{q_{-i}}{n-1}$; $p_l = p_m$ $\forall l, m \neq i$ Now, for any firm $j \neq i$ the inverse demand function can be written as,

$$p_j(q_i, q_{-i}) = a - \frac{q_{-i}}{n-1}\left(1 + \theta(n-2)\right) - \theta q_i \quad (2)$$

The cost of production for firm i is in *quadratic form*, written as,

$$C_i(q_i) = \frac{c}{2} q_i^2; \quad c \geq 0 \quad (3)$$

If the firm's decision variable is price, we can change our equations to,

$$q_i(p_i, p_j) = \frac{a(1-\theta) + p_j(n-1)\theta - p_i(1+(n-2)\theta)}{(1-\theta)(1+(n-1)\theta)} \quad (4)$$

$$\text{for } i \neq j$$

[4]In their model, the monopoly market outcome is socially optimal. However, while deriving the socially optimal outcome, they only consider the welfare of the agents that are playing the game, *i.e.* the producers of a good, and ignore the welfare of the consumers, who have an important role in determining the final market outcome.

$$q_j\left(p_i,p_j\right)=\frac{a(1-\theta)+p_i\theta-p_j}{(1-\theta)(1+(n-1)\theta)} \qquad \forall j\neq i \qquad (5)$$

Profit functions for either quantity or price competition for firm i can be derived from the equation, $\pi_i = p_i q_i - \frac{c}{2}q_i^2$, by substituting the right values.

3. Socially Optimal Outcome

When each firm in the market acts as a *price taker*, the total Social Welfare, *i.e.* the sum of Consumer Surplus and Producer Surplus is maximum with no welfare loss. By equating $q_i = q_j = Q_{SO}/n \ \forall i \neq j$ (as all *n* firms face the same demand and cost functions), and summing up, we get the Social Optimal Market output, Q_{SO} and price, P_{SO},

$$Q_{SO}(n)=\frac{na}{1+c+\theta(n-1)}$$
$$P_{SO}(n)=\frac{ca}{1+c+\theta(n-1)} \qquad (6)$$

In the limit when n tends to infinity, *i.e.* as the number of firms increase, we get

$$\lim_{n\to\infty} Q_{SO}(n)=\frac{a}{\theta};\ \lim_{n\to\infty} P_{SO}(n)=0 \qquad (7)$$

This is the Monopolistic Competition outcome with a large number of firms (and Perfectly competitive outcome for, $\theta=1$), with zero profits in the market.

4. Quantity Competition

4.1. Nash Equilibrium

The first order conditions, $\frac{\partial \pi_i(q_i,q_{-i})}{\partial q_i}=0$ and $\frac{\partial \pi_j(q_i,q_{-i})}{\partial q_j}=0$ where, $q_j=\frac{q_{-i}}{n-1}$, gives the following reaction function of firm i and the aggregate reaction function of the rest of the firms,

$$\rho_i(q_{-i};r_i)=\frac{a-\theta q_{-i}}{2+c+\theta r_i} \qquad (8)$$

$$\rho_{-i}(q_i;r_j)=\frac{(n-1)(a-\theta q_i)}{2+c+\theta(n-2)+\theta r_j} \qquad (9)$$

where, $r_i=\frac{\partial q_{-i}}{\partial q_i}$, $\forall i$ is the Conjectural Variation (CV) of firm i, *i.e.* the change expected in the aggregate quantity produced by all other firms in response to a change in its own quantity. The Nash Equilibrium, by solving the above reaction function is,

$$q_i^*(r_i,r_j)=\frac{a\left(R_{-i}-\theta(n-1)\right)}{R_iR_{-i}-\theta^2(n-1)};$$
$$q_{-i}^*(r_i,r_j)=\frac{a(n-1)\left(R_i-\theta\right)}{R_iR_{-i}-\theta^2(n-1)}; \qquad (10)$$

$$R_i=2+c+\theta r_i;$$
$$R_{-i}=2+c+\theta(n-2)+\theta r_j \qquad (11)$$

4.2. Consistent Conjectural Variations (CCV)

We will follow the method adopted by Perry (1982) [12], while trying to solve for the consistent CV assuming complete symmetry between firms. As mentioned in the previous section, we will consider symmetry between $(n-1)$ firms. This symmetry assumption is justified as, for consistency, all firms should have the same conjecture about firm i, which leads to same conjectures about aggregate output as well.

Using Bresnahan's (1981) definition of consistent CV, where firms correctly guess the reaction of their rival firms while maximizing their profits, we have the CV of a firm equal to the slope of the actual reaction function of the rival firm (here aggregate reaction function).

$$r_i=\frac{\partial \rho_{-i}(q_i;r_j)}{\partial q_i}=\frac{-(n-1)\theta}{2+c+\theta(n-2)+\theta r_j} \qquad (12)$$

Equating $r_i=r_j=r$, as we are dealing with symmetric consistent conjectures r^C, we get,

$$\theta r^2+r\left(2+c+\theta(n-2)\right)+\theta(n-1)=0 \qquad (13)$$

The root satisfying the second order condition is,

$$r^C=\frac{-\left(2+c+\theta(n-2)\right)+A}{2\theta} \qquad (14)$$

where,

$$A=\sqrt{\left(2+c+\theta(n-2)\right)^2-4\theta^2(n-1)} \qquad (15)$$

4.3. Evolutionarily Stable Strategy (ESS)

Firms can hold any conjectures initially and no rationality condition is imposed on them regarding this decision. However, given their conjectures they play the market game rationally. The evolutionary game then helps in making firms choose conjectures that maximizes their profits in each period (which can be thought of as their reproductive success). The conjectures which lead to a better outcome for a firm will then spread to the whole population. It can also be thought of in another way, the proportion of the firms with good conjectures increase in the population while those with bad conjectures and relatively low evolutionary success fall out of the market. The evolutionary game can be thought of as being played in two steps [9]. First, firms choose their decision variables given their conjectural variations (types) rationally (Nash equilibrium, $\left(q_i^*\left(r_i,r_j\right),q_j^*\left(r_i,r_j\right)\right)$). The evolutionary success of firms is given by their profits:

$$\pi_i^*\left(r_i,r_j\right)=\pi_i\left(q_i^*\left(r_i,r_j\right),q_{-i}^*\left(r_i,r_j\right)\right) \quad (16)$$

In the second step each firm maximizes their evolutionary success (profits) by choosing the ESS in the long run. For the same, we will apply the static concept of an ESS (Maynard Smith (1982) [11]).

An equilibrium with ESS conjectures is a set of quantities $\left(q_1^*,q_2^*,\cdots,q_n^*\right)=\left(q_i^*,q_{-i}^*\right)$ and conjecture r^* such that,

$$q_i^* = \rho_i\left(q_{-i}^*\right); q_{-i}^* = \rho_{-i}\left(q_i^*\right) \quad (17a)$$

and

$$\pi_i^*\left(r^*,r^*\right)\ge \pi_i^*\left(r,r^*\right) \quad \forall r \quad (17b)$$

and

$$\pi_i^*\left(r^*,r^*\right)> \pi_i^*\left(r^*,r\right) \quad \forall r\ne r^* \\ \text{with } \pi_i^*\left(r^*,r^*\right)= \pi_i^*\left(r,r^*\right) \quad (17c)$$

The interpretation of the above equations is as follows. The equilibrium with evolutionarily stable conjectures requires the outputs to be the Nash equilibrium (Equation (17a)). The ESS, r^* is the best response against itself (Equation (17b)). No r-mutant invading a society of r^*-players may be more successful than r^* (Equation (17c)).

Since the ESS has to be the *best response* against itself, the evolutionary game will have a symmetric equilibrium, allowing us to continue with the assumption of symmetry between players for ease of calculations.

Substituting Equation (10) in our profit functions gives us the evolutionary success given the firm types in a particular time period, $\pi_i^*\left(r_i,r_j\right)=\frac{q_i^{*2}}{2}\left(c+2\left(1+\theta r_i\right)\right)$. Firms maximize it with respect to their types (here conjectures) over periods. Since the ESS should be the *best response* against itself, we replace $r_j=r_i=r^*$ in the first order condition and obtain the following quadratic equation,

$$\theta r^{*2}+r^*\left(2+c+\theta\left(n-2\right)\right)+\theta\left(n-1\right)=0 \quad (18)$$

Note that the above condition is the same as the one derived for Consistency (Equation (13)). Hence, we have the Evolutionarily Stable Conjecture, r^*,

$$r^* = \frac{-\left(2+c+\theta\left(n-2\right)\right)+A}{2\theta} \quad (19)$$

with A as defined in Equation (15).

However for $c=0$ and $\theta=1$ (Constant marginal cost and homogeneous goods), the CCV is not evolutionarily stable as it does not satisfy the condition for stability (Equation (17c)).

Note that $r^*\in\left[-1,0\right)$. This means that any increase in quantity by a firm in the market is offset by a decrease in the quantity by the other firms, thereby, decreasing the influence each firm has on the market price. Hence, they are more competitive than the Cournot outcome $\left(r=0\right)$ but less competitive than perfect competition $\left(r=-1\right)$.

PROPOSITION 1: *The Evolutionarily Stable Strategy for a general n-player quantity game coincides with the Consistent Conjectural Variation.*

Now, let us calculate the equilibrium outcome in the evolutionary game. At the ESS, $r_i=r_j=r^*$. Substituting them in the Nash Equilibrium (Equation (10)) we find that $q_{-i}^*=\left(n-1\right)q_i^*$ confirming symmetric output by firms in the market. Total market equilibrium output $\left(Q^*=nq_i^*\right)$ and price are calculated to be,

$$Q^*\left(n\right)=\frac{2na}{2+c+n\theta+A} \\ P^*\left(n\right)=\frac{a\left(c-\theta\left(n-2\right)+A\right)}{2+c+n\theta+A} \quad (20)$$

4.4. Comparing with the Socially Optimal Market Outcome

It can be verified that the ESS equilibrium induces the socially optimal outcome, *i.e.*

$$Q^* = Q_{SO} \text{ iff } c=c^* \\ c^* = -\left(1-\theta\right)\left(1+\left(n-1\right)\theta\right)\le 0 \quad (21)$$

Moreover,

$$Q^* < Q_{SO}\left(\text{underproduction}\right)\text{iff } c>c^* \quad (22)$$

Using (21) and (22), it can be shown that if,

- θ = 1 (Homogeneous goods), then c^* = 0, and $Q^*=Q_{SO}$ iff $c=0$ (linear cost), while for $c>0$ (quadratic cost), $Q^*<Q_{SO}$.
- θ < 1 (Heterogeneous goods), then c^* < 0, and $\forall c\ge 0$ (linear and quadratic cost), $Q^*<Q_{SO}$.

PROPOSITION 2: *When firms play with consistent conjectures in a quantity competition oligopoly, only those markets where firms have constant marginal costs and produce homogeneous goods result in a perfectly competitive equilibrium, which is socially optimal. In heterogeneous goods markets, the market output falls short of the socially optimal level of output* ("*underproduction*").

As the number of firms increase and tend to infinity,

$$\lim_{n\to\infty} Q^*\left(n\right)=\frac{a}{\theta}; \ \lim_{n\to\infty} P^*\left(n\right)=0 \quad (23)$$

Note that the above result coincides with Equation (7),

the limit of the Socially Optimal outcome as n tends to infinity. Hence,

PROPOSITION 3: As the number of firms in the oligopoly increases to infinity, with firms playing an evolutionary game in quantities, the industry outcome approaches the socially optimal market outcome for the given market structure with linear demand and quadratic costs.

5. Price Competition

5.1. Nash Equilibrium

In price competition, each firm maximizes its profit with respect to its price. The reaction functions of firms i and j are respectively,

$$\rho_i\left(p_j;r_i\right)=\frac{\left(a(1-\theta)+p_j\theta(n-1)\right)\left(D-cR_i\right)}{\left(1+\theta(n-2)\right)\left(D-cR_i\right)-DR_i} \quad (24)$$

$$\rho_j\left(p_i;r_j\right)=\frac{\left(a(1-\theta)+p_i\theta\right)\left(D-cR_j\right)}{D-cR_j-DR_j} \quad (25)$$

where,

$$D=(1-\theta)\left(1+\theta(n-2)\right) \quad (26)$$

$$R_i=\theta r_i-\left(1+\theta(n-2)\right), R_j=\theta r_j-\left(1+\theta(n-2)\right) \quad (27)$$

r_i is the conjecture of firm i about the sum changes in the prices of all other firms due to a change in its own price. Thus,

$$r_i=\sum_{j\neq i}\frac{\partial p_j}{\partial p_i}=(n-1)\frac{\partial p_j}{\partial p_i}, r_j=\sum_{k\neq j}\frac{\partial p_k}{\partial p_j}=(n-2)+\frac{\partial p_i}{\partial p_j} \quad (28)$$

Note that as mentioned while describing the model, the symmetry between $(n-1)$ firms, which leads to the price of all firms other than firm i be equal *i.e.* p_j. Now solving for the above two simultaneous equations will give us the Nash Equilibrium,

$$\begin{aligned} p_i^*\left(r_i,r_j\right)&=\frac{a(1-\theta)\left(\chi_j+\theta(n-1)\boldsymbol{R}_j\right)\boldsymbol{R}_i}{\chi_i\chi_j-\theta^2(n-1)\boldsymbol{R}_i\boldsymbol{R}_j} \\ p_j^*\left(r_i,r_j\right)&=\frac{a(1-\theta)\left(\chi_i+\theta\boldsymbol{R}_i\right)\boldsymbol{R}_j}{\chi_i\chi_j-\theta^2(n-1)\boldsymbol{R}_i\boldsymbol{R}_j}\end{aligned} \quad (29)$$

in which,

$$\begin{aligned} &\boldsymbol{R}_i=D-cR_i; \quad \boldsymbol{R}_j=D-cR_j \\ &\chi_i=\left(1+\theta(n-2)\right)\boldsymbol{R}_i-DR_i; \chi_j=\boldsymbol{R}_j-DR_j\end{aligned} \quad (30)$$

5.2. Consistent Conjectural Variations (CCV)

We will follow the same method as in Section 4.2, of assuming symmetry between firms. Now, for consistency of conjectures in the above price game, we need the conjecture of firm i to be equal to the sum of the slopes of the reaction functions of all other firms,

$$r_i=(n-1)\frac{\partial p_j\left(p_i,r_j\right)}{\partial p_i}=\frac{(n-1)\theta\boldsymbol{R}_j}{\boldsymbol{R}_j-DR_j} \quad (31)$$

Replacing the above in terms of r_i and r_j, and letting $r_i=r_j=r^C$, we get,

$$\begin{aligned} &r^{C2}\theta(c+D) \\ &-r^C\left(D+(c+D)\left(1+\theta(n-2)+\theta^2c(n-1)\right)\right) \\ &+\theta(n-1)\left(D+c\left(1+\theta(n-2)\right)\right)=0\end{aligned} \quad (32)$$

The profit maximizing Consistent Conjectural Variation is given by,

$$r^C=\frac{D\left(2+\theta(n-2)\right)+c\left(D+2\theta^2(n-1)\right)-DA}{2\theta(c+D)} \quad (33)$$

with A as defined in Equation (15) and D as defined in Equation (26).

5.3. Evolutionarily Stable Strategy (ESS)

The evolutionary success of firms after they play a Nash equilibrium in each period, given by substituting equation (29) in the profit functions, is

$\pi_i^*\left(r_i,r_j\right)=-p_i^{*2}\left(\frac{R_i}{\boldsymbol{R}_i}+\frac{c}{2}\left(\frac{R_i}{\boldsymbol{R}_i}\right)^2\right)$, which the firms maximize with respect to their conjectures, thus evolving to have the stable conjecture. Replacing $r_i=r_j=r^*$ in the first order condition gives us,

$$\begin{aligned} &r^{*2}\theta(c+D) \\ &-r^*\left(D+(c+D)\left(1+\theta(n-2)+\theta^2c(n-1)\right)\right) \\ &+\theta(n-1)\left(D+c\left(1+\theta(n-2)\right)\right)=0\end{aligned} \quad (34)$$

Note that the above quadratic (Equation (34)) is same as the quadratic derived for the consistent conjectures (Equation (32)). The Evolutionary Stable Strategy, r^* for the price competition is given by,

$$r^*=\frac{D\left(2+\theta(n-2)\right)+c\left(D+2\theta^2(n-1)\right)-DA}{2\theta(c+D)} \quad (35)$$

with A defined as in Equation (15) and D as defined in Equation (26). Also,

$$\frac{\partial p_j}{\partial p_i}=\frac{r^*}{n-1}\in(0,1] \quad (36)$$

This means that, a decrease in price of any firm leads to a decrease in the price of the other firms as well, resulting in little possibility of any single firm to be able to capture a large market share by reducing its price. Thus, the outcome is more competitive than Cournot, but less competitive than Bertrand (Perfect Competition), with it being equal to Bertrand at $\frac{\partial p_j}{\partial p_i} = 1$.

PROPOSITION 4: *The Evolutionarily Stable Strategy for a general n-player Price game coincides with the Consistent Conjectural variation.*

Calculating the equilibrium outcome for this game, by substituting for $r_i = r_j = r^*$ in the Nash equilibrium gives us, $p_i^* = p_j^* = P^*$ and Q^*,

$$P^* = \frac{a(1-\theta)(2D + c(D + 2 + \theta(n-2)) + A)}{(c+D)(D + 2(1-\theta) + \theta(n-2) + A)},$$

$$Q^* = \frac{naD(D + \theta(n-2) + A)}{(c+D)(1+\theta(n-1))(D + 2(1-\theta) + \theta(n-2) + A)} \quad (37)$$

5.4. Comparing with the Socially Optimal Market Outcome

As θ tends to 1 (homogeneous goods), we have,

$$\lim_{\theta \to 1} \frac{r^*(\theta)}{n-1} = \frac{\partial p_j}{\partial p_i} = +1 \quad (38)$$

i.e. the equilibrium gives rise to the Bertrand outcome, which is perfectly competitive.

Also, in general it can be verified that the ESS equilibrium induces the socially optimal outcome, *i.e.*

$$P^* = P_{SO} \text{ iff } c = c^*, P^* > P_{SO} \text{ iff } c > c^*$$
$$c^* = -(1-\theta)(1+(n-1)\theta) \le 0 \quad (39)$$

Using (39), we have for $\theta < 1$ (heterogeneous goods), $c^* < 0$. Hence, *for all* $c \ge 0$ (linear and quadratic cost), $P^* > P_{SO}$.

PROPOSITION 5: *When firms in the oligopoly with homogeneous goods play an evolutionary game in prices, the market evolves to become perfectly competitive, which leads to the socially optimal outcome. This result holds irrespective of the cost of production of firms and the number of firms in the market. In heterogeneous goods markets, the market price is always greater than the socially optimal price.*

When the number of firms in the market increases and tends to infinity,

$$\lim_{n\to\infty} Q^*(n) = \frac{a}{\theta}; \quad \lim_{n\to\infty} P^*(n) = 0 \quad (40)$$

Note that the above result coincides with Equation (7), the limit of the Social Optimal Output and also Equation (23), the limit of the Quantity Competition Output.

PROPOSITION 6: *As the number of firms in the oligopoly increases to infinity, with firms playing an evolutionary game in prices, the industry outcome approaches the socially optimal market outcome for the given market structure with linear demand and quadratic costs.*

And finally, it is interesting to note that, *as the number of firms in the market increases to infinity, the industry outcome approaches the socially optimal market outcome, regardless of whether the firms are involved in quantity competition or price competition.*

6. Conclusions

The evolutionary approach to analyzing Conjectural Variations has revived the idea of the long forgotten Consistent CV, showing us that Consistent CV can be viewed as the ESS of a two-player evolutionary game (duopoly). We have generalized the above result for general n-firm oligopoly markets and have also analyzed the social optimality of ESS in a differentiated goods oligopoly framework, with both quantity competition and price competition. We have demonstrated that the coincidence of Consistent CV and ESS holds for general n-firm oligopolies as well. We have also derived conditions under which the ESS is social optimal.

The above analysis gives us a comprehensive view of how oligopoly markets function. In Cournot's analysis $(r = 0)$, extended to a n-firm quantity game, it is well known that the oligopoly market outcome approaches the perfect competitive market outcome as the number of firms increases to infinity. We obtain the same result for oligopoly markets with non-zero conjectures, with both quantity competition and price competition. The above result provides a justification for the use of Consistent CV and shows that the market outcome under Consistent CV (which coincides with ESS) approaches the perfectly competitive outcome as the number of firms increases to infinity.

7. Acknowledgements

An earlier version of the paper was presented at the "International Conference on Game Theory and Operations Research Applications (in honor of Prof. C. R. Rao and Prof. Lloyd Shapley)", held at Hyderabad, India, during 21-22 December 2012. We thank the conference participants and an anonymous journal referee for their valuable comments and suggestions.

REFERENCES

[1] A. L. Bowley, "The Mathematical Groundwork of Economics," Oxford University Press, Oxford, 1924.

[2] R. Frisch, "Monopole-Polypole: La Notion de Force dans l'Economie," *Nationalokonomisk Tidsskrift*, 1933.

[3] T. F. Breshnahan, "Duopoly Models with Consistent Conjectures," *The American Economic Review*, Vol. 71,

No. 5, 1981, pp. 934-945.

[4] E. J. Dockner, "A Dynamic Theory of Conjectural Variations," *The Journal of Industrial Economics*, Vol. 40, No. 4, 1992, pp. 377-395.

[5] J. Itaya and D. Dasgupta, "Dynamic, Consistent Conjectures and Heterogeneous Agents in the Private Provision of Public Goods," *Public Finance = Finances Publiques*, Vol. 50, No. 3, 1995, pp. 371-389.

[6] J. W. Friedman and C. Mezzetti, "Bounded Rationality, Dynamic Oligopoly, and Conjectural Variations," *Journal of Economic Behavior & Organization*, Vol. 49, No. 3, 2002, pp. 287-306.

[7] A. Jean-Marie and M. Tidball, "Adapting Behaviors through a Learning Process," *Journal of Economic Behavior & Organization*, Vol. 60, No. 3, 2006, pp. 399-422.

[8] H. D. Dixon and E. Somma, "The Evolution of Consistent Conjectures," *Journal of Economic Behavior and Organization*, Vol. 51, No. 4, 2003, pp. 523-536.

[9] W. Muller and H. Normann, "Conjectural Variations and Evolutionary Stability: A Rationale for Consistency," *Journal of Institutional and Theoretical Economics*, Vol. 161, No. 3, 2005, pp. 491-502.

[10] A. Possajennikov, "The Evolutionary Stability of Constant Consistent Conjectures," *Journal of Economic Behavior & Organization*, Vol. 72, No. 1, 2009, pp. 21-29.

[11] J. M. Smith, "Evolution and the Theory of Games," Cambridge University Press, Cambridge, 1982.

[12] M. K. Perry, "Oligopoly and Consistent Conjectural Variations," *The Bell Journal of Economics*, Vol. 13, No. 1, 1982, pp. 197-205.

Mixed Strategy Nash Equilibria in Signaling Games

Barry R. Cobb[1*], Atin Basuchoudhary[1], Gregory Hartman[2]
[1]Department of Economics and Business, Virginia Military Institute, Lexington, USA
[2]Department of Mathematics and Computer Science, Virginia Military Institute, Lexington, USA

ABSTRACT

Signaling games are characterized by asymmetric information where the more informed player has a choice about what information to provide to its opponent. In this paper, decision trees are used to derive Nash equilibrium strategies for signaling games. We address the situation where neither player has any pure strategies at Nash equilibrium, *i.e.* a purely mixed strategy equilibrium. Additionally, we demonstrate that this approach can be used to determine whether certain strategies are part of a Nash equilibrium containing dominated strategies. Analyzing signaling games using a decision-theoretic approach allows the analyst to avoid testing individual strategies for equilibrium conditions and ensures a perfect Bayesian solution.

Keywords: Game Theory; Decision Analysis; Decision Tree; Nash Equilibrium; Signaling Game

1. Introduction

Signaling games are a class of games with incomplete information. We use the tools of decision theory to provide a process for analyzing signaling games and divide the solution process into two phases: 1) *strategy selection*-determining the strategies for each player that are chosen at equilibrium; and 2) *equilibrium calculation*-finding the percentage of each time the players should choose the selected strategies. We address this second task by solving for a purely mixed strategy Nash equilibrium. Additionally, we suggest how the approach used to solve for a purely mixed Nash equilibrium may assist in the first task, that of identifying the strategies that form an equilibrium solution.

1.1. Background

A basic signaling game has two players. Player 1 (the "Sender") has private information about her type, while Player 2 (the "Receiver") does not know the type of Player 1. However, Player 2 knows the population distribution of types of Player 1. Player 1 sends messages that Player 2 receives. Player 2's actions depend on his beliefs about Player 1's type. In a classic example of a signaling game [1], education is a signal that can be obtained by workers of both high and low skill-level. Milgrom and Roberts [2] subsequently define a limit pricing game where an incumbent firm may temporarily charge lower prices to signal that the market is unprofitable. Descriptions of additional applications of signaling games have been provided by Kreps and Sobel [3] and Riley [4].

Previous research has been devoted to finding efficient Nash equilibrium solution algorithms for extensive form games. Von Stengel [5] summarizes much of the research on equilibrium calculation in extensive-form games as part of a text on algorithmic game theory [6]. While much of this research has not exclusively focused on signaling games, some of the algorithms can be used to calculate Nash equilibria in signaling games. For example, the Gambit software package developed by McKelvey *et al.* [7] can be used to solve signaling games. However, the developers state on the Gambit website that it is "...quite easy to write down games which will take Gambit an unacceptably long amount time to (solve)." This has been our experience in using this software to calculate Nash equilibria for signaling games. Thus, we feel there is a need to develop algorithms with heuristic approaches for determining Nash equilibria in signaling games, and this is the focus of our paper.

We suggest a method that combines modeling techniques from the fields of decision analysis and game theory. Previous research has combined game theory, decision analysis, and/or statistical risk analysis to address situations where the decision maker has an adaptive adversary, such as those in counterterrorism decisions. We mention some examples here. Rios Insua *et al.* [8] introduce a Bayesian approach to adversarial risk analysis where two or more opponents make decisions with uncertain outcomes. Decision trees and influence

*Corresponding author.

diagrams are used to simultaneously model the decision-making of each player. Parnell *et al.* [9] use decision tree and influence diagram models to illustrate a defender-attacker-defender problem where the United States selects actions both prior to and after a bioterrorism attack. Paté-Cornell and Guikema [10] use an influence diagram for the attacker's decision to provide input to an influence diagram model for the defender in a counter-terrorism measures selection problem.

The three articles cited above are similar to our method in that they use decision-theoretic models to examine a strategic problem from the perspective of each opponent. Our research differs in that we seek a Nash equilibrium solution (as opposed to a utility maximizing solution) and limit our analysis to problems that can be framed as a signaling game. Our primary objective is to enhance the methodology available for solving signaling games. We are optimistic that achievement of this objective will allow signaling game methodology to be applied to important decision problems that involve strategic interaction. We primarily address situations where a purely mixed Nash equilibrium exists in signaling games. Toward the end of the paper, we examine how our method can be extended to games with other types of equilibria.

Most game theory textbooks classify the equilibria for signaling games into three categories-separating on the message, pooling on the message, and semi-separating equilibria where some types of players select mixed strategies [11, pp. 326-328]. The typical analytical approach to solve for these equilibria is to assume that the equilibrium exists and then test whether either player has an incentive to deviate from the strategy or not. This process forces the game theorist to test each possible strategy pair for each of the three types of possible equilibria. In other words, the *strategy selection* task is by-passed and the *equilibrium calculation* task is simplified by testing only equilibria for which the mathematical conditions can be easily identified. In games with more than two types of players sending messages and/or more than two possible messages this approach can be tedious, time consuming and prone to errors.

1.2. Decision-Theoretic Approach

We suggest that a decision theoretic approach may provide a standardized process for analyzing signaling games that does not involve testing individual strategies for equilibrium qualities. Our approach can simplify both the *strategy selection* and *equilibrium calculation* tasks required to solve signaling games. This approach to solving signaling games uses the concept of Nash equilibrium. Thus, in the mixed-strategy equilibrium, each player acts in a way that makes other players indifferent between choosing among different actions. Thus conceptually, our approach is not that different from the usual PBE (Perfect Bayesian Equilibrium) approach to solving signaling games [12]. However, the actual solution process for PBE involves testing each possible strategy for "beliefs that are consistent with strategies, which are optimal given the beliefs" [11, p. 326]. This circularity in the solution process precludes the possibility of using backward induction as a way of solving signaling games. However, in our approach we do use backward induction.

This paper uses a decision tree approach to model the two-player, n-type symmetric signaling game. The use of decision trees for representing problems of strategic interaction was introduced by van Binsbergen and Marx [13]. In their model, a decision tree is constructed for each player. A player's own choices are modeled with decision nodes and the opponent's strategies are shown as chance variables.

Cobb and Basuchoudhary [14] modified the decision tree approach by modeling the choices of both players in each tree with chance nodes and using the probabilities in the trees to represent the strategies. This allowed use of the decision tree approach to solve the two-type signaling game; however, this prior research only discussed the determination of pooling, separating, and semi-separating equilibria. This paper extends the previous research by both addressing signaling games with more than two types of Senders and by finding a purely mixed Nash equilibrium (the *equilibrium calculation* task), which is one where neither player has any pure strategies.

We employ a decision tree representation of the signaling game to determine Nash equilibrium strategies for several reasons. First, the equations capturing the Nash equilibrium strategies are actually calculated while solving the decision tree, as opposed to being abstractly determined by analyzing the game tree. This is particularly advantageous in the signaling game because Bayes' rule is used routinely at the time the decision tree is constructed. Second, the Nash equilibrium conditions are intuitively apparent through inspection of the decision tree. Additionally, the decision tree representation is more easily expanded as the number of Sender types increases than a corresponding game tree representation.

1.3. Outline

After first introducing signaling games and notation used in the paper, we solve for Nash equilibrium strategies in a two-type signaling game. The purpose of this section is to illustrate how decision trees are constructed for signaling games. Next, we give general derivations of Nash equilibrium strategies in the n-type signaling game where both players select purely mixed strategies at Nash equilibrium. In general, for a strategy vector chosen by the Sender to be part of a purely mixed Nash equilibrium, the Receiver observing each possible message must be indifferent between all of its subsequent actions after assigning any dominated strategies for the Sender a value of zero. Similarly, for a strategy vector chosen by the Receiver to be part of a purely mixed Nash equilibrium, each type of Sender must be indifferent between transmitting each of its possible messages after assigning any dominated strategies for the Receiver a value of zero.

Later in the paper, we will discuss how to apply decision trees to signaling games where the players do not necessarily select purely mixed strategies at Nash equilibrium, *i.e.* we use decision trees to address the *strategy selection* task. In the final section, we discuss our results and describe the development of a comprehensive approach to determining all types of equilibria in signaling games as a direction for future research.

2. Preliminaries

This section outlines notation and definitions that will be used throughout the paper.

In the n-type signaling game, the Sender has n possible types, $t_1,\cdots,t_n$ and can choose one of n possible messages, $m_1,\cdots,m_n$, from a discrete strategy set. The Receiver responds with one of n possible actions, $a_1,\cdots,a_n$, that it chooses from its discrete strategy set once it observes the Sender's message. Descriptions and definitions of the parameters in the n-*type signaling game* are shown below.

Parameter	Description
p_i	Probability the sender is type i (t_i for $i=1,\cdots,n$)
m_{ij}	t_i Sender's strategy (% of time t_i, $i=1,\cdots,n$, plays message m_j for $j=1,\cdots,n$)
a_{jk}	Receiver's strategy after observing message m_j, $j=1,\cdots,n$ (% of time receiver takes action a_k for $k=1,\cdots,n$)
v_{ijk}	Payoff to the Receiver observing message m_j and taking action a_k when the Sender is t_i
w_{ijk}	Payoff to the t_i Sender playing message m_j when the Receiver takes action a_k

Let us summarize the strategies played by the Sender and the Receiver, respectively, in vector form as

$$\boldsymbol{m}=\begin{bmatrix}m_{11} & m_{21} & \cdots & m_{n1} & m_{12} & \cdots & m_{nn}\end{bmatrix}^{\mathrm{T}}$$

and

$$\boldsymbol{a}=\begin{bmatrix}a_{11} & a_{12} & \cdots & a_{1n} & a_{21} & \cdots & a_{nn}\end{bmatrix}^{\mathrm{T}}.$$

Note that $\boldsymbol{m}$ is indexed differently than $\boldsymbol{a}$. The first part of the index on m_{ij} refers to the Sender type and the second part refers to the message transmitted by the Sender. The first number in the index on a_{jk} refers to the message of the Sender, whereas the second stands for the action of the Receiver. This ordering is consistent with the order in which the nodes appear in the decision trees presented throughout the remainder of the paper.

The strategy m_{ij} for the Sender can be interpreted as the conditional probability $P(m_j \mid t_i)$ that the t_i Sender will transmit message m_j. Analogously, the strategy a_{jk} for the Receiver can be interpreted as the conditional probability $P(a_k \mid m_j)$.

We use a decision tree approach to identify Nash equilibrium strategies in signaling games. We first consider the case where neither player has any dominated strategies at Nash equilibrium and address the *equilibrium calculation* task. In this situation, the payoffs are structured so that there is an equilibrium where each type of Sender plays a mixture of all of its possible messages, so each Sender strategy satisfies $0<m_{ij}<1$ at Nash equilibrium. Correspondingly, the payoffs are also structured so that the Receiver plays a mixture of all its possible strategies after observing each message, which requires each Receiver strategy to satisfy $0<a_{jk}<1$.

By inspecting the decision tree models, we are able to intuitively observe the conditions that must exist for a solution to be a Nash equilibrium. The decision tree provides for easy calculation of the expected values for each player, which are ultimately used to derive the mathematical conditions necessary for a Nash equilibrium in purely mixed strategies.

3. Signaling Game Example

This section analyzes a two-type signaling game. For now, we assume nature's selection of each Sender type is equally likely, *i.e.* $p_1=p_2=0.5$. The Sender will choose one of two messages-Left or Right. The selection of the Left strategy by the t_1 Sender is the strategy m_{11}, whereas the choice of Left for the t_2 Sender is m_{21}. The alternate strategies (Right) are denoted by m_{12} and m_{22} for t_1 and t_2, respectively, and these probabilities satisfy $m_{12}=1-m_{11}$ and $m_{22}=1-m_{21}$.

Once the Receiver observes the signal, it decides whether or not to move Up or Down and this threat represents its strategy. If it observes the Left message, its

Up strategy is denoted by a_{11}. If it observes Right, its Up strategy is denoted by a_{21}. A Down strategy by the Receiver is denoted by either a_{12} or a_{22}, depending on the type of signal observed.

The payoffs for the Sender and Receiver are shown in **Table 1**. As an example, if the Receiver moves Up against a t_1 Sender, both players could suffer significant losses, thus $v_{111} = -8$ and $w_{111} = -3$. The Sender ends up with a worse outcome in this scenario by selecting Right, so $w_{121} = -4$.

3.1. Receiver's Nash Equilibrium Strategies

The decision tree for the Sender in this game is shown in the left panel of **Figure 1**. The model shows that nature chooses the Sender's type. After learning its type, the Sender chooses its message. Whereas the "Type" node is a chance node, the "Signal" nodes are *random strategy nodes* as defined by Cobb and Basuchoudhary [14], as the probabilities at these nodes represent Sender strategies. These nodes are shaded to distinguish them from typical chance nodes. After its strategy is chosen, the Sender's payoff in the game is determined by the action chosen by the Receiver.

To find its Nash equilibrium strategies, the Receiver rolls back the Sender's decision tree one level as shown in the left panel of **Figure 2**. Since all nodes in the tree are chance nodes, the roll-back procedure involves calculating expected values. For example, the t_1 Sender observing m_1 calculates its expected value as $-3 \cdot a_{11} + 2 \cdot a_{12}$ at the chance node representing the Receiver action at the top of its tree in **Figure 1**. This expected value is placed in the rolled back decision tree in **Figure 2** as the payoff on the branch representing the t_1 Sender and the m_1 observation. Other expected values are calculated similarly during the roll-back process.

Two conditions must be met by the strategies a_{11}, a_{12}, a_{21}, and a_{22} established at Nash equilibrium by the Receiver:

1) A t_1 Sender must be indifferent among all possible strategy assignments m_{11} and m_{12}.

2) A t_2 Sender must be indifferent among all possible strategy assignments m_{21} and m_{22}.

These conditions are met when the expected values at the end of either branch at the two Signal nodes in the decision tree in the left panel of **Figure 2** are equal, or

Table 1. The payoffs to each player in the signaling game.

	Type 1 Sender (t_1) with probability $p_1 = 0.5$			Type 2 Sender (t_2) with probability $p_2 = 0.5$	
	Left	Right		Left	Right
Receiver	m_1	m_2	Receiver	m_1	m_2
Up (a_1)	−8, −3	0, −4	Up (a_1)	1, −5	−1, −5
Down (a_2)	−2, 2	−1, 1	Down (a_2)	−2, 2	1, 0

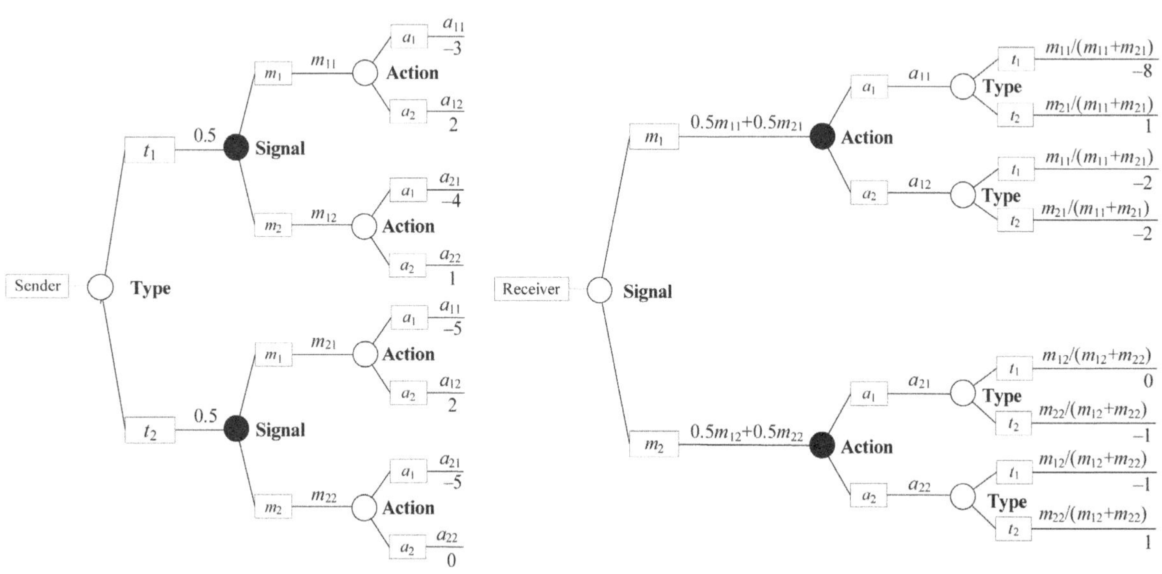

Figure 1. Decision trees for the general two-type signaling game.

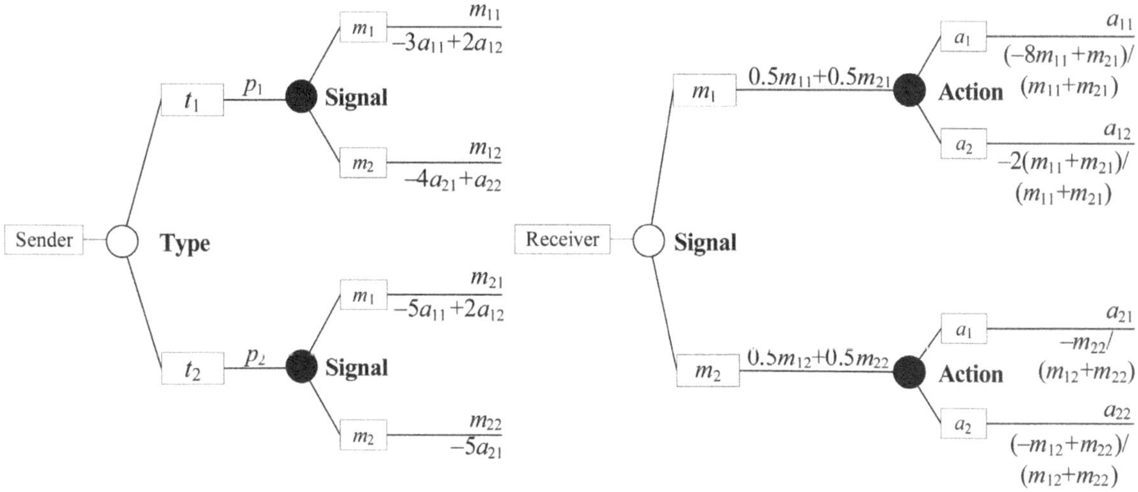

Figure 2. Decision trees rolled back one level.

when

$$-3a_{11}+2a_{12}=-4a_{21}+a_{22}$$

and

$$-5a_{11}+2a_{12}=-5a_{21}.$$

The solutions must also meet the conditions $a_{11}+a_{12}=1$ and $a_{21}+a_{22}=1$. The solution to this system of four equations in four unknowns is $a_{11}^*=0.5$, $a_{12}^*=0.5$, $a_{21}^*=0.3$, and $a_{22}^*=0.7$.

The *equilibrium calculation* task is easily accomplished by solving the decision tree, because the expressions required to solve for a_{11}^*, a_{12}^*, a_{21}^*, and a_{22}^* are precisely the expected values calculated during rollback.

The strategies a_{11}^*, a_{12}^*, a_{21}^*, and a_{22}^* determined using this method are only guaranteed to make the Sender indifferent between any assignment of its strategies if none of its pure strategies is dominant. However, if a dominant strategy exists in the game, the decision tree solution can assist in the *strategy selection* task described in the introduction. For example, suppose the Sender's payoffs in the example are changed so that $w_{212}=-5$. The solution process outlined previously yields $a_{11}^*=1.2$. Since this not a valid probability, a purely mixed strategy equilibrium does not exist and the Sender must have at least one pure strategy at equilibrium.

Observe from the tree in the left panel of **Figure 1** (with $w_{212}=2$ replaced by $w_{212}=-5$) that t_2 should never move Left, so $m_{22}=1$. Note from the Receiver's tree in **Figure 2** that with $m_{22}=1$, when the Receiver observes m_2 it will never move Up $(a_{22}=1)$ because $1-m_{12}>-1$. The Receiver's Nash equilibrium conditions are further reduced to $-3a_{11}+2a_{12}=1$ and $a_{11}+a_{12}=1$. The solution ($a_{11}=0.2$ and $a_{12}=0.8$) is given by Proposition 1 in Cobb and Basuchoudhary [14, p. 252].

3.2. Sender's Nash Equilibrium Strategies

The decision tree for the Receiver in this game is shown in the right panel of **Figure 1**. The Receiver does not directly learn the Sender's type, but does observe whether it chooses Left or Right. Once it observes this message, it decides whether to move Up or Down. The "Action" nodes are shaded to indicate these are random strategy nodes (as opposed to typical chance nodes). The payoff to the Receiver in the game is then determined by the Sender's actual type.

The marginal probabilities for the Sender's message type are calculated as

$$\begin{aligned}P(m_j)&=P(m_j\cap t_1)+P(m_j\cap t_2)\\&=P(m_j\mid t_1)P(t_1)+P(m_j\mid t_2)P(t_2)\\&=0.5m_{1j}+0.5m_{2j}\end{aligned}$$

for $j=1,2$. The conditional probabilities for the Sender's type given the observed message in this model are determined using Bayes' rule as

$$\begin{aligned}P(t_1\mid m_j)&=\frac{P(m_j\mid t_1)P(t_1)}{P(m_j)}\\&=\frac{0.5m_{1j}}{0.5m_{1j}+0.5m_{2j}}=\frac{m_{1j}}{m_{1j}+m_{2j}}\end{aligned}$$

with $P(t_2\mid m_j)=1-P(t_1\mid m_j)$.

To find its Nash equilibrium strategies, the Sender rolls back the Receiver's decision tree one level as shown in the right panel of **Figure 2**. For example, the Receiver observing m_1 and taking action a_1 calculates its expected value as

$$-8 \cdot m_{11}/(m_{11}+m_{21})+m_{21}/(m_{11}+m_{21})$$
$$=(-8m_{11}+m_{21})/(m_{11}+m_{21})$$

at the chance node representing the Sender type at the top of its tree in **Figure 1**. This expected value is placed in the rolled back decision tree in **Figure 2** as the payoff on the branch representing the Receiver observing m_1 and taking action a_1.

Two conditions must be met by the strategies m_{11}, m_{12}, m_{21}, and m_{22} established at Nash equilibrium by the Sender:

1) If the Receiver observes m_1, it must be indifferent between the strategies a_{11} and a_{12}.

2) If the Receiver observes m_2, it must be indifferent between the strategies a_{21} and a_{22}.

These conditions are met when the expected values at the end of either branch at the two Action nodes in the decision tree in the right panel of **Figure 2** are equal, or when

$$-8m_{11}+m_{21}=-2(m_{11}+m_{21})$$

and

$$-m_{22}=-m_{12}+m_{22}.$$

The solutions must also meet the conditions $m_{11}+m_{12}=1$ and $m_{21}+m_{22}=1$. Solving this system of four equations in four unknowns gives $m_{11}^*=1/3$, $m_{12}^*=2/3$, $m_{21}^*=2/3$, and $m_{22}^*=1/3$.

The strategies m_{11}^*, m_{12}^*, m_{21}^*, and m_{22}^* determined using the process outlined above are only guaranteed to make the Receiver indifferent between any assignment of its strategies if none of its strategies are dominant. Recall the example from the last section where the Sender's payoffs are such that it always plays $m_{21}=0$ and $m_{22}=1$. The revised probabilities in the Receiver's decision tree will indicate that $P(t_2 \mid m_1)=0$. We also established that in this scenario the Receiver observing m_2 should always play $a_{21}=0$ and $a_{22}=1$. By inserting the pure strategies that will always be played by both the Sender and Receiver in the decision trees and rolling back the trees, the Nash equilibrium strategies for a semi-separating equilibrium can be determined. The solution for the Receiver observing m_1 is given by Proposition 2 in Cobb and Basuchoudhary [14, p. 252].

In this next section, decision trees and the expected values obtained from the solution process are used to obtain a pure mixed strategy Nash equilibrium for the n-type signaling game.

4. General Signaling Game

In this section, we discuss the general n*-type signaling game*. Decision trees similar to those used in the $n=2$ case will be useful in demonstrating the conditions that are required to establish a Nash equilibrium.

4.1. Analysis of Sender's Decision Tree

Figure 3 shows a portion of the decision tree for the Sender in this game. The model is expanded beyond the

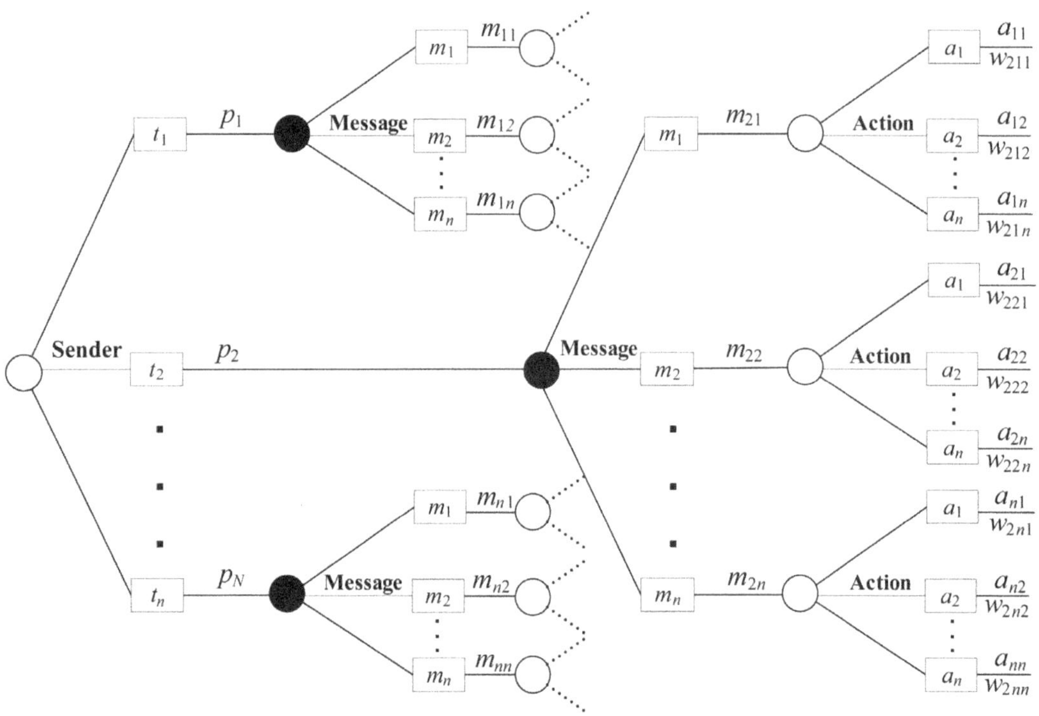

Figure 3. Sender's decision tree in the general signaling game.

"Message" branch for the t_2 Sender. This expansion shows that the t_2 Sender chooses from among n possible messages. Once it selects a message, it will which of the Receiver's n possible actions has been taken. An expansion of the decision tree for the other Sender types would appear similarly.

Rolling back the section of the decision tree in **Figure 3** for the t_2 Sender results in the expected values

$$EV_{2j}^S = a_{j1}w_{2j1} + a_{j2}w_{2j2} + \cdots + a_{jn}w_{2jn}$$

for $j = 1, \cdots, n$. A Nash equilibrium in this game must meet the $n-1$ separate conditions

$$\begin{aligned} &EV_{21}^S - EV_{22}^S = 0, \\ &EV_{22}^S - EV_{23}^S = 0, \cdots, EV_{2,n-1}^S - EV_{2n}^S = 0. \end{aligned} \quad (1)$$

More generally, the Receiver's strategies at Nash equilibrium must obey the conditions

$$\begin{aligned} &EV_{i1}^S - EV_{i2}^S = 0, \\ &EV_{i2}^S - EV_{i3}^S = 0, \cdots, EV_{i,n-1}^S - EV_{in}^S = 0 \end{aligned} \quad (2)$$

for $i = 1, 2, \cdots, n$.

To solve for the mixed strategy Nash equilibrium strategies for the Receiver, we construct the $n^2 \times n^2$ matrix W as

$$W = \begin{bmatrix} W_1 & \mathbf{0} & \cdots & \mathbf{0} \\ \mathbf{0} & W_2 & \cdots & \mathbf{0} \\ \vdots & \vdots & \ddots & \vdots \\ \mathbf{0} & \mathbf{0} & \cdots & W_n \end{bmatrix},$$

where each W_j is itself an $n \times n$ matrix and $\mathbf{0}$ is the $n \times n$ zero matrix. The i, kth entry of block W_j is simply w_{ijk}. The vector $\boldsymbol{EV}^S$ is $n^2 \times 1$, with

$$\boldsymbol{EV}^S = \begin{bmatrix} EV_{11}^S & EV_{21}^S & \cdots & EV_{n1}^S & EV_{12}^S & \cdots & EV_{nn}^S \end{bmatrix}^{\mathrm{T}}.$$

Note that $W\boldsymbol{a} = \boldsymbol{EV}^S$.

We can encode the conditions specified in (1) and (2) in the $(n^2 - n) \times n^2$ matrix

$$N = \begin{bmatrix} I & -I & \mathbf{0} & \cdots & \mathbf{0} \\ \mathbf{0} & I & -I & \cdots & \mathbf{0} \\ \vdots & \vdots & \vdots & \ddots & \vdots \\ \mathbf{0} & \mathbf{0} & \mathbf{0} & I & -I \end{bmatrix}.$$

where I is the $n \times n$ identity matrix.

To satisfy a Nash equilibrium, we need $NW\boldsymbol{a} = N(\boldsymbol{EV}) = \mathbf{0}$ This gives us $n^2 - n$ equations for our n^2 unknowns. We have yet to use the fact that the sum of the a_{jk} should be one (when j is fixed). The $n \times n^2$ matrix P takes this into account:

$$P = \begin{bmatrix} \mathbf{1}_{1\times n} & \mathbf{0}_{1\times n} & \cdots & \mathbf{0}_{1\times n} \\ \mathbf{0}_{1\times n} & \mathbf{1}_{1\times n} & \cdots & \mathbf{0}_{1\times n} \\ \vdots & \vdots & \ddots & \vdots \\ \mathbf{0}_{1\times n} & \mathbf{0}_{1\times n} & \cdots & \mathbf{1}_{1\times n} \end{bmatrix}.$$

Thus, we want $P\boldsymbol{a} = \mathbf{1}$. Let $G = \begin{bmatrix} NW \\ P \end{bmatrix}$ and define $\boldsymbol{b} = \begin{bmatrix} \mathbf{0}_{(n^2-n)\times 1} \\ \mathbf{1}_{n\times 1} \end{bmatrix}$. We want to solve for $\boldsymbol{a}$ in the equation

$$G\boldsymbol{a} = \boldsymbol{b}.$$

Thus, the Nash equilibrium strategies for the Receiver are determined as

$$\boldsymbol{a}^* = G^{-1}\boldsymbol{b}$$

provided these entries are all non-negative. When the Receiver plays the strategies in $\boldsymbol{a}^*$, the Sender cannot unilaterally change its strategy to earn a higher expected payoff.

The prior discussion describes how the decision tree formulation is used for *equilibrium calculation* in the case of a purely mixed strategy equilibrium. To aid in *strategy selection*, the vector $\boldsymbol{a}$ can be examined to determine whether there are any dominated strategies at equilibrium. This is indicated when $\boldsymbol{a}$ contains entries that are not strictly between 0 and 1, or when G is not invertible. In the n-type signaling game, if a Sender of any type has any *dominated* strategies, these should be assigned zero probabilities prior to finding the remaining strategies in $\boldsymbol{a}$ that comprise the Receiver's strategies in a Nash equilibrium. Since the Receiver can assume that the Sender will never play dominated strategies, it can adjust its strategies accordingly and may find dominated strategies of its own. The decision tree methodology can still be useful in determining Nash equilibrium strategies for the Receiver. A well-defined algorithm for finding Nash equilibria where each player chooses some pure strategies and mixes over the remaining strategies is beyond the scope of this paper and requires future research. An example of such a solution in the context of a specific example will be provided later in this section.

4.2. Analysis of Receiver's Decision Tree

The Receiver's decision tree in the general n-type signaling game is partially shown in **Figure 4**. This diagram shows the detail in the tree beyond the "Action" node when the Receiver observes message m_2. The detail shows that the Receiver will first learn the message selected from the Sender's n possible choices. Once it

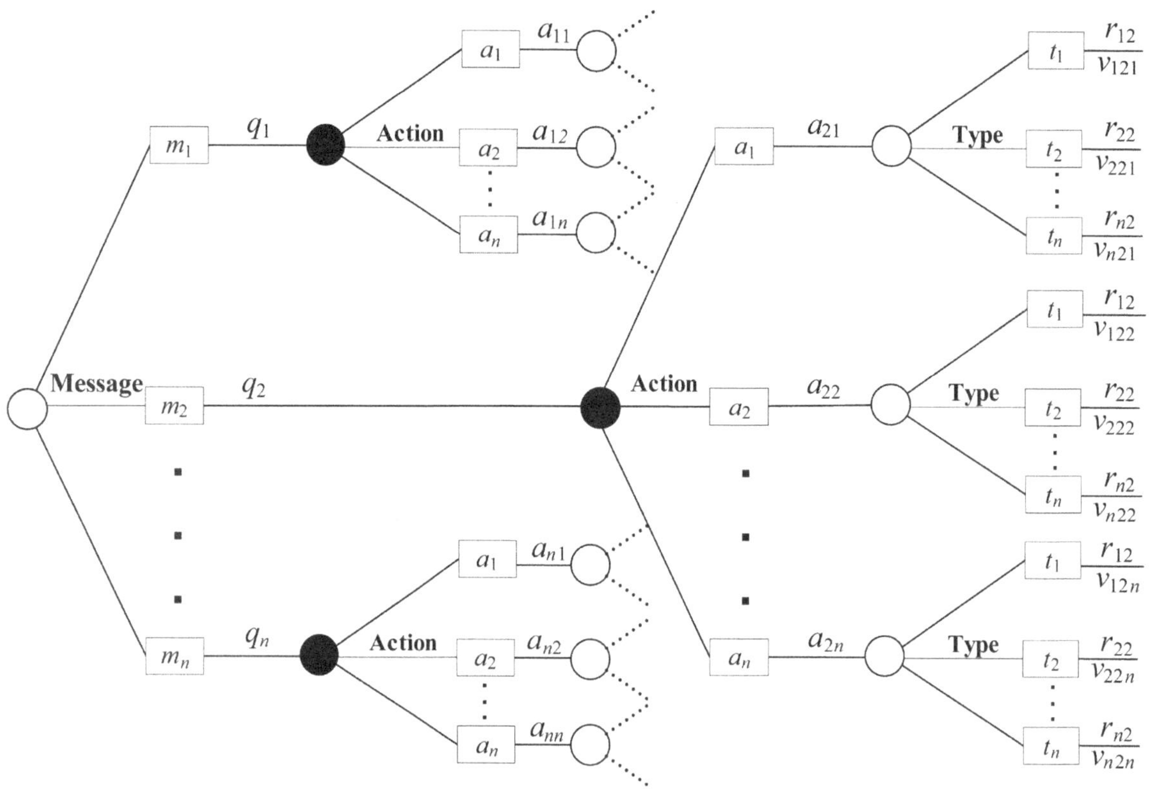

Figure 4. Receiver's decision tree in the general signaling game.

observes the message, it chooses an action from its n available possibilities. Only after the Receiver selects an action does it finally learn which of the n possible Sender types it opposes in the game.

In this section, P is an $n \times n$ diagonal matrix that holds the probabilities p_i on the diagonal, or $P = \text{diag}([p_1 \quad p_2 \quad \cdots \quad p_n])$. Let D be the $n^2 \times n^2$ diagonal matrix of n copies of P, or

$$D = \text{diag}([P \quad P \quad \cdots \quad P]).$$

The marginal probabilities for the message observed by the Receiver are calculated as

$$q_j = P(m_j) = \sum_{i=1}^{N} P(m_j \mid t_i) P(t_i) = \sum_{i=1}^{N} m_{ij} p_i.$$

The conditional probabilities for Sender type given the message observed by the Receiver are calculated as

$$r_{ij} = P(t_i \mid m_j) = \frac{P(m_j \cap t_i)}{P(m_j)} = \frac{m_{ij} p_i}{q_j}.$$

where r_{ij} is the conditional probability the Sender is t_i given message m_j is observed. Let

$$\boldsymbol{r} = [r_{11} \quad r_{21} \quad \cdots \quad r_{n1} \quad r_{12} \quad \cdots \quad r_{nn}]^{\mathrm{T}}.$$

Note that $\boldsymbol{r}$ is indexed in the same manner as $\boldsymbol{m}$. One can derive $\boldsymbol{r}$ from $\boldsymbol{m}$ by pre-multiplying $\boldsymbol{m}$ by the above matrix D and by the matrix Q defined as the $n^2 \times n^2$ diagonal matrix whose first n diagonal entries are $1/q_1$, whose second n diagonal entries are $1/q_2$, etc. One can view Q as being block diagonal, $Q = \text{diag}([Q_1 \quad Q_2 \quad \cdots \quad Q_n])$ where each Q_j is $n \times n$ diagonal, with the diagonal containing only $1/q_j$. We have that $\boldsymbol{r} = QD\boldsymbol{m}$. However, in calculating the Nash equilibrium strategies, we will not actually need the q_j's and hence we will not need Q. The matrix Q will be used to calculate the expected value in the game for the Receiver.

V is $n^2 \times n^2$ and contains the Receiver's payoffs. It is analogous to the matrix W from previous analysis of the Sender's tree, but is defined in a different manner. It can be viewed as a diagonal block matrix,

$$V = \begin{bmatrix} V_1 & \mathbf{0} & \cdots & \mathbf{0} \\ \mathbf{0} & V_2 & \cdots & \mathbf{0} \\ \vdots & \vdots & \ddots & \vdots \\ \mathbf{0} & \mathbf{0} & \cdots & V_n \end{bmatrix},$$

where each V_j is $n \times n$, and the k, i^{th} entry of V_j is v_{ijk}.

Let $\boldsymbol{EV}^R$ denote the $n^2 \times 1$ vector of expected values of the outcomes for the Receiver, or

$$\boldsymbol{EV}^R = \left[EV_{11}^R \quad EV_{12}^R \quad \cdots \quad EV_{1n}^R \quad EV_{21}^R \quad \cdots \quad EV_{nn}^R\right]^{\mathrm{T}}.$$

Note the indexing of $\boldsymbol{EV}^R$ differs from $\boldsymbol{EV}^S$. The components of $\boldsymbol{EV}^R$ are derived by rolling back the decision tree in **Figure 4**. For instance, rolling back the tree for the Receiver observing m_2 results in the following expected values:

$$EV_{21}^R = q_2^{-1}\left(m_{12}p_1v_{121} + m_{22}p_2v_{221} + \cdots + m_{n2}p_nv_{n21}\right)$$

$$EV_{22}^R = q_2^{-1}\left(m_{12}p_1v_{122} + m_{22}p_2v_{222} + \cdots + m_{n2}p_nv_{n22}\right)$$

$$\vdots$$

$$EV_{2n}^R = q_2^{-1}\left(m_{12}p_1v_{12n} + m_{22}p_2v_{22n} + \cdots + m_{n2}p_nv_{n2n}\right).$$

In general, we have $V\boldsymbol{r} = \boldsymbol{EV}^R$. At Nash equilibrium, the Receiver observing the message m_2 must be indifferent between each of its actions, so that

$$EV_{21}^R = EV_{22}^R = \cdots = EV_{2n}^R.$$

The matrix N will be $\left(n^2-n\right)\times n^2$ with

$$N = \begin{bmatrix} A & \mathbf{0} & \cdots & \mathbf{0} \\ \mathbf{0} & A & \cdots & \mathbf{0} \\ \vdots & \vdots & \ddots & \vdots \\ \mathbf{0} & \mathbf{0} & \cdots & A \end{bmatrix}.$$

with A an $(n-1)\times n$ "upper bidiagonal" matrix, with 1s on the diagonal and −1s on the upper bidiagonal. For instance, in the $n=4$ case, we have

$$A = \begin{bmatrix} 1 & -1 & 0 & 0 \\ 0 & 1 & -1 & 0 \\ 0 & 0 & 1 & -1 \end{bmatrix}.$$

We have $NV\boldsymbol{r} = N\boldsymbol{EV}^R = \mathbf{0}$.

Replacing $\boldsymbol{r}$ with $QD\boldsymbol{m}$ gives $NVQD\boldsymbol{m} = 0$. Because of the block diagonal structure of V and Q, we have that $VQ = QV$. Likewise, $NQ = Q^*N$, where Q^* is $\left(n^2-n\right)\times\left(n^2-n\right)$ diagonal, with $n-1$ copies of each $1/q_j$ on the diagonal instead of n copies.

Thus

$$NVQD\boldsymbol{m} = NQVD\boldsymbol{m} = Q^*NVD\boldsymbol{m} = \mathbf{0}$$

Since Q^* is invertible (as long as no $q_j = 0$), this implies that $NVD\boldsymbol{m} = \mathbf{0}$, and hence we can ignore Q and directly solve for $\boldsymbol{m}$.

We currently have n^2-n equations describing our n^2 unknowns. Our final n equations come from the fact that the m_{ij} form a distribution, hence $\sum_{j=1}^n m_{ij} = 1$ for $i = 1,\cdots,n$. Because of the way that we have indexed the matrix $\boldsymbol{m}$, this amounts to summing every n^{th} entry of $\boldsymbol{m}$ and getting 1. This can again be done conveniently through matrix multiplication.

Let S be the $n\times n^2$ matrix which is the concatenation of n copies of the $n\times n$ identity matrix I. That is, $S = [I \quad I \quad \cdots \quad I]$. Then $S\boldsymbol{m} = \mathbf{1}_{n\times 1}$.

Let $G = \begin{bmatrix} NVD \\ S \end{bmatrix}$. We want to solve for $\boldsymbol{m}$ in the equation

$$G\boldsymbol{m} = \boldsymbol{b},$$

where $\boldsymbol{b}$ is defined as in the previous section. Thus, the Nash equilibrium strategies for the Sender are determined as

$$\boldsymbol{m}^* = G^{-1}\boldsymbol{b}.$$

We can show an example of the conditions under which G will not be invertible. If for two values of i, say i_1 and i_2, we have that $v_{i_1j1} = v_{i_1j2} = \cdots = v_{i_1jn}$ and $v_{i_2j1} = v_{i_2j2} = \cdots = v_{i_2jn}$, then G will have two identical columns and hence will not be invertible.

In the n-type signaling game, if a Receiver observing any message has any *dominated* strategies, these should be assigned as zero in any Nash equilibrium solution. This may occur simply because of the structure of the Receiver's payoffs, or perhaps because the Receiver can assume that at least one type of Sender has dominated strategies that will never be played at Nash equilibrium. One such case mentioned earlier occurs when the Receiver has multiple actions that lead to exactly the same payoffs (this causes G to be invertible). All but one of such strategies can be considered dominated and assigned zero probabilities. As stated in the previous section, some additional discussion will be provided later in the paper regarding the use of decision trees to identify such equilibria, and further study of methods for using decision trees to solve for such equilibria will be the subject of ongoing research.

The same conclusions to those in Section 3 for the two-type signaling game about the solutions $\boldsymbol{a}^*$ and $\boldsymbol{m}^*$ outlined above can be made for the n-type signaling game. The solutions either compute a purely mixed Nash equilibrium or indicate that a Nash equilibrium containing at least some pure strategies exists.

5. Examples

In this section, the process from Section 4 is used to find Nash equilibrium strategies in the signaling game from Section 3 with $n=2$.

5.1. Determining the Receiver's Nash Equilibrium Strategies

In this problem, let $\boldsymbol{a} = \left[a_{11} \quad a_{12} \quad a_{21} \quad a_{22}\right]^{\mathrm{T}}$. Substituting the values from **Table 1** gives

$$W = \begin{bmatrix} -3 & 2 & 0 & 0 \\ -5 & 2 & 0 & 0 \\ 0 & 0 & -4 & 1 \\ 0 & 0 & -5 & 0 \end{bmatrix}.$$

Recall that $Wa = EV$. At Nash equilibrium $EV_{11} - EV_{12} = 0$ and $EV_{21} - EV_{22} = 0$. This idea is encoded in the matrix N. Combining N and W gives

$$NW = \begin{bmatrix} -3 & 2 & 4 & -1 \\ -5 & 2 & 5 & 0 \end{bmatrix}. \quad (3)$$

Therefore,

$$\begin{aligned} NWa &= N(Wa) = N(EV) \\ &= \begin{bmatrix} EV_{11} - EV_{12} \\ EV_{21} - EV_{22} \end{bmatrix} \quad (4) \\ &= \begin{bmatrix} -3a_{11} + 2a_{12} + 4a_{21} - a_{22} \\ -5a_{11} + 2a_{12} + 5a_{21} \end{bmatrix} = \begin{bmatrix} 0 \\ 0 \end{bmatrix}. \end{aligned}$$

Up to this point, we have two equations for four unknowns. The sum of the a_{jk} should be one (when j is fixed). This is ensured by the matrix P. Thus, we have that

$$Pa = \begin{bmatrix} a_{11} + a_{12} \\ a_{21} + a_{22} \end{bmatrix} = \begin{bmatrix} 1 \\ 1 \end{bmatrix}. \quad (5)$$

Combine Equations (4) and (5) together. The matrices NW and P are both 2×4, and hence the matrix

$$G = \begin{bmatrix} NW \\ P \end{bmatrix} \text{ is } 4 \times 4$$

and

$$G\mathbf{a} = \begin{bmatrix} 0 & 0 & 1 & 1 \end{bmatrix}^{\mathrm{T}}.$$

The Nash equilibrium strategies are

$$a^* = \begin{bmatrix} 0.5 & 0.5 & 0.3 & 0.7 \end{bmatrix}^{\mathrm{T}}.$$

5.2. Determining the Sender's Nash Equilibrium Strategies

This section illustrates the determination of the Sender's solution in the example from Section 3.

Let the Sender's strategy vector be denoted by $m = \begin{bmatrix} m_{11} & m_{21} & m_{12} & m_{22} \end{bmatrix}^{\mathrm{T}}$ and the vector of revised probabilities $P(t_i \mid m_j)$ be denoted by $r = \begin{bmatrix} r_{11} & r_{21} & r_{12} & r_{22} \end{bmatrix}^{\mathrm{T}}$. The matrix P holds the probabilities p_i on the diagonal. The matrix D is 4×4 block diagonal, with two copies of P on the diagonal.

The matrix V contains the payoffs v_{ijk} and is also block diagonal, $V = \mathrm{diag}([V_1 \quad V_2])$, or

$$V = \begin{bmatrix} -8 & 1 & 0 & 0 \\ -2 & -2 & 0 & 0 \\ 0 & 0 & 0 & -1 \\ 0 & 0 & -1 & 1 \end{bmatrix}.$$

The k, i^{th} entry of V_j is v_{ijk}. Thus, $Vr = EV^R$, where $EV^R = \begin{bmatrix} EV_{11}^R & EV_{21}^R & EV_{12}^R & EV_{22}^R \end{bmatrix}^{\mathrm{T}}$. We want to multiply EV^R by a matrix N that ensures we have a Nash equilibrium. This matrix is the same as N from the previous section.

The expression $NVDm = \mathbf{0}$ gives two equations for our four unknowns. Two more equations are required because m represents two probability distributions where $m_{i1} + m_{i2} = 1$. Let $S = [I_2 \quad I_2]$. The matrix S is formed such that $Sm = \mathbf{1}_{2\times 1}$. This gives two more equations that must be satisfied at Nash equilibrium.

We form G as before, concatenating our matrices. Set $G = \begin{bmatrix} NVD \\ S \end{bmatrix}$. Thus

$$Gm = \begin{bmatrix} 0 & 0 & 1 & 0 \end{bmatrix}^{\mathrm{T}}.$$

Forming G as directed gives

$$G = \begin{bmatrix} -3 & 1.5 & 0 & 0 \\ 0 & 0 & 0.5 & -1 \\ 1 & 0 & 1 & 0 \\ 0 & 1 & 0 & 1 \end{bmatrix}.$$

Finally, with G invertible, m can easily be found. With this, the q_i's can be easily determined as can r if needed.

The Nash equilibrium strategies are

$$m^* = \begin{bmatrix} 1/3 & 2/3 & 2/3 & 1/3 \end{bmatrix}^{\mathrm{T}}.$$

5.3. Nash Equilibria without Purely Mixed Strategies

When applied to an arbitrary set of Sender and Receiver payoffs, the solutions a^* and m^* can be classified into two mutually exclusive categories:

1) All elements of a^* and m^* are valid, non-zero probabilities (requiring that the matrices G used to determine the solution are both invertible), *i.e.* the solution is a purely mixed Nash equilibrium.

2) Some or all elements of a^* and m^* are *not* valid non-zero probabilities, or one or both of the vectors of solutions are not defined because one of the G matrices is *not* invertible.

All signaling games have either a pooling, separating, semi-separating or purely mixed Nash equilibrium. These equilibrium types are mutually exclusive. Solutions a^* and m^* from the first category above are identically associated with games with purely mixed strategies. Therefore, solutions from the second category above are identified with pooling, separating, or semi-separating equilibria. Thus, we can be certain that our solution technique will either identify a purely mixed strategy or verify the existence of a Nash equilibrium containing at least some pure strategies (the *strategy selection* task). In terms of the *equilibrium calculation* task, purely mixed strategy equilibria are the primary focus of this paper. We give an example in this section that uses decision trees to facilitate the determination of an equilibrium in the second category.

The payoffs and prior probabilities for Sender type in the game are listed in **Table 2**. The Sender may be one of three types and the Receiver has three possible actions. The first number in each pair is the payoff to the Receiver and the second number is the payoff to the Sender.

In this problem, calculating $\boldsymbol{a}^*$ or $\boldsymbol{m}^*$ in the *strategy selection* phase reveals that a purely mixed Nash equilibrium does not exist and dominated strategies must be identified to determine the Nash equilibrium. The procedure from Section 4 gives the solutions $a_{11} = 3.237$, $a_{12} = -1.156$, and $a_{13} = -1.082$ as the strategies for the Receiver observing m_1. Clearly, these are not probabilities and this result provides an indication that the Sender has a dominated strategy.

The part of the Sender's decision tree related to the t_1 Sender is shown in the left part of **Figure 5** and rolled back in the right part of **Figure 5**. Again, the roll-back procedure involves calculating expected values. For instance, the t_1 Sender selecting m_1 obtains expected value $-1 \cdot a_{11} - 1 \cdot a_{12} - 2 \cdot a_{13} = -a_{11} - a_{12} - 2a_{13}$. From these diagrams, we can clearly observe that the Sender will always play $m_{11} = 0$, as this strategy is dominated by both m_{12} and m_{13}. Specifically,

$$\min_{(a_{21},a_{22},a_{23})\in[0,1]} a_{21} - a_{22} + a_{23} \geq \max_{(a_{11},a_{12},a_{13})\in[0,1]} -a_{11} - a_{12} - 2a_{13}$$

and

$$\min_{(a_{32})\in[0,1]} a_{32} \geq \max_{(a_{11},a_{12},a_{13})\in[0,1]} -a_{11} - a_{12} - 2a_{13}.$$

Once the Receiver accounts for the fact that $m_{11} = 0$, it will adjust its payoffs and ascertain (through similar analysis as that performed above for the Sender) that it should always play $a_{12} = 0$ because a_{12} is dominated by a_{11} and a_{13}.

The method presented in Section 4 can be adapted to find the remaining equilibrium strategies in this game. Since $m_{11} = 0$, the expected value EV_{11}^S does not have to be considered in the Nash equilibrium conditions when the Receiver determines its optimal strategies using the Sender's decision tree. Since the first row of the matrix NW in (3) captures the condition $EV_{11}^S = EV_{12}^S$, this row can be removed from the matrix. Since $a_{12} = 0$ the second column of NW can be removed. The matrix is

$$NW = \begin{bmatrix} 1 & 2 & 1 & -1 & -2 & 0 & 0 & 0 \\ -0.5 & 0 & 0.5 & 0 & 1 & 0 & 0 & 0 \\ 0 & 0 & 1 & -1 & 1 & 0 & -1 & 0 \\ 0 & 0 & -1 & 1 & 2 & -1 & -2 & 1 \\ 0 & 0 & -0.5 & 0 & -1 & 0.6 & -1 & -1 \end{bmatrix}.$$

The Nash equilibrium strategies for the Receiver (with $a_{12} = 0$ replaced) are

$$\boldsymbol{a}^* = \begin{bmatrix} 0.926 & 0 & 0.074 & 0.156 & 0.459 & 0.385 & 0.914 & 0.082 & 0.004 \end{bmatrix}^{\mathrm{T}}.$$

To determine its equilibrium strategies, the Sender must adjust the Receiver's decision tree for the conditions $m_{11} = 0$ and $a_{12} = 0$. After adapting the process in Section 4 for these dominated strategies, solving

$$\boldsymbol{Gm} = \begin{bmatrix} \mathbf{0}_{5\times1} \\ \mathbf{1}_{3\times1} \end{bmatrix}$$ gives

$$\boldsymbol{m}^* = \begin{bmatrix} 0 & 0.831 & 0.333 & 0.990 & 0.110 & 0.550 & 0.010 & 0.059 & 0.117 \end{bmatrix}^{\mathrm{T}}.$$

The strategy $m_{11} = 0$ has been re-added to the vector.

The decision tree for the Receiver observing m_1 is shown in **Figure 6** with the optimal strategies and resulting conditional probabilities for both players inserted. The Sender's strategies make the Receiver indifferent between any possible assignment a_{11} and a_{13} (although it has selected $a_{11} = 0.926$ and $a_{13} = 0.074$ at equilibrium). Since m_{11}, the Receiver can never gain a higher payoff by assigning any positive probability a_{12}, so this was set to $a_{12} = 0$ prior to determining the other equilibrium strategies.

This example demonstrates that the decision trees are still useful for identifying Nash equilibria that are not purely mixed (the *strategy selection* task). The process for interpreting the results of Section 4 for an arbitrary signaling game where a purely mixed Nash equilibrium does not exist, then adapting the matrices representing the Nash equilibrium conditions is not well-defined and has only been demonstrated by example. Creating such an algorithm requires further investigation, but the decision tree approach appears to hold promise for developing a heuristic approach to determining a Nash equilibrium in signaling games.

6. Conclusions

The main contribution of this paper is to introduce a standard approach to constructing and solving the equa-

Table 2. Payoffs to each player in the example.

	Sender t_1				Sender t_2				Sender t_3		
	$P(t_1)=p_1=0.4$				$P(t_2)=p_2=0.4$				$P(t_3)=p_3=0.2$		
	m_1	m_2	m_3		m_1	m_2	m_3		m_1	m_2	m_3
a_1	−2, −1	−11, 1	2, 0	a_1	−2, 1	−1, −1	−1, 1	a_1	3, −0.5	2, −0.5	−2, −0.6
a_2	0.1, −1	−10, −1	−1, 1	a_2	−2, 0	0, 1	−2, 2	a_2	−1, −1	−2, 0	−1, 1
a_3	−1, −2	−11, 1	−1, 0	a_3	−1, 2	4, 2	2, −1	a_3	−2, 0	0, −1	−3, 1

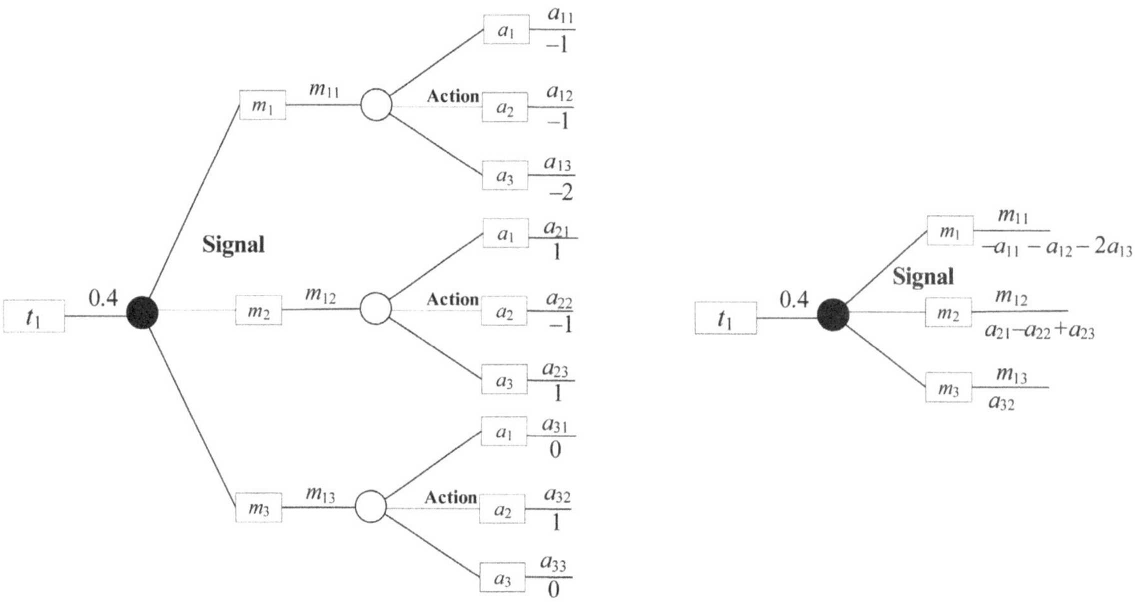

Figure 5. Decision tree for the t_1 Sender.

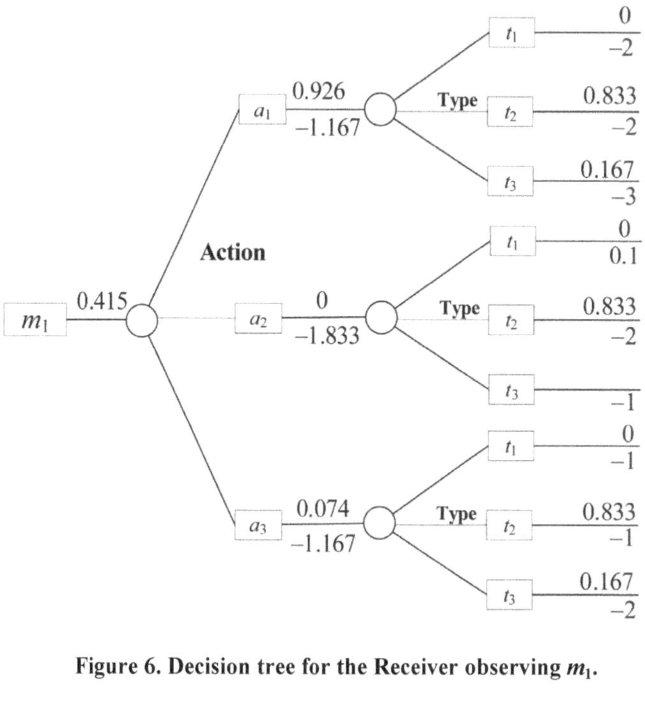

Figure 6. Decision tree for the Receiver observing m_1.

tions required to determine a mixed strategy Nash equilibrium in a signaling game. Some existing algorithms in the literature can solve two-type signaling games very fast. The problem is that once the game becomes even slightly more complex, finding equilibrium becomes increasingly difficult. This is acknowledged, for instance, by the developers of the Gambit software package [7].

In some sense, the purely mixed strategy is the most general solution for the n-type signaling game. Naturally, many signaling games have payoffs structured so that certain strategies for either player are dominated. In these cases, the decision tree can still be used to identify the Nash equilibrium conditions and solve for a mixed equilibrium over the remaining strategies. The eventual goal of future research is to provide new heuristic approaches for solving signaling games that can be derived from the solutions to the equations for the mixed strategy Nash equilibrium. This potential was demonstrated in Section 5.3 through an example where the Sender has a dominated strategy.

Decision trees provide a convenient modeling tool to facilitate the calculation of purely mixed Nash equilibria in signaling games. This paper extends decision tree results for the two-type signaling game presented by Cobb and Basuchoudhary [14] by finding general results for a purely mixed Nash equilibrium. Most game theory textbooks limit the possible types of solutions to pooling, separating, and semi-separating equilibria. The decision tree allows an analyst to simply compute a purely mixed Nash equilibrium, as opposed to testing a hypothesized Nash equilibrium by abstractly examining the payoffs or game tree for the problem.

The graphical representation of the decision tree models used to determine the purely mixed strategy Nash equilibria will clearly grow exponentially as the number of Sender types expands in the symmetric signaling game. However, the expected values required to solve such a decision tree are easily defined in matrix form. In a sense, we can dynamically construct nodes of interest in the decision tree, calculate expected values, then find the Nash equilibria using these expected values. This allows the decision tree solution to be used to find the purely mixed Nash equilibrium solution, even when the Sender has many possible types.

REFERENCES

[1] A. M. Spence, "Job Market Signaling," *Quarterly Journal of Economics*, Vol. 87, No. 3, 1974, pp. 355-374.

[2] P. Milgrom and J. Roberts, "Limit Pricing and Entry Under Incomplete Information: An Equilibrium Analysis," *Econometrica*, Vol. 50, No. 2, 1982, pp. 443-459.

[3] D. M. Kreps and J. Sobel, "Signalling," In: R. J. Aumann and S. Hart, Eds., *Handbook of Game Theory: With Economics Applications*, Elsevier, Amsterdam, Vol. 2, No. 11, 1994, pp. 849-868.

[4] J. G. Riley, "Silver Signals: Twenty-Five Years of Screening and Signaling," *Journal of Economic Literature*, Vol. 39, No. 2, 2001, pp. 432-478.

[5] B. von Stengel, "Equilibrium computation for Two-Player Games in Strategic and Extensive Form," In: N. Nisan, T. Roughgarden, E. Tardos and V. V. Vazirani, (Eds.), *Algorithmic Game Theory*, Cambridge University Press, New York, 2007, pp. 53-78.

[6] N. Nisan, T. Roughgarden, E. Tardos and V. V. Vazirani, "Algorithmic Game Theory," Cambridge University Press, New York, 2007.

[7] R. D. McKelvey, A. M. McLennan and T. Turocy, "Gambit: Software Tools for Game Theory, Version 0.2010.09.01," 2011. http://www.gambit-project.org

[8] D. Rios Insua, J. Rios and D. Banks, "Adversarial Risk Analysis," *Journal of the American Statistical Association*, Vol. 104, No. 486, 2009, pp. 841-854.

[9] G. S. Parnell, C. M. Smith and F. I. Moxley, "Intelligent Adversary Risk Analysis: A Bioterrorism Risk Management Model," *Risk Analysis*, Vol. 30, No. 1, 2010, pp. 32-48.

[10] E. Paté-Cornell and S. Guikema, "Probabilistic Modeling of Terrorist Threats: A Systems Analysis Approach to Setting Priorities among Countermeasures," *Military Operations Research*, Vol. 7, No. 4, 2002, pp. 5-20.

[11] D. Fudenberg and J. Tirole, "Game Theory," MIT Press, Cambridge, 1993.

[12] D. M. Kreps and R. Wilson, "Sequential Equilibria," *Econometrica*, Vol. 50, No. 4, 1982, pp. 863-894.

[13] J. H. van Binsbergen and L. M. Marx, "Exploring Relations between Decision Analysis and Game Theory," *Decision Analysis*, Vol. 4, No. 1, 2007, pp. 32-40.

[14] B. R. Cobb and A. Basuchoudhary, "A Decision Analysis Approach to Solving the Signaling Game," *Decision Analysis*, Vol. 6, No. 4, 2009, pp. 239-255.

An Extended Model of Currency Options Applicable as Policy Tool for Central Banks with Inflation Targeting and Dollarized Economies

Luis-Felipe Arizmendi[1,2]
[1]GPI Asset Management S.A., Lima, Perú
[2]Center for International Policy Studies, Department of Economics, Fordham University, New York, USA

ABSTRACT

The purpose of this paper is to provide a new set of tools for policy makers at central banks. Based on the Garman-Kohlhagen [1] formula for currency options, this research extends it with the Taylor-rule expression used for inflation targeting, thus obtaining the corresponding Call and Put options and the first and higher-degree partial derivatives known as "Greeks" for key variables such as the policy target domestic interest rate and the output gap.

Keywords: Inflation Targeting; Central Bank Policies; Exchange Rates; Currency Options

1. Introduction

In spite of the very recent debate in Caballero [2], Good friend [3], Taylor [4,5] and Woodford [6], on some limitations on how to apply it, the well-known Taylor-rule for inflation targeting (IT) has to be recognized as one of the most fruitful tools provided by macroeconomists to facilitate predictability and credibility related to changes in future price level. It is also claimed that for IT to be successful is required to include a high degree of exchange rate flexibility as in Ostry, Ghosh and Chamon [7]. In today's world, emerging markets economists and policy makers are no longer engaged in just choosing an exchange rate regime as a framework for the economic activity in a country, but rather to optimize growth, employment and private investment. In that sense, the adoption of the Taylor-rule for IT has become not only fashionable but also useful to relate the effects in the nominal interest rate with the desired and observed levels of inflation, changes in the Real GDP and the short-term trends in the business cycle, as seen in Apergis, Miller, Panethimitakis and Vamvakidis [8], and Salvatore [9,10].

There are, however, some potential long-term weaknesses and yet unresolved policy issues when applying IT to dollarized economies. Ozsoz, Rengifo and Salvatore [11] show additional challenges for the policy-makers that come from the dollarization phenomena and the potential currency competition. It brings complex situations, where the effectiveness of the monetary policy may appear partially or temporarily restricted, opening the case for increasing imbalances that may precipitate financial crises in the medium-term, with massive inflows of foreign speculative capital and abrupt local currency appreciation.

The use of market-related tools, such as currency options, is not strange to literature (see Veestraeten [12]), although they have been just partially employed in a few countries, and none has attempted to merge currency option models, such as the Garman-Kohlhagen [1], within an IT framework.

There are some cases that will help us to set the boundaries of this proposed research. As seen in works of Archer [13], Bernedo and Azañero [14], Breuer [15], Gürsu and Öncü [16], Mandeng [17], Orellana and Rodriguez [18], Suk and Malliaris [19], Taylor [20], and Uribe and Toro [21], there is some recent evidence to assume that exchange rate intervention by employing market-friendly tools such as currency options, can provide the additional instruments many central banks in small dollarized open-economies, are looking for.

2. The Model

We will employ the model presented by Taylor [22], Molodtsova and Papell [23], where the most widely used expression by central banks is usually written as:

$$i_t = \pi_t + \varphi(\pi_t - \bar{\pi}) + \gamma Y_t + R \quad (1)$$

where i_t is the policy target domestic interest rate, π_t is the actual inflation rate, $\bar{\pi}$ is the target inflation rate, Y_t is the Output gap (potential vs actual real GDP), and R is the equilibrium real interest rate.

Rearranging some terms to obtain a form easier to compute, we get:

$$i_t - \pi_t = R + \varphi\pi_t - \varphi\bar{\pi} + \gamma Y_t; \quad (1.a)$$

by separating in two terms, we get:

$$i_t = k_t + m, \quad (1.b)$$

where $k_t = (1+\varphi)\pi_t + \gamma Y_t$, (1.b.1)
and $m = R - \varphi\bar{\pi}$ (1.b.2)

As a suggestion to avoid multicollinearity, the regressional form may be set as:

$$(i_t - \pi_t) = R + \varphi(\pi_t - \bar{\pi}) + \gamma Y_t + \varepsilon_t \quad (1.a.1),$$

After obtaining the fitted values for $i_t - \pi_t$, and then substracting π_t, we obtain $\hat{i}_t$ as the estimated target nominal interest rate.

Renaming the terms and using T (for Taylor) instead of t for the purpose to identify them as instrumental values that come from the Taylor expression, the estimated regression can be written as:

$$\hat{i}_T = \hat{k}_T + \hat{m}. \quad (2)$$

Whereas, by grouping terms from (1.a.1), we get:

$$\hat{k}_T = (1+\varphi)\pi_T + \gamma Y_T + \varepsilon_T \quad (2.a)$$

$$\hat{m} = \hat{R} - \varphi\bar{\pi} \quad (2.b)$$

Being the Garman-Kohlhagen (GK) model an European option, with q being the risk-free foreign interest rate, and $\Phi(d)$, the cumulative distribution function for the standard normal distribution, the values d_1 and d_2 of the GK formula with the coefficients from the Taylor-rule, the modified d_1^T and d_2^T are:

$$d_1^T = \frac{\log(S/X) + \left(\hat{k}_T + \hat{m} - q + \left(\frac{\sigma^2}{2}\right)\right)t}{\sigma\sqrt{t}} \quad (3)$$

and,

$$d_2^T = d_1^T - \sigma\sqrt{t} \quad (4)$$

So, the expressions for the Call and the Put options of the GK-Taylor modified will be:

$$C = Se^{-qt}\Phi(d_1^T) - Xe^{-(\hat{k}_T+\hat{m})t}\Phi(d_2^T) \quad (5)$$

$$P = Xe^{-(\hat{k}_T+\hat{m})t}\Phi(-d_2^T) - Se^{-qt}\Phi(-d_1^T) \quad (6)$$

Being log the natural logarithm, and:

S = the current exchange rate (domestic currency per unit of foreign currency);

X = the strike exchange rate;

$\hat{k}_T + \hat{m}$ = the estimated domestic target interest rate $(\hat{i}_T)$ by the Taylor-rule regression;

q = the continuously compounded foreign risk-free interest rate;

t = the time in years until the expiration of the option;

σ = the implied volatility for the underlying exchange rate;

Φ = the standard normal cumulative distribution function.

Assuming option values at expiration time E to be $C_E = \text{Max}[0, S_E - X]$, and $P_E = \text{Max}[0, X - S_E]$, options having non-negative prices such as $C, P \geq 0$, upper boundaries $C \leq S, P \leq X$, and lower boundaries $C \geq e^{-qt}S - e^{(\hat{i}_T)t}X$, and $P \geq e^{(\hat{i}_T)t}X - e^{-qt}S$, as described by DeRosa [24], as well as Haup [25] and Steland [26], for further details.

3. First and Higher Order Partial Derivatives

In terms of the GK-Taylor modified model (GK-T), the new "Greeks" are defined in the following way:

Delta (Δ): $\partial C/\partial S$ and $\partial P/\partial S$ will show the change in the price of a corresponding Call or Put to the change in the price of the underlying asset. Delta is known as the "hedge ratio", since it indicates how much of the underlying asset needs to be bought or sold to hedge the option.

For a Call GK-T, $\partial C/\partial S \equiv \Delta_c = e^{-qt}\Phi(d_1^T), 0 < \Delta < 1$.

For a Put GK-T,

$\partial P/\partial S \equiv \Delta_P = e^{-qt}\left[\Phi(d_1^T) - 1\right] - 1 < \Delta < 0.$

Gamma (Γ): It shows the amount that delta (Δ) changes of C and P when the underlying price changes, in this case S, the current spot exchange rate.

For the GK-T Call,

$\partial^2\Delta_C/\partial S^2 \equiv \Gamma_C = \dfrac{\Phi(d_1^T)e^{-qt}}{S\sigma\sqrt{t}}, \Gamma_C = \Gamma_P > 0$ For the GK-T Put, $\partial\Delta_P/\partial S^2 \equiv \Gamma_P =$ as above

Vega (V): Vega is the amount that the theoretical value of an option changes when the volatility σ changes by one point (either money or percentage). So, $V = \partial C/\partial\sigma, \partial P/\partial\sigma$ being C and P the values of a Call option and a Put option.

By deriving, we obtain
$V_C = V_P = Se^{-qt}\Phi(d_1^T)\sqrt{t}, V_C = V_P > 0$

Theta (Θ): Theta represents the loss in value of the option in one time period, all other factors held constant. Then, $\Theta = \partial C/\partial t, \partial P/\partial t$.

By deriving, we obtain the following expressions:

$$\Theta_C = -\frac{S\mathrm{e}^{-qt}\Phi(d_1)\sigma}{2\sqrt{t}} + qS\mathrm{e}^{-qt}\Phi(d_1^T) - \hat{i}_T X\mathrm{e}^{-\hat{i}_T t}\Phi(d_2^T),$$

$$\Theta_P = -\frac{S\mathrm{e}^{-qt}\Phi(d_1)\sigma}{2\sqrt{t}} - qS\mathrm{e}^{-qt}\Phi(d_1^T) + \hat{i}_T X\mathrm{e}^{-it}\Phi(d_2^T),$$

Being usually Θ_C and $\Theta_P < 0$; and $\hat{i}_T = \hat{k}_T + \hat{m}$.

Rho (ρ): We will obtain several "rho" values for the GK-T model, since we have a domestic target interest rate $\hat{i}_T$ that depends on π and Y, and a foreign q interest rate. Rho is the change in the option price when there is a change in the interest rates. They may be critical for this research, since an important outcome of the "blended" IT model will rely on the central bank's ability to operate either open or "shadow" currency options, to stabilize the trend of the exchange rate by minimizing the loss of the inflation target forecasting. Then, rho $(\rho_q) = \frac{\partial C}{\partial q}$ will be the first derivative of the Call option price when there is a change in the foreign risk-free interest rate.

Deriving accordingly, we obtain:

1) For domestic rho, we will derive $\partial C/\partial i$ and $\partial P/\partial i$, as well as in terms of π and Y, such as $\partial C/\partial \pi, \partial P/\partial \pi$ and $\partial C/\partial Y, \partial P/\partial Y$, so

$$\partial C/\partial i \equiv \rho_C = Xt\mathrm{e}^{-(\hat{k}_T+\hat{m})t}\Phi(d_2^T), \rho_C > 0$$

$$\partial P/\partial i \equiv \rho_P = -Xt\mathrm{e}^{-it}\Phi(d_2^T), \rho_P < 0,$$

Since $\hat{i}_T = (1+\varphi)\pi_T + \gamma Y_T + \hat{m},$, then

$$\partial C/\partial \pi = -S(1+\varphi)t\mathrm{e}^{-(\hat{k}_T+\hat{m})t}\Phi(d_1^T), \text{ and,}$$

$$\partial P/\partial \pi = -S(1+\varphi)t\mathrm{e}^{-(\hat{k}_T+\hat{m})t}\left[1-\Phi(d_1^T)\right], \text{ while}$$

$$\partial C/\partial Y = -S\gamma t\mathrm{e}^{-((1+\varphi)\pi_T+\gamma T_T+\hat{m})t}\Phi(d_1^T), \text{ and,}$$

$$\partial P/\partial Y = -S\gamma t\mathrm{e}^{-((1+\varphi)\pi_T+\gamma T_T+\hat{m})t}\Phi(-d_1^T)$$

2) For foreign rho,

$$\partial C/\partial q \equiv \rho_C = -St\mathrm{e}^{-qt}\Phi(d_1^T), \rho_C > 0$$

$$\partial P/\partial q \equiv \rho_P = -St\mathrm{e}^{-qt}\Phi(-d_1^T), \rho_P < 0$$

Useful higher order partial derivatives for C and P, such as Vanna $(\partial^2 V/\partial S\partial\sigma)$, Volga $(\partial^2 V/\partial\sigma^2)$, Speed $(\partial^2 V/\partial\sigma^2)$, DvegaDtime $(\partial^2 V/\partial\sigma\partial t)$, and new "Greeks" (as in Arizmendi [27]), such as DrhoDpi $(\partial^2 C/\partial\pi\partial S; \partial^2 P/\partial e\partial S)$, and DrhoDoutput $(\partial^2 C/\partial Y\partial S; \partial^2 P/\partial Y\partial S)$, are also obtained as:

Vanna $= \frac{q}{S}\left[1-\frac{d_1^T}{\sigma\sqrt{t}}\right],$

Volga $= \frac{q}{\sigma}\left(d_1^T d_1^T\right),$

Speed $= -\frac{\mathrm{e}^{-(\hat{k}_T+\hat{m})t}\Phi(d_1^T)}{S^2\sigma\sqrt{t}}\left[\frac{d_1^T}{\sigma\sqrt{t}}+1\right],$

DvegaDtime

$$= S\mathrm{e}^{-(\hat{k}_T+\hat{m})t}\sqrt{t}\Phi(d_1^T)\left[\frac{d_1^T d_2^T - 1}{2t} - \frac{d_1^T(q-\hat{k}_T-\hat{m})}{\sigma\sqrt{t}} - (\hat{k}_T-\hat{m})\right]$$

DrhoDpi (Call)

$$= -(1+\varphi)t\mathrm{e}^{-((1+\varphi)\pi_T+\gamma Y_T+\hat{m})t}\left(\Phi(d_1^T)+\frac{\Phi(d_1^T)}{\sigma\sqrt{t}}\right),$$

DrohoDpi (Put)

$$= -(1+\varphi)t\mathrm{e}^{-((1+\varphi)\pi_T+\gamma Y_T+\hat{m})t}\left(\Phi(-d_1^T)+\frac{\Phi(d_1^T)}{\sigma\sqrt{t}}\right);$$

DrhoDoutput (Call)

$$= -\gamma t\mathrm{e}^{-((1+\varphi)\pi_T+\gamma Y_T+\hat{m})t}\left(\Phi(d_1^T)+\frac{\Phi(d_1^T)}{\sigma\sqrt{t}}\right), \text{ and}$$

DrhoDoutput (Put)

$$= \gamma t\mathrm{e}^{-((1+\varphi)\pi_T+\gamma Y_T+\hat{m})t}\left(\Phi(-d_1^T)-\frac{\Phi(d_1^T)}{\sigma\sqrt{t}}\right)$$

4. Conclusion

This model may be a useful set of tools for central banks and monetary authorities, especially those in countries with a relatively high level of dependency to a foreign currency, mainly through its local financial market and capital inflows. In particular, Call and Put option pricing—even if such derivatives market is not yet developed—may help central banks to intervene in the FX market when a combination of undesirable or untenable interest rate differentials, persistent inflows of capital, or a series of speculative attacks against the foreign currency in the local FX market, may cause the local currency to appreciate beyond certain level, introducing elements of potential instability, precisely opposed to what is sought by using the IT approach. In a free-float to dirty-float spot FX environment, the central bank of any given relatively dollarized country may diminish the cost of some sterilization through open-market-operations by calculating the relative value of its equivalent currency options, corresponding hedging and timely intervention.

5. Acknowledgements

The author wants to express its gratitude for the comments provided by Dominick Salvatore and Erick Rengifo, both at the Department of Economics, Fordham University, as well as Gianfranco Aguirre, Yerson Salcedo and Gabriel Samanez, from GPI Management S.A., that assisted him throughout the process of creating and writing this paper.

REFERENCES

[1] M. B. Garman and S. W. Kohlhagen, "Foreign Currency Options Values," *Journal of International Money and Finance*, Vol. 2, No. 3, 1983, pp. 231-237.

[2] R. J. Caballero, "Macroeconomics after the Crisis: Time to Deal with the Pretense-of-Knowlegde Syndrome," *Journal of Economic Perspectives*, Vol. 24, No. 4, 2010, pp. 85-102.

[3] M. Goodfriend, "How the World Achieved Consensus on Monetary Policy," *Journal of Economic Perspectives*, Vol. 21, No. 4, 2007, pp. 47-68.

[4] J. B. Taylor, "The Effectiveness of Central Bank Independence versus Policy Rules," American Economic Association Annual Meeting San Diego, California, January 2013, 22 p.

[5] J. B. Taylor, "Monetary Policy Rules Works and Discretion Doesn't: A Tale of Two Eras," *Journal of Money, Credit and Banking*, Vol. 44, No. 6, 2012, pp. 1017-1032.

[6] M. Woodford, "The Case for Forecast Targeting as a Monetary Policy Strategy," *Journal of Economic Perspectives*, Vol. 21, No. 4, 2007, pp. 3-24.

[7] J. Ostry, A. R. Ghosh and M. Chamon, "Two Targets, Two Instruments: Monetary and Exchange Rate Policies in Emerging Market Economies," *IMF Staff Discussion Note*, 29 February 2012, SDN/12/01.

[8] N. Apergis, S. M. Miller, A. Panethimitakis and A. Vamvakidis, "Inflation Targeting and Output Growth: Evidence from Aggregate European Data," University of Connecticut, Department of Economics, Working Paper Series No. 2005-06, 2005.

[9] D. Salvatore, "Exchange Rate Misalignments and the Present International Monetary System," *Journal of Policy Modeling*, Vol. 34, No. 4, 2012, pp. 594-604.

[10] D. Salvatore, J. W. Dean and T. D. Willett, "The Dollarization Debate," Oxford University Press, Oxford, 2003.

[11] E. Ozsoz, E. W. Rengifo and D. Salvatore, "Dollarization as an Investment Signal in Developing Countries: The Case of Croatia, Czech Republic, Peru, Slovak Republic and Turkey," Fordham University, Discussion Paper No. 2008-16, 2008.

[12] D. Veestraeten, "Currency Option Pricing in a Credible Exchange Rate Target Zone," University of Amsterdam, 2012.

[13] D. Archer, "Foreign Exchange Market Intervention: Methods and Tactics," *Foreign Exchange Market Intervention in Emerging Markets: Motives, Techniques and Implications*, BIS Papers No. 24, May 2005.

[14] M. del Rosario Bernedo and J. M. Azañero, "La Banca Central y los Derivados Financieros: El caso de las Opciones de Divisas," *Banco Central de Reserva del Perú, Estudios Económicos*, 2003, pp. 113-148.

[15] P. Breuer, "Central Bank Participation in Currency Options Markets," *International Monetary Fund*, Working Paper WP/99/140, 1999.

[16] G. Keles and T. S. Öncü, "Alternative Tools of Trade for Central Banks and Other Financial Institutions: Foreign Exchange Liquidity Options," IFC Bulletin No. 31, 2009, pp. 181-196.

[17] O. Mandeng, "Central Bank Foreign Exchange Market Intervention and Option Contract Specification: The Case of Colombia," *International Monetary Fund*, Working Paper WP/03/15, 2003.

[18] V. Orellana and P. Rodríguez, "Methodology for Measuring Derivatives at the Central Bank of Chile," IFC Bulletin, No. 31, 2009, pp. 165-180.

[19] S. H. Lee and A. G. Malliaris, "Currency Markets and International Interest Rate Parity," In: K. Baker and L. Riddick, Eds., *Survey of International Finance*, Oxford University Press, Oxford, 2011

[20] J. B. Taylor, "The Role of the Exchange Rate in Monetary-Policy Rules," *American Economic Review*, Vol. 91, No. 2, 2001, pp. 263-267.

[21] J. Uribe and J. Toro, "Foreign Exchange Market Intervention in Colombia," *Foreign Exchange Market Intervention in Emerging Markets: Motives, Techniques and Implications*, BIS Papers No. 24, May 2005.

[22] J. B. Taylor, "Discretion versus Policy Rules in Practice," *Carnegie-Rochester Conference Series on Public Policy*, Vol. 39, No. 1, 1993, pp. 195-214.

[23] T. Molodtsova and D. Papell, "Taylor Rule Exchange Rate Forecasting during The Financial Crisis," Working Paper 18330, National Bureau of Economic Research, 2012.

[24] D. F. DeRosa, "Options on Foreign Exchange," 3rd Edition, Wiley Finance, Hoboken, 2008.

[25] E. G. Haug, "The Complete Guide to Option Pricing Formulas," McGraw-Hill, New York, 2007.

[26] A. Steland, "Financial Statistics and Mathematical Finance. Methods, Models and Applications," John Willey & Sons, Ltd., Hoboken, 2012.

[27] L.-F. Arizmendi, "Open and Shadow Currency Options as Policy Tool for Central Banks with Inflation Targeting and Dollarized Economies: The Case for Peru," Fordham University, Internal Discussion Paper, January 2013.

15

Capacity Choice in a Private Duopoly: A Unilateral Externality Case*

Yasuhiko Nakamura
College of Economics, Nihon University, Tokyo, Japan

ABSTRACT

This paper studies capacity choice in a quantity-setting and price-setting private duopoly with differentiated goods wherein either of two firms has a price-raising effect on the price level of the product of the opponent firm. In both quantity-setting and price-setting competition, whether the price-raising effect of the product of one firm on the price level of the other firm's product is strong or weak strictly depends on the differences between the quantities and capacity levels of both firms. More precisely, in the quantity-setting competition, when the price-raising effect is sufficiently strong, both firms choose under-capacity, whereas when such an effect is sufficiently weak, both firms choose over-capacity. Furthermore, in the price-setting competition, when the price-raising effect is sufficiently strong, both firms choose over-capacity, whereas when such an effect is sufficiently weak, both firms choose under-capacity. Therefore, the presence of the price-raising effect as the unilateral externality strikingly changes the difference between each firm's quantity and capacity level in the contexts of both the quantity-setting competition and the price competition in a private duopoly with differentiated goods.

Keywords: Private Duopoly; Externality; Capacity Choice

1. Introduction

This paper considers the capacity choices of two profit-maximizer firms in a private duopoly with unilateral externality. More precisely, in the contexts of both quantity-setting competition and price-setting competition wherein one firm has a price-raising effect on the price level of the product of the opponent firm as the unilateral externality, we investigate the difference between the quantity and capacity level of each firm. We introduce the price-raising effect as the unilateral externality into each firm's demand function à la Choi and Lu [1]. The purpose of this paper is to check the robustness of the result on the difference between each firm's quantity and capacity level obtained in the standard private duopoly with differentiated goods against the introduction of the price-raising effect of the one firm's product on the price level of the opponent firm's product in the fashion of Choi and Lu [1].

In the model of this paper, following the model employed in Choi and Lu [1], we consider the situation where both firms produce a homogeneous good if there does not exist the price-raising effect of the product of the one firm as the unilateral externality[1]. Similar to Choi and Lu [1], since only the quantity of the product of the one firm (say firm 1) has the price-raising effect on the price level of the opponent firm's product, we refer to this effect as the unilateral externality. When the price-raising effect of firm 1's product is sufficiently strong, its product becomes a complement to the product of the firm without the price-raising effect (say firm 0). Hence, when the price-raising of firm 1's product as the unilateral externality is sufficiently strong, the strategic relations between the quantities/price levels and between the capacity levels as the strategic variables of both firms are changed in the context of both the quantity-setting competition and the price-setting competition. Cabral and Majure [2] found theoretical and empirical evidence on the asymmetry of the strategic relation in the Portuguese banking industry. More precisely, they indicated that for some banks, the number of branches of rival banks is a

*We are grateful for the financial support of KAKENHI (25870113). All remaining errors are our own.

[1]As indicated in Choi and Lu [1], although we can investigate the model such that the products of both firms can be differentiated even if there is the price-raising effect of the one firm as the unilateral externality, such an assumption does not change the qualitative results obtained in this paper.

strategic complement, whereas for other banks, it is a strategic substitute[2]. By considering a standard oligopolistic market without unilateral externality, Bulow *et al.* [3] and Bulow *et al.* [4] found that the dominant firm in an industry can consider the products of fringe firms as strategic complements, whereas the fringe firms can consider the output level of the dominant firm as strategic substitutes. In addition, Tombak [5] considered a two-stage game in which one firm regards its rival's second-stage strategic variable as a strategic complement whereas the other firm regards its rival's second-stage strategic variable as a strategic substitute[3].

In contrast to the works in this field including Choi and Lu [1], in this paper, we elaborate on the influences of the price-raising effect that the dominant firm has on not only the strategic variables in the market but also the additional strategies (the capacity levels) of the dominant firm and the fringe firm, that is, whether the over-capacity or under-capacity is achieved in both firms[4].

In this paper, we show that when the price-raising effect of the one firm's product on the price level of the other firm's product is sufficiently strong, in the quantity-setting competition, both firms choose under-capacity, while in the price-setting competition, both firms choose over-capacity. These results sharply contrast with those obtained in the standard quantity-setting and price-setting competitions with differentiated goods and without the price-raising effect[5]. As described above, the strength of the price-raising effect of firm 1's product changes the strategic relation between the strategic variables of both firms, *i.e.*, their quantities/price levels and capacity levels. More precisely, when the price-raising effect of the product of firm 1 is sufficiently strong (weak), in the quantity-setting competition, the strategic relation of firm 0's quantity with firm 1's quantity is a strategic complement (substitute) in firm 0's reaction function in the quantity-setting stage[6]. On the other hand, in the price-setting competition, when the price-raising effect of the product of firm 1 is sufficiently strong (weak), the strategic relation of firm 0's price level with firm 1's price level is a strategic substitute (complement) in firm 0's reaction function in the price-setting stage[7]. Furthermore, in the contexts of both quantity-setting competition and price-setting compe-tition, the influence of firm 1's capacity level on firm 0's quantity/price level is changed when the price-raising effect is sufficiently strong. Thus, when the price-raising effect is sufficiently strong, the changes of the strategic relations between the strategic variables yield changes of the signs of the differences between the quantities and capacity levels of both firms in the context of both quantity-setting competition and the price-setting competition.

The remainder of this paper is organized as follows. In Section 2, we formulate a private duopolistic model with the prise-raising effect of the one firm's product as the unilateral externality and with the capacity choices of both firms that will be investigated throughout this paper. In Section 3, from the viewpoints of quantity-setting competition and the price-setting competition, we consider the differences between the quantities and capacity levels of both firms using the model built in Section 2. Section 4 concludes with several remarks. The market outcomes including each firm's equilibrium price level and profit are relegated to the appendix.

2. Model

Following Choi and Lu [1], we formulate an asymmetric duopolistic model with unilateral externality wherein both firms determine not only their quantities/price levels but also their capacity levels. The products are perfect substitutes if the unilateral externality does not exist. When the unilateral externality is introduced, the quantity of firm 1's products can have an price-raising effect on the price level of firm 0's products. On the basis of Choi and Lu [1], we call the effect such that the output level of firm 1 can raise firm 0's price level the "unilateral externality". The inverse demand functions of firms 0 and 1 are given as follows:

$p_0 = a - q_0 + (\theta - 1)q_1$, $p_1 = a - (q_0 + q_1)$, respectively,

where p_i and q_i denote firm i's price level and output level, respectively, and parameter θ measures the

[2]The findings obtained in Cabral and Majure [2] are explained by the following two facts: i) the geographic differences (urban or rural areas) of the expansion patterns of incumbents (public banks) and entrants (private banks) and ii) the degree of customer honesty (in general, rural customers are more honest than urban customers).

[3]More precisely, Tombak [5] investigated the situation where only the dominant firm decides the investment for R&D in the first stage.

[4]By taking into account the managerial delegation in the fashion of Fershtman and Judd [6], Sklivas [7], and Vickers [8], although Choi and Lu [1] investigated the multi-stage game where the delegation parameters of both the firms as well as their quantities/price levels are determined, their main focus was to derive the result on the equilibrium timing of setting the quantities of both firms obtained in the endogenous timing game (the consequent order of the game). We consider how the setting of the strategic variable for the firm without the price-raising effect except for its strategic variable in the market is influenced by the setting of the strategic variables for the firm with the price-raising effect as the unilateral externality.

[5]In the appendix, we give the results on the differences in the quantities and capacity levels between both firms in the standard quantity-setting and price-setting competitions with differentiated goods and without the price-raising effect. More precisely, in a standard quantity-setting competition, both firms always choose over-capacity irrespective of the degree of product differentiation, whereas in a standard price-setting competition, both firms choose under-capacity irrespective of the degree of product differentiation.

[6]In firm 1's reaction function in the quantity-setting competition, the strategic relation of firm 1's quantity with firm 0's quantity is a strategic substitute irrespective of the strength of the price-raising effect of firm 1.

[7]In firm 1's reaction function in the price-setting competition, the strategic relation of firm 1's price level with firm 0's price level is a strategic complement irrespective of the strength of price-raising effect of firm 1.

degree of the price-raising effect as the unilateral externality, $(i=0,1)$. Note that a denotes the demand parameter and $\theta \in (0,1) \cup (1,2)$ [8]. $\theta \in (1,2)$ indicates that the price-raising effect of firm 1's output level is relatively strong whereas $\theta \in (0,1)$ indicates that the price-raising effect of firm 1's output level is relatively weak. Futhermore, $\theta \in (1,2)$ implies that firm 1's product becomes a complement to firm 0's product whereas $\theta \in (0,1)$ implies that firm 1's product becomes a substitute for firm 0's product.

Both firms adopt identical technologies represented by the cost function $C_i(q_i, x_i)$, where x_i is the capacity level of firm i, $(i=0,1)$. Following Vives [9], Ogawa [10], Bárcena-Ruiz and Garzón [11], Tomaru *et al.* [12], Nakamura and Saito [13], Nakamura and Saito [14], and Nakamura [15], we assume that the cost function is given by $C_i(q_i, x_i) = mq_i + (q_i - x_i)^2$, $(i=0,1)$. This cost function implies that if each firm's output level equals its capacity level, $q_i = x_i$, the long-run average cost is minimized. The profit of firm i is given by $\Pi_i = p_i q_i - C_i(q_i, x_i)$ $(i=0,1)$.

We investigate the game with the following orders of each firm's moves: In the first stage, firms 0 and 1 simultaneously set their capacity levels. In the second stage, after both firms observe their capacity levels, they engage in either quantity-setting competition or price-setting competition with each other.

3. Equilibrium Analysis

3.1. Quantity Competition

We first solve the quantity-setting game by backward induction from the second stage to obtain the subgame perfect Nash equilibrium. In the second stage, firm i maximizes its profit Π_i with respect to q_i, $(i=0,1)$. The best response functions of firms 0 and 1 in the second stage are given as follows:

$$q_0(q_1; x_0, x_1) = (a - m - q_1 + 2x_0 + q_1\theta)/4, \quad (1)$$

$$q_1(q_0; x_1) = (a - m - q_0 + 2x_1)/4. \quad (2)$$

From Equations (1) and (2), when $\theta \in (0,1)$, q_0 is decreasing in q_1, whereas when $\theta \in (1,2)$, q_0 is increasing in q_1. For any $\theta \in (0,1) \cup (1,2)$, q_1 is decreasing in q_0. Thus, the strategic relation of the quantity of firm 0 with the quantity of firm 1 strictly depends on the value of θ; that is, when $\theta \in (0,1)$, the quantity of firm 0 is a strategic substitute for the quantity of firm 1, whereas when $\theta \in (1,2)$, the quantity of firm 0 is a strategic complement to the quantity of firm 1. On the other hand, the strategic relation of the quantity of firm 1 is a strategic substitute for the quantity of firm 0 irrespective of $\theta \in (0,1) \cup (1,2)$.

Furthermore, we obtain the following equilibrium quantities of firms 0 and 1 as the functions of their capacity levels in the Nash equilibrium in the quantity-setting stage:

$$q_0 = \frac{8x_0 - 2x_1 + 2x_1\theta + a(3+\theta) - m(3+\theta)}{15+\theta}, \quad (3)$$

$$q_1 = \frac{3(a-m) - 2x_0 + 8x_1}{15+\theta}. \quad (4)$$

In the first stage, firms 0 and 1 realize that the choices of their capacity levels influence their quantity determined in the second stage. Provided Equations (3) and (4), respectively, firms 0 and 1 simultaneously and independently set their capacity levels with respect to their profits. Thus, by solving the first-order conditions of the profits of firms 0 and 1, we obtain

$$x_0(x_1) = \frac{16\left[2x_1(\theta-1) + a(3+\theta) - m(3+\theta)\right]}{97 + 30\theta + \theta^2}, \quad (5)$$

$$x_1(x_0) = \frac{16(3a - 3m - 2x_0)}{97 + 30\theta + \theta^2}, \quad (6)$$

yielding

$$x_0^q = \frac{16(a-m)(13 + 18\theta + \theta^2)}{559 + 419\theta + 45\theta^2 + \theta^3},$$

$$x_1^q = \frac{16(a-m)(13 + 3\theta)}{559 + 419\theta + 45\theta^2 + \theta^3}.$$

Note that superscript q is used to represent the subgame perfect Nash equilibrium market outcomes in the quantity-setting competition. Then, the equilibrium quantities of firms 0 and 1 are given as follows:

$$q_0^q = \frac{(a-m)(15+\theta)(13 + 18\theta + \theta^2)}{559 + 419\theta + 45\theta^2 + \theta^3},$$

$$q_1^q = \frac{(a-m)(15+\theta)(13 + 3\theta)}{559 + 419\theta + 45\theta^2 + \theta^3}.$$

Therefore, from easy calculations, we obtain the following equilibrium result on the differences between the quantities and capacity levels of firms 0 and 1:

$$q_0^q - x_0^q = \frac{(a-m)(\theta-1)(13 + 18\theta + \theta^2)}{559 + 419\theta + 45\theta^2 + \theta^3},$$

$$q_1^q - x_1^q = \frac{(a-m)(\theta-1)(13 + 3\theta)}{559 + 419\theta + 45\theta^2 + \theta^3}.$$

Proposition 1 *In the quantity-setting competition, when the price-raising effect of firm* 1*'s product on the price level of firm* 0*'s product is sufficiently strong, i.e.,* $\theta \in (1,2)$, *both firms* 0 *and* 1 *choose under-capacity. In contrast, in the quantity-setting competition, when such a price-raising effect of firm* 1*'s product is sufficiently*

[8]Similar to Choi and Lu [1], we omit the case of $\theta = 1$ since firm 0's price level is independent of firm 1's output level; this is a trivial case.

weak, i.e., $\theta \in (0,1)$, *both firms* 0 *and* 1 *choose over-capacity.*

Proposition 1 indicates that whether either of the two firms has a price-raising effect on the price level of the product of its opponent firm strictly determines the differences between the quantities and capacity levels of both firms. More precisely, when the price-raising effect of the one firm's product on the price level of the product of its opponent firm is sufficiently strong, both firms choose under-capacity, whereas when such an effect is sufficiently weak, both choose over-capacity. This result is strikingly different from that obtained in the standard quantity-setting competition with differentiated goods[9]. In the standard private duopolistic competition without the price-raising effect, since firm i pays attention to its market share in order to increase its profit, it attempts to decrease the quantity of its opponent firm j in order to increase its market share by increasing its capacity level when the relation between their output levels is substitutable, $(i,j=0,1;i\neq j)$. In addition, in the case wherein the relation between the products of both firms is complementary, firm i has an incentive to increase its market share by decreasing the quantity of its opponent firm j by decreasing its own capacity, and thus, this behavior of decreasing firm i's capacity also decreases firm j's capacity since their capacity levels are strategic complements in the first stage, $(i,j=0,1;i\neq j)$. Although the capacity levels of both firms tend to be low, their quantities are lower than their capacity levels since their capacity levels are positively associated with their own quantities. Thus, irrespective of whether the relation of the goods produced by both firms are substitutable or complementary, in a standard quantity-setting duopoly without the price-raising effect, they choose over-capacity.

In the quantity-setting competition wherein the one firm has the price-raising effect of its product on the price level of the product of the other firm, if such an effect is sufficiently weak, *i.e.*, $\theta \in (0,1)$, the intuition behind the result that both firms 0 and 1 choose over-capacity is similar to that given in the standard quantity-setting competition with substitutable goods and without the price-raising effect[10]. From Equations (3) and (4), when $\theta \in (0,1)$, both firms 0 and 1 have incentive to decrease the quantities of their respective opponent firms through increasing their own capacity in order to expand their respective market share, implying that both firms choose over-capacity. On the other hand, when the price-raising effect of firm 1's product is sufficiently strong, *i.e.*, $\theta \in (1,2)$, we obtain the result that the differences between the quantities and capacity levels of firms 0 and 1 are positive, which is strikingly different from the results obtained for i) the quantity-setting competition without the price-raising effect and ii) the case wherein such a price-raising effect is sufficiently weak, *i.e.*, $\theta \in (0,1)$. The intuition behind this result is as follows: from Equation (3), firm 1 which has the price-raising effect has an incentive to decrease firm 0's quantity by decreasing its own capacity, and consequently, firm 1 chooses under-capacity. On the other hand, from Equation (4), firm 0, which does not have the price-raising effect has an incentive to decrease firm 1's quantity by increasing its own capacity, similar to the case where $\theta \in (0,1)$. However, taking Equations (5) and (6) into account, firm 0's capacity tends not to become so high when $\theta \in (1,2)$. Therefore, since the quantity of firm 1 does not become so low because of the relatively low capacity of firm 0, from Equation (1), the quantity of firm 0 is higher relative to its capacity when $\theta \in (1,2)$. Consequently, firm 0 also chooses under-capacity. We emphasize that the strength of the price-raising effect and the change of the relation of the goods produced by firms 0 and 1 on the basis of such an effect determine the difference between the quantity and capacity of each firm in the quantity-setting competition with the price-raising effect as the unilateral effect.

3.2. Price Competition

We next solve the price-setting game by backward induction from the second stage to obtain the subgame perfect Nash equilibrium. In the second stage, firm i maximizes its profit with respect to p_i, $(i=0,1)$. The best-response functions of firms 0 and 1 in the second stage are given as follows:

$$p_0 = \frac{p_1\left(2-\theta-\theta^2\right)+\theta\left[m-2x_0+a(2+\theta)\right]}{2(1+\theta)}, \quad (7)$$

$$p_1 = \frac{2p_0+m\theta+p_0\theta-2x_1\theta}{2(1+\theta)}. \quad (8)$$

From Equations (7) and (8), when $\theta \in (0,1)$, p_0 is increasing in p_1, whereas when $\theta \in (1,2)$, p_0 is decreasing in p_1. For any $\theta \in (0,1)\cup(1,2)$, p_1 is increasing in p_0. Thus, the strategic relation of the price level of firm 0 with the price level of firm 1 strictly depends on the value of θ; that is, when $\theta \in (0,1)$, the strategic relation of the price level of firm 0 is a strategic complement to the price level of firm 1, whereas when $\theta \in (1,2)$, the strategic relation of the price level of firm 0 is a strategic substitute for the price level of firm 1. On

[9]This results on the differences between the quantities and capacity levels of firms 0 and 1, which are obtained in the standard quantity-setting competition with differentiated goods and without the price-raising effect, are given in the appendix. More concretely, in both cases wherein firms 0 and 1 produce substitutable goods or complementary goods, it was shown that they both always choose over-capacity.

[10]As described in the setting of this model, we recall that the fact that the price-raising effect is sufficiently weak implies that the products firms 0 and 1 are substitutable.

the other hand, the strategic relation of the price level of firm 1 is a strategic complement to the price level of firm 0 irrespective of $\theta \in (0,1) \cup (1,2)$.

Furthermore, we obtain the following price levels of firms 0 and 1 as the functions of the capacity levels in the Nash equilibrium in the price-setting stage.

$$p_0 = \frac{-4x_0 - 4x_1 - 4x_0\theta + 2x_1\theta + 2x_1\theta^2 + m(4+\theta-\theta^2) + 2a(2+3\theta+\theta^2)}{8+7\theta+\theta^2}, \quad (9)$$

$$p_1 = \frac{a(2+\theta)^2 + m(4+3\theta) - 2[2x_1(1+\theta) + x_0(2+\theta)]}{8+7\theta+\theta^2}. \quad (10)$$

In the first stage, firms 0 and 1 realize that the choices of their capacity levels influence their price levels in the second stage. Provided Equations (9) and (10), respectively, firms 0 and 1 set their capacity levels with respect to their profits. Thus, by solving the first-order conditions of the profits of firms 0 and 1 in the first stage, we obtain

$$x_0(x_1) = \frac{4(3+4\theta+\theta)[x_1(\theta-1) + a(1+\theta) - m(1+\theta)]}{28+52\theta+37\theta^2+10\theta^3+\theta^4}, \quad (11)$$

$$x_1(x_0) = \frac{2(3+4\theta+\theta^2)[-2x_0 + a(2+\theta) - m(2+\theta)]}{28+52\theta+37\theta^2+10\theta^3+\theta^4}, \quad (12)$$

yielding

$$x_0^p = \frac{4(a-m)(1+\theta)^2(6+17\theta+8\theta^2+\theta^3)}{80+264\theta+360\theta^2+231\theta^3+75\theta^4+13\theta^5+\theta^6},$$

$$x_1^p = \frac{2(a-m)(12+34\theta+43\theta^2+29\theta^3+9\theta^4+\theta^5)}{80+264\theta+360\theta^2+231\theta^3+75\theta^4+13\theta^5+\theta^6}.$$

Note that superscript p represents the subgame perfect Nash equilibrium market outcomes in the price-setting competition. Then, the equilibrium quantities of firms 0 and 1 are given as follows:

$$q_0^p = \frac{2(a-m)(8+7\theta+\theta^2)(2+7\theta+6\theta^2+\theta^3)}{80+264\theta+360\theta^2+231\theta^3+75\theta^4+13\theta^5+\theta^6},$$

$$q_1^p = \frac{(a-m)(8+7\theta+\theta^2)(4+6\theta+5\theta^2+\theta^3)}{80+264\theta+360\theta^2+231\theta^3+75\theta^4+13\theta^5+\theta^6}$$

Therefore, from easy calculations, we obtain the following equilibrium result on the differences between the quantities and capacity levels of firms 0 and 1:

$$q_0^p - x_0^p = \frac{2(a-m)(1-\theta)(1+\theta)(2+\theta)(2+5\theta+\theta^2)}{80+264\theta+360\theta^2+231\theta^3+75\theta^4+13\theta^5+\theta^6},$$

$$q_1^p - x_1^p = \frac{(a-m)(1-\theta)(2+\theta)(4+6\theta+5\theta^2+\theta^3)}{80+264\theta+360\theta^2+231\theta^3+75\theta^4+13\theta^5+\theta^6}.$$

Proposition 2 *In the price-setting competition, when the price-raising effect of firm* 1*'s product on the price level of firm* 0*'s product is sufficiently strong, i.e.,* $\theta \in (1,2)$, *both firms* 0 *and* 1 *choose over-capacity. In contrast, when such a price-raising effect of firm* 1*'s product is sufficiently weak, i.e.,* $\theta \in (0,1)$, *both firms* 0 *and* 1 *choose under-capacity.*

Similar to the quantity-setting competition with the price-raising effect of the product of firm 1, Proposotion 2 indicates that the differences between the quantities and capacity levels of firms 0 and 1 strictly depend on the strength of the price-raising effect of firm 1's product on the price level of firm 0's product. More concretely, it is shown that when the price-raising effect of firm 1's product is sufficiently strong, the differences between the quantities and capacity levels of firms 0 and 1 are negative, whereas when such an effect is sufficiently weak, the differences between their quantities and capacity levels are positive[11].

In the price-setting competition with the price-raising effect, when such an effect is sufficiently weak, *i.e.*, $\theta \in (0,1)$ from Equations (9) and (10), both firms 0 and 1 attempt to decrease the quantity of their respective opponent firm by decreasing their capacity in order to expand their own market share. Thus, when $\theta \in (0,1)$, both firms 0 and 1 choose under-capacity, which is the same result as that obtained in the standard price-setting competition with differentiated goods and without the

[11]These results on the differences between the quantities and capacity levels of firms 0 and 1, which are obtained in the standard price-setting competition with differentiated goods and without the price-raising effect, are given in the appendix. More concretely, in both cases wherein firms 0 and 1 produce substitutable goods or complementary goods with each other, it is shown that they always choose under-capacity together.

price-raising effect[12].

In contrast, the intuition behind the result that both firms 0 and 1 choose over-capacity in the price-setting competition when $\theta \in (1,2)$ is given as follows: from Equation (9), firm 1 which has the price-raising effect attempts to increase firm 0's price level by setting its capacity level high in order to decrease the quantity of firm 0, implying that it chooses over-capacity. Furthermore, similar to the case wherein $\theta \in (0,1)$, from Equation (10), firm 0 tends to decrease its own capacity level in order to decrease firm 1's quantity by increasing the price level of firm 1 when $\theta \in (1,2)$ as well. However, taking Equations (11) and (12) into account, firm 0's capacity level tends not to become low when $\theta \in (1,2)$. Therefore, since the price level of firm 1 does not become so high because of the relatively high capacity level of firm 0, from Equation (7), the price of firm 0 becomes relatively high, Consequently, since the quantity of firm 0 becomes low, firm 0 also chooses over-capacity when $\theta \in (1,2)$.

For both the quantity-setting competition with the price-raising effect and the price-setting competition with the price-raising effect, we find that the choices of the quantity/price level and the capacity level for the firm with the price-raising effect influences not only the selection of the quantity/price level for its opponent firm in the market, but also the selection of the capacity level for its opponent firm. These choices change the differences between the quantities and capacity levels of the two firm.

4. Conclusions

This paper investigated the differences between the output and capacity levels in a private duopoly composed of two profit-maximizer firms in both quantity-setting competition and price-setting competition, particularly when one firm has the price-raising effect on the price level of the product of its opponent firm as the unilateral externality. In both the standard quantity-setting competition and price-setting competition with differentiated goods and without the price-raising effect, the differences between the quantity and capacity levels of the two firms do not depend on the relation between their products, that is, whether they are substitutable or complementary. More precisely, in the standard quantity-setting competition with differentiated goods, both firms 0 and 1 always choose over-capacity, whereas in the standard price-setting competition with differentiated goods, they always choose under-capacity. In contrast, in the private duopoly with the price-raising effect of the product of the one firm, the differences between the quantities and capacity levels of both firms strictly depend on the strength of such an effect in not only the quantity-setting competition but also the price-setting competition. In particular, when the price-raising effect is sufficiently strong, both firms choose under-capacity in the quantity-setting competition whereas they both choose over-capacity in the price-setting competition. In the model of this paper, in the quantity-setting and price-setting competitions when the price-raising effect of the one firm is sufficiently strong, the product of the firm with such an effect is a complement to the product of the firm without such an effect, while the product of the firm without such an effect is always a substitute for the product of the firm with such an effect. Thus, the change of the strategic relation between the quantities/price levels and capacity levels of both firms along with the change of the relation of the product of the firm that has the price-raising effect as the unilateral externality with the product of the firm without such an effect (*i.e.*, substitutable or complementary) strikingly influences the differences between their quantities and capacity levels even if their strategic variables (q or p) are fixed in the market. The above findings comprise the most important contribution of this paper.

Finally, we mention an issue to be addressed in the future. Throughout this paper, we explored the differences between the quantity and capacity level of each firm by adopting the private duopolistic model with the unilateral externality à la Choi and Lu [1]. However, we did not consider the impact of the separation between ownership and management, which was investigated in Choi and Lu [1], on the difference between the quantities and capacity levels of the firms[13]. Future research must deal with the above problems.

[12]In the standard price-setting duopoly with differentiated goods, when the goods produced by both firms are substitutable, since each firm's capacity is negatively associated with the opponent firm's price level, each attempts to decrease the quantity of its opponent firm by increasing its opponent firm's price level by decreasing its own capacity level in order to increase its own market share, and hence, each firm's quantity is relatively higher than its capacity level. Thus, both firms choose under-capacity. On the other hand, when the relation between the products of the firms is complementary, each firm has an incentive to increase its opponent firm's price level by increasing its capacity level in order to increase its market share, and thus, such capacity-increasing behavior also increases its opponent firm's capacity since the capacity levels of both firms are strategic complements in the first stage. Although the capacity levels of both firms tend to become high, their quantities are higher than their capacity levels since their capacity levels are negatively associated with their own price levels. Thus, whether the relation of the goods produced by both firms is substitutable or complementary, in a standard price-setting duopoly without the price-raising effect, they choose under-capacity.

[13]Several types of strategic delegation, along with the separation between ownership and management, are presented as the objective functions of managers on the basis of the manager's bonus. For instances, Jansen *et al.* [16] introduced the weighted sum of the firm's profit and its market share as the objective function of its manager, and Miller and Pazgal [17] and Miller and Pazgal [18] considered the weighted sum of the firm's profit and (the sum of) the profit(s) of its opponent firm(s).

REFERENCES

[1] K. Choi and Y. Lu, "A Note on Endogenous Timing with Strategic Delegation: Unilateral Externality Case," *Bulletin of Economic Research*, Vol. 64, No. 2, 1983, pp. 253-264.

[2] L. Cabral and W. R. Majure, "An Empirical Analysis of Bank Branching: Portugal 1989-1991," In: D. Neven and L.-H. Roller, Eds., *The Empirical Analysis of Industrial Organization*, CEPR, London, 1994.

[3] J. I. Bulow, J. D. Geanakoplos and P. D. Klemperer, "Holding Idle Capacity to Deter Entry," *Economic Journal*, Vol. 95, No. 377, 1985, pp. 178-182.

[4] J. I. Bulow, J. D. Geanakoplos and P. D. Klemperer, "Multimarket Oligopoly: Strategic Substitutes and Complements," *Journal of Political Economy*, Vol. 93, No. 3, 1985, pp. 488-511.

[5] M. M. Tombak, "Strategic Asymmetry," *Journal of Economic Behavior & Organization*, Vol. 61, No. 3, 2006, pp. 339-350.

[6] C. Fershtman and K. Judd, "Equilibrium Incentives in Oligopoly," *American Economic Review*, Vol. 77, No. 5, 1987, pp. 927-940.

[7] S. D. Sklivas, "The Strategic Choice of Management Incentives," *RAND Journal of Economics*, Vol. 18, No. 3, 1987, pp. 452-458.

[8] J. Vickers, "Delegation and the Theory of the Firm," *Economic Journal*, Vol. 95, No. 380a, 1985, pp. 138-147.

[9] X. Vives, "Commitment, Flexibility, and Market Outcomes," *International Journal of Industrial Organization*, Vol. 4, No. 2, 1986, pp. 217-229.

[10] H. Ogawa, "Capacity Choice in the Mixed Duopoly with Product Differentiation," *Economics Bulletin*, Vol. 12, No. 8, 2006, pp. 1-6.

[11] J. C. Bárcena-Ruiz and M. B. Garzón, "Capacity Choice in a Mixed Duopoly under Price Competition," *Economics Bulletin*, Vol. 12, No. 26, 2007, pp. 1-7.

[12] Y. Tomaru, Y. Nakamura and M. Saito, "Capacity Choice in a Mixed Duopoly with Managerial Delegation," *Economics Bulletin*, Vol. 29, No. 3, 2009, pp. 1904-1924.

[13] Y. Nakamura and M. Saito, "Capacity Choice in a Price-Setting Mixed Duopoly: The Relative Performance Approach," *Modern Economy*, Vol. 4, No. 4, 2013, pp. 273-280.

[14] Y. Nakamura and M. Saito, "Capacity Choice in a Mixed Duopoly: The Relative Performance Approach," *Theoretical Economics Letters*, Vol. 3, No. 2, 2013, pp. 124-133.

[15] Y. Nakamura, "Capacity Choice in a Price-Setting Mixed Duopoly with Network Effects," *Modern Economy*, Vol. 4, No. 5, 2013, pp. 418-425.

[16] T. Jansen, A. V. Lier and A. V. Witteloostruijn, "A Note on Strategic Delegation: The Market Share Case," *International Journal of Industrial Organization*, Vol. 25, No. 3, 2007, pp. 531-539.

[17] N. Miller and A. Pazgal, "The Equivalence of Price and Quantity Competition with Delegation," *RAND Journal of Economics*, Vol. 32, No. 2, 2001, pp. 284-301.

[18] N. Miller and A. Pazgal, "Relative Performance as a Strategic Commitment Mechanism," *Managerial and Decision Economics*, Vol. 23, No. 2, 2002, pp. 51-68.

Appendix

Equilibrium Outcomes in a Standard Quantity-Setting Competition with Differentiated Goods

In this appendix, we formulate a standard private quantity-setting competition with differentiated goods wherein firms 0 and 1 choose not only their output levels but also their capacity levels. It is assumed that the inverse demand functions of firms 0 and 1 are $p_0 = a - q_0 - bq_1$ and $p_1 = a - bq_0 - q_1$, respectively. Note that a and b denote the demand parameter and the degree of product differentiation, respectively. Moreover, similar to the setting on the cost functions of firms 0 and 1 in the main body of this paper, their cost functions are represented as $C_i(q_i; x_i) = mq_i + (q_i - x_i)^2$, $(i = 0,1)$. Then, in the standard quantity-setting competition without the price-raising effect, we obtain the following equilibrium quantities and capacity levels of firms 0 and 1:

$$q_i^* = \frac{(16-b^2)(a-m)}{32+16b-4b^2-b^3},$$
$$x_i^* = \frac{16(a-m)}{32+16b-4b^2-b^3},$$
$$i = 0,1.$$

Note that superscript * is used to denote the equilibrium market outcomes in the standard quantity-setting competition without the price-raising effect.

Then we obtain the following equilibrium differences between the quantities and capacity levels of firms 0 and 1:

$$q_i^* - x_i^* = -\frac{b^2(a-m)}{32+16b-4b^2-b^3} < 0,$$
$$\forall b \in (-1,0) \cup (0,1),$$
$$i = 0,1.$$

Thus, we find that in the standard quantity-setting competition with differentiated goods and without the price-raising effect, firms 0 and 1 both choose over-capacity irrespective of the relation between the products.

Equilibrium Outcomes in a Standard Price-Setting Competition with Differentiated Goods

Similar to the standard quantity-setting competition without the price-raising effect, in the price-setting competition without the price raising effect, we give the following equilibrium outcomes including the quantities and capacity levels of firms 0 and 1:

$$q_i^{**} = \frac{(16-9b^2+b^4)(a-m)}{32+16b-28b^2-9b^3+9b^4+b^5-b^6},$$
$$x_i^{**} = \frac{2(8-6b^2+b^4)(a-m)}{32+16b-28b^2-9b^3+9b^4+b^5-b^6},$$
$$i = 0,1.$$

Note that superscript ** is used to denote the equilibrium market outcomes in the standard quantity-setting competition without the price-raising effect.

Thus, we obtain the following equilibrium differences between the quantities and capacity levels of both firms:

$$q_i^{**} - x_i^{**} = \frac{b^2(3-b^2)(a-m)}{32+16b-28b^2-9b^3+9b^4+b^5-b^6} > 0,$$
$$\forall b \in (-1,0) \cup (0,1), i = 0,1.$$

Thus, in the standard price-setting competition without the price-raising effect, we find that both firms 0 and 1 choose under-capacity irrespective of the relation between the products.

Equilibrium Outcomes of Firms 0 and 1 in Quantity-Setting Competition

In this subsection, we give the equilibrium following market outcomes, including the equilibrium price levels and profits of both firms 0 and 1 in the quantity-setting competition with the price-raising effect as the unilateral externality:

$$p_0^q = \frac{2m(195+73\theta-11\theta^2-\theta^3)+a(169+273\theta+67\theta^2+3\theta^3)}{559+419\theta+45\theta^2+\theta^3}$$

$$p_1^q = \frac{a(13+3\theta)^2+m(390+341\theta+36\theta^2+\theta^3)}{559+419\theta+45\theta^2+\theta^3},$$

$$\Pi_0^q = \frac{2(a-m)^2(13+18\theta+\theta^2)^2(97+30\theta+\theta^2)}{(559+419\theta+45\theta^2+\theta^3)^2},$$

$$\Pi_1^q = \frac{2(a-m)^2(13+3\theta)^2(97+30\theta+\theta^2)}{(559+419\theta+45\theta^2+\theta^3)^2}.$$

Equilibrium Outcomes of Firms 0 and 1 in Price-Setting Competition

In this subsection, we give the equilibrium following market outcomes, including the equilibrium price levels and profits of both firms 0 and 1 in the price-setting competition with the price-raising effect as the unilateral externality:

$$p_0^p = \frac{m\left(64+184\theta+208\theta^2+77\theta^3-11\theta^4-9\theta^5-\theta^6\right)+2a\left(8+40\theta+76\theta^2+77\theta^3+43\theta^4+11\theta^5+\theta^6\right)}{80+264\theta+360\theta^2+231\theta^3+75\theta^4+13\theta^5+\theta^6},$$

$$p_1^p = \frac{a\left(4+6\theta+5\theta^2+\theta^3\right)^2+m\left(64+216\theta+284\theta^2+163\theta^3+38\theta^4+3\theta^5\right)}{80+264\theta+360\theta^2+231\theta^3+75\theta^4+13\theta^5+\theta^6},$$

$$\Pi_0^p = \frac{4(a-m)^2(1+\theta)^3\left(2+5\theta+\theta^2\right)^2\left(28+52\theta+37\theta^2+10\theta^3+\theta^4\right)}{\left(80+264\theta+360\theta^2+231\theta^3+75\theta^4+13\theta^5+\theta^6\right)^2},$$

$$\Pi_1^p = \frac{(a-m)^2\left(4+6\theta+5\theta^2+\theta^3\right)^2\left(28+80\theta+89\theta^2+47\theta^3+11\theta^4+\theta^5\right)}{\left(80+264\theta+360\theta^2+231\theta^3+75\theta^4+13\theta^5+\theta^6\right)^2}.$$

Irrelevance of Conjectural Variation in a Mixed Duopoly: The Case of Relative Performance and Consistent Conjectures*

Yasuhiko Nakamura
College of Economics, Nihon University, Chiyoda, Japan

ABSTRACT

This study explores the equilibrium outcomes in the contexts of quantity-setting and price-setting mixed duopolies with consistent conjectures of both the social welfare maximizing public firm and the relative profit maximizing private firm. Similar to the private duopoly composed of only relative profit maximizing firms, we show that in the mixed duopoly, the equilibrium outcomes in the quantity-setting competition with the consistent conjectures of both firms are equivalent to those in the price-setting competition with the consistent conjectures of both firms.

Keywords: Mixed duopoly; Relative Profit Maximization; Conjectural Variation; Consistent Conjecture *JEL Classification*: L20, L32, D43

1. Introduction

In the context of a mixed duopolistic market with the differentiated and substitutable goods, this study addresses the problem of whether or not the consistent conjectures of the public firm and the private firm yield the same equilibrium outcomes in a quantity-setting competition and a price-setting competition. The topic of conjectural variations in oligopolistic markets has been investigated for a long time; for example, Bresnahan [1], Perry [2], Boyer and Moreaux [3], Tanaka [4], and Tanaka [5] considered the influence of the conjectural variations of firms on the equilibrium market outcomes in several economic contexts.[1] More recently, in a private duopoly with linear demand functions and constant marginal cost functions which is composed of the two symmetric private firms, Tanaka [6] showed that firms' equilibrium output and the price levels in the Cournot equilibrium under their relative profit maximization are equal to their equilibrium output and prices in the Bertrand equilibrium under their relative profit maximization.[2] Furethermore, in a private duopoly wherein symmetric private firms maximize their relative profits, Tanaka [8] found that 1) their conjectural variations are irrelevant to the equilibrium outcome, and both their quantity setting behaviors and their price setting behaviors are equivalent to any of their conjectural variations; and 2) all the conjectural variations common to both the firms are consistent.

On the other hand, the relative profit approach has been adopted in many modern theoretical oligopolistic works. In the context of evolutionary economics `a la Schaffer [9], Vega-Redondo [10] found that each firm's adoption of its relative profit maximizing behavior yields the Walrasian equilibrium in the general equilibrium framework. Furthermore, Lundgren [11] presented a new economic method for preventing incentives for collusion by making managerial compensation which depends on relative profits rather than absolute profits. Kockesen, *et al.* [12] derived the condition that a firm with interdependent preferences (*i.e.*, the relative profit preference) obtains a strictly higher profit than an independent (*i.e.*, the absolute profit preference) firm in any equilibrium.

*We are grateful for the financial support from KAKENHI (25870113). All remaining errors are our own.

[1] In particular, Perry [2] showed that each firm's competitive conjecture is the unique consistent conjecture in a private duopoly with a homogeneous good and its constant marginal cost function.

[2] In addition, Tanaka [7] found that in a private duopoly with linear demand and constant marginal cost functions, when the two symmetric private firms maximize their relative profits, the choices of their strategic variables are irrelevant to the outcome of the game in the sense that the equilibrium outcomes are the same in all three types of market structure, and then any combination of choices of strategic variables by the firms comprises a subgame perfect equilibrium in the two stage game.

Most recently, Matsumura and Matsushima [13] investigated the relationship between the degree of competition and the stability of collusive behavior by introducing the element of relative performance to the objective functions of firms and showed that an increase in the degree of competition destabilizes collusion[3].

Given the importance of both the relative profit approach and conjectural variations in an oligopolistic market, the purpose of this paper is to ascertain whether or not the irrelevance result that the equilibrium market outcomes in the quantity-setting competition are equivalent to those in the price-setting competition in a mixed duopoly with differentiated and substitutable goods and with the consistent conjectural variations of both the social welfare-maximizing public firm and the relative profit-maximizing private firm. In this paper, by following Tanaka [8], we consider a mixed duopoly with linear demand functions and constant marginal cost functions. Under the above assumptions, we show that in a mixed duopoly with the consistent conjectures of both the social welfare-maximizing public firm and the relative profit maximizing private firm, the equilibrium market outcomes in the quantity-setting competition including their output and price levels, absolute profits, consumer surplus, and social welfare are the same as those in the price-setting competition[4]. Thus, in a mixed duopoly wherein it is possible for both the public firm and the private firm to react consistently its opponent firm's strategic variable, *i.e.*, price or output levels, we must refrain from making the shortsighted judgment that the price-setting competition should be used rather than the quantity-setting competition, and *vice versa.*

The remainder of this paper is organized as follows. In Section 2, we formulate the basic model employed in this paper. In Section 3, we derive the equilibrium outcomes in both the quantity-setting competition and the price-setting competition with differentiated and substitutable goods wherein the public and private firms consistently react to their respective opponent firm's strategic variable. Section 4 concludes with several remarks.

2. Model

We consider a mixed duopolistic market composed of one social welfare maximizing public firm (firm 0) and one relative profit-maximizing private firm (firm 1). We use q_i and p_i to represent firm i's output and price levels, respectively, (i = 0,1). We adopt the constant marginal cost function, which c is a common marginal cost between firms 0 and 1, similar to Tanaka [8].

In addition, we assume that firms 0 and 1 incur no fixed costs. We use δ_i^{qq} and δ_i^{pp} to denote firm i's consistent conjectural variation and we suppose that $-1 < \delta_i^{qq} < 1$ and $-1 < \delta_i^{pp} < 1$, (i = 0,1). On the basis of the assumption of Tanaka [8], we employ the following inverse demand function of the goods produced by firm i `a la Singh and Vives [16]:

$$p_i\left(q_i, q_j\right) = a - q_i - bq_i, \quad i, j = 0,1; i \neq j$$

where $a > c$, 0 and $0 < b < 1$[5]. This inverse demand function results from the following representative consumer's utility:

$$U\left(q_0, q_1\right) = a\left(q_0 + q_1\right) - \frac{q_0^2 + 2bq_0q_1 + q_1^2}{2} + m,$$

where m denotes the income of the representative consumer. Furthermore, the ordinary demand functions for the goods of firms 0 and 1 are obtained from the above inverse demand functions as follows:

$$q_i = \frac{a(1-b) - p_i + bp_j}{1-b^2}, \quad i, j = 0,1; i \neq j.$$

Consumer surplus is expressed as the representative consumer's utility as follows:
$CS = U\left(q_0, q_1\right) - p_0q_0 - p_1q_1$, whereas producer surplus is given by the sum of the profits of firms 0 and 1, $\pi_0 + \pi_1$. Finally, we suppose that social welfare W is defined as the sum of the consumer surplus and the producer surplus[6], implying that $W = CS + \left(\pi_0 + \pi_1\right)$.

3. Equilibrium Analysis

In this section, we derive the equilibrium outcomes with public firm 0 and private firm 1 in the contexts of both the quantity-setting competition and the price-setting competition with consistent conjectures for both firms.

3.1. Quantity-Setting Framework

In this subsection, we consider the situation wherein the

[3]Moreover, existing works using the relative performance approach in the context of a mixed duopoly with one welfare maximizing public firm and one relative profit-maximizing private firm include Nakamura and Saito [14], who investigated each firm's capacity choice in the quantity-setting competition, and Nakamura and Saito [15], who considered each firm's capacity choice in price-setting competition.

[4]In the model of this paper, this result is satisfied in the standard mixed duopoly wherein the private firm maximizes its absolute profit since we allow the case wherein the degree of importance of its relative performance is zero.

[5]The value of $b \in (0,1)$ indicates that the relation between the goods of firms 0 and 1 are substitutable. Moreover, the assumption that $a > c \geq 0$ is made in order to ensure the non-negativity of all equilibrium outcomes.

[6]Similar to Matsumura and Okamura [17], Nakamura and Saito [14], and Nakamura and Saito [15], we consider social welfare not as the sum of consumer surplus and the relative profits of firms 0 and 1 but as the sum of consumer surplus and the profits of firms 0 and 1. Firms' CEOs frequently emphasize the relative performance of their firms rather than the absolute performance of their firms since relatively good performance increases current and future income. However, we regard such an increase of income as a simple income transfer. For this reason, we suppose that the social welfare in this paper is equal to the sum of consumer surplus and the profits of firms 0 and 1.

strategic variables of firms 0 and 1 are their output levels. The objective functions of firms 0 and 1 are given as follows:

$$V_0^{qq}(q_0,q_1) = W(q_0,q_1) = a(q_0+q_1) - \frac{2cq_0 + q_0^2 + 2cq_1 + 2bq_0q_1 + q_1^2}{2} + m,$$

$$V_1^{qq}(q_0,q_1) = \pi_1(q_0,q_1) - \alpha\pi_0(q_0,q_1) = (a-c-bq_0-q_1)q_1 - q_0(a-c-q_0-bq_1)\alpha$$

where $\alpha \in [0,1)$ [7].

Firm 0 decides its output level in order to maximize V_0^{qq}, assuming that the reaction of the output level of firm 1 to the output level of firm 0 is given as follows:

$$\frac{\partial q_1}{\partial q_0} = \delta_0^{qq}.$$

On the other hand, firm 1 decides its output level in order to maximize V_1^{qq} 1 assuming that the reaction of the output level of firm 0 to the output level of firm 1 is given as follows:

$$\frac{\partial q_0}{\partial q_1} = \delta_1^{qq}.$$

The first-order conditions of firms 0 and 1 in the quantity-setting market competition are given, and their real reaction functions are obtained as follows:[8]

$$\frac{\partial V_0^{qq}}{\partial q_0} = a - c - q_0 - bq_1 + a\delta_0 - c\delta_0 - bq_0\delta_0 - q_1\delta_0 = 0$$

$$\Leftrightarrow q_0(q_1) = \frac{a(1+\delta_0) - c - c\delta_0 - bq_1 - q_1\delta_0}{1+b\delta_0},$$

$$\frac{\partial V_1^{qq}}{\partial q_1} = a - bq_0 - 2q_1 + bq_0\alpha - bq_1\delta_1 - a\alpha\delta_1 + 2q_0\alpha\delta_1 + bq_1\alpha\delta_1 - c(1-\alpha\delta_1) = 0$$

$$\Leftrightarrow q_1(q_0) = \frac{a(1-\alpha\delta_1) - c + c\alpha\delta_1 - q_0(b - b\alpha - 2\alpha\delta_1)}{2+b(1-\alpha)\delta_1}.$$

From the real reaction function of the output level of firm *i* to the output level of firm *j*, we obtain the following result $(i,j=0,1;i\neq j)$:

$$\frac{\partial q_0}{\partial q_1} = -\frac{b+\delta_0}{1+b\delta_0}, \text{ and } \frac{\partial q_1}{\partial q_0} = -\frac{b-b\alpha-2\alpha\delta_1}{2+b(1-\alpha)\delta_1}, \text{ respectively.}$$

The conditions of the consistency of the conjectural variations of firms 0 and 1 are, respectively,

$$\begin{cases} -(b+\delta_0)/(1+b\delta_0) = \delta_1, \\ -[b-b\alpha-2\alpha\delta_1]/[2+b(1-\alpha)\delta_1] = \delta_0, \end{cases}$$

yielding

$$\delta_0^{qq} = -\frac{b^2(1-\alpha)+2\left(1-\sqrt{1-b^2}\right)\alpha}{b\left(1+\sqrt{1-b^2}+\alpha-\sqrt{1-b^2}\,\alpha\right)},$$

$$\delta_1^{qq} = \frac{-1+\sqrt{1-b^2}}{b}.$$

The above values of firms 0 and 1 are the equilibrium consistent conjectures in the quantity-setting competition under the assumption that $\delta_0^{qq} \in (-1,1)$ and $\delta_1^{qq} \in (-1,1)$. Thus, the equilibrium output levels and price levels of firms 0 and 1 under the assumption that $\delta_0 = \delta_0^{qq}$ and $\delta_1 = \delta_1^{qq}$ are obtained as follows:

$$q_0^{qq} = \frac{(a-c)\left\{b^3(1-\alpha)+2b\left(1-\sqrt{1-b^2}\right)\alpha+4\left(1-\sqrt{1-b^2}\right)\alpha^2+b^2\left[2\left(1+\sqrt{1-b^2}\right)+3\left(1-\sqrt{1-b^2}\right)\alpha+\left(3-\sqrt{1-b^2}\right)\alpha^2\right]\right\}}{2(1+b)\left\{4\left(1-\sqrt{1-b^2}\right)\alpha^2+b^2(1-\alpha)\left[1+\sqrt{1-b^2}+\left(3-\sqrt{1-b^2}\right)\alpha\right]\right\}},$$

$$q_1^{qq} = \frac{(a-c)\left\{b^3(1-\alpha)\alpha+8\left(1-\sqrt{1-b^2}\right)\alpha^2+2b\left(1-\sqrt{1-b^2}\right)\alpha^2+b^2\left[1+\sqrt{1-b^2}+3\left(1-\sqrt{1-b^2}\right)\alpha-2\left(3-\sqrt{1-b^2}\right)\alpha^2\right]\right\}}{2(1+b)\left\{4\left(1-\sqrt{1-b^2}\right)\alpha^2+b^2(1-\alpha)\left[1+\sqrt{1-b^2}+\left(3-\sqrt{1-b^2}\right)\alpha\right]\right\}},$$

and

[7] As indicated in Matsumura and Matsushima [13], if we adopt the sales delegation approach in Fershtman and Judd [18], Sklivas [19], and Vickers [20] and replace each firm's sales with the (negative) profit of the opponent firm, as in their models, it would use a positive value of *α*. Moreover, for the technical reason that all equilibrium outcomes of firms 0 and 1 must be positive, throughout this paper, we adopt their common positive values of a following Matsumura and Matsushima [13], Nakamura and Saito [14], and Nakamura and Saito [15].

[8] The second-order conditions of firms 0 and 1 are satisfied.

$$p_0^{qq}=\frac{\begin{array}{l}\Big[a\Big[2b\big(-1+\sqrt{1-b^2}\big)\alpha+b^4(-1+\alpha)\alpha+4\big(1-\sqrt{1-b^2}\big)\alpha^2+b^3\big(\sqrt{1-b^2}+2\alpha-\sqrt{1-b^2}\alpha\big)\\ +b^2\alpha\big(1-\sqrt{1-b^2}-5\alpha+3\sqrt{1-b^2}\alpha\big)\Big]+c\Big(b^4(1-\alpha)\alpha+4\big(1-\sqrt{1-b^2}\big)\alpha^2+2b\big(1-\sqrt{1-b^2}\big)\alpha(1+4\alpha)\\ +b^2\Big[2\big(1+\sqrt{1-b^2}\big)+\alpha\big(3-3\sqrt{1-b^2}-\alpha-\sqrt{1-b^2}\alpha\big)\Big]+b^3\Big\{2+\sqrt{1-b^2}+\alpha\Big[2-3\sqrt{1-b^2}-2\big(3-\sqrt{1-b^2}\big)\alpha\Big]\Big\}\Big)\Big]\end{array}}{2(1+b)\Big\{4\big(1-\sqrt{1-b^2}\big)\alpha^2+b^2(1-\alpha)\Big[1+\sqrt{1-b^2}+\big(3-\sqrt{1-b^2}\big)\alpha\Big]\Big\}},$$

$$p_1^{qq}=\frac{\begin{array}{l}\Big(ab\Big\{b^3(-1+\alpha)+2\big(1-\sqrt{1-b^2}\big)\alpha^2-b^2\alpha\Big[\sqrt{1-b^2}+\big(2-\sqrt{1-b^2}\big)\alpha\Big]+b\Big[1+\sqrt{1-b^2}-\big(1-\sqrt{1-b^2}\big)\alpha\Big]\Big\}\\ +c\Big\{b^4(1-\alpha)+8\big(1-\sqrt{1-b^2}\big)\alpha^2+6b\big(1-\sqrt{1-b^2}\big)\alpha^2+b^3\Big[2\big(1+\sqrt{1-b^2}\big)+\big(4-3\sqrt{1-b^2}\big)\alpha-\big(4-\sqrt{1-b^2}\big)\alpha^2\Big]\\ +b^2\Big[1+\sqrt{1-b^2}+5\big(1-\sqrt{1-b^2}\big)\alpha-2\big(3-\sqrt{1-b^2}\big)\alpha^2\Big]\Big\}\Big)\end{array}}{2(1+b)\Big\{4\big(1-\sqrt{1-b^2}\big)\alpha^2+b^2(1-\alpha)\Big[1+\sqrt{1-b^2}+\big(3-\sqrt{1-b^2}\big)\alpha\Big]\Big\}}.$$

3.2. Price-Setting Framework

In this subsection, we consider the situation wherein the strategic variables of firms 0 and 1 are their price levels. The objective functions of firms 0 and 1 are given as follows:

$$V_0^{pp}(p_0,p_1)=W(p_0,p_1)=\frac{2a^2(1-b)-4a(1-b)c-p_0^2+2bp_0p_1-p_1^2+2(1-b)c(p_0+p_1)}{2(1-b^2)}+m,$$

$$V_1^{pp}(p_0,p_1)=\pi_1(p_0,p_1)-\alpha\pi_0(p_0,p_1)=\frac{(p_1-c)\big[a(1-b)+bp_0-p_1\big)-(p_0-c)\big[a(1-b)-p_0+bp_1\big]\alpha}{1-b^2}.$$

Firm 0 decides its price level in order to maximize V_0^{pp}, assuming that the reaction of the price level of firm 1 to the price level of firm 0 is given as follows:

$$\frac{\partial p_1}{\partial p_0}=\delta_0^{pp}.$$

On the other hand, firm 1 decides its price level in order to maximize V_1^{pp} assuming that the reaction of the price level of firm 0 to the price level of firm 1 is given as follows:

$$\frac{\partial p_0}{\partial p_1}=\delta_1^{pp}.$$

The first-order conditions of firms 0 and 1 in the price-setting competition are given, and their real reaction functions are obtained as follows:[9]

From the real reaction of the price level of firm i to the price level of firm j, we obtain the following result ($i, j =$

$$\frac{\partial V_0^{pp}}{\partial p_0}=-\frac{p_0-bp_0\delta_0-(1-b)c(1+\delta_0)-p_1(b-\delta_0)}{1-b^2}=0\Leftrightarrow p_0(p_1)=\frac{-p_0+bp_0\delta_0+(1-b)c(1+\delta_0)+p_1(b-\delta_0)}{1-b^2},$$

$$\frac{\partial V_1^{pp}}{\partial p_1}=\frac{a(1-b)+bp_0-p_1+(c-p_1)(1-b\delta_1)-\alpha\big[(a+c-2p_0)\delta_1-b(c-p_0+a\delta_1-p_1\delta_1)\big]}{1-b^2}=0$$

$$\Leftrightarrow p_1(p_0)=\frac{c(1+b\alpha-b\delta_1-\alpha\delta_1)+a(1-b)(1-\alpha\delta_1)+p_0(b-b\alpha+2\alpha\delta_1)}{2-b(1-\alpha)\delta_1}.$$

[9]The second-order conditions of firms 0 and 1 are satisfied.

0, 1; $i=j$):

$$\frac{\partial p_0}{\partial p_1}=\frac{b-\delta_0}{1-b\delta_0}, \text{ and } \frac{\partial p_1}{\partial p_0}=\frac{b-b\alpha+2\alpha\delta_1}{2-b(1-\alpha)\delta_1}, \text{ respectively.}$$

The conditions of the consistency of the conjectural variations of firms 0 and 1 are, respectively

$$\begin{cases}(b-\delta_0)/(1-b\delta_0)=\delta_1, \\ (b-b\alpha+2\alpha\delta_1)/\left[2-b(1+\alpha)\delta_1\right]=\delta_0,\end{cases}$$

yielding

$$\delta_0^{pp}=\frac{b^2(1-\alpha)+2\left(1+\sqrt{1-b^2}\right)\alpha}{b(1-\sqrt{1-b^2}+\alpha+\sqrt{1-b^2}\alpha}, \quad \delta_1^{pp}=\frac{1-\sqrt{1-b^2}}{b}.$$

The above values of firms 0 and 1 are the equilibrium consistent conjectures in the price-setting competition under the assumption that $\delta_0^{pp}\in(-1,1)$ and $\delta_1^{pp}\in(-1,1)$. Note that each firm's consistent conjectural variation in the price-setting competition is different from that in the quantity-setting competition.[10] Thus, the equilibrium price level and output level under the assumption that $\delta_0=\delta_0^{pp}$ and $\delta_1=\delta_1^{pp}$ are obtained as follows:

By summing up the equilibrium market outcomes and including the output and price levels of firms 0 and 1 between the quantity-setting competition and the price-setting competition, we obtain the following proposition:

$$p_0^{pp}=\frac{\begin{gathered}\Big[a\Big[2b\left(-1+\sqrt{1-b^2}\right)\alpha+b^4(-1+\alpha)\alpha+4\left(1-\sqrt{1-b^2}\right)\alpha^2+b^3\left(\sqrt{1-b^2}+2\alpha-\sqrt{1-b^2}\alpha\right) \\ +b^2\alpha\left(1-\sqrt{1-b^2}-5\alpha+3\sqrt{1-b^2}\alpha\right)\Big]+c\Big(b^4(1-\alpha)\alpha+4\left(1-\sqrt{1-b^2}\right)\alpha^2+2b\left(1-\sqrt{1-b^2}\right)\alpha(1+4\alpha) \\ +b^2\left[2\left(1+\sqrt{1-b^2}\right)+\alpha\left(3-3\sqrt{1-b^2}-\alpha-\sqrt{1-b^2}\alpha\right)\right]+b^3\left\{2+\sqrt{1-b^2}+\alpha\left[2-3\sqrt{1-b^2}-2\left(3-\sqrt{1-b^2}\right)\alpha\right]\right\}\Big)\Big]\end{gathered}}{2(1+b)\left\{4\left(1-\sqrt{1-b^2}\right)\alpha^2+b^2(1-\alpha)\left[1+\sqrt{1-b^2}+\left(3-\sqrt{1-b^2}\right)\alpha\right]\right\}},$$

$$p_1^{pp}=\frac{\begin{gathered}\Big(ab\Big\{b^3(-1+\alpha)+2\left(1-\sqrt{1-b^2}\right)\alpha^2-b^2\alpha\left[\sqrt{1-b^2}+\left(2-\sqrt{1-b^2}\right)\alpha\right]+b\left[1+\sqrt{1-b^2}-\left(1-\sqrt{1-b^2}\right)\alpha\right]\Big\} \\ +c\Big\{b^4(1-\alpha)+8\left(1-\sqrt{1-b^2}\right)\alpha^2+6b\left(1-\sqrt{1-b^2}\right)\alpha^2+b^3\left[2\left(1+\sqrt{1-b^2}\right)+\left(4-3\sqrt{1-b^2}\right)\alpha-\left(4-\sqrt{1-b^2}\right)\alpha^2\right] \\ +b^2\left[1+\sqrt{1-b^2}+5\left(1-\sqrt{1-b^2}\right)\alpha-2\left(3-\sqrt{1-b^2}\right)\alpha^2\right]\Big\}\Big)\end{gathered}}{2(1+b)\left\{4\left(1-\sqrt{1-b^2}\right)\alpha^2+b^2(1-\alpha)\left[1+\sqrt{1-b^2}+\left(3-\sqrt{1-b^2}\right)\alpha\right]\right\}},$$

and

$$q_0^{pp}=\frac{(a-c)\left\{b^3(1-\alpha)+2b\left(1-\sqrt{1-b^2}\right)\alpha+4\left(1-\sqrt{1-b^2}\right)\alpha^2+b^2\left[2\left(1+\sqrt{1-b^2}\right)+3\left(1-\sqrt{1-b^2}\right)\alpha+\left(3-\sqrt{1-b^2}\right)\alpha^2\right]\right\}}{2(1+b)\left\{4\left(1-\sqrt{1-b^2}\right)\alpha^2+b^2(1-\alpha)\left[1+\sqrt{1-b^2}+\left(3-\sqrt{1-b^2}\right)\alpha\right]\right\}},$$

$$q_1^{pp}=\frac{(a-c)\left\{b^3(1-\alpha)\alpha+8\left(1-\sqrt{1-b^2}\right)\alpha^2+2b\left(1-\sqrt{1-b^2}\right)\alpha^2+b^2\left[1+\sqrt{1-b^2}+3\left(1-\sqrt{1-b^2}\right)\alpha-2\left(3-\sqrt{1-b^2}\right)\alpha^2\right]\right\}}{2(1+b)\left\{4\left(1-\sqrt{1-b^2}\right)\alpha^2+b^2(1-\alpha)\left[1+\sqrt{1-b^2}+\left(3-\sqrt{1-b^2}\right)\alpha\right]\right\}}.$$

[10]As shown in Tanaka [8], in a private duopoly composed of two absolute profit maximizing firms, their consistent conjectural variations in the quantity-setting competition are different from those in the price-setting competition.

Proposition 1. In a mixed duopoly with the consistent conjectural variations of both the welfare maximizing public firm and the relative profit maximizing private firm, the equilibrium outcomes in the quantity-setting competition including output and price levels, profit, consumer surplus, and social welfare, are equivalent to those in the price-setting competition.

Note that the statement of Proposition 1 is relevant to a standard mixed duopoly composed of one social welfare maximizing public firm and one absolute profit maximizing private firm since it includes the case of $\alpha = 0$.

Thus, in a mixed duopoly with the consistent conjectural variations of both the welfare maximizing public firm and the relative profit maximizing private firm, we must pay attention to the fact that there is no advantage between the price-setting competition and the quantity-setting competition, since the equilibrium market outcomes in both the competitions are the same with each other.

4. Concluding Remarks

In this paper, we considered the equilibrium outcomes in a mixed duopoly with differentiated and substitutable goods and with firms' consistent conjectures, which are composed of one social welfare maximizing public firm and one relative profit maximizing private firm. Then, similar to the private duopolies composed of two absolute profit maximizing firms and of two relative profit maximizing firms shown in Tanaka [8], we show that the equilibrium outcomes in the quantity-setting competition are equivalent to those in the price-setting competition even in a mixed duopoly composed of one social welfare-maximizing public firm and one relative profit-maximizing private firm.

Finally, we indicate several topics that are left to our future studies. First, we must check whether or not the results obtained in this paper also hold given the assumptions of the general number of private firms and the general inverse and ordinary demand functions. Second, we should investigate the issue of capacity choice in a mixed duopoly with consistent conjectural variations, which is composed of one social welfare maximizing public firm and one relative profit maximizing private firm `a la Nakamura and Saito [14] and Nakamura and Saito [15]. These studies are left for future works.

REFERENCES

[1] T. Bresnahan, "Duopoly Models with Consistent Conjectures," *American Economic Review*, Vol. 71, No. 5, 1981, pp. 934-945.

[2] M. Perry, "Oligopoly and Consistent Conjectural Variations," *Bell Journal of Economics*, Vol. 13, No. 1, 1982, pp. 197-205.

[3] M. Boyer and M. Moreaux, "Consistent versus Non-Consistent Conjectures in Duopoly Theory: Some Examples," *Journal of Industrial Economics*, Vol. 32, No. 1, 1983, pp. 97-110.

[4] Y. Tanaka, "Consistent Conjectures in Free Entry Oligopoly," *Economics Letters*, Vol. 17, No. 1-2, 1985, pp. 15-18.

[5] Y. Tanaka, "On Multiplicity of Consistent Conjectures in Free Entry Oligopoly," *Economics Letters*, Vol. 28, No. 2, 1985, pp. 109-115.

[6] Y. Tanaka, "Equivalance of Cournot and Bertrand Equilibria in Differentiated Duopoly under Relative Profit Maximization with Linear Demand," *Economics Bulletin*, Vol. 33, No. 2, 2013a, pp. 1479-1486.

[7] Y. Tanaka, "Irrelevance of the Choice of Strategic Variables in Duopoly under Relative Profit Maximization," *Economics and Business Letters*, Vol. 2, No. 2, 2013b, pp. 75-83.

[8] Y. Tanaka, "Irrelevance of Conjectural Variation in Duopoly under Relative Profit Maximization and Consistent Conjectures," 2013c (mimeo).

[9] M. E. Schaffer, "Are Profit Maximizers the Best Survivors?" *Journal of Economic Behavior and Organization*, Vol. 12, No. 1, 1989, pp. 29-45.

[10] F. Vega-Redondo, "The Evolution of Walrasian Behavior," *Econometrica*, Vol. 65 No. 2, 1997, pp. 375-384.

[11] C. Lundgren, "Using Relative Profit Incentives to Prevent Collusion," *Review of Industrial Organization*, Vol. 11, No. 4, 1996, pp. 533-550.

[12] L. Kockesen, E. A. Ok and R. Sethi, "The Strategic Advantage of Negatively Interdependent Preferences," *Journal of Economic Theory*, Vol. 92, No. 2, 2000, pp. 274-299.

[13] T. Matsumura and N. Matsushima, "Competitiveness and Stability of Collusive Behavior," *Bulletin of Economic Research*, Vol. 64, Suppl. S1, 2012, pp. 22-31.

[14] Y. Nakamura and M. Saito, "Capacity Choice in a Mixed Duopoly: The Relative Performance Approach," *Theoretical Economics Letters*, Vol. 3, No. 2, 2013a, pp. 124-133.

[15] Y. Nakamura and M. Saito, "Capacity Choice in a Price-Setting Mixed Duopoly: The Relative Performance Approach," *Modern Economy*, Vol. 4, No. 4, 2013b, pp. 273-280.

[16] N. Singh and X. Vives, "Price and Quantity Competition in a Differentiated Duopoly," *RAND Journal of Economics*, Vol. 15, No. 4, 1984, pp. 546-554.

[17] T. Matsumura and M. Okamura, "Competition and Privatization Policy: The Relative Performance Approach," 2010 (mimeo).

[18] C. Fershtman and K. Judd, "Equilibrium Incentives in Oligopoly," *American Economic Review*, Vol. 77, No. 5, 1987, pp. 927-940.

[19] S. D. Sklivas, "The Strategic Choice of Managerial In-

centives," *RAND Journal of Economics*, Vol. 18, No. 3, 1987, pp. 452-458.

[20] J. Vickers, "Delegation and the Theory of the Firm," *Economic Journal*, Vol. 95, No. 380, 1985, pp. 138-147.

17

What Is the Natural Weight of the Current Old?*

Damien Gaumont[1#], Daniel Leonard[2]
[1]Pantheon-Assas, Sorbonne Universities, ERMES EAC 7181 CNRS, CRED, Institute for Labor Studies and Public Policies, Paris, France
[2]Flinders Business School, Flinders University, Adelaide, Australia

ABSTRACT

We consider a simple overlapping generations model with an externality à la Arrow-Romer [1,2] and a government with fiscal powers. If it wishes to maximize a criterion depending on the lifelong utility of agents, is there a natural weight for the utility of the current old? We show in a simple example that this weight depends on the specific features of the model, in particular the length of the horizon, and cannot be chosen arbitrarily. Our result has a neat economic interpretation [2].

Keywords: Overlapping Generations Model; Learning-by-Doing; Social Welfare

1. Introduction

The overlapping generations model of Allais [3], Samuelson [4,5] and Diamond [6] is ideally suited to the exploration of inter-generational issues. For a more recent and thorough presentation of these models, see the classic reference: De la Croix and Michel [7].

Most models assume that agents live for two periods; the training of the young may or may not be explicitly modeled. Steady states, temporary equilibria and intertemporal equilibria are studied and a role for government intervention appears naturally if market imperfections such as externalities are present. Public finance issues can also be considered.

As it is assumed that agents live for two periods, an objective measure of time is inherent to the model. Thus the length of one period can be taken to be around 30 years. This observation has deep consequences for the interpretation of policy recommendations.

The traditional approach of the literature on overlapping generations models has been to consider the welfare of all generations from the present onward (De La Croix and Michel [7], pp. 91-93). In such models, and with a separable utility function, the planner's criterion is

$$W_{\infty} = \sum_{t=0}^{\infty} \gamma^{t} \left(u(c_t) + \frac{\beta}{\gamma} u(d_t) \right),$$

where c_t and d_t refer to the consumption of young and old in period t respectively; β is their subjective rate of time preference and γ is the planner's social discount rate.

Economics is a moral science. Welfare economics should be a central part of the discipline (Atkinson [8], p. 192). Since there is usually more than one adult generation at any on time, one may reasonably ask—whose welfare function is it? Are we saying to 50-year-old that their welfare is judged by their 75-year-old parents? Or the reverse? If the reverse, when does the baton pass? The uneasiness surrounding this construction is apparent when we consider the issue of the rate at which future utility is discounted[1] (see Atkinson [7], p. 195). Bernheim [9] also mentions that many of the usual concepts of welfare are difficult to implement, since the concerned individuals do not necessarily have the opportunity to vote for them.

Here, our argument is that if government intervention is warranted, the proposed policies should be acceptable to people who are alive at the time. Policies that optimize over the very long run but lower the welfare of the current generations—compared with the status quo of no intervention at all—have little chance of being adopted. Hu [10] (p. 283) was well aware of this point. To sharpen

*We are grateful to Russell Davidson and participants of the economics seminar at McGill University.
#Corresponding author.

[1]Note that Atkinson [8] is talking here about the discount rate applied to utility, not to the rate at which future consumption is discounted, which takes account of differences in how well-off future generations will be.

our argument, we use the simplest criterion that reflects this notion, namely the lifelong utility of people alive in period 0[2]. (The welfare function can be made to include more generations as we discuss later.) In the usual notation, it is

$$W_1 = \frac{\beta}{\gamma} u(d_0) + u(c_0) + \beta u(d_1),$$

where β and γ are exogenous parameters.

The purpose of this note is to show that, when a specific horizon is adopted, there is a natural endogenous value for β/γ (which we denote by η for simplicity of notation) that is consistent with efficient government intervention and cannot be arbitrary, contrary to the traditional approach of letting both β and γ be exogenous. *Other horizons produce different specific results but the main conclusion remains the same*: η *cannot be chosen arbitrarily*.

We begin with a standard Diamond-like model with an externality of the learning-by-doing type (Arrow [1], Sheshinski [11] and Romer [2]). The external effect is that the aggregate stock of capital has a beneficial effect on the efficiency of production by each firm. It can be internalized through government intervention in the form of fiscal policies that subsidize capital investment and are financed by a tax on labor.

2. The Individuals

Individuals live for two periods: in the first period they consume, save and inelastically supply one unit of labor. In the second period they live off the revenue from their savings. There is no population growth, $L_t = L, \forall t$ The consumptions of young and old in period t are, respectively, c_t and d_t; s_t is savings; θ_t is the rate of tax on wage income w_t; $(1-\theta_t)w_t$ is the net wage rate and R_t is the rent of capital. The individual's subjective discount factor is $\beta < 1$. An individual born in period t solves the following program:

$$\max_{c_t, d_{t+1}} u(c_t) + \beta u(d_{t+1})$$

$$c_t + s_t = (1-\theta_t) w_t$$

$$d_{t+1} = R_{t+1} s_t$$

The optimality condition is

$$u'(c_t) = \beta u'(d_{t+1}). \quad (1)$$

3. The Firm

The production function exhibits constant returns to scale to the factors hired by the firm but there is an externality. The firm hires l_t units of labor and produces q_t units of good with k_t units of capital; $B(K_t)$ is a productivity factor that represents the externality where K_t is the aggregate stock of capital; however the firm is unaware of the structure of this productivity factor.

$$q_t = B(K_t) F(k_t, l_t),$$

where $F(.,.)$ is homogeneous of degree one; therefore

$$q_t = l_t B(K_t) F(k_t / l_t, 1).$$

Normalizing the size of the firm at $l_t = 1$, we have, in the usual notation:

$$\begin{aligned} q_t &= B(K_t) f(k_t) \\ &= B(Lk_t) f(k_t), \end{aligned} \quad (2)$$

The firm maximizes profit

$$\begin{aligned} \pi(k_t) &= B(Lk_t) f(k_t) \\ &\quad - w_t - (R_t - \tau_t) k_t, \end{aligned}$$

where τ_t is a government subsidy designed to internalize the externality. Therefore

$$R_t = \tau_t + B(Lk_t) f'(k_t), \quad (3)$$

$$w_t = B(Lk_t)\left[f(k_t) - f'(k_t) k_t\right]. \quad (4)$$

An informed government that wishes to internalize the externality in each period t would choose the efficient subsidy as

$$\tau_t = LB'(Lk_t) f(k_t),$$

in order to account for the role capital plays in enhancing overall productivity.

Capital depreciates entirely in one period, hence the dynamics of the economy are given by

$$k_{t+1} = s_t.$$

4. The Government

The government is responsible for implementing the planner's policies and has fiscal authority. The government balances its budget in each period, thus the constraint on its fiscal policy (θ_t, τ_t) is,

$$\theta_t w_t = \tau_t k_t, \quad (5)$$

where θ_t is the rate of payroll tax and τ_t is the subsidy to capital. Therefore we shall be able to express one of the tax/subsidy parameters in terms of the other. Together the wage rate equation, the efficient subsidy and the budget constraint in period t yield an expression for the payroll tax θ_t.

$$\begin{aligned} \theta_t w_t &= \theta_t B(Lk_t)\left[f(k_t) - f'(k_t) k_t\right] = \tau_t k_t \\ &= LB'(Lk_t) f(k_t) k_t, \end{aligned}$$

[2]The utility of the young born in period -1 (hence those who are old in period 0) can be included, but treated as exogenous, therefore it is irrelevant. See for instance De la Croix and Michel [7], p. 91.

$$\theta_t = \frac{LB'(Lk_t) f(k_t) k_t}{B(Lk_t)\left[f(k_t) - f'(k_t) k_t\right]} = \frac{K_t B'(K_t)}{B(K_t)} \frac{1}{1 - f'(k_t) k_t / f(k_t)}. \qquad (6)$$

This expression for θ_t can be interpreted as follows. It is the ratio of the elasticity of the externality factor with respect to aggregate capital over 1 minus the elasticity of the firm's output with respect to its capital stock. Clearly, with a general CRS production-function and an arbitrary externality effect, this ratio depends on current capital stock and varies over time. The dynamic path of θ_t is nonetheless constrained.

At this stage we must emphasize the following point in order to show the essential nature of our argument: The logic consequence of three elements, a competitive wage, an efficient capital subsidy and a balanced budget in every period, by itself determines the dynamic structure of fiscal policies. This is done without any reference to the planner's objective.

In this extensive literature (Samuelson, [4,5], Lerner, [12,13], De La Croix and Michel, [7]) the criterion is often an infinite horizon welfare function or sometimes, more simply, the steady state outcome. These views have the advantage of supplying clear answers to real problems in an abstract world. However, steady state criteria and infinite horizon optimal paths suffer from an implementation problem, namely that policies designed to maximize such criteria may entail losses of utility for several generations, including those alive at the time of planning (See Gaumont& Leonard, [14], for some compelling evidence). We argue that such policies stand little chance of being implemented *and therefore we look for a more feasible criterion.*

Here we assume that the government objective is simply to maximize the lifelong utility of people who are alive at the time (see footnote 2). Therefore, it takes into account the utility of the old and young in period zero, plus the utility of those who will be old in period one. In the traditional formulation the exogenous weight of the old is $\eta \equiv \beta/\gamma$, the ratio of the subjective rate of time preference of households and the planner's social discount factor. Our purpose is to show that, for the optimal choice of θ_t to be consistent with an efficient fiscal policy, the weight of the current old must take on a natural value that depends on the specific features of the model and the length of the horizon.

In order to make our argument simple and concise we show by counterexample that the value of η cannot be exogenous, even in a very standard version of the model.

5. A Simple Case

We use a logarithmic utility and a Cobb-Douglas production with $B(K_t) = K_t^{\sigma}$ where $0 < \sigma < 1$ measures the strength of the externality[3]. Therefore conditions (1), (2), (3), and (4) become, respectively,

$$d_{t+1} = \beta R_{t+1} c_t,$$

$$q_t = L^{\sigma} k_t^{\sigma} k_t^{\alpha},$$

$$R_t = \tau_t + \alpha L^{\sigma} k_t^{\sigma+\alpha-1},$$

$$w_t = (1-\alpha) L^{\sigma} k_t^{\sigma+\alpha}.$$

We use (5) to eliminate τ_t from our calculations and obtain

$$d_0 = \left[\alpha + (1-\alpha)\theta_0\right] L^{\sigma} k_0^{\sigma+\alpha}, \qquad (7)$$

$$c_0 = \frac{1-\alpha}{1+\beta}(1-\theta_0) L^{\sigma} k_0^{\sigma+\alpha},$$

$$d_1 = \beta R_1 c_0,$$

$$d_1 = \frac{\beta R_1}{1+\beta}(1-\theta_0)(1-\alpha) L^{\sigma} k_0^{\sigma+\alpha},$$

with

$$R_1 = \left[\alpha + (1-\alpha)\theta_1\right] \cdot L^{\sigma} \left[\frac{\beta}{1+\beta}(1-\theta_0)(1-\alpha) L^{\sigma} k_0^{\sigma+\alpha}\right]^{\alpha+\sigma-1} \qquad (8)$$

The planner's objective is to maximize a welfare function that incorporates the utility of the current old and the lifetime utility of the current young,

$$W = \eta \ln d_0 + \ln c_0 + \beta \ln d_1 \qquad (9)$$

where η is, for the time being, treated as exogenous.

For the chosen production function the equation that dictates the dynamicstructure of fiscal policies (6) simplifies to

$$\theta_t = \frac{\sigma}{1-\sigma} \equiv \theta., \qquad (10)$$

Therefore in this specific model an efficient θ_t is constant over time. This is because the two elasticities are constant due to the Cobb-Douglas production function and the power function form of the externality factor. *This is so, irrespective of the planner's choice of welfare function*[4].

Turning now to the planner's choice of an optimal fiscal policy to characterize the θ value that maximizes (9) and using the solved consumption Equations (7) and (8), the first-order condition is:

[3]This is a very simplified version of Gaumont and Leonard [14], which addresses the question of knowledge transmission among generations.

[4]Note that this is a convenient result as it guarantees inter-temporal consistency, were the planner to redo this exercise in the next period and thereafter.

$$\frac{(\beta+\eta)(1-\alpha)}{\alpha+(1-\alpha)\theta}=\frac{1+\beta(\sigma+\alpha)}{1-\theta}.$$

Therefore the welfare-maximizing θ value is

$$\theta^*=\frac{\beta[1-\alpha(1+\alpha+\sigma)]-\alpha(1+\eta)}{(1-\alpha)[1+\beta(\alpha+\sigma)+\beta+\eta]}. \quad (11)$$

This welfare-maximizing tax depends on the values of the parameters of the problem, including the weight of the old generation, η, which has so far been treated as exogenous. Given θ^*, all the consumption variables can be calculated and a complete solution obtained.

Finally, combining the dynamic fiscal structure (10) and the planner's choice of policy (11) we find that there is only one value of η that is consistent with both. It is therefore endogenous to the model and depends, among other things, on the strength of the externality, σ. We denote it by η_σ:

$$\eta_\sigma=\frac{(\alpha+\sigma)(1+(\alpha+\sigma)\beta)}{1-\alpha-\sigma}-\beta. \quad (12)$$

We insist that our argument does not depend on the existence of an externality, although it can accommodate it. In order to make our point sharper, we now look at the special case of no externality when there is no need for government intervention as (10) makes clear, and the natural η value is

$$\eta_0=\frac{\alpha(1+\alpha\beta)}{1-\alpha}\beta. \quad (13)$$

The expression in (13) is always less than 1 for sensible values of $\alpha\in[0,1/2]$. There is a similar result for (12) but $\alpha+\sigma\in[0,1/2]$ cannot be assumed.

Proposition: *The natural weight of the current old cannot be exogenous but depends on the specific features of the model (including the length of the planning horizon).*

With discount rates of 1% - 2% p.a. compounded over a generation and a capital share of around 1/3, the values of η_0 are around 10%. When, and if, there is an externality, $\sigma>0$, a government that wishes to optimize (9) and impose an efficient tax/subsidy scheme in a competitive economy must choose a weight for the old of the current generation as given by (12). This weight, and only this weight, will insure that welfare is maximized and that the tax/subsidy scheme is efficient.

When there is no externality, there is no role for government, tax or subsidy. Therefore, η_0—which is the only weight consistent with no taxes—is the weight which the central planner must give to the current old if its plans are to coincide with the competitive outcome. The value of η (or, equivalently γ) cannot be determined exogenously.

This makes clear the meaning of our result in the simplest terms: a short-term horizon, coupled with an efficient tax/subsidy fiscal policy, cannot use an arbitrary exogenous weight for the old generation.

The expressions in (12) and (13) clearly depend on the features of the model as well as on the length of the horizon selected by the government. Possible extensions and alternatives have been explored. Additional calculations using (12), and in the simplest case(13), shows that the natural value of η can vary enormously. Cases when W also includes terms such as $\ln(c_1)$ and $\ln(d_2)$ yield more complicated expressions. Another type of production function such as $q_t=Ak_t+B_tl_t$, with $B_t=L^\sigma k_t^\sigma$ also yields simple results. A model with a different production function might require more complex calculations but the constraint on the dynamic structure of θ_t given by (6) would still need to be accommodated with the optimal choice of θ_t.

6. Conclusion

In a simple two-period overlapping generations model with an externality (*à la* Arrow-Romer [1,2]), when the government has the power to tax the wage of the young, we have shown that the "natural" value of the weight of the current old—the value of the weight that reconciles the maximization of the chosen welfare function with the use of the efficient externality-correcting fiscal policy—is endogenous to the model and depends on the strength of the externality as well as on the government's chosen criterion. It is also true when the external effects are non-existent. It is not possible to choose both the subjective rate of time preference of households and the planner's social discount factor arbitrarily. The choice of the value of the weight of the current old crucially depends on the length of the social planner's horizon.

REFERENCES

[1] K. Arrow, "The Economic Implications of Learning-by-Doing," *Review of Economic Studies*, Vol. 29, 1962, pp. 155-173.

[2] P. Romer, "Increasing Returns and Long Run Growth," *Journal of Political Economy*, Vol. 94, No. 5, 1986, pp. 1002-1037.

[3] M. Allais, "EconomieetIntérêt," Imprimerie Nationale, Paris, 1947.

[4] P. A. Samuelson, "An Exact Consumption-Loan Model of Interest with or without the Social Contrivance of Money," *Journal of Political Economy*, Vol. 66, No. 6, 1958, pp. 467-482.

[5] P. A. Samuelson, "Reply," *Journal of Political Economy*, Vol. 67, No. 5, 1959, pp. 518-522.

[6] P. Diamond, "National Debt in Neoclassical Growth

Models," *American Economic Review*, Vol. 55, No. 5, 1965, pp. 1126-1150.

[7] D. De La Croix and Ph. Michel, "A Theory of Economic Growth: Dynamics and Policy in Overlapping Generations," Cambridge University Press, Cambridge, 2002.

[8] A. B. Atkinson "Economics as a Moral Science," *Economica*, Vol. 76, No. 304, 2009, pp. 791-804.

[9] B. D. Bernheim, "Behavioral Welfare Economics," *Journal of the European Economic Association*, Vol. 7, No. 2-3, 2009, pp. 267-319.

[10] S. C. Hu, "Social Security, the Supply of Labor and Capital Accumulation," *American Economic Review*, Vol. 69, No. 3, 1979, pp. 274-284.

[11] E. Sheshinski, "Test of the Learning by Doing Hypothesis," *The Review of Economics and Statistics*, Vol. 49, No. 4, 1967, pp. 568-678.

[12] A. Lerner, "Consumption-Loan Interest and Money," *Journal of Political Economy*, Vol. 67, No. 5, 1959, pp. 512-518.

[13] A. Lerner, "Consumption-Loan Interest and Money: Rejoinder," *Journal of Political Economy*, Vol. 67, No. 5, 1959, pp. 523-524.

[14] D. Gaumont and D. Leonard, "Human Capital, Externalities and Growth in an Overlapping Generations Model," *Research in Economics*, Vol. 60, No. 3, 2010, pp. 186-200.

18

A Generalization of Berry's Probability Function

André de Palma[1], Soumyanetra Munshi[2]
[1]Economics and Management Department, ENS Cachan, France and KU Leuven, Belgium
[2]Economics and Social Science Area, Indian Institute of Management Bangalore (IIMB), Bangalore, India

ABSTRACT

In a multi-prize contest, we consider the space of all outcomes and define a probability on it by hypothesizing the probability of an outcome to depend on resources expended by all the players. In this probability space, we then derive the probability of an individual player winning. It turns out that this probability is a generalized Berry (1993) probability function. Specifically, when 0 weight is attached to the resources spent by the "unsuccessful players" (losers), the probability of winning of an individual player is proposed exactly by Berry (1993). Such a formulation also helps to alleviate charges against the probability function of Berry levied by Clark and Riis (1996) in the context of sequential distribution of prizes since prizes by our very hypothesis, are awarded simultaneously.

Keywords: Probability Function in Multi-Prize Contests; Generalization of Tullock's Contest Success Function

1. Introduction

Berry [1] analyses a rent-seeking model with multiple prizes/winners. By doing so, he generalizes Tullock's contest success function (the technology or function that translates a player's expended resources into his probability of winning) for one prize to the probability of winning in a multi-prize situation. If there are n players and k (denoted as $\bar{n}$ in this note) many prizes, then Berry postulates that "the probability that firms 'n' wins is dependent upon its rent-seeking expenditures *in combination* with the expenditures of all other possible combinations of '$k-1$' firms (out of 'n' firms) divided by the combinations of all *possible* 'k' firms' expenditures." (p. 438).

The main gap in Berry's analysis is that it starts directly by postulating the probability of an "event" (that a player wins a prize) without specifying the set of "outcomes" (where an outcome means the distribution of the limited number of prizes among the competing players. See section II for a mathematical definition) and the corresponding probabilities, which is necessary for a mathematical formulation of the problem. Clark and Riis [2] criticize the ad hoc-ness of Berry's approach from a different perspective (see below) and they also miss to lay down the underlying probability space of Berry's model. This paper resolves this issue completely and proposes a concrete probabilistic foundation of Berry's approach.

Clark and Riis [2] note that Berry's probability of winning function is a valid probability function (though not deriving it from the underlying probability space) but they criticize it on the ground that it implies an "unreasonable selection process" of the winners in which "rent-seeking outlays affect only the distribution of the first prize; after this is awarded, rent-seeking outlays are forgotten and each player has an equal probability of winning" (p. 179). But their criticism holds only when the process perceived is one where the announcement of outlays by the players is *simultaneous* while the distribution of prizes is *sequential* (like the distribution of quotas by the government, or the promotion of several workers. See Clark and Riis [3]).

However, often the process in contests can be perceived to be one of not only simultaneous announcements of efforts but also *simultaneous distribution of prizes*. Examples include occupying seats in a congested transport vehicle by passengers, getting admitted to limited number of seats in elite educational institutions, or getting housing allotments in the regulated housing market. (Keeping these examples in mind, we use the terms "resources", "expenditures" and "efforts" interchangeably, in the sense of outlays expended by the players participating in the contest.) Our probability space, by the very way it is defined, is more amenable to model such simultaneous distribution of prizes and since we can derive Berry's formulation from it, our model can dispel Clark and Riis' criticism leveled against it (see especially footnote 1).

We start from the space of all possible outcomes and make the following plausible hypothesis: let the probability of an outcome depend on the (weighted) sum of efforts of all the players. In the resulting probability space, we derive the probability of success (winning a prize) for an individual player (which is in contrast to both Berry [1] and Cark and Riis [2], who start from the probability of winning of individual players).

We find that if the efforts of the unsuccessful players are weighed equally like those of the successful players, then we end up with an *equal probability model* where each player has an equal chance of winning, irrespective of their expended resources. On the other hand, if the resources expended by the unsuccessful players receive no weight at all (that is 0 weight) in bringing about a realized outcome (that is the probability of the outcome depends only on the resources expended by the successful players), then the resulting probability of winning of an individual player turns out exactly to be *Berry's formulation.* Thus, in particular, our model generalizes Berry's probability function.

The next section begins from the probability space and derives a probability function by postulating a plausible hypothesis (Assumption 1) for the probability of outcomes, and demonstrates that Berry's formula can be derived from it as a special case.

2. The Model

Let there be *n* players and $\bar{n} < n$, many prizes. The set of all possible outcomes can be represented by the collection of vectors

$$\Omega := \left\{ \nu = \left(\varepsilon_1(\nu), \cdots, \varepsilon_n(\nu)\right) \in \{0,1\}^n : \sum_{i=1}^{n} \varepsilon_i(\nu) = \bar{n} \right\}. \tag{1}$$

here $\varepsilon_i(\nu) = 1$ means that in the outcome ν the *i*-th person is successful in winning a prize, and otherwise $\varepsilon_i(\nu) = 0$. The restriction $\sum_{i=1}^{n} \varepsilon_i(\nu) = \bar{n}$ reflects the fact that in any outcome all prizes are taken. Also note that the number of different outcomes[1] in the space is given by

$$|\Omega| = \binom{n}{\bar{n}} = \frac{n!}{\bar{n}!(n-\bar{n})!}.$$

A probability on the space Ω is given by a collection P of non-negative real numbers p_ν allotted to each outcomes $\nu \in \Omega$, satisfying the two conditions

$$p_\nu \geq 0, \quad \text{and} \quad \sum_{\nu\in\Omega} p_\nu = 1.$$

The pair (Ω, P) is said to form a probability space.

The question we are asking is the following: Can we have a probability space (on the sample space Ω given above) such that the probability of any outcome reflects the collective effort of the mode of the outcome (the way the outcome comes about)? To answer the question, let us hypothesize the following:

Assumption 1. Let probability p_ν be proportional to the weighted sum of the efforts of all the competing players. That is,

$$p_\nu \propto \left[\sum_{i=1}^{n} \varepsilon_i(\nu) e_i + \lambda \sum_{i=1}^{n} \left(1 - \varepsilon_i(\nu)\right) e_i \right] \tag{2}$$

where e_i be the effort exerted by the i th player to obtain a prize out of $\bar{n}$ available units, with $\bar{n} \leq n$, $i = 1, \cdots, n$, and $0 \leq \lambda \leq 1$ is the weight attached to the efforts of the players who are not successful in winning any prize.

This assumption means that there exists a positive constant (not depending on the outcome) K such that

$$p_\nu = K \left[\sum_{i=1}^{n} \varepsilon_i(\nu) e_i + \lambda \sum_{i=1}^{n} \left(1 - \varepsilon_i(\nu)\right) e_i \right].$$

The following proposition lays down the value of K, the probability of an outcome, p_ν, and the probability of "success" for player *i*, $\Pr\{\varepsilon_i = 1\}$:

Proposition 1. Consider the probability space given by (1). Then, under Assumption (1), the probability of outcome ν is given by

$$p_\nu = K \left[\sum_{i=1}^{n} \varepsilon_i(\nu) e_i + \lambda \sum_{i=1}^{n} \left(1 - \varepsilon_i(\nu)\right) e_i \right], \tag{3}$$

where the constant of proportionality K is given by

$$K = \frac{1}{\dfrac{(n-1)!}{(\bar{n}-1)!(n-\bar{n})!} \left(\dfrac{\bar{n} + \lambda(n-\bar{n})}{\bar{n}} \right) \sum_{i=1}^{n} e_i}. \tag{4}$$

Moreover, the probability of success for player *i* is:

$$\Pr\{\varepsilon_i = 1\} = \frac{\bar{n}\left(\bar{n} - 1 + \lambda(n-\bar{n})\right)}{(n-1)\left(\bar{n} + \lambda(n-\bar{n})\right)} + \frac{e_i}{\sum_j e_j} \frac{(n-\bar{n})}{(n-1)} \frac{\bar{n}(1-\lambda)}{\left(\bar{n} + \lambda(n-\bar{n})\right)}. \tag{5}$$

Proof. **Derivation of** ***K*:** The derivation of the constant

[1]Note that in any particular outcome, we have $\bar{n}$ many one's and $(n-\bar{n})$ many zeroes in a certain order, but the one's (or the zeroes) are unordered among themselves. Hence the situation depicts $\bar{n}$ prizes awarded simultaneously. In contrast, if we had sequential distribution of prizes, then the set of outcomes would be given by

$$\Omega_{seq} := \left\{ \nu = \left(\theta_1(\nu), \cdots, \theta_n(\nu)\right) \right\}$$

where $\theta_i(\nu) = 0$ means the *i*-th player is unsuccessful whereas $\theta_i(\nu) = j$ means the *i*-th player has won the *j*-th prize, $j = 1, \cdots, \bar{n}$, in the outcome ν. That is, Ω_{seq} is the set of all possible permutations of $(1, 2, \cdots, \bar{n}, 0, \cdots, 0)$.

of proportionality K is as follows: The non-negativity of p_v just means that K has to be non-negative (as the efforts $e_i \geq 0$). The second criterion is satisfied if and only if

$$1=\sum_{v\in\Omega} p_v=\sum_{v\in\Omega}\left[K\left[\sum_{i=1}^{n}\varepsilon_i(v)e_i+\lambda\sum_{i=1}^{n}(1-\varepsilon_i(v))e_i\right]\right].$$

Since K is an absolute constant and not depending i or v we can take it out of the summations to get

$$1=K\sum_{v\in\Omega}\left[\sum_{i=1}^{n}\varepsilon_i(v)e_i+\lambda\sum_{i=1}^{n}(1-\varepsilon_i(v))e_i\right].$$

Next we interchange the order of summations

$$1=K\left\{\left[\sum_{i=1}^{n}\sum_{v\in\Omega}\varepsilon_i(v)e_i\right]+\left[\lambda\sum_{i=1}^{n}\sum_{v\in\Omega}(1-\varepsilon_i(v))e_i\right]\right\}.$$

In the inner sum, since the effort e_i does not depend on v (this is by assumption, since we do not allow different efforts for different outcomes), we can take it out to get

$$1=K\left\{\sum_{i=1}^{n}e_i\left[\sum_{v\in\Omega}\varepsilon_i(v)\right]+\lambda\sum_{i=1}^{n}e_i\left[\sum_{v\in\Omega}(1-\varepsilon_i(v))\right]\right\}.$$

Now consider the inner sums over v. Here, $\sum_{v\in\Omega}\varepsilon_i(v)$ is just the count for the number of outcomes $v\in\Omega$ for which $\varepsilon_i(v)=1$. That is,

$$\sum_{v\in\Omega}\varepsilon_i(v)=\sum_{\substack{v\in\Omega\\ \varepsilon_i(v)=1}}1.$$

From simple combinatorics, we get that this count is same as the number of vectors of length $n-1$, with 0, 1 entries such that $\bar{n}-1$ entries have value 1 and others have value 0. This is given by $\binom{n-1}{\bar{n}-1}$ Similarly, $\sum_{v\in\Omega}(1-\varepsilon_i(v))$ is just the count for the number of outcomes $v\in\Omega$ for which $\varepsilon_i(v)=0$ (since otherwise the contribution is 0). That is,

$$\sum_{v\in\Omega}(1-\varepsilon_i(v))=\sum_{\substack{v\in\Omega\\ \varepsilon_i(v)=0}}1.$$

From simple combinatorics, we get that this count is same as the number of vectors of length $n-1$, with 0, 1 entries such that $\bar{n}$ entries have value 1 and others have value 0. This is given by $\binom{n-1}{\bar{n}}$. Substituting we get the following calculations

$$1=K\left\{\sum_{i=1}^{n}e_i\binom{n-1}{\bar{n}-1}+\lambda\sum_{i=1}^{n}e_i\binom{n-1}{\bar{n}}\right\}$$

$$=K\left(\sum_{i=1}^{n}e_i\right)\frac{(n-1)!}{(\bar{n}-1)!(n-\bar{n})!}\left[\frac{1}{n-\bar{n}}+\frac{\lambda}{\bar{n}}\right].$$

Hence,

$$K=\frac{1}{\frac{(n-1)!}{(\bar{n}-1)!(n-\bar{n})!}\left(\frac{\bar{n}+\lambda(n-\bar{n})}{\bar{n}}\right)\sum_{i=1}^{n}e_i}.$$

Substituting we can get p_v. This completes the derivation of the probability space in the case of our model. Now we come to the next part of the proposition.

Derivation of individual's probability of success: Consider person 1. Let us compute the probability that person 1 is successful using the above probability model:

$$\Pr\{\varepsilon_1=1\}$$

$$=\sum_{\substack{v\in\Omega\\ \varepsilon_1(v)=1}}p_v=\sum_{\substack{v\in\Omega\\ \varepsilon_1(v)=1}}K\left[\sum_{i=1}^{n}\varepsilon_i(v)e_i+\lambda\sum_{i=1}^{n}(1-\varepsilon_i(v))e_i\right]$$

where K is as given by (4)

$$=K\left[\sum_{i=1}^{n}e_i\sum_{\substack{v\in\Omega\\ \varepsilon_1(v)=1}}\varepsilon_i(v)+\lambda\sum_{i=1}^{n}e_i\sum_{\substack{v\in\Omega\\ \varepsilon_1(v)=1}}(1-\varepsilon_i(v))\right]$$

$$=K\left[\sum_{i=1}^{n}e_i\sum_{\substack{v\in\Omega\\ \varepsilon_1(v)=1\\ \varepsilon_i(v)=1}}1+\lambda\sum_{i=1}^{n}e_i\sum_{\substack{v\in\Omega\\ \varepsilon_1(v)=1\\ \varepsilon_i(v)=0}}1\right].$$

Now

$$\sum_{\substack{v\in\Omega\\ \varepsilon_1(v)=1\\ \varepsilon_i(v)=1}}1=\begin{cases}\binom{n-1}{\bar{n}-1} & \text{if } i=1\\ \binom{n-2}{\bar{n}-2} & \text{if } i\neq 1\end{cases},$$

and

$$\sum_{\substack{v\in\Omega\\ \varepsilon_1(v)=1\\ \varepsilon_i(v)=0}}1=\begin{cases}0 & \text{if } i=1\\ \binom{n-2}{\bar{n}-1} & \text{if } i\neq 1\end{cases},$$

Substituting and simplifying, we get

$$\Pr\{\varepsilon_1=1\}$$

$$=\frac{\bar{n}(\bar{n}-1+\lambda(n-\bar{n}))}{(n-1)(\bar{n}+\lambda(n-\bar{n}))}+\frac{e_1}{\sum_i e_i}\frac{(n-\bar{n})}{(n-1)}\frac{\bar{n}(1-\lambda)}{(\bar{n}+\lambda(n-\bar{n}))}.$$

Substituting subscript 1 with i, we can get (5). This completes the proof.

Notice that in this model, if $\lambda=0$, we see that the probability of any outcome depends on the efforts of the people who are successful only, while $\lambda=1$ means the probability of any outcome depends equally on the efforts of those who are successful as well as those who are not so. For any $0<\lambda<1$, it means the efforts of those who are successful contribute more towards bringing about the outcome than the efforts of those who remain unsuccessful.

Notice the following easily derivable properties of our model. If $\lambda = 1$, we get $\Pr\{\varepsilon_i = 1\} = \frac{\bar{n}}{n}$, which is the *equal probability model*. This means that if people's efforts are equally weighted in the probability of an outcome, irrespective of whether they are ultimately successful or not, then each individual has the same probability of being successful, irrespective of effort levels.

Derivation of Berry's probability function: Note if $\lambda = 0$, we get

$$\Pr\{\varepsilon_i = 1\} = \frac{\bar{n}-1}{n-1} + \frac{e_i}{\sum_i e_i}\frac{n-\bar{n}}{n-1}. \quad (6)$$

This is the same expression as introduced by Berry [1] and also rearranged and reproduced in Clark and Riis [2]. (An example of the above probability model can be found in **Appendix A**.) As noted by Berry [1], in case of a single prize, the probability of success of the *i*th individual reduces to the classic Tullock's contest success function (obtained by substituting $\bar{n} = 1$ in (6)), given by

$$\Pr\{\varepsilon_i = 1\} = \frac{e_i}{\sum_i e_i}. \quad (7)$$

The probability function also exhibits the usual properties (as also noted in Clark and Riis [2] and (1998)) in that it is bounded between 0 and 1, the probability of winning of a particular player is increasing in one's own resources, decreasing in other's resources, and the sum of all players' probability of winning one of the prizes equals $\bar{n}$, the number of prizes.

An interpretation for $\lambda = 0$: Suppose we are interested in the finding out how the probability of being successful changes as the weight given to efforts of people who are unsuccessful, λ, changes[2]. That is, we calculate $\frac{\partial \Pr\{\varepsilon_i = 1\}}{\partial \lambda}$ as follows:

$$\frac{\partial \Pr\{\varepsilon_i = 1\}}{\partial \lambda} = \frac{\bar{n}(n-\bar{n})}{(n-1)(\bar{n}+\lambda(n-\bar{n}))^2}\left(1 - \frac{e_i}{\sum_{i=1}^{n} e_i} n\right).$$

Hence the probability increases or decreases with λ, depending on individual effort e_i, relative to the average $\frac{\sum_{i=1}^{n} e_i}{n}$. In particular, if $1 > \frac{e_i}{\sum_{i=1}^{n} e_i} n$, that is $e_i < \frac{\sum_{i=1}^{n} e_i}{n}$, then $\frac{\partial \Pr\{\varepsilon_i = 1\}}{\partial \lambda} > 0$. (Similarly, if $1 < \frac{e_i}{\sum_{i=1}^{n} e_i} n$, the opposite holds.) This means that if individual i is exerting less than average effort, then as desired, his probability of success falls, as λ falls. Similarly, for someone exerting more than the average effort, the above derivative is negative, which means that his probability of success increases as λ falls.

The last observation means that in our probability model, the smaller λ gets, the more the probability of success of someone who is exerting above average effort, and lesser is the probability of success of someone who is exerting less than average effort. In the extreme case we have $\lambda = 0$ which means the probability of an outcome is sensitive only to the efforts of those who have succeeded. Hence $\lambda = 0$ makes for a good case to work with, which again means that our probability of success turns out to be that of Berry's.

3. Conclusion

In this note, we derive a probability function by hypothesizing a possible relation between outcomes and efforts/resources of players in the context of a multi-prize contest. When efforts are simultaneously exerted by players, multiple prizes are simultaneously awarded, we hypothesize that the probability of an outcome is proportional to all efforts exerted. In the special case, where the probability of an outcome is proportional to the effort exerted by the winners only (that is to say the weight attached to the efforts of the unsuccessful players is 0), the probability of an individual player winning is proposed exactly by Berry [1]. Hence we provide a probabilistic foundation for the probability function in a multi-prize rent-seeking contest as introduced by Berry. Moreover our probability model, by the very way it is defined, is a good depiction when prizes are simultaneously distributed.

[2]Notice that in our probability model, the space Ω is essentially given by a collection P_λ of non-negative real numbers $p_{v,\lambda}$ allotted to each outcomes $v \in \Omega$, satisfying the two conditions

$$p_{v,\lambda} \geq 0, \text{ and } \sum_{v\in\Omega} p_{v,\lambda} = 1.$$

Hence for every λ, the pair (Ω, P_λ) is said to form a probability space. Now here we want to see if we can choose a particular λ (and hence the corresponding probability space) to work with.

REFERENCES

[1] S. K. Berry, "Rent-seeking with Multiple Winners," *Pub-*

lic Choice, Vol. 77, No. 2, 1993, pp. 437-443.

[2] D. J. Clark and C. Riis, "A Multi-Winner Nested Rent-Seeking Contest," *Public Choice*, Vol. 87, No. 1-2, 1996, pp. 177-184.

[3] D. J. Clark and C. Riis, "Influence and the discretionary allocation of several prizes," *European Journal of Political Economy*, Vol. 14, No. 4, 1998, pp. 605-625.

Appendix

Derivation of the Probability Model with an Example

Consider the basic probability model with $\lambda = 0$ (which gives Berry's probability function). Let $n = 3$,, $\bar{n} = 2$. Then the possible outcomes and associated probabilities are as follows:

$$\bar{v}_1 = (1,1,0): p_1 = K\left(\varepsilon_1(\bar{v}_1)e_1 + \varepsilon_2(\bar{v}_1)e_2 + \varepsilon_3(\bar{v}_1)e_3\right) = K(e_1 + e_2)$$

$$\bar{v}_2 = (1,0,1): p_2 = K\left(\varepsilon_1(\bar{v}_2)e_1 + \varepsilon_2(\bar{v}_2)e_2 + \varepsilon_3(\bar{v}_2)e_3\right) = K(e_1 + e_3)$$

$$\bar{v}_3 = (0,1,1): p_3 = K\left(\varepsilon_1(\bar{v}_3)e_1 + \varepsilon_2(\bar{v}_3)e_2 + \varepsilon_3(\bar{v}_3)e_3\right) = K(e_2 + e_3)$$

Hence summing over all outcomes we get,

$$1 = p_1 + p_2 + p_3 = K \times \sum_{i=1}^{3} e_i \left(\sum_{\bar{v}\in\Omega} \varepsilon_i(\bar{v}) \right)$$

$$= K \times \left(e_1 \left(\sum_{\bar{v}\in\Omega} \varepsilon_1(\bar{v}) \right) + e_2 \left(\sum_{\bar{v}\in\Omega} \varepsilon_2(\bar{v}) \right) + e_3 \left(\sum_{\bar{v}\in\Omega} \varepsilon_3(\bar{v}) \right) \right).$$

Now:

$$\sum_{\bar{v}\in\Omega} \varepsilon_1(\bar{v}) = \sum_{\substack{\bar{v}\in\Omega \\ \varepsilon_1(\bar{v})=1}} 1 = 2$$

and similarly $\sum_{\bar{v}\in\Omega} \varepsilon_2(\bar{v}) = \sum_{\bar{v}\in\Omega} \varepsilon_3(\bar{v}) = 2$. Hence substituting we get $1 = K \times 2 \times (e_1 + e_2 + e_3)$.

And $2 = \binom{3}{2}$, for this example.

Now consider an example with $n = 3$, $\bar{n} = 2$, $e_1 = 8$, $e_2 = e_3 = 1$. Then we get the following:

$$P_1 = \frac{1}{2} + \frac{8}{10}\frac{1}{2} = \frac{18}{20}$$

$$P_2 = \frac{1}{2} + \frac{1}{10}\frac{1}{2} = \frac{11}{20}$$

$$P_3 = \frac{1}{2} + \frac{1}{10}\frac{1}{2} = \frac{11}{20}$$

Again the sum equals $\bar{n} = 2$. This means (roughly) that person 1 exerting high effort gets to win a prize with a very high probability, while the other two players exerting the same low probability gets to win the remaining prize with almost equal probability.

Corporate Social Responsibility from Friedman to Porter and Kramer

Maria Teresa Bosch-Badia, Joan Montllor-Serrats, Maria Antonia Tarrazon
Department of Business Economics, Autonomous University of Barcelona, Barcelona, Spain

ABSTRACT

We analyze, from the viewpoint of value creation, the evolution of Corporate Social Responsibility (CSR) thought from Friedman critical view of CSR to Porter and Kramer "shared-value" proposition, emphasizing, at the same time, its parallelism with the evolution of asset valuation models from the viewpoint of common stocks value. On this basis, we show how CSR has adapted to value creation, the corporate goal that has substituted the old goal of profit maximization. A review of the studies about the impact of CSR on corporate financial performance complements this analysis.

Keywords: Corporate Social Responsibility; Corporate Financial Performance; Real Options; Stakeholders

1. Introduction[1]

Corporate Social Responsibility (CSR) is a key issue for modern corporations and, of course, for modern society. Since it began to be regarded as a relevant topic to nowadays, its practice and the theory behind it have substantially changed. The aim of this article is to analyze the evolution of economic and strategic thought on CSR from Friedman's [1] critical view to Porter and Kramer [2] shared value proposition. We draw the conclusion that value creation has evolved in parallel to CSR: the former does not longer exclusively consists of profit maximization, and the latter has turned from an expense into an investment. CSR consists of the courses of action that firms undertake to become environmentally and socially sustainable beyond their legal obligations. From the financial viewpoint, in the short run, CSR means a decrease in profits for the sake of a social or environmental end. Its roots lie in demands from society and law makers for correcting market failures as the essential driver of both individual and corporate social responsebilities (Bénabou and Tirole [3]). Thus, we can say that CSR has added a third dimension to the two primitive coordinates of demand, *i.e.* to price and quality. The paper is organized as follows: Section 2 analyses the evolution of CSR thought from Milton Friedman to stakeholder's theory. In Section 3, we study the links between CSR and value creation. First we center on the works that identify CSR as a value driver and, next, we focus on Porter and Kramer shared value proposition. Section 4 is devoted to the parallel evolution of asset valuation models and CSR thought. Section 5 complements the previous analysis by revising the evolution of CSR from the perspective of the empirical works. Section 6 closes the article.

2. Friedman vs. Stakeholder's Theory

At nineteen sixties, when interest for CSR began, it was regarded as an expense on philanthropy which aim was returning profits to society. Thus, from the financial viewpoint it meant a decrease in profits for the sake of a social or environmental end. On this basis, Milton Friedman [1] wrote the famous article entitled The Social Responsibility of Business is to Increase its Profits, where he held that those executives who imposed social expenses to the corporations they managed should be regarded as disloyal agents to their principals, the shareholders. In fact, if profits are the only value driver, it becomes clear that any reduction in earnings without any complementary effect, whether it comes from philanthropy, destroys value. Nevertheless, since value comes from discounting expected profits at the required rate of return, with risk premium inside, we have to consider the impact of CSR on risk, and, therefore, on the discounting

[1]We thank an anonymous referee for helpful comments.

rate. Several works, (Orlitzky and Benjamin [4]; Husted [5]; Kitzmueller and Shimshack [6]) point out that CSR hedges social risk, *i.e.* the risk that comes from social activism or private politics. The logical next step is to acknowledge that it creates value through risk reduction. Kitzmueller and Shimshack [6] also underline that CSR is an instrument to reduce public political risk. To this extent, CSR, even if it exclusively consists of philanthropic expenses, it creates value through risk reduction.

The main argument against Friedman's criticism has come from stakeholders' theory introduced by Freeman [7]. Corporate governance does not only take into account shareholders' interests, but also the interests of other stakeholders, like employees, customers, suppliers and communities directly affected by corporate actions. The Halal Return-on-Resources Model [8] clarifies the resources invested by each stakeholders group and their benefits, costs and return. Halal [8] points out the centrality of integrating the various social interests into corporate goals and shows the myopia that pervades the philosophy that considers profits alone as the unique legitimate goal of business. Haigh and Jones [9] identify as the CSR drivers the pressures that come from different stakeholders: the corporation itself, competence, investors, consumers, regulators and popular mobilizations. A CSR policy that takes into account stakeholder requirements may add competitive advantage in some corporate areas. For instance, non-monetary conditions of employment can be regarded as a positive signal to attract quality work force (Kitzmueller and Shimshack [6]) while environmental care and better relationships with government and communities may smooth the requirements for opening new plants. CSR also facilitates to attract investments from ethical mutual funds.

3. Corporate Social Responsibility and Value Creation

3.1. Identifying CSR as a Value Driver

The conceptual enlargement brought by stakeholder's theory has lead to identify CSR as a value driver. Burker and Logsdon [10] find five dimensions of corporate strategy that enable to relate CSR to value creation: Centrality (*closeness to the firm's mission and objectives*), specificity (*ability to capture private benefits by the firm*), proactivity (*planning in anticipation of social trends*), voluntarism, and visibility (*projects observable by stakeholders*). Epstein, Buhovac, and Yuthas [11] approach CSR from the paradox theory perspective showing that the tensions between CSR and Corporate Financial Performance (CFP) are a source of creative ideas for managers. Vilanova, Lozano, and Arenas [12] argue that CSR and competitiveness relate through learning and innovation cycle. Fernández and Luna [13] examine how corporate reputation contributes to create value. Freeman, Harrison, Wicks, Parmar, and Colle [7] make a distinction between the residual concept of CSR, focused on returning profits to society, and integrated CSR. The integrated approach regards CSR as a part of the corporate competitive strategy: *it conceptualizes CSR as the integration of social, ethical and environmental concerns into the management criteria for corporate strategy*. The role of managers consists of interweaving stakeholders demands with corporate capacities in order to create value by respecting the rules that regulate corporate behaviour. Nevertheless, the relationship between CSR and value creation is mainly due to the articles by Michael Porter and his co-authors Kramer and Van der Linde. Porter and Van der Linde [14] regard expenses in reduceing environmental impact as an opportunity to improve competitiveness. Porter and Kramer [15], writing on corporate philanthropy, also advocate for strategic giving, *i.e.* for charitable efforts that contribute to society and improve the corporate competitive context, instead of giving pure donations that, at most, enable cause-related marketing. The same authors [16] hold that CSR, analyzed using the same framework that guides corporate business choice becomes *a source of opportunity, innovation, and competitive advantage*. The basis of this statement is the distinction between *responsive CSR* and *strategic CSR*. The former is addressed to returning profits to society. The latter is addressed to identifying societal problems that the corporation can contribute to solve, and, as a consequence, create value simultaneously for society and shareholders.

3.2. The Porter and Kramer Proposition: Shared Value

The last step of the evolution of Porter and Kramer [2] thought on the relationships between corporations and society is the concept of shared value. The corporation-centered value creation perspective gives way to a corporation-stakeholders perspective. The basis of this new approach is to recognize that *societal needs, not just conventional economic needs, define markets*. Ultimately corporations, by assuming shared-value strategies, have the opportunity to turn capitalism into an environmentally, socially and financially sustainable economic system. In the long run, shared value leads to a stronger and more sustainable value chain, but, in the short run it faces the capital markets pressure for short term profits. At this point, it is worth remembering that common stock prices reflect available information (Fama [17], although they can be distorted by noise (Black [18]), anomalies, and bubbles (Malkiel [19]). Long term sustainability can be assimilated to information and pressures for short term profits to noise. For this reason, a central goal of corporate communication policy is to make investors aware of the fact that long term sustainability deserves a greater weight than short term profits in any sensible stock value estimation.

To sum up, the evolution of the theoretical thought on CSR can be synthesized in three stages: philanthropy, evolution from philanthropy to value creation, and shared value. The latter can be regarded as the whole integration of CSR into corporate strategy. The problem with regarding and managing CSR as a policy exclusively aimed at returning profits to society is that, in the end, shares value would become a decreasing function of CSR, and; thus, CSR would not be financially sustainable. The managerial challenge with respect to CSR is to turn it from an expense into an investment (Husted and Allen [20]), to create value through it and to make shareholders aware of this value creation.

4. The Parallel Evolution of Asset Valuation Models

4.1. Discounting Cash Flow Models: Dividend Growth vs. the Present Value of Growth Opportunities

Asset valuation models have experienced an evolution that parallels the evolution of CSR thought. At the moment at which Friedman wrote his article on CSR, the discounting cash flow technique was, by large, the dominant model. The two main models in this field are the dividend growth model and the present value of growth opportunities. The dividend growth model[2] (Williams [22], Gordon and Shapiro [23]) considers dividends, their growth and the required rate of return as the variables that determine common stock prices. Therefore, it exactly fits with the profit maximization paradigm and Friedman's viewpoint.

Miller and Modigliani [24], in their article on dividend policy and shares valuation, develop a model in which the value of common stock is obtained as the addition of the discounted earnings generated by current assets and the future opportunities of undertaking new projects with positive net present value. The theoretical approach by Miller and Modigliani has lead to applied models that follow this line, such as the ones developed by Brealey and Myers [25] in the first edition of their textbook, Leibowitz and Kogelman [26] and O'Brien [27]. These models widen the valuation scope by making explicit the relevance of new opportunities. Since their perspective, value maximization is not only the outcome of the maximization of the profits generated by current operations. It also depends on the outcome of one of the central functions of managerial strategic thinking: capturing and creating new opportunities. Thus, they provide the basis to connect CSR to value creation.

[2]As Brealey, Myers and Allen [21] point out, the dividend growth model was first deduced by Williams [22], and later rediscovered by Gordon and Shapiro [23].

4.2. Flexibility and the Value of New Opportunities: Real Options

In the second half of the nineties option valuation began to be applied beyond the option contracts traded in derivatives markets. Real options were introduced in financial literature (Trigeorgis [28]) and on strategic thinking (Luehrman [29]; Amran and Kulatilaka [30]). The new valuation approach emphasized that value not only comes from undertaking projects that maximize the present value of profits, but also from projects that bring the opportunity to start new projects in the future. Although only few articles directly relate CSR with real options (Husted [5]), the link between the new value creation opportunities embedded in CSR strategies and real options is fairly clear. In other words, if from the discounted cash flow viewpoint the value creation capacity of CSR often remains fuzzy, real options enlighten the relationship between CSR and value creation.

5. The Empirical Analysis on CSR

Empirical analysis on CSR has been mainly concerned with its relationship with corporate financial performance (CFP). Three conclusions can be drawn from revising the literature on the empirical evidence on the effects of CSR on CFP. First, the relationship between CSR and CFP has evolved from a nil or low correlation to a positive correlation. Second, CSR positively impacts on CFP in the long run. Third, CSR creates value mainly when it is focused on primary stakeholders, but it has an insurance effect when it has a wider orienta1tion. McWilliams and Siegel [31] find that the impact of CSR on CFP is neutral after separating it from the influence of R&D. The meta-analysis performed by Orlitzky, Schmidt and Rynes [32], and Margolis and Walsh [33], conclude that CSR predominantly shows a low positive impact on CFP. The latter is reviewed by Margolis and Elfenbein [34], where the authors conclude that *investments need to be judged solely on the merits, and leaders can and should explore their own motivations before buying into the hype*. The more recent literature review by Beurden and Gössling [35], finds that there exists a positive correlation between CSR and CFP in the studies they consider, and draw the conclusion that there is a change in this correlation with respect to its observed value in previous works. Roberts and Dowling [36] argue that CSR positively contributes to the long term sustainability of CFP. Shank, Manullang and Hill [37] find that, in the long run, CSR and CFP have a significant correlation, but not in the short run. According to Hillman and Keim [38], there is a significant positive correlation between CSR and CFP when the former is focused on primary stakeholders, but a nil correlation in other circumstances. On the other hand, Godfrey, Merrill and Hansen [39], find that CSR focused on secondary stakeholders has an insurance effect that creates value for shareholders in case of negative events. The synthesis of these three conclusions leads to realize the relevance of real options to link CSR with CFP. The temporal lag between the growth of CSR and its association to value creation can be attributed to the fact that financial markets may not have become aware of the financial value of CSR expenses until they have begun to regard them as a source of opportunities to undertake new investments, *i.e.* as real options. The long run impact of CSR on corporate value fits with the interaction of creating real options and, after some years, exercising the ones that have become really valuable. This is a value chain that attracts investors who look for the long run profitability, instead of trying to make profits from short run volatility. Finally, real options arise mainly from the relationships between the corporation and its primary stakeholders. The insurance effect pointed out by Godfrey, Merrill and Hansen also has option features that we consider below. Shared value, in turn, opens a new field for value creation.

6. Conclusion

From this overview of the evolution of CSR thought, we can draw the conclusion that it has evolved from returning profits to society to creating shared value with stakeholders in order to improve the environmental and social corporate sustainability. The collateral activity that CSR was at the beginning has become part of the core corporate strategy. Financially, philanthropic expenses have turned into investments with shared value creation ends. Friedman criticized CSR for its capacity to spoil corporate value assuming that it was limited to philanthropic expenses that enhanced the managerial ego. Nevertheless, capitalism has found the way of integrating CSR into value creation. In effect, even if CSR does not maximize earnings directly, it contributes to the end that profit maximization had assigned in old valuation methods: value creation.

REFERENCES

[1] M. Friedman, "The Social Responsibility of Business Is to Increase Its Profits," *The New York Times Magazine*, 13 September 1970.

[2] M. E. Porter and M. R. Kramer, "Creating Shared Value," *Harvard Business Review*, Vol. 89, No. 1, 2011, pp. 2-17.

[3] R. Bénabou and J. Tirole, "Individual and Corporate Social Responsibility," *Economica*, Vol. 77, No. 305, 2010, pp. 1-19.

[4] M. Orlitzky and J. D. Benjamin, "Corporate Social Performance and Firm Risk, a Meta-Analytic Review," *Business and Society*, Vol. 40, No. 4, 2001, pp. 369-396.

[5] B. V. Husted, "Risk management, Real Options, and Corporate Social Responsibility," *Journal of Business Ethics*, Vol. 60, No. 2, 2005, pp. 175-183.

[6] H. Kitzmueller and J. Shimshack, "Economic Perspectives on Corporate Social Responsibility," *Journal of Economic Literature*. Vol. 50, No. 1, 2012, pp. 51-84.

[7] R. E. Freeman, J. S. Harrison, A. C. Wicks, B. L. Parmar and S. de Colle, "Stakeholder Theory," Cambridge University Press, Cambridge, 2010.

[8] W. E. Halal, "Business and Government—A New Partnership?" *Long Range Planning*, Vol. 20, No. 1, 1987, pp. 123-130.

[9] M. Haigh and M. T. Jones, "The Drivers of Corporate Social Responsibility, a Critical Review," *The Business Review*, Vol. 5, No. 2, 2006, pp. 245-251.

[10] L. Burke and J. M. Logsdon, "How Corporate Social Responsibility Pays off," *Long Range Planning*, Vol. 29, No. 4, pp. 495-502.

[11] M. J. Epstein, A. R. Buhovac and K. Yuthas, "Managing Social, Environmental and Financial Performance Simultaneously," *Long Range Planning*, Unpublished.

[12] M. Vilanova, J. Lozano and D. Arenas, "Exploring the Nature of the Relationship between CSR and Competitiveness," *Journal of Business Ethics*, Vol. 87, No. 1, 2009, pp. 57-69.

[13] J. L. F. Sánchez and L. L. Sotorrío, "The Creation of Value through Corporate Reputation," *Journal of Business Ethics*. Vol. 76, No. 3, 2007. pp. 335-346.

[14] M. E. Porter, M. E. and C. Van der Linde, "Green and Competitive, Ending the Stalemate," *Harvard Business Review*, Vol. 73, No. 5, 1995, pp. 120-121.

[15] M. E. Porter and M. R. Kramer, "The Competitive Advantage of Corporate Philanthropy," *Harvard Business Review*, Vol. 80, No. 9, 2002, pp. 56-69.

[16] M. E. Porter and M. R. Kramer, "Strategy & Society, the Link between Competitive Advantage and Corporate Social Responsibility," *Harvard Business Review*, Vol. 84, No. 12, 2006, pp. 78-92.

[17] E. Fama, "Efficient Capital Markets: A Review or Theory and Empirical Work," *Journal of Finance*, Vol. 25, No. 2, 1970, pp. 383-417.

[18] F. Black, "Noise," *Journal of Finance*, Vol. 41, No. 3, 1986, pp. 529-543.

[19] B. Malkiel, "A Random Walk down Wall Street," W. W. Norton & Company, New York, 2011.

[20] B. W. Husted and D. B. Allen, "Strategic Corporate Social Responsibility and Value Creation among Large Firms, Lessons from the Spanish Experience," *Long Range Planning*, Vol. 40, No. 6, 2007, pp. 594-610.

[21] R. Brealey, S. C. Myers and F. Allen, "Corporate Finance," 8th Edition, McGraw Hill, New York, 2006.

[22] J. B. Williams, "The Theory of Investment Value," Harvard University Press, Cambridge, 1938.

[23] M. J. Gordon and E. Shapiro, "Capital Equipment Analysis: The Required Rate of Profit," *Management Science*, Vol. 3, No. 1, 1956, pp. 102-110.

[24] M. Milller and F. Modigliani, "Dividend Policy, Growth and the Valuation of Shares," *The Journal of Business*, Vol. 34, No. 4, 1961, pp. 411-433.

[25] R. Brealey and S. C. Myers, "Principles of Corporate Finance," McGraw Hill, New York, 1981.

[26] M. L. Leibowitz and S. Kogelman, "Inside the P/E Ratio: The Franchise Factor," *Financial Analysts Journal*, Vol. 46, No. 6, 1990, pp. 17-35.

[27] T. O'Brien, "A Simple and Flexible DCF Valuation Formula," *Journal of Applied Finance*, Vol. 13, No. 2, 2003, pp. 54-62.

[28] L. Trigeorgis, "Real Options and Interactions with Financial Flexibility," *Financial Management*, Vol. 22, No. 3, 1993, pp. 202-224.

[29] T. A. Luehrman, "Strategy as a Portfolio of Real Options," *Harvard Business Review*, Vol. 76, No. 5, 1998, pp. 89-99.

[30] M. Amram and N. Kulatilaka, "Disciplined Decisions, Aligning Strategy with the Financial Markets," *Harvard Business Review*, Vol. 77, No. 1, 1999, pp. 95-104.

[31] A. McWilliams and D. Siegel, "Corporate Social Responsibility and Financial Performance, Correlation or Misspecification?" *Strategic Management Journal*, Vol. 21, No. 5, 2000, pp. 603-609.

[32] M. Orlitzky, L. Schmidt and S. L. Rynes, "Corporate Social and Financial Performance, a Meta-Analysis," *Organization Studies*, Vol. 24, No. 3, 2003, pp. 403-441.

[33] J. D. Margolis and J. P. Walsh, "Misery Loves Companies, Rethinking Social Initiatives by Business," *Administrative Science Quarterly*, Vol. 48, No. 2, 2003, pp. 268-305.

[34] J. D. Margolis and H. A. Elfenbein, "Do Well by Doing Good? Don't Count on It," *Harvard Business Review*, Vol. 86, No. 1, 2008, pp. 19-20.

[35] P. Beurden and T. Gössling, "The Worth of Values—A Literature Review on the Relation between Corporate Social and Financial Performance," *Journal of Business Ethics*, Vol. 82, No. 2, 2008, pp. 407-424.

[36] P. W. Roberts and G. R. Dowling, "Corporate Reputation and Sustained Superior Financial Performance," *Strategic Management Journal*, Vol. 23, No. 1, 2002, pp. 1077-1093.

[37] T. Shank, D. Manullang and R. Hill, "Doing Well While Doing Good Revisited, a Study of Socially Responsible Firms' Short-Term versus Long-Term Performance," *Managerial Finance*, Vol. 31, No. 8, 2005, pp. 33-46.

[38] A. J. Hillman and G. D. Keim, "Shareholder Value, Stakeholder Management, and Social Issues, What's the Bottom Line?" *Strategic Management Journal*, Vol. 22, No. 2, 2001, pp. 125-139.

[39] P. C. Godfrey, C. B. Merrill and J. M. Hansen, "The Relationship between Corporate Social Responsibility and Shareholder Value, an Empirical Text of the Risk Management Hypothesis," *Strategic Management Journal*, Vol. 30, No. 4, 2009, pp. 425-445.

20

Optimal Foreign Exchange Risk Hedging: A Mean Variance Portfolio Approach

Yun-Yeong Kim
Department of International Trade, Dankook University, Yong-In, Korea

ABSTRACT

This paper introduces the optimal foreign exchange risk hedging model following a standard portfolio theory. The results indicate that a lower level of risk can be achieved, given a specified level of expected return, from using optimization modeling. In the paper the expected hedging return is defined from the expected cost of the foreign currency using a specified hedging strategy minus the expected cost of the foreign currency when it is purchased form the spot market. The focal point of the technique is its ability to identify optimal combinations of hedging vehicles, those are currency options, forward contracts, leaving the position open (foreign exchange risk hedging tools suggested by the US. Department of Commerce) in a closed form.

Keywords: Foreign Exchange; Risk; Optimal Hedging; Closed Form

1. Introduction

Beginning in the early 1970s, floating foreign exchange (FX) rates became more common, among the major currencies. Now the recent global financial crisis including euro zone instability have clearly illustrated the critical importance of hedging for risks in foreign exchange rate. See following figures of monthly Euro/Dollar and Yen/Dollar foreign exchange rates during 1999.1-2011.7, where both FX rates are fluctuating especially after global financial crisis.[1]

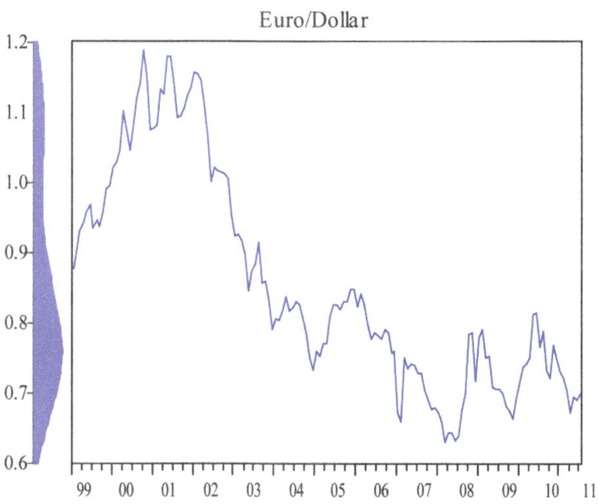

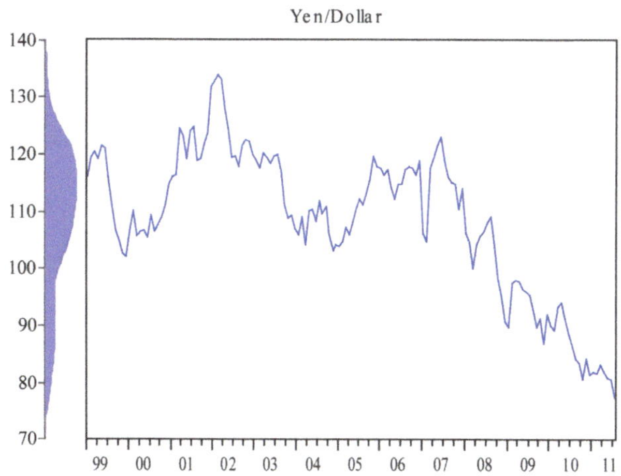

So foreign currency fluctuations are one of the key sources of risk in multinational operations. The various tools which have emerged to deal with foreign exchange risk have been treated extensively in the finance literature. The nature, uses, and efficiency of their markets are quite well understood today (See [1]). The US Department of Commerce is also warning that "The volatile nature of the FX market poses a great risk of sudden and drastic FX rate movements, which may cause significantly damaging financial losses from otherwise profitable export sales (Trade finance guide, http://trade.gov/publications/pdfs/tfg2008ch12.pdf)." The same guide suggests three FX risk management techniques considered suitable for new-to-export US small and medium-

[1]The axsis border graphs are kernel density functions.

sized enterprises companies as non-hedging FX risk management techniques,[2] FX forward hedges[3] and FX options hedges.[4]

However, what has been ignored, as correctly pointed out [2], are the factors an investor should consider when choosing from among the various available hedging tools to reduce the risk resulting from a certain type of exposure to foreign exchange risk for a given expected return.

[2] gauges the preferences of finance officers in terms of the specific characteristics of a hedging tool relying on a questionnaire survey. [3,4] illustrate the technique of computerized optimization and simulation modeling to manage foreign exchange risk. However they did not derive the closed form optimal hedging solution analytically and thus it obviously requires the additional computational burden.

So this paper introduces the optimal foreign exchange risk hedging model following a standard portfolio theory. The results indicate that a lower level of risk can be achieved, given a specified level of expected return, from using optimization modeling. In the context of this paper the expected hedging return is defined from the expected cost of the foreign currency using a specified hedging strategy minus the expected cost of the foreign currency when it is purchased form the spot market. The focal point of the technique is its ability to identify optimal combinations of most frequently using hedging vehicles, those are (European) currency options, forward contracts, leaving the position open (foreign exchange risk hedging tools suggested by the US Department of Commerce) in a closed form.[5]

The rest of this paper proceeds as follows. Section 2 derives the expected return and variance of hedging vehicles. Section 3 analyzes the optimal hedging selection. Section 4 concludes.

2. Moments of Triple Hedging Tools' Returns

Assume, at time 0, an investor hopes to buy one unit of foreign exchange at a future time T. Denotes S_t as the foreign exchange rate at time t in terms of domestic currency. For instance, S_t is the dollar price of one euro where the dollar is the domestic currency. Further we suppose that there are three hedging tools, *i.e.*, European currency call option, forward contracts and leaving the position open.[6] Define a forward contract rate F_t, a striking price K and its premium P at time *t* of European call option with the maturity T, respectively.[7]

Now we would like to construct the efficient hedging frontier composed of expected return and variance of each hedging vehicle. So, it is exactly matched with the portfolio possibilities curve. An optimal combination of hedging vehicles is one, which maximizes the expected return given a desired level of risk.

Before proceeding, we assume the logarithm of exchange rate follows a random walk following [5]:

Assumption 2.1. *We suppose*

$$s_{t+1} = s_t + u_t$$

where $s_t \equiv \ln(S_t)$ *and* $\{u_t\}$ *is independent, identically and normally distributed sequence with the mean zero and variance* σ^2.

Above Assumption 2.1 represents the efficient market hypothesis for the foreign exchange rate. Now we derive the return and its variance of different hedging tools, where the return is computed based upon the purchasing a foreign currency by the spot rate S_0. The expected return is defined from the conditional expectation[8] based on the information of past exchange rates $\Omega \equiv \{S_0, S_{-1}, \cdots\}$.[9]

2.1. Derivation of Mean and Variance

At first, we derive the expected return [R_n] and its variance [V_n] of non-hedging (leaving the position open) as:

Proposition 2.2. *Suppose Assumption* 2.1 *holds. Then the expected return for non-hedging is* $R_n = 0$ *and its variance is* $V_n = T\sigma^2$.

Proof. Note the return of non-hedging is the negative[10] value of following:[11]

[2]The exporter can avoid FX exposure by using the simplest non-edging technique: price the sale in a foreign currency. The exporter can then demand cash in advance, and the current spot market rate will deterne the US dollar value of the foreign proceeds.

[3]The most direct method of hedging FX risk is a forward contract, which enables the exporter to sell a set amount of foreign currency at a pre-agreed exchange rate with a delivery date from three days to one year into the future.

[4]Under an FX option, the exporter or the option holder acquires the right, but not the obligation, to deliver an agreed amount of foreign currency to the lender in exchange for dollars at a specified rate on or before the expiration date of the option. As opposed to a forward contract, an FX option has an explicit fee, which is similar to a premium paid for an insurance policy.

[5]At least author's knowledge, there are not any the same researches in this direction.

[6]It is a non-hedging and to buy the foreign currency at time T.

[7]The value of call option was derived by [6].

[8]Note the conditional expectation is the optimal forecasting of return which minimizes the mean squared forecasting error.

[9]So an investor exploits the information Ω when she determines the optimal hedging tool.

[10]It is negative because buying of foreign currency means the outflow of domestic currency.

[11]We do not consider the cost-of-carry for the spot purchasing of foreign currency since it is applied for the other hedging vehicles by the same amount. In particular, suppose an interest r is required to borrow the S_0 till time T and then the non-hedging return Formula (1) may be revised as;

$$\frac{S_T - (1+r)S_0}{(1+r)S_0} = \frac{1}{(1+r)}\frac{S_T - S_0}{S_0} - \frac{r}{1+r}$$

Thus it does not matter even if we just focus on the $(S_T - S_0)/S_0$ since the other terms $1/(1+r)$ and $r/(1+r)$ are same for the other hedging tools.

$$\frac{S_T - S_0}{S_0} \cong s_T - s_0 \qquad (1)$$

assuming $S_T - S_0$ is small. Then, under Assumption 2.1, the claimed results hold as:

$$E(s_T - s_0 | \Omega) = 0$$

and

$$E\left[(s_T - s_0)^2 | \Omega\right] = T\sigma^2.$$

At second, we derive the expected return $[R_f]$ and its variance $[V_f]$ of forward contract as:

Proposition 2.3. *Suppose Assumption* 2.1 *holds. Then the expected return of forward is* $R_f = s_0 - f_T$ *and its variance is* $V_f = 0$ *where* $f_T = \log(F_T)$.

Proof: Note the expected return for forward is the negative value of following:

$$\frac{F_T - S_0}{S_0} \cong f_T - s_0$$

assuming $F_T - S_0$ is small. Its variance is obviously zero since the return is not random.

Above forward contract may dominate the non-hedging if its expected return is positive, which is riskless. Such dominance may be closely related with the interest rates whenever the covered interest parity holds. See following result.

Corollary 2.4. *Suppose Assumption* 2.1 *holds and* $r < r^*$. *Then the forward contracts dominates the non-hedging where* r *and* r^* *denote the domestic and foreign risk free interest rates respectively.*

Proof. From the covered interest parity, note $r - r^* = f_T - s_0$. So if $f_T - s_0 < 0$ or $r < r^*$, then there is positive expected return without risk. In this case, the forward contract dominates the non-hedging case.

Above result also implies that if the domestic interest rate is higher than the foreign interest rate, then the non-hedging may better than the forward contract.[12]

Now we derive the expected return $[R_o]$ and its variance $[V_o]$ of currency call option as:

Proposition 2.5. *Suppose Assumption* 2.1 *holds. Then*

1) *the expected return of currency call option is given as*:

$$R_o = -x_0\left[1 - \Phi(z_0)\right] - \sigma\sqrt{T}\lambda(z_0)\Phi(z_0) - p$$

and 2) *its variance is*

$$V_o = x^2\left(1 - \Phi(z_0)\right) + \sigma\sqrt{T}\frac{1}{\sqrt{2}}\frac{\vartheta_3(z_0)}{\vartheta_1(z_0)}\Phi(z_0) - \left(x_0\left[1 - \Phi(z_0)\right] + \sigma\sqrt{T}\lambda(z_0)\Phi(z_0)\right)^2$$

where $k = \log K$, $p = P/S_0$, $x_0 = k - s_0$, $z_0 = x_0/\sigma\sqrt{T}$ *and* $\lambda(z_0) = -\phi(z_0)/\Phi(z_0)$ *where* ϕ *and* Φ *are the standard normal density and distribution function respectively and* ϑ_q *denotes the distribution function of* χ_q^2 *density function with the degree of freedom* q.

Proof. 1) Note the outflow of call option at time T is given as $\min(S_T, K) + P$ where P is the option premium. Thus its return is the negative value of following:

$$\frac{\min(S_T, K) + P - S_0}{S_0}$$
$$= \min\left(\frac{S_T - S_0}{S_0}, \frac{K - S_0}{S_0}\right) + \frac{P}{S_0}$$
$$\cong \min(s_T - s_0, k - s_0) + p$$

assuming $S_T - S_0$ and $K - S_0$ are small.

Now the expected return conditional on Ω is the negative value of following:

$$E\left[\min(s_T - s_0, k - s_0) + p | \Omega\right]$$
$$= E\left[\min(x_T, x_0) | \Omega\right] + p$$
$$= x_0\left[1 - \Phi(z_0)\right] + \sigma\sqrt{T}\lambda(z_0)\Phi(z_0) + p$$

where $x_T \equiv s_T - s_0$, since

$$\begin{aligned} &E\left[\min(x_T, x_0) | \Omega\right] \\ &= E\left[\min(x_T, x_0) | x_T > x_0, \Omega\right]\Pr(x_T > x_0) \\ &\quad + E\left[\min(x_T, x_0) | x_T \le x_0, \Omega\right]\Pr(x_T \le x_0) \qquad (2) \\ &= x_0 \Pr(x_T > x_0) + E(x_T | x_T \le x_0, \Omega)\Pr(x_T \le x_0) \\ &= x_0\left[1 - \Phi(z_0)\right] + \sigma\sqrt{T}\lambda(z_0)\Phi(z_0) \end{aligned}$$

from the definition of conditional expectation, where $x_T \sim N(0, T\sigma^2)$ from Assumption 2.1 and

$$E(x_T | x_T \le x_0, \Omega) = \sigma\sqrt{T}\lambda(z_0) \qquad (3)$$

for the Equality (2) from [7] (p. 759), and

$$\Pr(x_T \le x_0) = \Pr\left(\frac{x_T}{\sigma\sqrt{T}} \le \frac{x_0}{\sigma\sqrt{T}}\right)$$
$$= \Pr(z_T \le z_0) \equiv \Phi(z_0)$$

where $z_T = x_T/\sigma\sqrt{T}$.

2) The return's variance of call option conditional on Ω is defined as:

$$\begin{aligned} &E\left(\min(x_T, x_0) - E\left[\min(x_T, x_0) | \Omega\right] | \Omega\right)^2 \\ &= E\left(\left[\min(x_T, x_0)\right]^2 | \Omega\right) - \left(E\left[\min(x_T, x_0) | \Omega\right]\right)^2 \end{aligned} \qquad (4)$$

Note the second term of (4) is derived from (2) directly. Then the first term of (4) is arranged as:

[12]This result well explains why a lot of firms of the developing countries with the high interest rate do not use the forward contract. The problem is the cost to use the forward is bigger than the non-hedging if $f_T > s_0$ even though there is the risk difference.

$$
\begin{aligned}
&E\left(\left[\min\left(x_T,x_0\right)\right]^2|\Omega\right)\\
&=E\left(\left[\min\left(x_T,x_0\right)\right]^2|x_T>x_0,\Omega\right)\Pr\left(x_T>x_0\right)\\
&\quad+E\left(\left[\min\left(x_T,x_0\right)\right]^2|x_T\le x_0,\Omega\right)\Pr\left(x_T\le x_0\right) \qquad (5)\\
&=x_0^2\Pr\left(x_T>x_0\right)+E\left(x_T^2|x_T\le x_0,\Omega\right)\Pr\left(x_T\le x_0\right)\\
&=x_0^2\left(1-\Phi\left(z_0\right)\right)+E\left(x_T^2|x_T\le x_0,\Omega\right)\Phi\left(z_0\right)
\end{aligned}
$$

from the definition of conditional expectation for the first equality.

However we may show

$$
E\left(x_T^2|x_T\le x_0\right)=\sigma\sqrt{T}\frac{1}{\sqrt{2}}\frac{\vartheta_3\left(z_0\right)}{\vartheta_1\left(z_0\right)} \qquad (6)
$$

from following facts (b-i) and (b-ii):

$$
\begin{aligned}
E\left(x_T^2|x_T\le x_0\right)&=\int_{x_T\le x_0}x_T^2\frac{g\left(x_T\right)}{G\left(x_T\le x_0\right)}\mathrm{d}x_T\\
&=T\sigma^2\int_{z_T\le z_0}z_T^2\frac{g\left(\sigma\sqrt{T}z_T\right)}{G\left(z_T\le z_0\right)}\sigma\sqrt{T}\mathrm{d}z_T \qquad \text{(b-i)}\\
&=T\sigma^2E\left(z_T^2|z_T\le z_0\right)
\end{aligned}
$$

since $\frac{g\left(\sigma\sqrt{T}z_T\right)}{G\left(z_T\le z_0\right)}\sigma\sqrt{T}$ is the truncated density function of variable z_T since

$$
1=\int_{x_T\le x_0}\frac{g\left(x_T\right)}{G\left(x_T\le x_0\right)}\mathrm{d}x=\int_{z_T\le z_0}\frac{g\left(\sigma\sqrt{T}z_T\right)}{G\left(z_T\le z_0\right)}\sigma\sqrt{T}\mathrm{d}z_T
$$

from the change of variable formula where g and G denote the density and distribution functions of x_T respectively, and $\sigma\sqrt{T}\mathrm{d}z_T=\mathrm{d}x_T$ since $z_T=x_T/\sigma\sqrt{T}$ by definition.

$$
\begin{aligned}
&E\left(z_T^2|z_T\le z_0\right)\\
&=2\frac{\Gamma\left(\frac{3}{2}\right)}{\Gamma\left(\frac{1}{2}\right)}\frac{\vartheta_3\left(z_0\right)-\vartheta_3\left(0\right)}{\vartheta_1\left(z_0\right)-\vartheta_1\left(0\right)}=\frac{1}{\sqrt{2}}\frac{\vartheta_3\left(z_0\right)}{\vartheta_1\left(z_0\right)} \qquad \text{(b-ii)}
\end{aligned}
$$

from [8] (Remark 3), where

$$
\Gamma\left(\frac{1}{2}\right)=\sqrt{\pi}\ \text{ and }\ \Gamma\left(\frac{3}{2}\right)=\sqrt{\pi}\frac{1}{\sqrt[3/2]{2}},
$$

where

$$
h\left(0,1,0\right)=\vartheta_1\left(z_0\right)-\vartheta_1\left(0\right)
$$

and

$$
h\left(0,3,0\right)=\vartheta_3\left(z_0\right)-\vartheta_3\left(0\right)
$$

in [8] (Remark 3) where $\vartheta_1\left(0\right)=\vartheta_3\left(0\right)=0$.

Finally if we plug (6) into (5), then we get the claimed result as:

$$
\begin{aligned}
&E\left(\left[\min\left(x_T,x_0\right)\right]^2|\Omega\right)\\
&=x_0^2\left(1-\Phi\left(z_0\right)\right)+\sigma\sqrt{T}\frac{1}{\sqrt{2}}\frac{\vartheta_3\left(z_0\right)}{\vartheta_1\left(z_0\right)}\Phi\left(z_0\right)
\end{aligned}
$$

2.2. Derivation of Covariances

At second, we derive the covariance among three hedging tools. Note the covariance of returns between non-hedging (or option) and forward is obviously zero since the forward return is not random. Then the covariance of returns between option and non-hedging is given as:

Proposition 2.7. *Suppose* Assumption 2.1 *holds. Then the covariance of returns between option and non-hedging is*

$$
\begin{aligned}
\mathrm{Cov}_{on}&=x_0\sigma\sqrt{T}\lambda\left(z_0\right)\left(1-\Phi\left(z_0\right)\right)\\
&\quad+\sigma\sqrt{T}\frac{1}{\sqrt{2}}\frac{\vartheta_3\left(z_0\right)}{\vartheta_1\left(z_0\right)}\Phi\left(z_0\right).
\end{aligned}
$$

Proof. Note the covariance between non-hedging and option conditional on Ω is defined as:

$$
\begin{aligned}
&E\left[\left(\min\left(x_T,x_0\right)+p-E\left[\min\left(x_T,x_0\right)+p|\Omega\right]\right)x_T|\Omega\right]\\
&=E\left[\left(\min\left(x_T,x_0\right)-E\left[\min\left(x_T,x_0\right)|\Omega\right]\right)x_T|\Omega\right]\\
&=E\left[\min\left(x_T,x_0\right)x_T|\Omega\right]-E\left[\min\left(x_T,x_0\right)|\Omega\right]E\left(x_T|\Omega\right)\\
&=E\left[\min\left(x_T,x_0\right)x_T|\Omega\right]
\end{aligned}
$$

since the fourth equality holds from $E\left(x_T|\Omega\right)=0$.

Now the claimed result is derived since

$$
\begin{aligned}
&E\left[\min\left(x_T,x_0\right)x_T|\Omega\right]\\
&=E\left[\min\left(x_T,x_0\right)x_T|x_T>x_0,\Omega\right]\Pr\left(x_T>x_0\right)\\
&\quad+E\left[\min\left(x_T,x_0\right)x_T|x_T\le x_0,\Omega\right]\Pr\left(x_T\le x_0\right)\\
&=x_0E\left(x_T|x_T>x_0,\Omega\right)\Pr\left(x_T>x_0\right)\\
&\quad+E\left(x_T^2|x_T\le x_0,\Omega\right)\Pr\left(x_T\le x_0\right)\\
&=x_0E\left(x_T|x_T>x_0,\Omega\right)\left(1-\Phi\left(z_0\right)\right)\\
&\quad+E\left(x_T^2|x_T\le x_0,\Omega\right)\Phi\left(z_0\right)\\
&=x_0\sigma\sqrt{T}\lambda\left(z_0\right)\left(1-\Phi\left(z_0\right)\right)+\sigma\sqrt{T}\frac{1}{\sqrt{2}}\frac{\vartheta_3\left(z_0\right)}{\vartheta_1\left(z_0\right)}\Phi\left(z_0\right).
\end{aligned}
$$

from (3) and (6) for the last equation and

$$
\vartheta_1\left(0\right)=\vartheta_3\left(0\right)=0.
$$

3. Exact Efficient Hedging Frontier Construction

Based upon above derivation of return structure, now we may derive the efficient hedging frontier. It is exactly matched with the portfolio possibilities curve in a standard portfolio theory (see [9] for a nice introduction).

For this purpose, first of all, we consider a portfolio composed of non-hedging and call option that are all risky. Let the weight of non-hedging be as w and $1 - w$ for the option where w is a number. Then, from the above derivation, its expected return is defined as:

$$\bar{R}_w = wR_n + (1-w)R_o$$

and its variance is given as:

$$\bar{V}_w = w^2 V_n + (1-w)^2 V_o + 2w(1-w)\text{Cov}_{on}$$

where Cov_{on} denotes a covariance between the returns of non-hedging and call option.

In our case, the return of forward has the zero variance with the expected return is R_f. Thus it is regarded as the riskless asset in the standard portfolio theory. Now the hedging allocation line[13] connecting the riskless forward contract and a combination of non-hedging and call option is defined as:

$$R = R_f + \left(\frac{\bar{R}_w - R_f}{\bar{V}_w}\right)V \tag{7}$$

where R denotes the return and V denotes the risk; $(\bar{R}_w - R_f)/\bar{V}_w$ is a slope.

Then the efficient hedging allocation line[14] is given by solving following problem:

$$\max_w \frac{\bar{R}_w - R_f}{\bar{V}_w} \tag{8}$$

that is maximizing the slope of Equation (7) with the argument w.

The problem (8) may be solved without restriction by [9] (pp. 100-103) as:

$$w^* = \frac{m_1}{m_1 + m_2} \tag{9}$$

where

$$\begin{pmatrix} m_1 \\ m_2 \end{pmatrix} = \begin{pmatrix} V_n & \text{Cov}_{on} \\ \text{Cov}_{on} & V_o \end{pmatrix}^{-1} \begin{pmatrix} R_n - R_f \\ R_o - R_f \end{pmatrix}.$$

If $w^* < 0$ or $1 < w^*$, then the maximization problem (8) should be solved under the restriction $0 \le w \le 1$ using a typical Kuhn-Tucker condition.

[13]It is called as the capital allocation line in the portfolio theory.
[14]It is called as the capital market line in the portfolio theory.

Finally, the efficient hedging frontier is given by

$$R = R_f + \left(\frac{\bar{R}_{w^*} - R_f}{\bar{V}_{w^*}}\right)V \text{ of the left of } (\bar{R}_{w^*}, \bar{V}_{w^*}) \\ = (\bar{R}_w, \bar{V}_w) \text{ of the right of } (\bar{R}_{w^*}, \bar{V}_{w^*}) \tag{10}$$

where $0 \le w^* \le 1$.

For the given efficient frontier in (10), optimal hedging (c.f., separation theorem) is conducted as follows. At first, the hedging ratio between non-hedging and option re set as $(w^*, 1-w^*)$. At second, $\rho(\equiv rho)$ is set for the forward and $(1-\rho)$ is set for the first combination of non-hedging and option. Expected utility maximization may be a rule to determine a ρ. Finally $[\rho, w^*(1-\rho), (1-w^*)(1-\rho)]$ becomes the optimal hedging ratio of the forward, non-hedging and call option with a sum as one. See following **Figure 1**.

Now we suggest an example that shows how above result may be applied in the field.

Example 3.1. Above result is applied to the dollar as domestic currency and the yen as the foreign currency. To compute the efficient hedging frontier in (10), we let $T = 3$ months, $S_0 = 0.8547$ (August 18, 2010), $F_3 = 0.9000$, $K = 0.9000$, $P = 0.0100$ dollar/100yen and an estimator of $\sigma^2 = 0.0888$ (during 2005.1-2009.12).

Then, at first, we get $R_f = -0.1106$, $V_f = 0$, $R_n = 0$, $V_n = 0.0025$, $R_0 = -0.0816$ and $V_0 = 0.0008$ from the above results. Then we obtain the return $\bar{R}_{w^*} = -0.0679$ and variance $\bar{V}_{w^*} = 0.0037$ of the portfolio non-hedging and option where $w^* = 0.1678$.

From this result, the Equation (10) in the efficient hedging frontier becomes:

$$R = -0.1106 + 11.62V \\ \text{of the left of } (-0.0679, 0.0037) \tag{11}$$

Suppose an extremely risk-averse investor maximizes

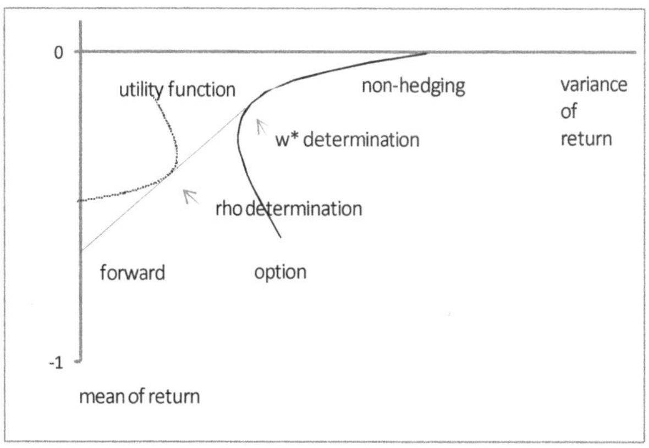

Figure 1. Efficient hedging frontier.

a utility function $u = R - 2000V^2$ subject to (11).[15] The resultant portfolio induces $V = 0.0029$ and $R = -0.0769$. It implies $\rho = 0.0029/0.0037 = 0.7837$ where the utility is maximized with the constraint (11). Thus the forward, non-hedging and option are finally selected as

$$\left[\rho, w^*(1-\rho), (1-w^*)(1-\rho)\right]$$
$$= (0.7837, 0.0362, 0.1800)$$

4. Conclusion

We introduced the optimal foreign exchange risk hedging model following a standard portfolio theory. The results indicate that a lower level of risk can be achieved, given a specified level of expected return, from using optimization modeling. The structure may be extended to cover the futures and American options and we will take it as a future research topic. However I am sure the similar logic may be readily applied to these extensions. Further a development of convenient computer program for FX risk hedging users based on above results might be a useful project.

REFERENCES

[1] P. Sercu and R. Uppal, "International Financial Markets and the Firm," South-Western College Publishing, Cincinnati, 1995.

[2] S. Khoury and K. Chan, "Hedging Foreign Exchange Risk: Selecting the Optimal Tool," *Midland Corporate Finance Journal*, Vol. 5, 1988, pp. 40-52.

[3] N. Beneda, "Optimal Hedging and Foreign Exchange Risk," *Credit and Financial Management Review*, 2004.

[4] Z. Bodie, A. Kane and A. Marcus, "Investments," McGraw Hill, New York, 2002.

[5] F. X. Diebold and J. A. Nason, "Nonparametric Exchange Rate Prediction?" *Journal of International Economics*, Vol. 28, No. 3-4, 1990, pp. 315-332.

[6] M. Garman and S. Kohlhagen, "Foreign Currency Option Values," *Journal of International Money and Finance*, Vol. 2, No. 3, 1983, pp. 231-238.

[7] W. Greene, "Econometric Analysis," Pearson Education, Upper Saddle River, 2003.

[8] E. Marchand, "Computing the Moments of a Truncated Noncentral Ch-Square Distribution," *Journal of Statistical Computation and Simulation*, Vol. 55, No. 4, 1996, pp. 23-29.

[9] E. Elton, M. Gruber, S. Brown and W. Goetzmann, "Modern Portfolio Theory and Investment Analysis," Wiley, New York, 2007.

[15]This utility function largely penalizes the risk and reflects deep risk aversions (e.g., under recent financial crisis). Of course other utility functions may be readily applied.

21

A Note on Timing of Endogenous Wage Bargaining: The Case of Complements*

Kangsik Choi[1], **Minhwan Lee**[2#]
[1]Graduate School of International Studies, Pusan National University, Pusan, South Korea
[2]Division of Global Finance and Banking, Inha University, Incheon, South Korea

ABSTRACT

By introducing Cournot and Bertrand competition in adifferentiated goods with the case of complements into Nash bargaining solution problem, we investigate timing of endogenous wage setting where wages can be negotiated either simultaneously or sequentially. Contrary to the case of substitutes, we show that regardless of the bargaining power, the type of product market competition (Cournot or Bertrand) and the degree of complementarity, 1) bargaining over wages is always simultaneous when the goods are complements; and 2) the social welfare under both Cournot and Bertrand competitions can improve when bargaining over wages is simultaneous.

Keywords: Bargaining; Complements; Cournot-Bertrand Competition; Social Welfare

1. Introduction

In the literature on unionized oligopolies, there has been analyzed regarding the bargaining process between the firm and the union. For instance, in a spatial context, Brekke and Straume [1] haveanalyzed how equilibrium locations in location-price games under Hotelling's model are affected when wage negotiations occur simultaneously. Specifically, Barcena-Ruiz and Casado-Izaga [2] extend the findings of Brekke and Straume [1] by analyzing a duopoly in which firms choose their location and bargain over wages with their unions when the goods are substitutes. Thus, they showed that both unions prefer sequential wage-setting and that the timing of wage setting does not alter the location equilibrium. Moreover, Barcena-Ruiz and Casado-Izaga [2] demonstrate that bargaining over wages is simultaneous if and only if both firms decide when negotiation takes place; otherwise, negotiation takes place sequentially.

However, none of these papers have considered the case in which firms choose to bargain over wages of the endogenous timing when goods are complements. Specifically, Horn and Wolinsky [3] showed that when there is a single input upstream firm, the total profit of downstream industry is smaller or greater under monopoly than under duopoly according to whether the goods are substitutes or complements[1]. However, Horn and Wolinsky [3] restricted their attention to the case of substitutes of sequential wage negotiating and they do not analyze how firms and unions choose to bargain over wages of the endogenous timing when goods are complements. Therefore, by introducing differentiated goods with complements under either Cournot or Bertrand competition, we attempt to examine the situation where both firms or unions or one firm and one union can either simultaneously or sequentially bargain over wages. Thus, we extend Horn and Wolinsky [3], and Barcena-Ruiz and Casado-Izaga [2] by considering the timing of endogenous wage-setting and both Cournot and Bertrand competitions in a duopoly context where outputs and prices are chosen simultaneously.

Consequently, we demonstrate that regardless of the bargaining power, the type of product market competition (Cournot or Bertrand) and the degree of complementarity, bargaining over wages in unionized duopoly is always simultaneous when the goods are complements. This is because when the goods are complements, each union has a strictly dominant strategy for simultaneous wage-setting, under which the firms pay lower wages and produce more outputs and obtain more profits is obtained in the unionized duopolistic market. Hence, when the

*This work was supported by INHA University Research Grant (INHA40279-01).
#Corresponding author.

[1]Barcena-Ruiz and Garzon [4] analyzed a theoretical model for case of multiproduct firms in which both unions and firms can choose their bargaining structures according to whether the goods are substitutes or complements.

goods are complements to each other, it does not matter whether the timing of wage setting is established by: only the two unions; only the two firms; the two unions and only one firm or one union and both firms. Second, we find that regardless of the bargaining power, the type of product market competition (Cournot or Bertrand) and the degree of complementarity, the social welfare under both Cournot and Bertrand competitions can improve when bargaining over wages in a unionized duopoly is simultaneous. These results, when the choice of timing of endogenous wage setting is set in a unionized duopoly, differ from the standard findings of De Fraja [5], Corneo [6], and Barcena-Ruiz and Casado-Izaga [2]. They show that if the goods are substitutes, unions prefer to play sequentially when wage bargaining is decentralized at the level of the firm.

2. Relationship to the Literature

In this section, we discuss the relationship between our paper and some other previous theoretical papers on the bargaining process between the firm and the union.

For non-spatial contexts, theoretical studies that introduce the timing of endogenous wage-setting (*i.e.*, the setting of input costs) into Cournot type of oligopolistic markets include De Fraja [5] and Corneo [6], among others when the goods are substitutes. De Fraja [5] and Corneo [6] show that in aoligopoly, when wage bargaining is decentralized at the level of the firm, unions prefer to play sequentially and vice versa. On the other hand, there have been some attempts, namely, Davidson [7], Naylor [8], Dorwrick [9], Horn and Wolinsky [3,10] and Lommerud *et al.* [11], to introduce the downstream firm negotiating with its labor union into a model of Nash bargaining. Further, as De Fraja [5] and Corneo [6] suggested, Horn and Wolinsky [3] showed that a single supplier prefers to set the input price with one firm and only then with the other firm in where a single supplier faces two firms that produce substitutes.

In a companion paper, the formal structure of the model is closely related to Choi [12]. Choi [12] considers the case in which both private and public firms choose to set over wages of the endogenous timing in a unionized mixed duopoly *without generalized Nash bargaining* between union-firm pair regarding both utility of union and firm's profit (*i.e.*, wage-setting is modelled as that of a monopoly union). Furthermore, introducing only Cournot-type of product market competition into the endogenous timing of wage-setting, Choi [12] investigates social welfare and privatization depending on the nature of goods and the timing of wage-setting in either a unionized-mixed or a unionized-privatized duopolistic market. Thus, Choi [12] demonstrates that regardless of the type of unionized duopoly competition (mixed or privatized duopoly) and the degree of complementarity, wage-setting is always simultaneous if the goods are complements under only Cournot competition. Otherwise, the standard results occur when the goods are substitutes, as De Fraja [5], Corneo [6], and Barcena-Ruiz and Casado-Izaga [2] point out[2]. Instead, by introducing the generalized Nash bargaining power into unionized duopoly, we investigate how firms and unions choose to bargain over wages of the endogenous timing when goods are complements under either Cournot or Bertrand competition. Therefore, present paper is complement to Choi [12], which guarantees the robustness of our result when bargaining between the utility of union and firm's profit takes places.

3. The Model

Consider a unionized duopoly situation for a differentiated good that is supplied by two firms $i = 1,2$. On the demand side of the market, the representative consumer's utility is a quadratic function given by

$$U = x_i + x_j - \frac{1}{2}\left(x_i^2 - 2cx_i x_j + x_j^2\right), i \neq j; i, j = 1,2,$$

where x_i denotes the output of firm $i(i = 1,2)$. Let $c \in (0,1)$ denote the extent of product differentiation with goods assumed to beim perfect complements[3]. Thus, when the goods are complements, the inverse demand is characterized by

$$p_i = 1 + cx_j - x_i, i \neq j : i, j = 1,2, \quad (1)$$

where p_i is firm i's market price.

To analyze the union's wage bargaining, we also assume that both firms are unionized and that the wages, $w_i : i = 1,2$, are determined as a consequence of bargaining between firms and their respective unions. The utility of unions is wage bill: $u_i = (w_i - \bar{w})L_i$. For ease of exposition, let $\bar{w} = 0$ and L_i denote the reservation wage and the number of workers who are employed by firm i, respectively. On the other hand, the firms are homogeneous with respect to productivity. Each firm adopts a constant returns-to-scale technology where one unit of labor is turned into one unit of the final good; thus, $x_i = L_i$. We consider a variant of the right to manage model, where employment is set unilaterally by the firm (see also Booth [14]). Taking $\bar{w} = 0$ as a given, we assume that the wages are determined through Nash bargaining. The solution is wages w_i such that w_i is the Nash solu-

[2]Barcena-Ruiz and Campo [13] showed that unions may choose to set wages simultaneous spending most on R&D if the size of the market is small enough and the efficiency of the R&D technology is great enough.

[3]In the main body of analysis, we exclude the imperfect substitutability viz., the case when $c \in (-1,0)$ since the detailed computations of substitutes are considered by De Fraja [5] and Corneo [6] without the timing of endogenous wage setting. We will discuss the case of substitutes later in this paper.

tion to the bargaining problem between union i and the firm i, given that both expect to agree upon the price w_j. That is, given w_j, the bargaining problem between union i and the firm i is described by the payoff pairs $B=\{[w_i x_i, \pi_i] | w_i \geq 0\}$ and the disagreement point (0,0), where π_i is the profit of the firm i. The solution is given by:

$$w_i = \arg\max_{w_i} a_i \log w_i x_i + (1-a_i)\log \pi_i \quad (2)$$

where $a_i \in [0,1]$ measures the bargaining power of union i relative to that of the firm i. For ease of exposition, we assume that $a_i = a_j$ to show our results in a simple way. The papers that are closest to our representation of the unions' utilities are Davidson [7], Naylor [8], Dorwrick [9], Horn and Wolinsky [3,10] and Lommerud *et al.* [11]. As they suggest, each downstream firm negotiates with its labor union, which maximize the input wage level and number of workers. This is a departure from the framework of traditional models that involves each union has the same bargaining power across the firms.

Each firm's profit is as following function

$$\pi_i = (p_i - w_i)x_i; i = 1,2 \quad (3)$$

where the price of labor (*i.e.*, wage) that firm i has to pay is denoted by w_i, $i=1,2$.

Timing of the second-stage game is as follows. In the first stage, either firms or unions simultaneously decide whether to negotiate over wages in either period 1 or period 2. Note that decision of timing of wage bargaining could be taken in each case by the firms, by the union or a firm and its union in lieu of being chosen by firms or unions to decide the production quantities (or equivalently, the workforce levels). If the periods of negotiation happen to be identical, the wage bargaining process is simultaneous, in which cases a Cournot- and Bertrand-type game occur respectively; otherwise, the wage bargaining process is sequential. In the second stage, each firm simultaneously chooses its quantity or price to maximize its respective objective knowing each union's choice of the wage level.

4. Cournot Equilibrium under Unionized Duopoly

In this paper, since we focus on symmetric Nash equilibrium, we assume that all firms choose the same type of bargaining. Thus, the game is solved by backward induction, *i.e.*, the solution concept used is the subgame perfect Nash equilibrium.

This section examined the impact of a duopoly in terms of the extent of the timing of wage bargaining, which would be established in the case of a unionized duopoly. We discuss one Cournot- and two Stackelberg-type unionized-duopoly models of fixed timing.

4.1. Simultaneous Bargaining over Wages under Cournot Competition

In the second stage, taking as w_i and solving the first-order conditions (3), we obtain,

$$x_i = \frac{1 - w_i + cx_j}{2} \quad (4)$$

Straightforward computation yields each equilibrium output as follows:

$$x_i = \frac{2 + c - 2w_i - cw_j}{4 - c^2} \quad (5)$$

From (5), the each firm's profit, π_i, in the unionized duopoly can be rewritten as follows:

$$\pi_i = \frac{(2 + c - 2w_i - cw_j)^2}{(4-c^2)^2}. \quad (6)$$

We now move to the first stage of the game. Using (5), the problem for union i is defined as

$$u_i = w_i x_i = \frac{w_i(2 + c - 2w_i - cw_j)}{4 - c^2}$$

The wage w_i is determined through Nash bargaining. Applying the maximization problem in (2) to this situation, we have

$$\max_{w_i} a \log\left[\frac{w_i(2+c-2w_i-cw_j)}{4-c^2}\right] + (1-a)\log\left[\frac{(2+c-2w_i-cw_j)^2}{(4-c^2)^2}\right].$$

This implies the following first-order condition

$$w_i = \frac{a(2+c-cw_j)}{4} \quad (7)$$

The symmetry across unions yields that (in following the superscript "c" stands for the case of simultaneous bargaining over wages under Cournot competition)

$$w_i = \frac{a(2+c)}{4+ac} \quad (8)$$

Substituting each wage equilibrium value into (5) yields each equilibrium output x_i^c, firm's profit and utility of union yields that

$$x_i^c = \frac{2(2-a)}{(2-c)(4+ac)},$$
$$\pi_i^c = \frac{4(2-a)^2}{(2-c)^2(4+ac)^2}, u_i^c = \frac{2a(2+c)(2-a)}{(2-c)(4+ac)^2}. \quad (9)$$

4.2. Sequential Bargaining over Wages under Cournot Competition

In this case, we discuss that the firm i or its union acts as the leader regarding wage setting. To solve for the backwards-induction wage setting of this game, we use the firm j's union reaction function $w_j = a(2+c-cw_i)/4$ as in the case of simultaneous bargaining over wages under Cournot competition[4]. To distinguish notations, let the superscript "l" stand for the leader and "f" for the follower. Thus, we obtain each output level as follows;

$$x_i^l = \frac{(2+c)(4-ac)-(8-ac^2)w_j}{4(4-c^2)},$$
$$x_j^f = \frac{(2+c)(2-a)+c(a-2)w_i}{2(4-c^2)}. \tag{10}$$

Hence, the utility of union i is obtained as follows:

$$u_i^l = \frac{w_i\left[(2+c)(4-ac)-(8-ac^2)w_i\right]}{4(4-c^2)}. \tag{11}$$

Straightforward computation yields each firm's profit;

$$\pi_i^l = \frac{\left[(2+c)(4-ac)-(8-ac^2)w_i\right]^2}{16(4-c^2)^2}. \tag{12}$$

As mentioned earlier, the wage w_i is determined through Nash bargaining. Applying the maximization problem in (2) to this situation, we have

$$\max_{w_i} a\log\left\{\frac{w_i\left[(2+c)(4-ac)-(8-ac^2)w_i\right]}{4(4-c^2)}\right\}$$
$$+(1-a)\log\left\{\frac{\left[(2+c)(4-ac)-(8-ac^2)w_i\right]^2}{16(4-c^2)^2}\right\}$$

Straightforward computation yields each equilibrium wage as follows:

$$w_i^l = \frac{a(2+c)(4-ac)}{2(8-ac^2)},$$
$$w_j^f = \frac{a(2+c)\left(16-2ac(2+c)+a^2c^2\right)}{8(8-ac^2)}. \tag{13}$$

Therefore, substituting (13) into (10), (11) and (12) yields each equilibrium output, utility of union and firm's profit yields that

$$x_i^l = \frac{(4-ac)(2-a)}{8(2-c)},$$
$$x_j^f = \frac{(2-a)\left(16-2ac(2+c)+a^2c^2\right)}{4(2-c)(8-ac^2)}, \tag{14}$$

$$u_i^l = \frac{a(2+c)(2-a)(4-ac)^2}{16(2-c)(8-ac^2)},$$
$$u_j^f = \frac{a(2+c)(2-a)\left(16-2ac(2+c)+a^2c^2\right)^2}{32(2-c)(8-ac^2)^2} \tag{15}$$

$$\pi_i^l = \frac{(4-ac)^2(2-a)^2}{64(2-c)^2},$$
$$\pi_j^f = \frac{(2-a)^2\left(16-2ac(2+c)+a^2c^2\right)^2}{16(2-c)^2(8-ac^2)^2} \tag{16}$$

5. Bertrand Equilibrium under Unionized Duopoly

In this section, we assume that the product market game in the stage 2 is characterized by Bertrand competition by firms. Thus, we examined the impact of a duopoly in terms of the extent of the timing of wage bargaining, which would be established in the case of a unionized duopoly.

We discuss one Bertrand- and two Stackelberg-type unionized-duopoly models of fixed timing. From (1) and its rival firm j, we can rewrite product demand function facing firm i as

$$x_i = \frac{1+c-p_i-cp_j}{1-c^2}. \tag{17}$$

Thus, profits of firm i are given by

$$\pi_i = \frac{(p_i-w_i)(1+c-p_i-cp_j)}{1-c^2} \tag{18}$$

when goods are complements.

5.1. Simultaneous Bargaining over Wages under Bertrand Competition

In the second stage, taking as w_i and solving the first-order conditions (18), we obtain,

$$p_i = \frac{1+c+w_i-cp_j}{2}. \tag{19}$$

Straightforward computation yields each equilibrium price and output as follows:

[4]The case in which wages are bargained first in frim j is symmetric. Hence, we omit it.

$$p_i = \frac{(1+c)(2-c)+2w_i - cw_j}{4-c^2},$$
$$x_i = \frac{(1+c)(2-c)-(2-c^2)w_i - cw_j}{(4-c^2)(1-c^2)} \quad (20)$$

From (20), the each firm's profit, π_i, in the unionized duopoly can be rewritten as follows:

$$\pi_i = \frac{\left[(1+c)(2-c)-(2-c^2)w_i - cw_j\right]^2}{(4-c^2)^2(1-c^2)}. \quad (21)$$

We now move to the first stage of the game. Using (20), the problem for union i is defined as

$$u_i = w_i x_i = \frac{w_i\left[(1+c)(2-c)-(2-c^2)w_i - cw_j\right]}{(4-c^2)(1-c^2)}.$$

The wage w_i is determined through Nash bargaining. Applying the maximization problem in (2) to this situation, we have

$$\max_{w_i} a\log\left\{\frac{w_i\left[(1+c)(2-c)-(2-c^2)w_i - cw_j\right]}{(4-c^2)(1-c^2)}\right\}$$
$$+(1-a)\log\left\{\frac{\left[(1+c)(2-c)-(2-c^2)w_i - cw_j\right]^2}{(4-c^2)^2(1-c^2)}\right\}.$$

This implies the following first-order condition

$$w_i = \frac{a(1+c)(2-c)-acw_j}{2(2-c^2)}. \quad (22)$$

The symmetry across unions yields that (in following the superscript "B" stands for the case of simultaneous bargaining over wages under Bertrand competition)

$$w_i^B = \frac{a(1+c)(2-c)}{2(2-c^2)+ac},$$
$$x_i^B = \frac{(2+a)(2-c^2)}{(1-c)(2+c)\left[2(2-c^2)+ac\right]}. \quad (23)$$

Substituting each wage equilibrium values into (20) yields each equilibrium output x_i^B, firm's profit and utility of union as follows;

$$\pi_i^B = \frac{(1+c)\left[(2+a)(2-c^2)\right]^2}{(1-c)(2+c)^2\left[2(2-c^2)+ac\right]^2},$$
$$u_i^B = \frac{a(2-a)(2-c^2)(1+c)(2-c)}{(1-c)(2+c)\left[2(2-c^2)+ac\right]^2}. \quad (24)$$

5.2. Sequential Bargaining over Wages under Bertrand Competition

In this case, we discuss that the firm i or its union acts as the leader regarding wage setting. To solve for the backwards-induction wage setting of this game, we use the firm j's union reaction function

$$w_j = \frac{a(1+c)(2-c)-acw_i}{2(2-c^2)}$$

as in the case of simultaneous bargaining over wages under Bertrand competition. To distinguish notations, let the superscript "L" (respectively, "F") denote the equilibrium value in the case of leadership (respectively, followership) wage bargaining that the rival firm takes as given. Thus, we obtain each output level as follows:

$$x_i^L = \frac{(1+c)(2-c)\left[2(2-c^2)-ac\right]}{2(1-c^2)(2-c^2)(4-c^2)} + \frac{w_i\left[ac^2-2(2-c^2)^2\right]}{2(1-c^2)(2-c^2)(4-c^2)},$$
$$x_j^F = \frac{(2-a)\left[(1+c)(2-c)-cw_i\right]}{2(1-c^2)(4-c^2)}. \quad (25)$$

Hence, the utility of union i is obtained as follows:

$$u_i^L = \frac{w_i(1+c)(2-c)\left[2(2-c^2)-ac\right]}{2(1-c^2)(2-c^2)(4-c^2)} + \frac{w_i^2\left[ac^2-2(2-c^2)^2\right]}{2(1-c^2)(2-c^2)(4-c^2)} \quad (26)$$

Straightforward computation yields each firm's profit;

$$\pi_i^L = \frac{(1+c)(2-c)\left[2(2-c^2)-ac\right]}{(1-c^2)\left[2(2-c^2)(4-c^2)\right]^2} + \frac{w_i\left[ac^2-2(2-c^2)^2\right]^2}{(1-c^2)\left[2(2-c^2)(4-c^2)\right]^2} \quad (27)$$

As mentioned earlier, the wage w_i is determined through Nash bargaining. Applying the maximization problem in (2) to this situation, we have

$$\max_{w_i} a\log\left\{\frac{w_i(1+c)(2-c)\left[2\left(2-c^2\right)-ac\right]+w_i^2\left[ac^2-2\left(2-c^2\right)^2\right]}{2\left(1-c^2\right)\left(2-c^2\right)(4-c^2)}\right\}$$

$$+(1-a)\log\left\{\frac{\left[(1+c)(2-c)\left[2\left(2-c^2\right)-ac\right]+w_i\left[ac^2-2\left(2-c^2\right)^2\right]\right]^2}{\left(1-c^2\right)\left[2\left(2-c^2\right)\left(4-c^2\right)\right]^2}\right\}$$

Straightforward computation yields each equilibrium wage as follows:

$$w_i^L=\frac{a(1+c)(2-c)\left[2\left(2-c^2\right)-ac^2\right]}{2\left[2\left(2-c^2\right)^2-ac^2\right]},\ w_j^F=\frac{a(1+c)(2-c)\left[4\left(2-c^2\right)^2-2ac(2-c^2)-ac^2(2-a)\right]}{4\left(2-c^2\right)\left[2\left(2-c^2\right)^2-ac^2\right]}. \qquad (28)$$

Therefore, substituting (28) into (25), (26) and (27) yields each equilibrium outputs, utilities of unions and firms' profits as follows:

$$x_i^L=\frac{(2-a)\left[2\left(2-c^2\right)-ac\right]}{4(1-c)(2+c)\left(2-c^2\right)},\ x_j^F=\frac{(2-a)\left[4\left(2-c^2\right)^2-2ac(2-c^2)-ac^2(2-a)\right]}{4(1-c)(2+c)\left[2\left(2-c^2\right)^2-ac^2\right]}$$

$$u_i^L=\frac{a(2-a)(1+c)(2-c)\left[2\left(2-c^2\right)-ac\right]^2}{8(1-c)(2+c)\left(2-c^2\right)\left[2\left(2-c^2\right)-ac^2\right]},\ u_j^F=\frac{a(2-a)(1+c)(2-c)\left[4\left(2-c^2\right)^2-2ac\left(2-c^2\right)-ac^2(2-a)\right]^2}{16\left(2-c^2\right)(1-c)(2+c)\left[2\left(2-c^2\right)^2-ac^2\right]^2}$$

$$\pi_i^L=\frac{(1+c)(2-a)^2\left[2\left(2-c^2\right)-ac\right]^2}{16(1-c)(2+c)^2\left(2-c^2\right)^2},\ \pi_j^F=\frac{(1+c)(2-a)^2\left[4\left(2-c^2\right)^2-2ac\left(2-c^2\right)-ac^2(2-a)\right]^2}{(1-c)\left[4(2+c)\left[2\left(2-c^2\right)^2-ac^2\right]\right]^2}.$$

6. Choice of Bargaining Timing and Social Welfare

Having derived the equilibrium for three fixed-timing games in the previous section and using the same notation for the timings as before, we can determine firm's endogenous timing that each takes the utilities of unions and firms' profits and social welfare as a given.

Let "*F*" and "*S*" represent first period and second period with regard to timing choice of wage setting respectively. When agents (the firms or the unions) have chosen "*F*" or "*S*", they will play a Cournot- or Bertrand-type game of the wage setting in the first stage; when one firm's agent has chosen "*F*" while the other's agent has chosen "*S*", Stackelberg-type game of the wage setting arises in the second stage and vice versa.

In this section, we will find the Nash equilibrium in the first stage for any given utilities of the unions and the profits of firms under duopoly. The reduced endogenous-timing game among unions can be represented by the following payoff table.

To find the subgame-perfect Nash equilibrium, we need to compare utilities of unions. From **Table 1**, straitforward computations show that

$$u_i^c<u_i^l \Leftrightarrow -\left[32-a(32-ac)\right]<0;$$

$$u_i^c>u_i^f \Leftrightarrow 128-8ac^2-2a^2c^3+a^3c^3>0,$$

$$u_i^B<u_i^L \Leftrightarrow -8\left(2-c^2\right)^2(1-a)<ac^2;$$

$$u_i^B>u_i^F \Leftrightarrow 0>-ac(2-a).$$

These inequalities tell us that regardless of whether the type of product market is Cournot or Bertrand competition, each firm's union prefers simultaneous wage setting to sequential wage setting. So there is a unique subgame perfect Nash equilibrium of wage-setting: (*F*, *F*). Thus, we have the following lemma:

Lemma 1. *Suppose that the goods are complements and that the decision of the timing of wage setting is delegated to unions in duopoly market. Then, there can be sustained a unique endogenous order of wage setting. The order is* (*F*, *F*).

The intuition in the case of complements is as follows. The fact that the first opportunity of wage setting in duopoly market is the strictly dominant strategy for all unions plays an important role in the derivation of the re-

Table 1. Timing of wage setting between Union *i* and Union *j*.

Union *i* \ Union *j*	F	S
F	u_i^*, u_j^*	u_i^α, u_j^β
S	u_i^β, u_j^α	u_i^*, u_j^*

Note that $* = c$, $\alpha = l$, $\beta = f$ if Cournot competition and $* = B$, $\alpha = L$, $\beta = F$ if Bertrand competition.

sult.

It is clearly always better to be a leader than a follower. Contrary to the case of substitutes of wage setting, we show that unions choose to wages in the first opportunity when goods are complements: Although the number of workers employed in the simultaneous case is more than the number employed when the union is a follower (*i.e.*, $x_i^c > x_i^f > x_i^l$ and $x_i^B > x_i^F > x_i^L$), each union gets higher wages in the leader union (*i.e.*, $w_i^l > w_i^c > w_i^f$ and $w_i^L > w_i^B > w_i^F$). This implies that both unions obtain greater utilities under the simultaneous case than under the sequential case. Therefore, regardless of both the bargaining power, the type of product market competition (Cournot or Bertrand) and the degree of complementarity, all unions prefer to set the wages simultaneously in duopoly market[5].

Similar to the timing of wage setting among unions, the reduced endogenous-timing game among firms can be represented by the following payoff tables.

To find the subgame-perfect Nash equilibrium, we need to compare each firm's profit. Straightforward computations show in **Table 2** that

$$\pi_i^c > \pi_i^l \Leftrightarrow 2 > a; \pi_i^c > \pi_i^f \Leftrightarrow a^2c^2 > 0;$$
$$\pi_i^l < \pi_i^f \Leftrightarrow c < 2; \pi_i^B < \pi_i^F \Leftrightarrow 0 > -ac;$$

$$\pi_i^B > \pi_i^L \Leftrightarrow -(ac)^2;$$
$$\pi_i^B > \pi_i^L \Leftrightarrow (2-c^2)\left[ac - 2(1-c^2)\right] < ac^2$$

These inequalities tell us that each firm prefers simultaneous wage setting to sequential wage setting. So there are multiple subgame perfect Nash equilibria in the timing of endogenous wage-setting: (*F*, *F*), (*S*, *S*). Thus, we have the following lemma:

Lemma 2. *Suppose that the decision of the timing of wage setting is not delegated to the unions in duopoly market. Then, when the goods are complements, duopoly market can always sustain multiple subgame-perfect equilibria; the order is either (S, S) or (F, F).*

Table 2. Timing of wage setting between Firm *i* and Firm *j*.

Firm *i* \ Firm *j*	F	S
F	π_i^*, π_j^*	$\pi_i^\alpha, \pi_j^\beta$
S	$\pi_i^\beta, \pi_j^\alpha$	π_i^*, π_j^*

Note that $* = c$, $\alpha = l$, $\beta = f$ if Cournot competition and $* = B$, $\alpha = L$, $\beta = F$ if Bertrand competition.

The intuition of Lemma 2 is as follows. Lemma 2 confirms that regardless of the bargaining power, the type of product market competition and the degree of complementarity, the simultaneous negotiation of wages yields greater profits. In Lemma 1, we have considered that when the goods are complements, the workers employed in the simultaneous case are more than those in the sequential case and the unions get lower wages in the simultaneous case[6]. From the viewpoint of the firms, in the simultaneous case, they pay lower wages, produce more outputs, and realize more profits, which leads to the results $\pi_i^c > \pi_i^f > \pi_i^l$ and $\pi_i^B > \pi_i^F > \pi_i^L$. As a result, the firms in the simultaneous case get greater profits than that in the sequential case. Thus, both firms prefer to simultaneously set wages.

Given Lemma 1 and 2, we obtain the following result.

Proposition 1. *When the goods are complements, bargaining over wages is always simultaneous, regardless of bargaining power, the degree of complementarity and the type of product market competition (Cournot or Bertrand).*

Proof. Regardless of whether the type of product market is Bertrand or Cournot competition, the proof is the same from the result of Lemmas 1 and 2. Hence, we do not distinguish the type of product market competition.

First, consider the case when both unions decide the timing of wage setting. Then, both unions do not have incentives to play sequentially since there is a dominant strategy for each union, which is to bargain at the first opportunity.

Second, consider that both firms decide the timing of wage setting. As shown in Propositions 1 and 2, both firms prefer to play simultaneously regardless of c and a, *i.e.*, they wish to bargain at either the first or the second opportunity. This case shows that both firms prefer to play simultaneously even though there is no dominant strategy.

Third, consider that the firm *i* and the firm *j*'s union decide on the timing of endogenous wage-setting. There is a dominant strategy for the firm *j*'s union, which is to

[5]In contrast to Barcena-Ruiz and Campo [15], this result is because wages are strategic "substitutes". When the goods are substitutes, due to the fact that $w_i^l > w_i^f > w_i^c$, $w_i^L > w_i^F > w_i^C$, $x_i^f > x_i^c > x_i^l$ and $x_i^B > x_i^B > x_i^L$, we obtain the results that union prefers sequential wage setting: multiple subgame-perfect Nash equilibria can be sustained as (*F*, *S*) and (*S*, *F*).

[6]When the goods are substitutes, due to the fact that $\pi_i^f > \pi_i^c > \pi_i^l$ and $\pi_i^F > \pi_i^B > \pi_i^L$, a unique endogenous wage setting can always be sustained as (*S*, *S*).

bargain at the first opportunity. Given this, the firm igets a higher profit in the simultaneous case. Then, we have a simultaneous game at the bargaining stage.

Finally, suppose that the game is played by both firms and unions. In this case, neither union deviates from the first opportunity because both unions have a dominant strategy, which is to play at the first opportunity and be a leader. On the other hand, if one firm prefers to delay wage bargaining, then both unions have a dominant strategy, which is to play at the first opportunity and be a leader. Further, the firm does not have an incentive to deviate from the simultaneous case because its firm always prefers to play simultaneously. The same result can be obtained if the game is played by one firm and its union and vice versa. Q.E.D.

When the goods are complements, Proposition 1 is in contrast to one of the findings when the goods are substitutes, namely, that only two firms have incentives to play simultaneously (*i.e.*, to bargain at only the second opportunity) regarding endogenous wage-setting, which can be sustained as an equilibrium outcome. In our setting, since there is a strictly dominant strategy for each union and there is no strictly dominant strategy for each firm in duopoly market when the goods are complements, all the firms and unions prefer to play simultaneously at first opportunity[7]. It does not matter whether the timing of wage setting is established only by the two unions, by the unions and only one firm, or by one union and both firms. That is, bargaining over wages is always simultaneous when the goods are complements.

Noting that the social welfare

$$W = U - \sum_{i=1}^{2} p_i x_i + \sum_{i=1}^{2} (\pi_i + u_i)$$

which consists of consumer surplus $\left(U - \sum_{i=1}^{2} p_i x_i\right)$ and producer surplus $\left(\sum_{i=1}^{2} (\pi_i + u_i)\right)$, we can compute the social welfare W under either Cournot or Bertrand competition[8]. As shown in Propositions 1, the social welfare when the goods are complements is always determined by simultaneous timing of wage bargaining in a duopoly. Therefore, we immediately have the following proposition.

Proposition 2. *Suppose that each union has same bargaining power. Then, each level of social welfare is determined by*

$$W^c > W^l = W^f \text{ and } W^B > W^L = W^F.$$

Proof. See Appendix A. Q.E.D.

Proposition 2 suggests that regardless of the bargaining power, the type of product market competition and the degree of complementary, the social welfare is higher in the simultaneous case than in the sequential one. Therefore, when the goods are complements, larger social welfare can be obtained regardless of whether the timing of wage setting is established only by the two unions, by the unions and only one firm, or by one union and all firms. The intuition behind Proposition 2 is as follows. In this paper, we have assumed that the social welfare depends positively upon quantities produced, which consists of the representative consumer's utility. Since equilibrium quantities are higher under either Cournot or Bertrand competition, each firm can gain a higher profit, and total output is larger by choosing simultaneous case and equilibrium price becomes smaller by choosing sequential case, social welfare is larger in the simultaneous case than in the sequential one. Proposition 2 suggests that differences in the implementation of leadership depend on the nature of goods. That is, we find that when the goods are complements, social welfare of simultaneous bargaining over wages is obtained regardless of whether the type of product market is Bertrand or Cournot competition.

7. Concluding Remarks

This study has investigated the changes in the timing of endogenous wage setting when the goods are complements under either Cournout or Bertrand competition. By introducing the timing of endogenous wage setting into the unionized duopoly-framework when the goods are complements, this study provides new insight into the timing of endogenous wage setting. We have found that regardless of the bargaining power and the degree of complementarity, bargaining over wages is always simultaneous if the goods are complements. This result indicates differences in the implementation of endogenous wage setting according to whether the goods are substitutes or complements.

Finally, in this paper, we have used simplifying assumption that each firm's union is allowed to engage in decentralized bargaining. Furthermore, a limitation of this study is that there is different bargaining structure among the firms, which can be considered the preferred bargaining structure. Therefore, this paper does not investigate the existence of degree of centralization of union bargaining matters for all firms to choose different bargaining regime for different firms. The extension of our model in these directions remains an agendum for future research.

REFERENCES

[1] K. Brekke and O. R. Straume, "Bilateral Monopolies and Location Choice," *Regional Science and Urban Economics*, Vol. 34, No. 3, 2004, pp. 275-288.

[7]When the goods are substitutes, bargaining over wages is simultaneous if and only if both firm decide on the period of time in which bargaining takes place. Otherwise, bargaining takes place sequentially.

[8]Utilities of unions are included as the part of producer surplus, which is usual in literature.

[2] J. C. Barcena-Ruiz and F. J. Casado-Izaga, "Timing in Endogenous Bargaining over Costs and Firm Location," *Journal of Economics*, Vol. 95, No. 2, 2008, pp. 149-166.

[3] H. Horn and A. Wolinsky, "Bilateral Monopolies and Incentives for Merger," *Rand Journal of Economics*, Vol. 19, No. 3, 1988, pp. 408-419.

[4] J. C. Barcena-Ruiz and M. B. Garzon, "The Organisation of Wage Bargaining in Divisionalised Firms," *Australian Economic Papers*, Vol. 41, No. 3, 2002, pp. 305-319.

[5] G. De Fraja, "Staggered vs Synchronized Wage Setting in Oligopoly," *European Economic Review*, Vol. 37, 1993, pp. 1507-1522.

[6] G. Corneo, "National Wage Bargaining in an International Integrated Product Markets," *European Journal of Political Economy*, Vol. 11, No. 3, 1995, pp. 503-520.

[7] C. Davidson, "Multiunit Bargaining in Oligopolistic Industries," *Journal of Labor Economics*, Vol. 6, No. 3, 1988, pp. 397-422.

[8] R, A. Naylor, "Industry Profits and Competition under Bilateral Oligopoly," *Economics Letters*, Vol. 77, No. 2, 2002, pp. 169-175.

[9] S. Dorwrick, "Union-Oligopoly Bargaining," *Economic Journal*, Vol. 99, No. 398, 1989, pp. 1123-1142.

[10] H. Horn and A. Wolinsky, "Worker Substitutability and Patterns of Unionization," *Economic Journal*, Vol. 98, 1988, pp. 484-497.

[11] K. E. Lommerud, F. Meland and L. Sorgard, "Unionised Oligopoly, Trade Liberalisation and Location Choice," *Economic Journal*, Vol. 113, No. 490, 2003, pp. 782-800.

[12] K. Choi, "Timing of Endogenous Wage Setting and Privatization in a Differentiated Industry: A Mixed Duopoly Approach," Mimeo, Pusan National University, Pusan, 2009.

[13] J. C. Barcena-Ruiz and M. L. Campo, "R&D Investment and Sequential Wage Negotiation," *Australian Economic Papers*, Vol. 48, No. 3, 2009, pp. 183-202.

[14] A. Booth, "The Economics of the Trade Union," Cambridge University Press, Cambridge, 1995.

[15] J. C. Barcena-Ruiz and M. L. Campo, "Short-Term or Long-Term Labor Contracts," *Labour Economics*, Vol. 7, No. 3, 2000, pp. 249-260.

Appendix

Proof of Proposition 2: Noting that social welfare W^c (respectively, W^c) of simultaneous wage bargaining under Cournot (respectively, Bertrand) competition and social welfare $W^l = W^f$ (respectively, $W^L = W^F$) of sequential wage bargaining under Cournot (respectively, Bertrand) competition, we can compute the social wel- fare W^c, $W^l = W^f$ as follows;

$$W^c = \frac{2(2-a)(14+a-6c+3ac-2ac^2)}{(2-c)^2(4+ac)^2},$$

$$W^l = \frac{(2-a)\left[(8-ac^2)^2(4-ac)(24-16c+2ac+4a-a^2c)\right]}{128(2-c)^2(8-ac^2)^2} + \frac{(2-a)\left[4(16-2ac(2+c)+a^2c^2)^2(6-ac^2+a)\right]}{128(2-c)^2(8-ac^2)^2}.$$

Comparing social welfare under the simultaneous withthat under sequential wage setting, straightforward computations show under Cournot competition that[9]

$$\begin{aligned} & W^c - W^l\left(W^f\right) > 0 \\ & \Leftrightarrow 29768 - 16384a - 32768c + 16654ac - 8192ac^2 + 8192ac^3 + 8192a^2c^2 - 2048a^2c^3 \\ & \quad - 7680a^2c^4 - 512a^2c^5 + 2048a^3c^2 + 5888a^3c^4 - 512a^3c^5 - 512a^4c^3 - 384a^4c^4 + 256a^4c^5 \\ & \quad + 224a^4c^6 + 64a^4c^7 - 64a^5c^4 + 64a^5c^5 + 80a^5c^6 - 32a^5c^7 + 8a^6c^6 - 14a^6c^8 - 4a^7c^6 + 34a^7c^8 > 0. \end{aligned}$$

On the other hand, since comparing W^B with $W^L = W^F$ becomes complicated, so we need to use numerical examples to illustrate the impact of the degree of complementartity. Using this computation, the numerical analysis of **Table A-1** shows that the social welfare of W^B is larger than that of $W^L = W^F$ under Bertrand competition.

Table A-1. Numerical examples under Bertrand competition.

	$W^B - W^L$	$W^B - W^L$	$W^B - W^L$	$W^B - W^L$	$W^B - W^L$	$W^B - W^L$	$W^B - W^L$	$W^B - W^L$	$W^B - W^L$
	$\alpha = 0.01$	$\alpha = 0.2$	$\alpha = 0.3$	$\alpha = 0.4$	$\alpha = 0.5$	$\alpha = 0.6$	$\alpha = 0.7$	$\alpha = 0.8$	$\alpha = 0.99$
$c = 0.01$	1.58614	6.27235	1.39242	2.42928	3.70402	5.17347	6.78511	8.47713	1.16513
$c = 0.2$	8.87815	3.42475	7.50354	0.000129	0.000194	0.000267	0.000346	0.000427	0.000573
$c = 0.3$	2.5002	9.5305	0.0002	0.00035	0.00053	0.00072	0.00093	0.0011	0.0015
$c = 0.4$	5.8112	0.00021	0.00047	0.00080	0.0011	0.0016	0.0020	0.0025	0.0003
$c = 0.5$	1.2554	0.00046	0.0010	0.0017	0.0025	0.0033	0.0043	0.0052	0.0067
$c = 0.6$	2.6942	0.00099	0.00212	0.0035	0.0054	0.0070	0.00886	0.0106	0.01356
$c = 0.7$	6.0860	0.00221	0.00472	0.00787	0.01148	0.0153	0.0192	0.0229	0.02882
$c = 0.8$	1.5696	0.0056	0.01198	0.0198	0.02884	0.03828	0.0476	0.05653	0.0701
$c = 0.99$	0.0010	0.3692	0.7784	1.2897	1.8673	2.4768	3.0850	3.6610	4.5635

The positive number in each cell depicts that given the degree of complementarity, c or the bargaining power of union, α, the comparisons of social welfare implies $W^B > W^L = W^F$.

[9]Comparing W^c with $W^l = W^f$ is obtained using Microsoft Office Excel.

State-Dependence and Conditional Audit Policy

Ruey-Ji Guo, Yenpao Chen, Chun Chen Lee
Department of Accounting, Soochow University, Taipei, Taiwan

ABSTRACT

This paper investigates how the state-dependence between two periods affects the optimal audit decision. Using a principal-agent model, based on a state-dependent assumption, we find that it is desirable to use a conditional (punitive) audit mechanism when the agent's under-declaration benefit is significant and the principal's audit cost is moderate. In that case, the audit policy for the current period will be contingent on the audit result in the preceding period.

Keywords: Information Asymmetry; Agency Problem; Audit Policy

1. Introduction

To alleviate the problem resulting from information asymmetry, the principal tends to use audit mechanism to abate the related agency costs, or to maximize the net revenues concerned. The past studies have paid considerable attention to the audit issues, including Antle [1], Baron and Besanko [2], Demski and Sappington [3], and Baiman, Evans and Noel [4]. Variables of particular interest are the audit probability and the conditions upon which it depends. Using the data from the American pulp and paper industry, Helland [5] found that firms which are discovered in violation of environmental regulations experience a one- or two-quarter period of more frequent inspections from regulators. Placing higher inspection probability on agents with the record of incompliance appears to be a scheme preferred by the regulators.

Audit rules conditional on compliance history are broadly adopted by researchers as well. For instance, Landsberger and Meilijson [6] proposed that an agent's current audit results affect its probability of future audits. By targeting audits based on current audit outcomes, They demonstrated that conditional auditing is more cost-effective than random auditing and that agencies could increase tax revenue given the same enforcement budget and fine scheme. The use of such endogenous and dynamic enforcement mechanisms that use information obtained through prior audit to assign the agent's probability of future audits are extended to the literature of pollution regulation and tax compliance (e.g. Greenberg [7], Harrington [8], Friesen [9], and Stafford [10]).

In this paper, we present a two-period model with a state-dependent scenario, *i.e.* the nature state in period two is correlated with that in period one, to address the principal's audit decision and study the potential effect of state-dependence between different periods. Essentially, audit mechanism is associated with penalty system. As Landsberger and Meilijson [6] note that penalty systems usually include two elements of both penalty function and probability of detection, while from the practical point of view, the latter more than the former is under the control of the authorities. Accordingly, this paper focuses on the issue of optimal audit probability (probability of detection), and aims to identify the desirability of conditional audit.

By controlling the state-dependent degree of return, we demonstrate that a conditional audit policy can make the audit implementation more efficient only when the auditee's benefit of under-declaring return is larger than the expected penalty under complete audit and the audit cost is relatively moderate. In that case, by using conditional audit mechanism, the principal can concentrate costly audit resources on the auditees with higher probability to under-declare their actual returns. Additionally, we find that the state-dependent degree of return indeed plays a prominent role in whether to use conditional audit policy or not. This paper points out it may not be desirable for the principal to implement any conditional audit especially in a situation that the returns in two periods are totally independent.

2. The Model

In this paper, we use a principal-agent hierarchy, including a principal, an auditor and a manager, to address the issue of conditional audit in a two-period scenario. It is assumed that, in a vertical structure owned by the principal, the manager operates a business unit and holds private information concerning its realized returns. The principal can obtain the true return information only by assigning the auditor to undertake audit task. For sim= plicity, it is assumed that all parties are risk neutral, and the auditor is absolutely independent.

In the two-period scenario, nature is assumed to be the only one factor affecting the realized return, *i.e.* high return (R_H) or low return (R_L). In period one, the probability of high return is p (and $0 < p < 1$). However, under the assumption of state-dependence, the probability of high return occurring in period two will be contingent on the realized return in period one. If the realized return in period one is high (low), the probability of high return occurring in period two will be p_h(p_l). It is assumed that $0 < p_l < p < p_h < 1$. While the realized return in either period one or period two is the manager's private information, the probabilities p, p_h and p_l can be estimated objectively according to the past operating results, and regarded as common information. In the paper, the principal will take the information into account while planning the related audit policy. Specifically, we incorporate the exogenous variables p, p_h and p_l into the principal's objective function to develop the optimal two-period audit policy. At the end of each period, the manager is required to declare a return level (either high return (R_H) or low return (R_L)) to the principal, and transfers a portion (α) of the return to the latter. The transferring agreement brings about an incentive for the manager to under-declare the return.

This paper allows the principal to consider a two- period conditional audit mechanism to deter the manager's possible under-declaration of return. At the end of each period, the principal needs to determine whether to employ the auditor at cost C to audit the low return declared by the manager. If the auditor finds the under-declaration of return, the manager will be required to pay a penalty of $\overline{P}$. Following the previous literature (e.g. Malik [11]), the penalty of $\overline{P}$ is set as a maximal possible amount to minimize the expected audit cost, and it can be regarded as a legally specified limit on liability. Under a conditional audit mechanism, the audit policy for the second period is likely to be dependent on the audit result in the first period. In period one, the probability to audit the low return declared by the manager is assumed to be A. However, if the under-declaration of return in period one is found and revealed by the auditor, the audit probability for the second period will be enhanced up to $A'(\equiv A+a)$ provided the manager declares a low return once more in period two; otherwise, the audit probability will remain to be A, where $0 \le A \le 1$, $0 \le a \le 1-A$, and $A \le A'$. That is so-called "conditional audit" used in this paper.

Furthermore, the auditor's audit quality is defined as a probability, r that the manager's under-declaration can be found by the auditor. In other words, there remains a probability, $1-r$ that the auditor will be unable to disclose the manager's dishonest behavior even if the former has accomplished the related audit task. In this paper, we exclude the possibility of blackmail or collusion between the auditor and the manager. Both C and r are assumed to be the common information of all parties involved. The following is the timing on the relevant events.

1) The principal and the manager achieve an agreement that the latter will transfer a certain portion (α) of the return to the former.

2) Nature determines the realized return in period one, which is a high return (R_H) with the probability of p or a low return (R_L) with the probability of $1-p$.

3) The manager declares the return in period one ($\hat{R}_1$) to the principal and will transfer $\alpha \cdot \hat{R}_1$ to the latter.

4) The principal assigns the auditor to undertake audit task at cost C with an audit probability A if the manager declares a low return in period one (*i.e.* $\hat{R}_1 = R_L$).

5) The auditor presents an audit report. If the under-declaration of return is disclosed, the manager will have to pay the principal a penalty of $\overline{P}$, assumed to be larger than $\alpha \cdot (R_H - R_L)$ for compensation and punishment. Also, the manager's dishonest record will be kept for reference in next period.

6) Nature determines the realized return in period two once more. If the realized return in period one is R_H(R_L), the probability of high return occurring in period two will be p_h(p_l), where $p_l < p < p_h$.

7) The manager declares the return in period two, $\hat{R}_2$, and will transfer $\alpha \cdot \hat{R}_2$ to the principal.

8) The principal sends the auditor at cost C with a probability A if the manager was not found under-declaring the return in period one and declares a low return in period two (*i.e.* $\hat{R}_2 = R_L$), but with a probability A' if the manager was found under-declaring the return in period one and declares a low return in period two, where $A \le A'$.

9) The auditor presents an audit report, and the manager will be required to pay a penalty of $\overline{P}$ if the under-declaration of return is disclosed.

10) Transfer takes place.

Based on the self-interested and rational assumption, if the outcome in either period one or period two is a low realized return, the manager will necessarily choose to declare a low return to the principal. However, if the outcome is a high realized return, the manager will be likely to truthfully declare a high return or dishonestly declare a low return, depending on the result of cost and benefit analysis. In the first period, if the realized return is a high one, the manager will need to evaluate the difference of transferring amounts ($\alpha(R_H - R_L)$), the expected penalty ($Ar\overline{P}$), and the unfavorable effect on the audit probability in period two (possibly adjusted from A to A') in order to make an optimal declaring decision. In the second period, if the outcome is a high realized return, whether the manager chooses under-declaration or not will be contingent on the comparison between two factors, *i.e.* the benefit from the difference of transferring amounts ($\alpha(R_H - R_L)$) and the loss from the expected penalty ($Ar\overline{P}$ or $A'r\overline{P}$ depending on the previous audit result).

Since the realized return is the manager's private information, the principal's audit policy will be dependent on the return declared by the manager. On the basis of cost and benefit, the principal will take audit action only when the manager declares a low return. It is assumed that the auditor is required to present some evidence to support her audit report on the under-declared return, and the evidence cannot be falsified. Hence, the audit result will necessarily be a low return if the realized return is low, but if the realized return is high, the audit result will be subject to the effect of the audit quality (r).

3. The Analyses

3.1. The Agent's Strategy

In this section, we first characterize the manager's possible strategies under the variety of parameter combinations. As the aforementioned, on the basis of the self-interested and rational assumption, the manager will consistently declare low return to the principal if the realized return in either period one or period two is low. Moreover, the factors influencing the manager's declaration behavior include the transferring ratio of return declared (α), the penalty ($\overline{P}$), the audit probabilities (A and A') and the audit quality (r). Using the relative relations among those parameters, we infer three possible strategies that the manager will take into account. They are shown in *Lemmas* 1 to 3, respectively. To simplify the denotation, we let $R_H - R_L$ be ΔR in the latter analyses, and $\alpha\Delta R$ denotes the manager's maximal possible benefit while choosing to under-declare the return.

Lemma 1:

If $\alpha\Delta R \le Ar\overline{P}$, the manager will honestly declare the return in each period. That is, when the realized return in period one (or in period two) is high (*i.e.* $R_1 = R_H$ or $R_2 = R_H$), the manager will consistently declare high return to the principal (*i.e.* $\hat{R}_1 = R_1 = R_H$ or $\hat{R}_2 = R_2 = R_H$).

[Proof] See **Appendix 1**.

Lemma 2:

Under the condition of $Ar\overline{P} < \alpha\Delta R \le A'r\overline{P}$, when the realized return in period two is high (*i.e.* $R_2 = R_H$), the manager will under-declare the return if she has no under-declaration record; but she will honestly declare high return if she was found under-declaring return in period one. Nevertheless, when the realized return in period one is high (*i.e.* $R_1 = R_H$), the manager will choose to under-declare the return in period one.

[Proof] See **Appendix 2**.

Lemma 3:

Under the condition of $\alpha\Delta R > A'r\overline{P}$, when the realized return in period one (or in period two) is high (*i.e.* $R_1 = R_H$ or $R_2 = R_H$), the manager will choose to under-declare the return to the principal (*i.e.* $\hat{R}_1 = R_L < R_1$ or $\hat{R}_2 = R_L < R_2$).

[Proof] See **Appendix 3**.

3.2. The Principal's Strategy

On the other hand, while facing the manager's possible strategy responses, the principal first needs to consider if it is economically desirable to use audit measure as an incentive mechanism. The precondition concerned is that the expected payoff from auditing should exceed the related cost (*i.e.* $rp\overline{P} > C$). Otherwise, the audit mechanism will not be conducted. Hence, we regard $rp\overline{P} > C$ as an implied assumption in the latter analysis.

To highlight the difference between A and A' $(\equiv A + a)$ and search for the optimal value of a, we rewrite the preconditions in the *Lemmas* aforementioned as:

$$\alpha\Delta R \le Ar\overline{P} \Rightarrow 0 < \alpha\Delta R / r\overline{P} \le A \le 1 \quad (1)$$

$$Ar\overline{P} < \alpha\Delta R \le (A+a)r\overline{P} \Rightarrow 0 \le A < \alpha\Delta R / r\overline{P} \le A + a \le 1 \quad (2)$$

where $0 \le a \le 1 - A$

$$\alpha\Delta R > (A+a)r\overline{P} \Rightarrow 0 \le A \le A + a < \alpha\Delta R / r\overline{P} \quad (3)$$

where $0 \le A \le 1$ and $0 \le a \le 1 - A$.

Intuitively, if $\alpha\Delta R < r\overline{P}$ (or $\alpha\Delta R / r\overline{P} < 1$), there can exist the Situations (1), (2) or (3). Specifically, the Situation (1) can be called as a "deterrent audit policy" since the audit policy will effectively deter the manager's under-declaring behavior. The Situation (2) can be referred to as a "punitive conditional audit policy" in that the audit probability in period two will be adjusted up to a deterrent (higher) audit probability from a normal (lower) audit probability if the manager was found under-declaring the return in period one. Finally, the Situation (3) can be regarded as a "laissez-faire audit policy," in which the manager will choose to under-declare the return due to no sufficient audit influence. It is assumed that the principal can obtain the expected payoffs π_1, π_2 and π_3 under Situations (1), (2) and (3), respectively. In Lemmas 4 and 5, it will be shown that the audit policy from situation (1) will dominate that from either situation (2) or Situation (3). Hence, provided $\alpha\Delta R < r\overline{P}$, the audit policy from situation (1) will be the principal's optimal strategy in light of maximizing her expected payoff.

Lemma 4:

If $\alpha\Delta R < r\bar{P}$, then the principal's maximal expected payoff in the Situation (1), π_1^*, will be larger than that in the Situation (2), π_2^*.

[Proof] See **Appendix 4**.

Lemma 4 indicates that, as the incentive from under-declaring is insignificant (*i.e.* $\alpha\Delta R < r\bar{P}$), the deterrent audit policy (from Situation (1)) will be better than the punitive conditional audit policy (from Situation (2)) such that the principal can obtain a larger expected payoff.

Lemma 5:

If $\alpha\Delta R < r\bar{P}$, then the principal's maximal expected payoff in the situation (1), π_1^*, will be larger than that in the Situation (3), π_3^*.

[Proof] See **Appendix 5**.

Similarly, as the incentive from under-declaring is insignificant, *Lemma* 5 points out that the deterrent audit policy (from Situation (1)) will dominate the laissez-faire audit policy (from Situation (3)) as well. Accordingly, we can infer the following result in *Proposition* 1.

3.3. Deterrent Audit Policy

Proposition 1:

If the benefit of under-declaring return is relatively insignificant (*i.e.* $\alpha\Delta R < r\bar{P}$), the principal's optimal audit policy will be conducting random audit with the audit probability of $A = \alpha\Delta R / r\bar{P}$, provided audit is cost-effective (*i.e.* $C < rp\bar{P}$), and a will have no effect on the manager's declaration of the return in period two.

[Proof] By the *Lemmas* 4 and 5, it's straightforward that the principal can maximize the expected payoff by using the audit policy from the Situation (1) and achieve a maximal expected payoff, π_1^*.

As *Proposition* 1 shows, if the manager's benefit of under-declaring return is less than the expected penalty under complete audit (*i.e.* $\alpha\Delta R < r\bar{P}$), the optimal audit policy will be the deterrent audit policy (from Situation (1)). In that case, the principal will implement random audit action (*i.e.* $A = \alpha\Delta R / r\bar{P}$) to induce the manager to honestly declare her return, and to totally deter the under-declaring behavior. Obviously, since the manager necessarily chooses the honest declaration in period one, it is unnecessary to use a conditional audit probability in period two.

The deterrent audit policy may be not desirable *ex post* since audit is costly, but it reduces the expected audit cost and maximize the principal's expected payoff *ex ante*. Although it is doubtful that the principal would be able to adhere to her announced audit policy, the reputational forces could contribute toward inducing the principal to make such a commitment, especially in a repeated game setting such as royalty or tax collection. Hence, if the probability of random audit doesn't change dramatically over time, the manager could resort to inferences according to the principal's previous behavior.

As for when the manager's benefit of under-declaring return is *not* less than the expected penalty under complete audit (*i.e.* $\alpha\Delta R \geq r\bar{P}$), the optimal audit policy will need a different consideration. Firstly, we present a few technical definitions in the following *Lemma* 6.

Lemma 6:

Let

$$C_1 \equiv \left[rp\bar{P} + (1-p)rp_l\bar{P} + (1-r)rpp_h\bar{P}\right] / (2 - rp),$$

$$C_2 \equiv \left[rp\bar{P} + (1-p)rp_l\bar{P} + (1+r)rpp_h\bar{P}\right] / (2 + rp),$$

$$A_1 \equiv \left[2\left(r^2pp_h\bar{P} - C\right) - rpC + rp\bar{P} + (1-p)rp_l\bar{P} + (1-r)rpp_h\bar{P}\right] / \left[2rp\left(rp_h\bar{P} - C\right)\right]$$

and

$$a_1 \equiv \left[(2-rp)C - rp\bar{P} - (1-p)rp_l\bar{P} - (1-r)rpp_h\bar{P}\right] / \left[2rp\left(rp_h\bar{P} - C\right)\right] = 1 - A_1$$

under $\alpha\Delta R \geq r\bar{P}$ and $p_l < p < p_h$, we have $C_1 < C_2$. Also, if $C_1 < C < C_2$, both $0 < A_1 < 1$ and $0 < a_1 < 1$ are assured.

[Proof] See **Appendix 6**.

3.4. Conditional Audit Policy

In *Lemma* 6, C_1 and C_2 are used to set up the triggering points for different audit policies in light of audit cost. Additionally, A_1 denotes a certain random audit probability, and a_1 is used as a punitive audit factor. Using the related denotation, we characterize the principal's optimal audit policies in *Proposition* 2a.

Proposition 2a:

Following the denotation in *Lemma* 6, as the benefit of under-declaring return is sufficiently large (*i.e.* $\alpha\Delta R \geq r\bar{P}$) and there is a state-dependent return in period two (*i.e.* $p_l < p < p_h$), the principal's optimal audit policy will be conducting,

1) uniformly complete audit (*i.e.* $A = A' = 1$ and $a = 0$) if $C \leq C_1$;

2) some kind of conditional audit (*i.e.* $A = A_1$, $a = a_1$,

and $A' = A_1 + a_1 = 1$) if $C_1 < C < C_2$, or;

3) no audit (*i.e.* $A = 0$) if $C \geq C_2$.

[Proof] See **Appendix 7**.

Provided the benefit of under-declaring return is considerably significant (*i.e.* $\alpha\Delta R \geq r\bar{P}$), based on *Lemma* 3, the manager necessarily chooses to under-declare her return when a high return is realized. As *Proposition 2a* shows, to respond to the manager's strategy, the principal will implement an uniformly complete audit policy (*i.e.* $A = A' = 1$) in each period if audit cost is relatively negligible (*i.e.* $C \leq C_1$). But if audit cost is relatively larger (*i.e.* $C \geq C_2$), no audit action (*i.e.* $A = 0$) will be a desirable policy. In contrast, as the audit cost is moderate (*i.e.* $C_1 < C < C_2$), the optimal policy will be a conditional audit policy (*i.e.* $A = A_1 < 1$ and $A' = 1 > A$). In this case, the principal will first take a random audit action in period one, and then decide whether to adjust up the audit probability in period two, depending on the audit result in previous period.

Since $a_1 (= 1 - A_1)$ corresponds to the punitive effect of conditional audit policy, a larger a_1 implies the principal can conduct a random audit in period one with a lower audit probability, and then implement a complete audit in period two when the manager has a under-reporting record and declares a low return once more. In *Proposition* 2*b*, we examine the impacts of audit cost, audit quality, and under-reporting penalty on the punitive effect of conditional audit policy.

Proposition 2*b*:

As conditional audit policy is the principal's optimal choice, ceteris paribus, an increase in audit cost results in a larger punitive effect of conditional audit (*i.e.* $\partial a_1 / \partial C > 0$). However, a rise in audit quality or penalty results in a decrease in the punitive effect of conditional audit (*i.e.* $\partial a_1 / \partial r < 0$ and $\partial a_1 / \partial \bar{P} < 0$). The former leads to a lower random audit probability in period one (A_1), but the latter leads to a higher one (since $A_1 = 1 - a_1$).

[Proof] See **Appendix 8**.

As conditional audit policy is an optimal one, an increase in audit cost will be more unfavorable to audit action and result in a lower random audit probability in period one (a more punitive effect). Conversely, as audit quality or penalty grows, the expected benefit of random audit in period one will increase, and it leads to a higher random audit probability in period one (a less punitive effect). In *Proposition* 2*c*, we further investigate how the degree of return dependence in two consecutive periods influences the punitive effect of conditional audit policy.

Proposition 2*c*:

Let $\Delta p_h \equiv p_h - p$ and $\Delta p_l \equiv p - p_l$. Following the preconditions in *Proposition* 2*b*, if the realization of high return in period one brings about a much more chance of realizing a high return in period two (*i.e.* a larger Δp_h), the principal will reduce the punitive effect in conditional audit policy (*i.e.* a smaller a_1). Nevertheless, if the realization of low return in period one results in a much more chance of realizing a low return in period two or a much less chance of realizing a high return in period two (*i.e.* a larger Δp_l), the principal will enlarge the punitive effect in conditional audit policy (*i.e.* a larger a_1). The former leads to a higher random audit probability in period one (A_1), but the latter leads to a lower one (since $A_1 = 1 - a_1$).

[Proof] See **Appendix 9**.

As *Proposition* 2*c* shows, Δp_h and Δp_l have opposite impacts on the punitive effect of conditional audit policy. Intuitively, since Δp_h grows means that a high return in period one will lead to a much more chance of realizing a high return in period two, it become more favorable to increase the frequency of audit in period one and results in a higher random audit probability in the period (a less punitive effect). In contrast, if a low return in period one leads to a much less chance of realizing a high return in period two, it will be less favorable to enlarge the audit in period one and results in a lower random audit probability in the period (a more punitive effect).

3.5. No Conditional Audit Scenario

Finally, we are interested in how the optimal audit policy will be if the return-dependence in two periods vanishes totally. Is there any possibility for conditional audit policy to be desirable? As shown in the following proposition, the answer seems negative in light of the assumptions in the paper.

Proposition 3:

Using the denotation in *Proposition* 2*a*, if the benefit of under-declaring return is relatively significant (*i.e.* $\alpha\Delta R \geq r\bar{P}$), and the return in period two is independent of that in period one (*i.e.* $p_l = p = p_h$), it will be not desirable for the principal to conduct any conditional audit, and the optimal audit strategy will be either

1) complete audit policy (*i.e.* $A = A' = 1$ and $a = 0$) provided $C \leq rp\bar{P}$, or

2) no audit policy (*i.e.* $A = 0$) provided $C > rp\bar{P}$.

[Proof] Following the proof of *Proposition* 2*a*, under $p_l = p = p_h$, both C_1 and C_2 converge to $rp\bar{P}$, *i.e.* $C_1 = C_2 = rp\bar{P}$. Hence, the result (2) in *Proposition 2a* will vanish.

In *Proposition* 3, we let both p_l and p_h converge to p so that the returns in periods one and two are independent each other. In the specific case, we obtain a result that a conditional audit policy is uneconomical and inadequate if the realized return in period one has no effect on the realization of return in period two. As a result, the principal will choose either a complete-audit policy or a no-audit policy, depending on the size of audit cost (*i.e.* $C \le rp\bar{P}$ or $C > rp\bar{P}$).

4. Conclusion

In a state-dependent audit situation, we find that the principal's optimal audit policy will be a deterrent audit policy if the manager's benefit of under-declaring return is less than the expected penalty under complete audit and audit cost is insignificant. Nevertheless, if the benefit of under-declaring return is considerably significant, and the manager necessarily chooses to under-declare the return, the principal's optimal audit policy will be dependent on audit cost. Ceteris paribus, if audit cost is relatively negligible, the principal will take a uniformly complete audit policy; but if audit cost is relatively larger, the principal will tend to totally abandon audit action in consideration of costs and benefits related. More interestingly, as the audit cost is moderate, we find that a conditional audit policy will be an optimal choice. In that case, while the principal's audit action cannot deter the manager's under-declaring behavior, the conditional audit policy indeed can make audit action more efficient and cost-effective.

REFERENCES

[1] R. Antle, "The Auditor as an Economic Agent," *Journal of Accounting Research*, Vol. 20, No. 2, 1982, pp. 503-527.

[2] D. P. Baron and D. Besanko, "Regulation, Asymmetric Information and Auditing," *RAND Journal of Economics*, Vol. 15, No. 4, 1984, pp. 447-470.

[3] J. S. Demski and D. E. M. Sappington, "Hierarchical Regulatory Control," *RAND Journal of Economics*, Vol. 18, No. 3, 1987, pp. 369-383.

[4] S. Baiman, J. H. Evans III and J. Noel, "Optimal Contracts with a Utility-Maximizing Auditor," *Journal of Accounting Research*, Vol. 25, No. 2, 1987, pp. 217-244.

[5] E. Helland, "The Enforcement of Pollution Control Laws: Inspections, Violations, and Self-Reporting," *Review of Economics and Statistics*, Vol. 80, No. 1, 1998, pp. 141-153.

[6] M. Landsberger and I. Meilijson, "Incentive Generating State Dependent Penalty System: The Case of Income Tax Evasion," *Journal of Public Economics*, Vol. 19, No. 3, 1982, pp. 333-352.

[7] J. Greenberg, "Avoiding Tax Avoidance: A (Repeated) Game-Theoretic Approach," *Journal of Economic Theory*, Vol. 32, No. 1, 1984, pp. 1-13.

[8] W. Harrington, "Enforcement Leverage When Penalties Are Restricted," *Journal of Public Economics*, Vol. 37, No, 1, 1988, pp. 29-53.

[9] L. Friesen, "Targeting Enforcement to Improve Compliance with Environmental Regulations," *Journal of Environmental Economics and Management*, Vol. 46, No. 1, 2003, pp. 72-85.

[10] S. L. Stafford, "Self-Policing in a Targeted Enforcement Regime," *Southern Economic Journal*, Vol. 74, No. 4, 2008, pp. 934-951.

[11] A. S. Malik, "Self-Reporting and the Design of Policies for Regulating Stochastic Pollution," *Journal of Environmental Economics and Management*, Vol. 24, No. 3, 1993, pp. 241-257.

Appendix 1 (*Proof of Lemma* 1)

Under $\alpha\Delta R \le Ar\overline{P}(\le A'r\overline{P})$, if $R_2 = R_H$, then $\hat{R}_2 = R_H$ since the expected penalty will be too large for the manager to under-declare the return. By the same token, if $R_1 = R_H$, then $\hat{R}_1 = R_H$ since any audit result in period one will not affect her declaration decision as well as expected payoff in period two, and

$$\begin{aligned}
&\mathrm{E}\left(\hat{R}_1 = R_H \middle| R_1 = R_H\right) - \mathrm{E}\left(\hat{R}_1 = R_L \middle| R_1 = R_H\right) \\
&= (R_H - \alpha R_H) + p_h(R_H - \alpha R_H) + (1-p_h)(R_L - \alpha R_L) - (R_H - \alpha R_L - Ar\overline{P}) \\
&\quad - Ar\left[p_h(R_H - \alpha R_H) + (1-p_h)(R_L - \alpha R_L)\right] - (1 - Ar)\left[p_h(R_H - \alpha R_H) + (1-p_h)(R_L - \alpha R_L)\right] \\
&= \alpha R_L - \alpha R_H + Ar\overline{P} = -\alpha\Delta R + Ar\overline{P} \ge 0 \ \left(\text{if } \alpha\Delta R \le ArP\right)
\end{aligned}$$

Appendix 2 (*Proof of Lemma* 2)

If the realized return in period two is R_H, under the condition of $\alpha\Delta R > Ar\overline{P}$, the manager will choose to under-declare the return if she has a clean record; however, she won't do that if she was found under-declaring return in period one since $\alpha\Delta R \le A'r\overline{P}$.

On the other hand, if the realized return in period one is R_H, the manager will be inclined to under-declare the return since

$$\begin{aligned}
&\mathrm{E}\left(\hat{R}_1 = R_H \middle| R_1 = R_H\right) - \mathrm{E}\left(\hat{R}_1 = R_L \middle| R_1 = R_H\right) = \alpha R_L - \alpha R_H + Ar\overline{P} + Arp_h\left(\alpha R_H - \alpha R_L - Ar\overline{P}\right) \\
&= -\alpha\Delta R + Ar\overline{P} + Arp_h\left(\alpha\Delta R - Ar\overline{P}\right) = \left(\alpha\Delta R - Ar\overline{P}\right)\left(Arp_h - 1\right) < 0 \ \left(\because \alpha\Delta R > Ar\overline{P} \text{ and } Arp_h < 1\right).
\end{aligned}$$

Appendix 3 (*Proof of Lemma* 3)

Under the condition of $\alpha\Delta R > A'r\overline{P}(\ge Ar\overline{P})$, if the realized return in period two is high (*i.e.* $R_2 = R_H$), the manager will be inclined to under-declare the return whether she was found under-declaring return in period one or not. Meanwhile, if the realized return in period one is R_H, the manager will be also inclined to under-declare the return since

$$\begin{aligned}
&\mathrm{E}\left(\hat{R}_1 = R_H \middle| R_1 = R_H\right) - \mathrm{E}\left(\hat{R}_1 = R_L \middle| R_1 = R_H\right) \\
&= (R_H - \alpha R_H) - (R_H - \alpha R_L - Ar\overline{P}) \\
&\quad + p_h(R_H - \alpha R_L - Ar\overline{P}) - Arp\left[R_H - \alpha R_L - (A+a)r\overline{P}\right] \\
&\quad - p_h(R_H - \alpha R_L - Ar\overline{P}) + Arp_h(R_H - \alpha R_L - Ar\overline{P}) \\
&= \alpha R_L - \alpha R_H + Ar\overline{P} - Arp_h\left[Ar\overline{P} - (A+a)r\overline{P}\right] \\
&= -\alpha\Delta R + Ar\overline{P} + Arp_h \cdot ar\overline{P} \\
&\quad < 0 \ \left(\because \alpha\Delta R \ge (A+a)r\overline{P} > Ar\overline{P} + (Arp_h)ar\overline{P}\right)
\end{aligned}.$$

Appendix 4 (*Proof of Lemma* 4)

In Situation (1), the principal's expected payoff is

$$\begin{aligned}
\pi_1 = {} & p\left[\alpha R_H + p_h\alpha R_H + (1-p_h)(\alpha R_L - AC)\right] \\
& + (1-p)\left[\alpha R_L - AC + p_l\alpha R_H\right. \\
& \left. + (1-p_l)(\alpha R_L - AC)\right]
\end{aligned}$$

To maximize π_1, subject to $A \ge \alpha\Delta R/r\overline{P}\,(>0)$, $A + a \le 1$ and $a \ge 0$, we find the only optimal combination of $A^* = \alpha\Delta R/r\overline{P}$ and $0 \le a^* \le 1 - (\alpha\Delta R/r\overline{P})$, satisfying all of the Kuhn-Tucker conditions. Actually, the a^* will never be used in that case since the manager will honestly declare her return in period one under $A^* = \alpha\Delta R/r\overline{P}$ ($\equiv \underline{A}$). Thus we get the maximal expected payoff

$$\begin{aligned}
\pi_1^* = {} & 2\alpha R_L + p(1+p_h)\alpha\Delta R + (1-p)p_l\alpha\Delta R \\
& - (2 - p - p_l - pp_h + pp_l)\alpha\Delta RC/r\overline{P}
\end{aligned}.$$

On the other hand, in Situation (2), the principal's expected payoff is

$$\begin{aligned}\pi_2 &= p\Big\{\alpha R_L + A\left(r\bar{P}-C\right) + p_h\Big\{Ar\alpha R_H + (1-Ar)\left[\alpha R_L + A\left(r\bar{P}-C\right)\right]\Big\} \\ &\quad + (1-p_h)\Big\{Ar\left[\alpha R_L - (A+a)C\right] + (1-Ar)(\alpha R_L - AC)\Big\}\Big\} \\ &\quad + (1-p)\Big\{\alpha R_L - AC + p_l\left[\alpha R_L + A\left(r\bar{P}-C\right)\right] + (1-p_l)(\alpha R_L - AC)\Big\} \\ &= 2\alpha R_L + pp_h Ar\alpha\Delta R - 2AC + pp_h ArAC - p(1-p_h)AraC \\ &\quad + \left[pp_h(1-Ar)A + (1-p)p_l A + pA\right] r\bar{P}\end{aligned}$$

To maximize π_2, subject to $0 \le A < \alpha\Delta R/r\bar{P}$, $\alpha\Delta R/r\bar{P} \le A + a \le 1$ and $a \ge 0$, it is derived that only the combination of $A^* = \alpha\Delta R/r\bar{P} - \varepsilon$ ($\equiv \underline{A} - \varepsilon$) and $a^* = \varepsilon$ (where $\varepsilon > 0$ and $\varepsilon > 0$) can satisfy all of the Kuhn-Tucker conditions. Hence, the maximal expected payoff becomes

$$\begin{aligned}\pi_2^* &= 2\alpha R_L + pp_h(\underline{A}-\varepsilon)r\alpha\Delta R - 2(\underline{A}-\varepsilon)C + pp_h(\underline{A}-\varepsilon)^2 rC - p(1-p_h)(\underline{A}-\varepsilon)raC \\ &\quad + \left[pp_h\left(1-(\underline{A}-\varepsilon)r\right)(\underline{A}-\varepsilon) + (1-p)p_l(\underline{A}-\varepsilon) + p(\underline{A}-\varepsilon)\right] r\bar{P}\end{aligned}$$

Hence, overlooking the terms involved with ε we have

$$\pi_1^* - \pi_2^* \cong pp_h\underline{A}C(1-\underline{A}r) + \left[p(1-p_l) + p_l\right]\underline{A}C > 0,$$

where $0 < \underline{A} = \alpha\Delta R/r\bar{P} < 1$.

Appendix 5 (*Proof of Lemma* 5)

In Situation (3), the principal's expected payoff is

$$\begin{aligned}\pi_3 &= 2\alpha R_L - 2AC - pAraC + pAr\bar{P} \\ &\quad + pp_h Ar\bar{P} + (1-p)p_l Ar\bar{P} + pp_h Arar\bar{P}\end{aligned}.$$

To maximize π_3, subject to $A + a < \alpha\Delta R/r\bar{P}$, $A \ge 0$ and $a \ge 0$, we find that only the optimal combination of $A^* = \alpha\Delta R/r\bar{P} - \varepsilon$ (where $\varepsilon > 0$ and $\varepsilon \to 0$) and a^*=0 can satisfy all of the Kuhn-Tucker conditions. Hence, the maximal expected payoff become

$$\pi_3^* = 2\alpha R_L - 2AC + (p + pp_h + p_l - pp_l)(\underline{A}-\varepsilon)r\bar{P},$$

where $\underline{A} \equiv \alpha\Delta R/r\bar{P}$.

According to the proof of lemma 4,

$$\begin{aligned}\pi_1^* &= 2\alpha R_L + p(1+p_h)\underline{A}r\bar{P} + (1-p)p_l\underline{A}r\bar{P} \\ &\quad - (2 - p - p_l - pp_h + pp_l)\underline{A}C\end{aligned}.$$

Hence, overlooking the terms involved with ε,

$$\pi_1^* - \pi_3^* \cong \left[pp_h + p(1-p_l) + p_l\right]\underline{A}C > 0,$$

where $0 < \underline{A} = \alpha\Delta R/r\bar{P} < 1$.

Appendix 6 (*Proof of Lemma* 6)

Since

$$\begin{aligned}& C_1 < C_2 \\ &\Leftrightarrow (2+rp)\left[rp\bar{P} + (1-p)rp_l\bar{P} + (1-r)rpp_h\bar{P}\right] \\ &\quad < (2-rp)\left[rp\bar{P} + (1-p)rp_l\bar{P} + (1+r)rpp_h\bar{P}\right] \\ &\Leftrightarrow rp\bar{P} + rpp_h\bar{P} + (1-p)rp_l\bar{P} < 2rp_h\bar{P} \\ &\Leftrightarrow p + pp_h + (1-p)p_l < 2p_h \\ &\Leftrightarrow (p_h - p) + \left[p_h - pp_h - (1-p)p_l\right] \\ &\quad > 0 \ (\because p_l < p < p_h)\end{aligned},$$

$C_1 < C_2$ holds under $\alpha\Delta R \ge r\bar{P}$.

On the other hand,

$$\begin{aligned}& A_1 > 0 \\ &\Leftrightarrow 2\left(r^2 pp_h\bar{P} - C\right) - rpC + rp\bar{P} + (1-p)rp_l\bar{P} \\ &\quad + (1-r)rpp_h\bar{P} > 0 \ \left(\because rp_h\bar{P} > C\right) \\ &\Leftrightarrow rp\bar{P} + (1-p)rp_l\bar{P} + (1+r)rpp_h\bar{P} \\ &\quad > (2+rp)C \Leftrightarrow C < C_2,\end{aligned}$$

and

$$\begin{aligned}& A_1 < 1 \\ &\Leftrightarrow 2\left(r^2 pp_h\bar{P} - C\right) - rpC + rp\bar{P} + (1-p)rp_l\bar{P} \\ &\quad + (1-r)rpp_h\bar{P} < 2rp\left(rp_h\bar{P} - C\right) \\ &\Leftrightarrow rp\bar{P} + (1-p)rp_l\bar{P} + (1-r)rpp_h\bar{P} < (2-rp)C \\ &\Leftrightarrow C > C_1\end{aligned}.$$

Hence, $0 < A_1 < 1$ if $C_1 < C < C_2$.

Meanwhile,

$$\begin{aligned} & a_1 > 0 \\ & \Leftrightarrow (2-rp)C - rp\overline{P} - (1-p)rp_l\overline{P} - (1-r)rpp_h\overline{P} > 0 \\ & \Leftrightarrow (2-rp)C > rp\overline{P} + (1-p)rp_l\overline{P} + (1-r)rpp_h\overline{P} \\ & \Leftrightarrow C > C_1, \end{aligned}$$

and

$$\begin{aligned} & a_1 < 1 \\ & \Leftrightarrow (2-rp)C - rp\overline{P} - (1-p)rp_l\overline{P} - (1-r)rpp_h\overline{P} \\ & \quad < 2rp\left(rp_h\overline{P} - C\right) \\ & \Leftrightarrow (2+rp)C < rp\overline{P} + (1-p)rp_l\overline{P} + (1+r)rpp_h\overline{P} \\ & \Leftrightarrow C < C_2 \end{aligned}$$

Hence, $0 < a_1 < 1$ if $C_1 < C < C_2$.

Appendix 7 (*Proof of proposition 2a*)

According to the result of *Lemma* 6, as $\alpha\Delta R \geq r\overline{P}$, the principal's expected payoff will be

$$\pi = 2\alpha R_L + Arp\overline{P} - 2AC - AarpC + Arpp_h\overline{P} + Aar^2pp_h\overline{P} + Ar(1-p)p_l\overline{P}$$

To maximize π, subject to $A + a \leq 1$, $A \geq 0$, and $a \geq 0$, we find the following results. Firstly, as $C_1 < C < C_2$, only the optimal combination of $A^* = A_1$, $a^* = a_1$, and $A'^* = A_1 + a_1 = 1$ can satisfy all of the Kuhn-Tucker conditions. In that case, $0 < A_1 < 1$ and $0 < a_1 < 1$ will also be assured by *Lemma* 6 (since $C_1 < C < C_2$). Secondly, as $C \leq C_1$, the combination of $A^* = 1$ and $a^* = 0$ (*i.e.* $A'^* = 1$) will be the optimal solution, satisfying all of the Kuhn-Tucker conditions; but if $C \geq C_2$, the optimal solution will be $A^* = 0$ (and a has no effect).

Appendix 8 (*Proof of proposition 2b*)

$$\partial a_1/\partial C = 2rp\left\{\left(rp_h\overline{P}-C\right)(2-rp)+\left[(2-rp)C-rp\overline{P}-(1-p)rp_l\overline{P}-(1-r)rpp_h\overline{P}\right]\right\}\Big/\left[4r^2p^2\left(rp_h\overline{P}-C\right)^2\right]>0 \text{ (if } C>C_1)$$

$$\begin{aligned} \partial a_1/\partial r = & -\left\{2rp\left(rp_h\overline{P}-C\right)\left[pC+(1-p)p_l\overline{P}+(1-rp_h)p\overline{P}+(1-r)pp_h\overline{P}\right]\right. \\ & \left.+2p\left(2rp_h\overline{P}-C\right)\left[(2-rp)C-rp\overline{P}-(1-p)rp_l\overline{P}-(1-r)rpp_h\overline{P}\right]\right\}\Big/\left[4r^2p^2\left(rp_h\overline{P}-C\right)^2\right]<0 \text{ (if } C>C_1) \end{aligned}$$

$$\begin{aligned} \partial a_1/\partial \overline{P} = & -\left\{2rp\left(rp_h\overline{P}-C\right)\left[\left(1-(1-r)p_h\right)rp+(1-p)rp_l\right]\right. \\ & \left.+2r^2pp_h\left[(2-rp)C-rp\overline{P}-(1-p)rp_l\overline{P}-(1-r)rpp_h\overline{P}\right]\right\}\Big/\left[4r^2p^2\left(rp_h\overline{P}-C\right)^2\right]<0 \text{ (if } C>C_1). \end{aligned}$$

Appendix 9 (*Proof of proposition 2c*)

$$\begin{aligned} \partial a_1/\partial\Delta p_h = & -\left\{2r^2p^2\overline{P}(1-r)\left(rp_h\overline{P}-C\right)+2r^2p\overline{P}\left[(2-rp)C-rp\overline{P}\right.\right. \\ & \left.\left.-(1-p)rp_l\overline{P}-(1-r)rpp_h\overline{P}\right]\right\}\Big/\left[4r^2p^2\left(rp_h\overline{P}-C\right)^2\right]<0 \text{ (if } C>C_1) \end{aligned}$$

$$\partial a_1/\partial\Delta p_l = r\overline{P}(1-p)\Big/\left[2rp\left(rp_h\overline{P}-C\right)\right]>0.$$

23

Which Spouse First Decides in the Household? The Dynamics of Bargaining

Joaquín Andaluz Funcia[1], Miriam Marcén[1], José Alberto Molina Chueca[1,2]
[1]Departamento de Análisis Económico, Facultad de Economía y Empresa, Universidad de Zaragoza, Zaragoza, Spain
[2]Institute for the Study of Labour-IZA, Bonn, Germany

ABSTRACT

This paper examines the effects of which spouse first decides in the intrahousehold decision on the time that each spouse devotes to the provision of a family good. Specifically, we adopt a dynamic approach by developing a supergame, with the status quo being sequential, to study the influence of the discount factor, which measures the importance of the future, on the set of sustainable agreements in intrahousehold bargaining. We first show that cooperation is easily sustained. We then observe a positive relationship between the discount factor and the proportion of time that the follower devotes to housework, when focusing on sustainable agreements, with this finding being maintained even if the follower has higher wages than the spouse leader.

Keywords: Family Bargaining; Stackelberg Game; Family Good

1. Introduction

Although the comparative advantage of women in household production may have explained specialization in the past, Becker [1], this traditional theory is unable to explain the current empirical evidence on the contribution to housework. Despite the increase in female labor force participation and female human capital, specialization within the household has remained relatively unchanged, Aguiar and Hurst [2]. Many women choose working arrangements that are compatible with caring for their children. Hersch [3], and indeed, women who work more hours than their husbands outside the home, or those who have higher earnings than their husbands do relatively more housework, Akerlof and Kranton [4].

Bargaining theories also fail to predict these findings. Under this approach, it would be expected a more egalitarian allocation of time within the household as female human capital increases. Even more recent works on bargaining models of family decision-making, which extend the one-period approach to a dynamic setting, predict a reduction in the incentives to specialize in household production, Lundberg and Pollak [5]. In this setting, a consumption-smoothing problem arises, which may lead to the inability of spouses to engage in inter-temporal agreements, and that could lead to an inefficient allocation of household resources. The problem here is that a credible promise to compensate family public good production with future consumption cannot be made. The sustainability of family bargaining agreements in a dynamic setting is also analyzed in Andaluz and Molina [6]. By considering the trigger strategy, Friedman [7], as a punishment scheme, they show that the spouse with the higher bargaining power has a greater incentive to reach an agreement.[1] Since bargaining power is not the only relevant factor in a dynamic family decision-making process, we add to this work by analyzing the influence of the discount factor, which measures the importance of the future, on the set of sustainable agreements, and on the time that each spouse devotes to the provision of a family good.

Our paper builds on the work of Andaluz and Molina [6], with one important distinction: we extend the analysis of the dynamic aspects of the family bargaining process, developing a supergame in which the status quo is not only defined as non-cooperative, but also as sequential. We suppose that the spouses play a non-cooperative Stackelberg game, where the leader decides, first, contributions to a certain quantity of provision of family good, and thereby sets restrictions for the follower.

In our paper, we first solve the one-shot game, a Stackelberg game, and we then use this as the state game of an infinitely repeated game. To choose among the multiple equilibria of the repeated game, we focus on sustainable solutions and we determine the efficient allocation by way of the symmetric Nash bargaining solu-

[1]Note that sustainability here means the absence of incentives to deviate from the Nash bargaining solution.

tion. Using methodologies similar to ours, other studies such as Espinosa and Rhee, [8], have examined the relationship between a union and a firm by developing a supergame with a threat to return to a noncooperative Stackelberg equilibrium.

How does a spouse become a Stackelberg leader or a Stackelberg follower? In the literature of the economics of the family, we find several examples of marital relationships modeled as a Stackelberg game. Bolin [9,10] suggests that a wife may be a Stackelberg follower if she considers the decisions taken by her husband as a fait accompli. Bolin analyzes the division of family work as the outcome of a Stackelberg game, showing that not only comparative advantage but also dominance are important factors in time allocation. Another argument is proposed by Elul *et al.* [11], who consider that the age difference between spouses gives the husband a time advantage in the sequential decision game of time allocation, through an analysis of the gender wage gap. Beblo and Robledo [12] also study the wage gap, but jointly with the gender leisure gap, providing empirical evidence that husbands enjoy more leisure time, all other things being equal, than their wives. They explain this empirical finding as a result of the husband being the Stackelberg leader in a sequential private provision game. In our case, we could also consider a situation in which the household division of labor is affected by social norms. The prescription that women should do the work at home may alter the family decision-making process, since one spouse, normally the husband, can make a credible commitment to contribute no more than a possibly very small amount to the provision of a family good. Thus, this spouse, usually the husband, becomes a Stackelberg leader and the other spouse, the wife, becomes a Stackelberg follower.

As regards the main results, we observe an increase in the set of sustainable agreements derived from the bargaining, in a family setting, when the discount factor is higher. Thus, cooperation is more easily sustained. We also study the impact of the discount factor on the gains to well-being derived from cooperation, in order to analyze whether the leader or the follower has incentives to reach an agreement. Although, in this case, our results are ambiguous, we show that the time devoted by the leader to the production of the family good is a key element in determining the sign of the relationship between the welfare gains and the discount factor.

Focusing on the sustainable solutions, we examine the relationship between the discount factor and the time devoted to the provision of a family good. What is clearly observed is that the contribution of the follower to the family good is increasing with respect to the discount factor. Then, if the woman is the follower (for instance, she decides second because of the existence of social norms), we would expect her contribution to a family good to be greater when the discount factor increases (when women place more value on the future), even if there are no differences in the wages for men and women.[2] This prediction appears to be confirmed by current empirical research that finds that wives undertake larger shares of the housework, regardless of their earnings.

2. Preferences

We suppose that the utility of each agent takes the following functional form (see Konrad and Lommerud [14]):

$$u_1 = x_1 + Q - q_1^{\beta}; u_2 = x_2 + Q - q_2^{\alpha} \tag{1}$$

where $x_1 = w_1(1-q_1)$ and $x_2 = w_2(1-q_2)$, $w_j \in [0,1]$ represents the wage rate for agent j, x_j indicates the private consumption of agent j, $j = 1,2$; Q represents the family good, $Q = q_1 + q_2$, with q_j being the proportion of hours that agent j devotes to the provision of this good.

The maximum time available for each spouse is normalized to 1. In line with Konrad and Lommerud [14], we suppose that individuals increasingly dislike spending more time on the production of the family good. The contribution to the family good not only reduces the time available to the labor market, but also has a psychologycal cost, represented by an increasing and convex function in each of these arguments $(q_1^{\beta}, q_2^{\alpha})$, with α and β being greater than 1. The family good, Q, can include any situation which requires the joint performance of the spouses, e.g., raising the children or the maintenance of the home, but it excludes the possibility that the provision of the family good would be obtained in the market. This assumption can be reasonable if it takes into consideration that, for some couples, the private provision of family goods is not a substitute for their own contribution to the family good. (Though it is not the aim of this paper, our model can be extended by considering both kinds of provision of family goods).

We choose this special functional form for simplicity, although we acknowledge that this form can be restrictive. When the spouses act non-cooperatively, the provision of the family good by both agents is strategically independent, even though their utilities are intertwined through the existence of a family good. Then, this specification establishes the non-cooperative outcome as a benchmark for understanding the family decision-making process.

[2]The discount factor of the leader is not a key element in this analysis, thus it is not necessary to observe gender differences in discounting (for a review of this literature see Benjamin *et al.* [13]).

3. The One-Shot Game

To analyze how the discount factor affects both the set of sustainable agreements and time that each individual devotes to the provision of a family good, we first solve the one-shot game, a Stackelberg game, and we then use this as the state game of an infinitely-repeated game, using reversion to this non-cooperative Stackelberg equilibrium as the punishment for deviators. To determine the optimum levels of consumption and the contribution to the family good among the multiple stationary paths of the repeated game, we focus on sustainable solutions and we determine the efficient allocation as a result of the symmetric Nash bargaining solution, (see De la Rica and Espinosa [15]).

In each period t, the non-cooperative equilibrium is the outcome of a Stackelberg game, in which the leader (spouse 1) commits to a certain quantity of provision of family good, while anticipating the optimal contribution of the follower (spouse 2).

Applying the backward induction procedure, we begin by obtaining the equilibrium corresponding to spouse 2 (the follower). Formally:

$$\begin{aligned} \underset{x_2, q_2}{\text{Max}} \quad & u_2 = x_2 + Q - q_2^{\alpha} \\ \text{s.to} \quad & x_2 = w_2(1 - q_2) \\ & q_1 = \bar{q}_1 \end{aligned} \tag{2}$$

From here, we deduce the levels of consumption and the provision of the family good:

$$q_2^* = \left(\frac{1-w_2}{\alpha}\right)^{1/\alpha-1}; x_2^* = w_2\left[1-\left(\frac{1-w_2}{\alpha}\right)^{1/\alpha-1}\right] \tag{3}$$

and the utility level:

$$u_2^d = w_2 + \bar{q}_1 + (\alpha-1)\left(\frac{1-w_2}{\alpha}\right)^{\frac{\alpha}{\alpha-1}} \tag{4}$$

For spouse 1 (the leader) we formulate the following maximization problem:

$$\begin{aligned} \underset{x_1, q_1}{\text{Max}} \quad & u_1 = x_1 + Q - q_1^{\beta} \\ \text{s.to} \quad & x_1 = w_1(1 - q_1) \\ & q_2 = q_2^* \end{aligned} \tag{5}$$

and we obtain the level of private consumption, and the provision of the household good made by spouse 1:

$$q_1^* = \left(\frac{1-w_1}{\beta}\right)^{1/\beta-1}; x_1^* = w_1\left[1-\left(\frac{1-w_1}{\beta}\right)^{1/\beta-1}\right] \tag{6}$$

Therefore, the levels of utility in the non-cooperative solution for both spouses are:

$$u_1^*(q_1^*, q_2^*) = w_1 + (\beta-1)\left(\frac{1-w_1}{\beta}\right)^{\beta/\beta-1} + \left(\frac{1-w_2}{\alpha}\right)^{1/\alpha-1} \tag{7}$$

$$u_2^*(q_1^*, q_2^*) = w_2 + (\alpha-1)\left(\frac{1-w_2}{\alpha}\right)^{\alpha/\alpha-1} + \left(\frac{1-w_1}{\beta}\right)^{1/\beta-1} \tag{8}$$

The solution obtained in (3) and (6), is an interior solution.[3] In addition, we may determine the situations in which only one of the spouses is the contributor to the family good, to see whether there is a dominant strategy (see Bucholz *et al.*, [16]). We can distinguish two additional Stackelberg equilibria:

The leader is the only contributor.

In this case, $\bar{Q}$*, the family good, is only supplied by spouse* 1, *from* (5) *and with* $q_2 = 0$, *we can obtain the total family good:* $\bar{Q} = \left(\frac{1-w_1}{\beta}\right)^{\frac{1}{\beta-1}}$. *and the levels of utility of both spouses*:

$$\bar{u}_1(\bar{Q}, 0) = w_1 + (\beta-1)\left(\frac{1-w_1}{\beta}\right)^{\beta/\beta-1};$$

$$\bar{u}_2(\bar{Q}, 0) = w_2 + \left(\frac{1-w_1}{\beta}\right)^{1/\beta-1}$$

The follower is the only contributor.

From the maximization problem of spouse 2, (2), *and with* $q_1 = 0$, *we may determine the levels of provision of family good which are only provided by spouse* 2:

$$\tilde{Q} = \left(\frac{1-w_2}{\alpha}\right)^{\frac{1}{\alpha-1}}.$$

with the levels of utility for both spouses in this case being:

$$\hat{u}_1(0, \hat{Q}) = w_1 + \left(\frac{1-w_2}{\alpha}\right)^{\frac{1}{\alpha-1}};$$

$$\hat{u}_2(0, \hat{Q}) = w_2 + (\alpha-1)\left(\frac{1-w_2}{\alpha}\right)^{\alpha/\alpha-1}$$

Under the structure of preferences defined above, for all values of the parameters, the interior solution constitutes a dominant strategy for both agents in the Stackelberg equilibrium.[4] It is straightforward to deduce that

[3]Note that, under the preferences specified above, the reaction functions for both spouses have null slope, and thus, the provision of the family good by both agents is strategically independent. As a consequence, the levels of consumption and the provision of the family good obtained in the Stackelberg equilibrium coincide with those obtained in a Nash equilibrium.

[4]This result differs from that obtained by Bucholz *et al.* [16]. However, note that, in our model, the type of Stackelberg equilibrium does not depend on the aggregate income of the spouses, or on the redistribution of income between spouses. This is due to the fact that the incomes of the agents are endogenously determined, and that one spouse cannot compensate the other spouse.

$$u_1^*\left(q_1^*,q_2^*\right)>\bar{u}_i\left(\bar{Q},0\right)$$

and that

$$u_i^*\left(q_1^*,q_2^*\right)>\hat{u}_i\left(0,\hat{Q}\right),$$

$\forall 0<w_i<1;(\alpha,\beta)>1,(i=1,2)$. This is a reasonable result, since we do not consider the possibility that one spouse compensates the other.

However, the interior solution, the dominant strategy, is clearly inefficient, as can be seen in **Figure 1** where it is represented the curves of indifference of the spouses in the non-cooperative solution. For spouse 1, the slope of the curve of indifference in the non-cooperative equilibrium is zero in $\left(q_1^*,q_2^*\right)$, and is increasing and convex if $q_1>q_1^*$ and $q_2>q_2^*$, $\left.\frac{\mathrm{d}q_2}{\mathrm{d}q_1}\right|_{u_1^*}>0$, $\left.\frac{\mathrm{d}^2q_2}{\mathrm{d}q_1^2}\right|_{u_1^*}>0$. Analogously, for spouse 2, the slope of the curve of indifference that contains the solution of the one-shot game is equal to minus infinity in the combination $\left(q_1^*,q_2^*\right)$, and is increasing and concave when $q_1>q_1^*$ and $q_2>q_2^*$, $\left.\frac{\mathrm{d}q_2}{\mathrm{d}q_1}\right|_{u_2^*}>0;\left.\frac{\mathrm{d}^2q_2}{\mathrm{d}q_1^2}\right|_{u_2^*}<0$. All the points located inside the area formed by both curves of indifference are Pareto superior to the equilibrium of the one shot game, as Kapteyn and Kooreman [17] demonstrated. Those points located in the contract curve CC' are efficient solutions.

4. Dynamic Setting

We consider an infinitely-repeated game, in which the two members of a family, spouse 1 and spouse 2, may contribute voluntarily to the provision of a family good whose consumption is non-rival, as in [3]. We suppose that the spouses do not know the moment of the dissolution of the marriage, and that the objective of each is to maximize the discounted value of their current utilities.[5] Formally:

$$\sum_{t=1}^{\infty}\delta^{t-1}u_j\left(x_j,Q\right);\ (j=1,2)$$

where $\delta\in[0,1]$ denotes the discount factor, common to both agents.

Is it possible to reach an efficient equilibrium in a dynamic setting? When the decisions are taken in a multi-period framework, the loss from non-cooperation accumulates, and strong incentives appear to reach a Pareto Superior agreement. However, repetition alone is not enough to eliminate the non-cooperative static equilibrium, and thus the one-shot Stackelberg equilibrium is another possible outcome of the repeated game. To arrive at a combination that is Pareto superior to the one-shot non-cooperative equilibrium, it is necessary that both spouses implicitly create a credible strategy that deters deviations from a cooperative solution. As in Andaluz and Molina [6], we consider the so-called trigger strategy (Friedman [7]). In this case, when there is a deviation from the cooperative solution, the levels of private consumption, and the provision of the family good revert to those of non-cooperative equilibrium. The threat of retaliation, through reversion to this punishment path, sustains Pareto Superior outcomes and is credible, since it is in the best interest of each agent not to deviate unilaterally from the cooperative equilibrium.

For the sake of simplicity, we focus on stationary paths for all t. In a subgame perfect equilibrium, a stationary path is sustainable if it satisfies the following conditions:

$$u_i\left(x_i,Q\right)-u_i^*\geq 0;i=1,2 \tag{9}$$

$$\frac{u_2\left(x_2,Q\right)}{1-\delta}\geq u_2^d\left(q_1\right)+\frac{\delta u_2^*}{1-\delta} \tag{10}$$

Condition (9) establishes that both spouses have incentives to cooperate, since the well-being these agents obtain in the cooperative solution is greater than, or equal to, the well-being obtained in the non-cooperative solution. Condition (10) determines that the spouse who decides second has no incentive to deviate from the efficient solution. Condition (9) is not enough to obtain stationary paths, since the follower, given q_1, could react by deviation to maximize his/her own utility. To solve this problem, it is necessary to introduce inequality (10), which states that the discounted value of the well-being of the follower, conforming to the specified path, the left-hand side of the inequality, is greater than the well-being from the optimal one-shot deviation and the subsequent reversion from the following period, onwards

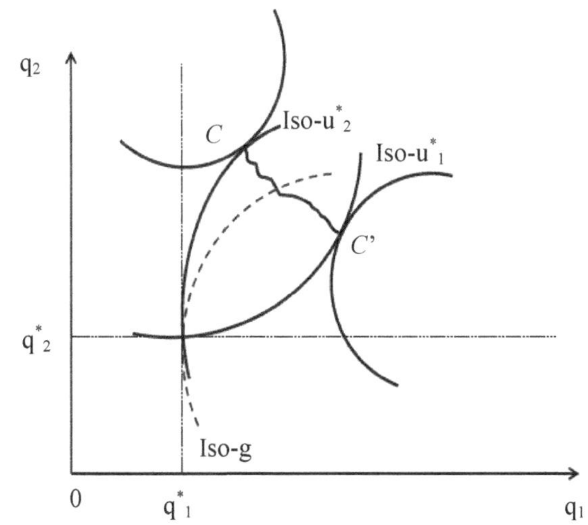

Figure 1. Set of Pareto-Superior Solutions.

[5]Our approach is developed in an environment where marital partners have separate preferences, and are involved in a long-term relationship.

to the punishment path, the right-hand side of the inequality.[6]

In this setting, the maintenance of the cooperative equilibrium depends on the agent who decides second. If spouse 1 deviates from a cooperative agreement, this is immediately observed by spouse 2, thus eliminating any possible short-term well-being gains for spouse 1. Moreover, the leader's discount rate plays no role, since the one-shot game is sequential. However, the follower's discount rate is a key element in the maintenance of the cooperative solution.

Unless δ is very high, constraint (10) is always binding in equilibrium, whereas (9) is not. Denote $\tilde{\delta}$ the minimum value of discount factor for which (10) is not binding, and let the function $g = g(q_1, q_2, \delta)$ represent the long-term gain from the follower's cooperation determined from (10). Formally:

$$g(q_1,q_2,\delta) = (1-w_2)q_2 - q_2^{\alpha} + \delta q_1 - (\alpha-1)\left(\frac{1-w_2}{\alpha}\right)^{\frac{\alpha}{\alpha-1}} - \delta\left(\frac{1-w_1}{\beta}\right)^{\frac{1}{\beta-1}} \quad (11)$$

When $q_1 > q_1^*$ and $q_2 > q_2^*$, the function g is increasing and concave, with the value of its slope being minus infinity in the non-cooperative solution (q_1^*, q_2^*). The function g is represented by a broken line in **Figure 1**. Among the Pareto-superior combinations (q_1, q_2), which are those points located in the contract curve CC', the function g allows us to identify a subset of sustainable solutions, all the combinations of (q_1, q_2) located to the right of the dashed line, which can be achieved by way of repeated interaction. This subset of Pareto-superior solutions to the equilibrium of the one-shot game is greater when the discount factor is higher, since the function g is increasing in δ. Thus, cooperation is more easily sustained as δ increases.

5. Bargaining Solution

In order to determine a single equilibrium among the multiple stationary paths, we suppose that there exists a bargaining process, not modeled explicitly here, and as a result, both spouses take their decisions by way of the symmetric Nash bargaining solution.[7] Focusing on the sustainable solutions, spouses choose the stationary paths of private consumption and family good provision that maximize the product of the utilities, after being normalized by the utility levels of the non-cooperative solution. Formally, the problem becomes, for $\delta < \tilde{\delta}$

$$\begin{aligned} &\max_{x_1,x_2,q_1,q_2} J(x_1,x_2,q_1,q_2) = (u_1 - u_1^*)(u_2 - u_2^*) \\ &\text{s.to} \qquad g(q_1,q_2,\delta) = 0 \end{aligned} \quad (12)$$

When δ takes value zero, the non-cooperative solution satisfies restrictions (9) and (10). Alternatively, if this factor takes value one, all the Pareto-superior solutions are indeed sustainable and, consequently, the bargaining agreement constitutes an efficient solution. Between these two extremes, the solution of the previous problem depends on the discount factor through constraint $g(q_1,q_2,\delta)=0$. The bargaining solution is determined by way of the tangency between an Iso-J line and an Iso-g line, as shown in **Figure 2**.[8]

Under some regularity assumptions (see Appendix) we obtain the following proposition:

Proposition 1.

For $\delta < \tilde{\delta}$

The contribution to the family good of the spouse who decides second (follower) is increasing with respect to the discount factor: $\frac{dq_2}{d\delta} > 0$.

The influence of the discount factor on the contribution to the family good of the spouse who decides first (leader) is ambiguous: $\frac{dq_1}{d\delta} \le 0$ or $\frac{dq_1}{d\delta} \ge 0$.

Proof. (See Appendix).

This proposition indicates that the agent who decides second will devote more time to the provision of the family good when he/she values the future heavily (a

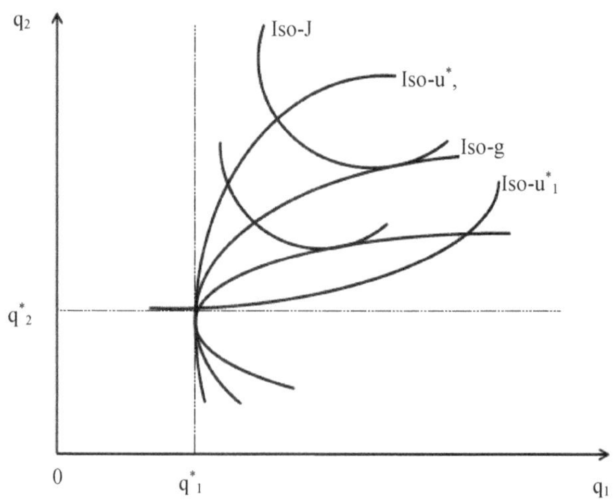

Figure 2. Set of possible sustainable bargaining solutions.

[6]This is not applicable to the situation of the standard case of Nash reversion, since, in this situation, decisions are taken simultaneously, and to obtain stationary paths it is necessary to include an additional inequality similar to that introduced for spouse 2, (10), but in this case it must also be established for spouse 1.

[7]This solution implicitly assumes a bargaining process resulting in the generalised bargaining solution (see Binmore *et al.* [18]; Harsanyi [19]).

[8]It is straightforward to deduce that under the structure of preferences used in this analysis, the provision of the family good is independent of the discount factor when we use the Cournot-Nash equilibrium as the threat point in the analysis.

high discount factor). However, the path of the contribution to the family good made by the spouse who decides first can be increased or decreased. An increasing evolution would imply that the difference between the hours this agent devotes to the family good in the cooperative solution, and the hours determined in the non-cooperative equilibrium, will not be significant.

Note that we have found that the discount factor can increase the provision of the family good without imposing any restriction on the follower's relative earnings, or on the psychological cost produced by devoting time to the family good. Thus, if the woman is the follower, the higher the discount factor, the higher the provision of the family good, even with the wage rate being the same for both spouses.

For the leader, spouse 1, we find a subset of sustainable solutions where the spouse who decides first increases or decreases provision of the family good, depending on the discount factor. There exists a level of provision of the family good, $\hat{q}_1$, with $\hat{q}_1 > q_1^*$, which represents the minimum value from which the relationship between the discount factor and the level of provision of the family good made by this agent becomes negative. By contrast, for $q_1^* < q_1 \leq \hat{q}_1$ when the discount factor increases, the provision of the family good by the leader increases. Thus, situations in which the husband devotes much less time to the family good than does the wife can be possible sustainable agreements, even without differences in the salaries of the spouses, as a result of a high discount factor.

The discount factor also reflects the subjective probability that the game will end. The higher the discount factor, the lower the probability that the game will end in the near future. Even when there is a possibility that the game will end sometime in the future, as in the case of intertemporal agreements within the family subject to renegotiation, our optimum provision of the family good can support a near-efficient outcome, as long as each spouse believes, with a high enough probability, that the game will continue. Thus, although we have considered an infinitely repeated game, it is possible to make agreements in a dynamic setting with a finite horizon (see Espinosa and Rhee [8]).

Knowing the evolution of the paths of the provision of the family good, we can deduce the influence of the discount factor on the level of utility derived from the cooperation.

Corollary:

For $\delta < \tilde{\delta}$

In the bargaining solution, a variation of the discount factor can increase or reduce the levels of utility for both spouses: $\frac{du_1}{d\delta} \geq 0; \frac{du_1}{d\delta} \leq 0; \frac{du_2}{d\delta} \geq 0; \frac{du_2}{d\delta} \leq 0$

Proof. (See Appendix).

Specifically, we observe that, for $q_1 > \hat{q}_1$ when the discount factor increases, the provision of the family good by the leader decreases, generating opposite effects on the level of utility of the spouses. The level of utility increases for the leader and decreases for the follower. By contrast, for $q_1^* < q_1 \leq \hat{q}_1$ when the discount factor increases, the provision of the family good by the leader increases, and the levels of utility can increase or decrease for both spouses.

6. Conclusions

Family bargaining models have usually presented the household allocation problem in a static setting. However, households endure for more than a single period, which can potentially, and substantially, affect the family decision-making process and it is thus necessary to view bargaining in a multi-period context.

In this dynamic setting, we have set up a supergame in an intrahousehold framework, in which both spouses may contribute voluntarily to the provision of a family good. Assuming that the status quo is not only defined as non-cooperative, but also as sequential (equilibrium of Stackelberg), and that the efficient allocation is given by way of the symmetric Nash bargaining solution, we deduce the influence of the discount factor on the sustainability of agreements, and on the time that each individual devotes to the provision of the family good. We acknowledge that we have not included all the factors that affect the dynamics of intrahousehold bargaining, and some of our assumptions are potentially restrictive, but we view this work as a benchmark for understanding long-term marital relationships.

The following conclusions are obtained. First, the set of possible sustainable agreements derived from bargaining is greater when the discount factor of the spouse who decides second is higher; cooperation is more easily sustained. However, it is not clear whether a greater discount factor increases the incentives to make an agreement, since we show that the discount factor has an ambiguous impact on the gains of well-being derived from the bargaining. The effect of the discount factor will be positive or negative, depending on the increase in the time devoted by the leader to the production of the family good in the bargaining solution.

Second, the contribution of the follower to the family good is increasing with respect to the discount factor, whereas the relationship between the discount factor and the contribution made by the leader is ambiguous. Then, we would expect a greater contribution of the follower to the family good than that predicted in a static context. If the woman is the follower, it is likely that she will devote more time to a family good as her discount factor increases, despite the absence of differences in the wages for both spouses.

7. Acknowledgements

Support from the Spanish Ministry of Economics is gratefully acknowledged (grant reference number ECO2012-34828).

REFERENCES

[1] G. S. Becker, "A Treatise on the Family," Enlarged Edition, Harvard University Press, Cambridge, 1991.

[2] M. Aguiar and E. Hurst, "Measuring Trends in Leisure: The Allocation of Time over Five Decades," *The Quarterly Journal of Economics*, Vol. 122, No. 3, 2007, pp. 969-1006.

[3] J. Hersch, "The Impact of Nonmarket Work on Market Wages," *American Economic Review Papers and Proceedings*, Vol. 81, 1991, pp. 157-160.

[4] G. Akerlof and R. Kranton, "Economics and Identity," *Quarterly Journal of Economics*, Vol. 115, No. 3, 2000, pp. 715-753.

[5] S. Lundberg and R. A. Pollak, "Efficiency in Marriage," *Review of Economic of the Household*, Vol. 1, No. 3, 2003, pp. 153-167.

[6] J. Andaluz and J. A. Molina, "On the Sustainability of Bargaining Solutions in Family Decision Models," *Review of Economics of the Household*, Vol. 5, No. 4, 2007, pp. 405-418.

[7] J. Friedman, "A Non-Cooperative Equilibrium for Supergames," *Review of Economic Studies*, Vol. 38, No. 113, 1971, pp. 1-12.

[8] M. P. Espinosa and C. Rhee, "Efficient Wage Bargaining as a Repeated Game," *Quarterly Journal of Economics*, Vol. 104, No. 3, 1989, pp. 565-588.

[9] K. Bolin, "An Economic Analysis of Marriage and Divorce," *Lund Economic Studies*, University of Lund, Lund, 1996, p. 62.

[10] K. Bolin, "A Family with One Dominating Spouse," In: I. Persson and C. Jonung, Eds., *Economics of the Family and Family Policies*, Routledge, New York, 1997, pp. 84-99.

[11] R. Elul, J. Silva-Reus and O. Volij, "Will You Marry Me? A Perspective on the Gender Gap," *Journal of Economic Behaviour and Organization*, Vol. 49, No. 4, 2002, pp. 549-572.

[12] M. Beblo and J. R. Robledo, "The Wage Gap and the Leisure Gap for Double-Earner Couples," *Journal of Population Economics*, Vol. 21, No. 2, 2008, pp. 281-304.

[13] D. J. Benjamin, J. J. Choi and A. J. Strickland, "Social Identity and Preferences," *American Economic Review*, Vol. 100, No. 4, 2010, pp. 1913-1928.

[14] K. A. Konrad and K. E. Lommerud, "The Bargaining Family Revisited," *Canadian Journal of Economics*, Vol. 33, No. 2, 2000, pp. 471-487.

[15] S. De la Rica and M. P. Espinosa, "Testing Employement Determination in Unionised Economies as a Repeated Game," *Scottish Journal of Political Economy*, Vol. 44, No. 2, 1997, pp. 134-152.

[16] W. Buchholz, K. A. Konrad and K. E. Lommerud, "Stackelberg Leadership and Transfers in Private Provision of Public Goods," *Review of Economic Design*, Vol. 3, No. 1, 1997, pp. 29-43.

[17] A. Kapteyn and P. Kooreman, "On the Empirical Implementation of Some Game Theoretic Models of Household Labor Supply," *The Journal of Human Resources*, Vol. 25, No. 4, 1990, pp. 584-598.

[18] K. Binmore, A. Rubinstein and A. Woolinsky, "The Nash Bargaining Solution in Economic Modeling," *Rand Journal of Economics*, Vol. 17, No. 2, 1986, pp. 176-188.

[19] J. C. Harsanyi, "Rational Behaviour and Bargaining Equilibria in Games and Social Situations," Cambridge University Press, Cambridge, 1977.

Appendix

Proof of Proposition

To be able to characterize the solution of the maximization problem proposed in (12), we introduce the following assumptions:

We suppose that $J(x_1, x_2, q_1, q_2)$ is strictly concave.

The level curves of $J(x_1, x_2, q_1, q_2)$ are monotone:

$$\frac{\partial(J_1/J_2)}{\partial q_1} < 0 \qquad (13)$$

For $q_1 > 0, q_2 > 0$, the first order conditions are:

$$J_1 + \lambda g_1 = 0$$

$$J_2 + \lambda g_2 = 0$$

$$g(q_1, q_2, \delta) = 0$$

with $\lambda > 0$, the multiplier of the problem of maximization. Thus, it is possible to deduce the following equation:

$$\frac{J_1}{J_2} = \frac{g_1}{g_2} \qquad (14)$$

Differentiating with respect to δ, we obtain that:

$$(J_{11} + \lambda g_{11})\frac{dq_1}{d\delta} + (J_{12} + \lambda g_{12})\frac{dq_2}{d\delta} + g_1 \frac{d\lambda}{d\delta} = -\lambda g_{1\delta}$$

$$(J_{21} + \lambda g_{21})\frac{dq_1}{d\delta} + (J_{22} + \lambda g_{22})\frac{dq_2}{d\delta} + g_2 \frac{d\lambda}{d\delta} = -\lambda g_{2\delta}$$

$$g_1 \frac{dq_1}{d\delta} + g_2 \frac{dq_2}{d\delta} = -g_\delta$$

These equations can be written in matrix form as:

$$\begin{pmatrix} (J_{11} + \lambda g_{11}) & (J_{12} + \lambda g_{12}) & g_1 \\ (J_{21} + \lambda g_{21}) & (J_{22} + \lambda g_{22}) & g_2 \\ g_1 & g_2 & 0 \end{pmatrix} \begin{pmatrix} \frac{dq_1}{d\delta} \\ \frac{dq_2}{d\delta} \\ \frac{d\lambda}{d\delta} \end{pmatrix} = \begin{pmatrix} -\lambda g_{1\delta} \\ -\lambda g_{2\delta} \\ -g_\delta \end{pmatrix}$$

The matrix on the left hand side is the bordered Hessian. Applying Cramer's rule it is possible to obtain the changes in q_2 when δ changes:

$$\frac{dq_2}{d\delta} = \frac{1}{|D|} \begin{vmatrix} (J_{11} + \lambda g_{11}) & -\lambda g_{1\delta} & g_1 \\ (J_{21} + \lambda g_{21}) & -\lambda g_{2\delta} & g_2 \\ g_1 & -g_\delta & 0 \end{vmatrix} \qquad (15)$$

where $|D|$ is the determinant of the bordered Hessian. The second order conditions of the maximization problem require that $|D|$ be positive.

Therefore, the sign of $\frac{dq_2}{d\delta}$ is determined by the sign of (15):

$$\operatorname{sign}\left(\frac{dq_2}{d\delta}\right) = \operatorname{sign}\left[-\lambda\delta\left(1 - w_2 - \alpha q_2^{\alpha-1}\right) + \left(q_1 - q_1^*\right)\left(J_{11}\left(1 - w_2 - \alpha q_2^{\alpha-1}\right) - \delta J_{12}\right)\right] \qquad (16)$$

Given that $\left(1 - w_2 - \alpha q_2^{\alpha-1}\right) < 0 \wedge q_2 > q_2^*$, and under (13) and (14), we deduce that (16) is positive: $\frac{dq_2}{d\delta} > 0$.

Differentiating the restriction with respect to δ, we have:

$$\frac{dq_1}{d\delta} = -\frac{1}{\delta}\left[\left(q_1 - q_1^*\right) + \left(1 - w_2 - \alpha q_2^{\alpha-1}\right)\frac{dq_2}{d\delta}\right] \qquad (17)$$

Thus, the sign of $\frac{dq_1}{d\delta}$ is the sign of the numerator:

$$\operatorname{sign}\left(\frac{dq_1}{d\delta}\right) = \operatorname{sign}\left[-\left(q_1 - q_1^*\right) - \left(1 - w_2 - \alpha q_2^{\alpha-1}\right)\frac{dq_2}{d\delta}\right]$$

Given that

$$\left(q_1 - q_1^*\right) > 0, \left(1 - w_2 - \alpha q_2^{\alpha-1}\right) < 0 \wedge \frac{dq_2}{d\delta} > 0,$$

we deduce that

$$\frac{dq_1}{d\delta} \geq 0. \quad \text{or} \quad \frac{dq_1}{d\delta} \leq 0.$$

From (15) and (17), we can determine a value $\hat{q}_1$, with $\hat{q}_1 > q_1^*$, which represents the minimum value from which the relationship between the discount factor and the level of provision of the family good made by this agent becomes negative. So, when $q_1 > \hat{q}_1$, we obtain that $\frac{dq_1}{d\delta} < 0$ and when $\hat{q}_1 \geq q_1 > q_1^*$ what we obtain is that $\frac{dq_1}{d\delta} > 0$.

Proof of Corollary

Applying the envelope theorem, we derive the utility function of both spouses with respect to δ:

For spouse 1, we obtain:

$$\frac{du_1}{d\delta} = \frac{\partial u_1}{\partial q_1}\frac{dq_1}{d\delta} + \frac{\partial u_1}{\partial q_2}\frac{dq_2}{d\delta} \qquad (18)$$

Taking into account (17), this expression takes the following form:

$$\frac{du_1}{d\delta} = \frac{-\left(1 - w_1 - \beta q_1^{\beta-1}\right)\left(q_1 - q_1^*\right)}{\delta} + \left[1 - \frac{\left(1 - w_1 - \beta q_1^{\beta-1}\right)\left(1 - w_2 - \alpha q_2^{\alpha-1}\right)}{\delta}\right]\frac{dq_2}{d\delta} \qquad (19)$$

Given that

$\left(1-w_1-\beta q_1^{\beta-1}\right)<0$, $\left(1-w_2-\alpha q_2^{\alpha-1}\right)<0, \frac{\mathrm{d}q_2}{\mathrm{d}\delta}>0$, $\left(q_1-q_1^*\right)>0$, $0<\delta<1$, $0<q_i<1$ $(i=1,2)$, we deduce that: $\frac{\mathrm{d}u_1}{\mathrm{d}\delta}\geq 0$ or $\frac{\mathrm{d}u_1}{\mathrm{d}\delta}\leq 0$

Analogously, given that $\frac{\mathrm{d}q_2}{\mathrm{d}\delta}>0$ and with $\frac{\mathrm{d}q_1}{\mathrm{d}\delta}<0$, we obtain that $\frac{\mathrm{d}u_1}{\mathrm{d}\delta}\geq 0$ with $q_1>\hat{q}_1$. When $\frac{\mathrm{d}q_1}{\mathrm{d}\delta}>0$, we obtain that $\frac{\mathrm{d}u_1}{\mathrm{d}\delta}\leq 0$ with $\hat{q}_1\geq q_1>q_1^*$.

For spouse 2,

$$\frac{\mathrm{d}u_2}{\mathrm{d}\delta}=\frac{\partial u_2}{\partial q_1}\frac{\mathrm{d}q_1}{\mathrm{d}\delta}+\frac{\partial u_2}{\partial q_2}\frac{\mathrm{d}q_2}{\mathrm{d}\delta}$$

Introducing (17), we deduce that:

$$\frac{\mathrm{d}u_2}{\mathrm{d}\delta}=\left(1-\frac{1}{\delta}\right)\left(1-w_2-\alpha q_2^{\alpha-1}\right)\frac{\mathrm{d}q_2}{\mathrm{d}\delta}-\frac{\left(q_1-q_1^*\right)}{\delta}.$$

Analogously, we obtain that

$$\frac{\mathrm{d}u_2}{\mathrm{d}\delta}=\left(1-w_2-\alpha q_2^{\alpha-1}\right)\frac{\mathrm{d}q_2}{\mathrm{d}\delta}+\frac{\mathrm{d}q_1}{\mathrm{d}\delta}.$$

Given that $\frac{\mathrm{d}q_2}{\mathrm{d}\delta}>0$ and with $\frac{\mathrm{d}q_1}{\mathrm{d}\delta}<0$, we obtain that $\frac{\mathrm{d}u_2}{\mathrm{d}\delta}\leq 0$. Remember that it is necessary that $q_1>\hat{q}_1$ to obtain a negative relationship between the discount factor and the level of provision of the family good made by spouse 1. When $\frac{\mathrm{d}q_1}{\mathrm{d}\delta}>0$, we obtain that $\frac{\mathrm{d}u_2}{\mathrm{d}\delta}\geq 0$, with $\hat{q}_1\geq q_1>q_1^*$.

Social Welfare under Quantity Competition and Price Competition in a Mixed Duopoly with Network Effects: An Analysis*

Yasuhiko Nakamura
College of Economics, Nihon University, Tokyo, Japan

ABSTRACT

In their recent work, Matsumura and Ogawa (2012) showed that in the context of a mixed duopoly, equilibrium social welfare is higher in price-setting competition than in quantity-setting competition. We found that when the strength of network effects is sufficiently high, the above result is totally reversed; thus, in a mixed duopoly, the presence of network effects weakens the superiority of price-setting competition with respect to equilibrium social welfare.

Keywords: Mixed Duopoly; Network Effect; Price Competition; Quantity Competition

1. Introduction

This study compares equilibrium social welfare between price-setting competition and quantity-setting competition in a mixed duopoly with network effects. The network effects that we consider in this paper were introduced in Katz and Shapiro [1] and applied in Hoernig [2], Nakamura [3], and Nakamura [4]. These effects reflected a simple mechanism where the surplus obtained by a firm's client increases directly with the number of other clients of this firm. In this study, we show that when the strength of such network effects is sufficiently high, the equilibrium social welfare is higher in a quantity-setting competition than in a price-setting competition; this finding is strikingly different from those in the existing literature in this field including Ghosh and Mitra [5] and Matsumura and Ogawa [6].

Although we can consider the European automobile industry as a representative example in a mixed oligopolistic industry, as described in Katz and Shapiro [1], network effects as positive consumption externalities are likely to arise in the automobile market[1]. In such an industry, foreign automobile firms' sales may be less than expected because of the perceptions that consumers hold about the less experienced and smaller service networks of new or less popular brands. Thus, in a mixed oligopoly, the presence of network effects as positive consumption externalities should be analyzed since they influence the equilibrium market outcomes in both price-setting and quantity-setting competitions.

By building a simple extention of the model from Matsumura and Ogawa [6] in line with Hoernig [2], Nakamura [3], and Nakamura [4], we find that a sufficiently high level of network effects reverses the ranking order of the equilibrium social welfare between price-setting competition and quantity-setting competition. Thus, when the strength of network effects is sufficiently high, the equilibrium social welfare can be higher in quantity competition than in price-setting competition, because the relatively large total output levels in the former yield a strictly positive influence on equilibrium social welfare in accordance with the sufficiently high level of network effects. Therefore, in a mixed market, the superiority of price-setting competition is weakened if network effects such as consumers' expectations about each firm's equilibrium market share are sufficiently strong.

2. Model

We formulate a mixed duopolistic model composed of one public firm and one private firm, with an additional term that reflects the network effects introduced in Katz

*We are grateful for the financial support by KAKENHI (25870113). All remaining errors are our own.

[1]As one example, a Spanish public-owned automobile manufacturer, SEAT competes with Volkswagen which is one of the most famous German private automobile manufacturers. In addition, Renault which is the most famous partially French public-owned firm competes with many private firms in Europe. Recently, Romanian private firm, Dacia merged with Renault, and it became a second marque for the Renault group. See Barcena-Ruiz and Garzon [7] for other examples and detail discussions of the European automobile industry as a mixed oligopolistic market.

and Shapiro [1] and applied by Hoernig [2], Nakamura [3], and Nakamura [4]. We assume that firm 0 is a welfare-maximizing public firm, whereas firm 1 is a pure profit-maximizing private firm. Similar to Hoernig [2], Nakamura [3], and Nakamura [4], firm i faces a linear demand of the following form:

$$q_i = a + ny_i - p_i + bp_j \text{ and } i = 0,1; i \neq j, \quad (1)$$

where $a > 0$ and $b \in (0,1)$ are demand parameters. $n \in [0,1)$ indicates the strength of network effects, and y_i is consumers' expectations on firm i's equilibrium market share. As explained in Hoernig [2], Nakamura [3], and Nakamura [4], the above demand system can be derived from the following quasi-linear concave utility function of a representative consumer:

$$U(q_0, q_1; y_0, y_1) = m + \frac{a(q_0 + q)}{1-b} - \frac{q_0^2 + q_1^2}{2(1-b^2)} - \frac{bq_0q_1}{1-b^2}$$
$$+ n\frac{(y_0 + by_1)q_0 + (y_1 + by_0)q_1}{1-b^2} + f(y_0, y_1),$$

where m denotes the income of the representative consumer and $f(\cdot,\cdot)$ represents some symmetric function of expectations. In this paper, in the same manner as in Hoernig [2], Nakamura [3], and Nakamura [4], we suppose that

$$f(y_0, y_1) = -n(y_0^2/2 + by_0y_1 + y_1^2/2)/(1-b^2)^2.$$

The marginal cost of production of both firms 0 and 1 is commonly assumed to be c. The profit function of firm i is given by $\Pi_i = (p_i - c)q_i$, $(i, j = 0,1; i \neq j)$ where q_i is given as (1)[3]. Consumer surplus is expressed as the representative consumer's utility as follows:

$$CS = U(q_0, q_1; y_0, y_1) - p_0q_0 - p_1q_1,$$

whereas producer surplus is given by the sum of the profits of both firms 0 and 1, $\Pi_0 + \Pi_1$. Finally, we suppose that social welfare is defined as the sum of consumer surplus and producer surplus.

We consider "rational expectations" to be a subgame perfect Nash equilibrium by imposing the rational expectations condition that $y_0 = q_0$ and $y_1 = q_1$ à la Katz and Shapiro [1], Hoernig [2], Nakamura [3], and Nakamura [4].

3. Welfare Analysis

3.1. *p-p* Game

In this subsection, we discuss the *p-p* game where firms 0 and 1 simultaneously choose their price levels. By considering y_0 and y_1 as given, public firm 0 maximizes the social welfare with respect to p_0 whereas private firm 1 maximizes its profit with respect to p_1. In this case, the social welfare is given as follows:

$$W(p_0, p_1; y_0, y_1)$$
$$= -\frac{(1-b^2)p_0^2}{2(1-b^2)} + \frac{p_0[2(1-b)(1-b^2)c + 2bp_1 - 2b^3p_1]}{2(1-b^2)}$$
$$+ \frac{2a^2(1+b) - p_1^2 + b^2p_1^2 - ny_0^2 + n^2y_0^2 - 2bny_0y_1}{2(1-b^2)}$$
$$+ \frac{2bn^2y_0y_1 - ny_1^2 + n^2y_1^2}{2(1-b^2)}$$
$$- \frac{2a(1+b)[2(1-b)c - n(y_0 + y_1)]}{2(1-b^2)}$$
$$+ \frac{2(1-b^2)c[(1-b)p_1 - n(y_0 + y_1)]}{2(1-b^2)}.$$

Note that the term of the price level of firm 0, p_0 is independent of the term of consumers' expectations about the market share of both firms 0 and 1, y_0 and y_1[4]. On the other hand, the profit of firm 1 is given as follows:

$$\Pi_1(p_0, p_1; y_0, y_1) = (p_1 - c)(a + bp_0 - p_1 + ny_1).$$

The respective reaction functions of firms 0 and 1, r_i, are given as follows $(i = 0,1)$:

$$p_0 = r_0(p_1) = c - bc + bp_1, \quad (2)$$

$$p_1 = r_1(p_0; y_1) = (a + c + bp_0 + ny_1)/2. \quad (3)$$

Note that the price level of firm 0 does not depend on consumers' expectations about the market share of both firms 0 and 1 in its reaction function.

We obtain the rational expectations Nash equilibrium outcomes by substituting the rational expectations assumption that $y_0 = q_0$ and $y_1 = q_1$ into Equations (2) and (3). The equilibrium market outcomes namely the output and price levels of firms 0 and 1, profit of firm 0, producer surplus and consumer surplus are given as follows:

$$q_0^{pp} = \frac{a-(1-b)c}{1-n}, \; q_1^{pp} = \frac{a-(1-b)c}{2-b^2-n},$$

$$p_0^{pp} = \frac{ab + c(2-b-n)}{2-b^2-n}, \; p_1^{pp} = c + \frac{a-(1-b)c}{2-b^2-n},$$

[2]This assumption in the form of $f(\cdot,\cdot)$ implies that the representative consumer's utility is the highest with respect to the consumption vector of the goods produced by both the public firm and the private firm, (q_0, q_1), when expectations are rational and correct.

[3]We assume that $a/(1-b) > c \geq 0$ in order to ensure the non-negativity of all equilibrium outcomes.

[4]Thus, as described below, in firm 0's reaction function, its price level does not depend on consumers' expectations about the market share of both firms 0 and 1, y_0 and y_1.

$$\Pi_0^{pp} = \frac{b\left[a-(1-b)c\right]^2}{(1-n)\left(2-b^2-n\right)},$$

$$PS^{pp} = \frac{(1+b)\left[a-(1-b)c\right]^2\left(1+b-b^2-n\right)}{(1-n)\left(2-b^2-n\right)^2},$$

$$CS^{pp} = \frac{\left[a-(1-b)c\right]^2\left[5-b+b^3-6n+2n^2-b^2(3-2n)\right]}{2(1-b)(1-n)\left(2-b^2-n\right)^2}+m.$$

Furthermore, the payoffs of both firms 0 and 1 are given as follows:

$$W^{pp} = \frac{\left[a-(1-b)c\right]^2\left[7+b-b^3+2b^4-2(4-n)n-b^2(7-4n)\right]}{2(1-b)(1-n)\left(2-b^2-n\right)^2}+m,$$

$$\Pi_1^{pp} = \frac{\left[a-(1-b)c\right]^2}{\left(2-b^2-n\right)^2}$$

3.2. *q-q* Game

In this subsection, we discuss the *q-q* game where firms 0 and 1 simultaneously choose their output levels. By considering y_0 and y_1 as given, public firm 0 maximizes the social welfare with respect to q_0 whereas private firm 1 maximizes its profit with respect to q_1. In this case, the social welfare is given as follows:

$$W\left(q_0,q_1;y_0,y_1\right) = \frac{2a(1+b)\left(q_0+q_1\right)-q_0^2+2bq_0q_1+q_1^2-2\left(1-b^2\right)c\left(q_0+q_1\right)}{2\left(1-b^2\right)} + \frac{2nq_0y_0+2bnq_1y_0-ny_0^2+2bnq_0y_1+2nq_1y_1-2bny_0y_1-ny_1^2}{2\left(1-b^2\right)}.$$

On the other hand, the profit of firm 1 is given as follows:

$$\Pi_1\left(q_0,q_1;y_0,y_1\right) = q_1\left[\frac{a(1+b)-bq_0-q_1+bny_0+ny_1}{1-b^2}-c\right]$$

The respective reaction functions of firms 0 and 1, r_i are given as follows $(i=0,1)$:

$$q_0 = r_0\left(q_1;y_0,y_1\right) = a(1+b)-\left(1-b^2\right)c-bq_1+ny_0+bny_1 \quad (4)$$

$$q_1 = r_1\left(q_0,y_0,y_1\right) = \left[a(1+b)-\left(1-b^2\right)c-bq_0+bny_0+ny_1\right]/2. \quad (5)$$

We obtain the rational expectations Nash equilibrium outcomes by substituting the rational expectations assumption that $y_0=q_0$ and $y_1=q_1$ into Equations (4) and (5), The equilibrium market outcomes including the output and price levels of firms 0 and 1, profit of firm 0, and consumer surplus are given as follows:

$$q_0^{qq} = \frac{(1+b)\left[a-(1-b)c\right]\left[2-b(1-n)-n\right]}{\left[2-b^2(1-n)-n\right](1-n)},\ q_1^{qq} = \frac{\left(1-b^2\right)\left[a-(1-b)c\right]}{2-b^2(1-n)-n},\ p_0^{qq}=c,$$

$$p_1^{qq} = c+\frac{a-(1-b)c}{2-b^2(1-n)-n},\ \Pi_0^{qq}=0,$$

$$PS^{qq} = \frac{\left(1-b^2\right)\left[a-(1-b)c\right]^2}{\left[2-b^2(1-n)-n\right]^2},$$

$$CS^{qq} = \frac{(1+b)\left[a-(1-b)c\right]^2\left[5-2b^2(2-n)(1-n)-2b(1-n)^2+2b^3(1-n)^2-2(3-n)n\right]}{2(1-b)\left[2-b^2(1-n)-n\right]^2(1-n)}+m.$$

Furthermore, the payoffs of both firms 0 and 1 are given as follows:

$$W^{qq} = \frac{\left[a-(1-b)c\right]^2\left[7+b-4b^2(2-n)(1-n)+2b^4(1-n)^2-2(4-n)n\right]}{(1-b)\left[2-b^2(1-n)-n\right]^2(1-n)}+m,$$

$$\Pi_1^{qq} = \frac{\left(1-b^2\right)\left[a-(1-b)c\right]^2}{\left[2-b^2(1-n)-n\right]^2}.$$

On comparing the equilibrium social welfare between price-setting competition and quantity competition, we obtain the following result:

$$W^{pp}-W^{qq} = \frac{b^2\left[a-(1-b)c\right]^2\left[4+b^4(1-n)^2-8n+3n^2-b^2\left(4-8n+3n^2\right)\right]}{2\left[2-b^2(1-n)-n\right]^2(1-n)\left(2-b^2-n\right)^2} \gtrless 0$$

$$\Leftrightarrow n \lesseqgtr \frac{4-4b^2+b^4-\left(2-b^2\right)\sqrt{1-b^2}}{3-3b^2+b^4}\left(\in(0,1),\ \forall b\in(0,1)\right).$$

Then, we obtain the proposition on the ranking order of equilibrium social welfare between price-setting competition and quantity-setting competition.

Proposition 1 *When the strength of network effects in a mixed duopoly is sufficiently high, that is,* $n > \left[4-4b^2+b^4-\left(2-b^2\right)\sqrt{1-b^2}\right]/\left(3-3b^2+b^4\right)$, *the equilibrium social welfare is higher in quantity-setting competition than in price-setting competition; otherwise the opposite is the case.*

In **Figure 1**, the difference in the equilibrium social welfare between price-setting competition and quantity-setting competition is described. Surprisingly, Proposition 1 implies that when the strength of network effects is sufficiently high, the result on the ranking order of the equilibrium social welfare between a price-setting competition and a quantity-setting competition obtained in Ghosh and Mitra [5] and Matsumura and Ogawa [6] is totally reversed; hence, the equilibrium social welfare can be higher in quantity-setting competition than in price-setting competition. The intuition behind this result is given by using the following lemma:

Lemma 1 *For the rational expectations Nash equilibrium in price and quantity competitions, the ranking orders of the equilibrium market outcomes are given as follows*:

1) $p_0^{pp} > p_0^{qq}$, $p_1^{pp} \geq p_1^{qq}$, $q_0^{qq} > q_0^{pp}$, and $q_1^{pp} > q_1^{qq}$,

2) $\left(q_0^{qq}+q_1^{qq}\right) > \left(q_0^{pp}+q_1^{pp}\right)$ and $\left(q_0^{qq}-q_1^{qq}\right) > \left(q_0^{pp}-q_1^{pp}\right)$,

3) $PS^{pp} > PS^{qq}$ and $CS^{qq} > CS^{pp}$.

Note that the above equality of the price level of private firm 1 is satisfied only when $n=0$ [5].

From Lemma 1, even if network effects are introduced, the ranking orders of equilibrium outcomes except for the price level of firm 1 are the same as those obtained in Ghosh and Mitra [5]. The introduction of network effects widens the difference in the price level of firm 0 between price-setting competition and quantity-setting competition, implying that such a low level of p_0^{qq} creates a strong downward pressure on firm 1's price level. Thus, when n takes some sort of positive value, firm 0's price level is strictly higher in price-setting competition than in quantity-setting competition. Therefore, in particular when the strength of network effects is sufficiently low, since the ranking order of the equilibrium market outcomes seldom changes against the introduction of network effects, the equilibrium social welfare is higher in price competition than in quantity competition owing to the large difference of the equilibrium producer surplus relative to that of the equilibrium consumer surplus, which is similar to Ghosh and Mitra [5] and Matsumura and Ogawa [6].

On the other hand, by following the formula of equilibrium social welfare à la Ghosh and Mitra [5], and by imposing the rational expectations condition that $y_0 = q_0$ and $y_1 = q_1$, we can represent the equilibrium social welfare as follows:

$$W\left(q_0,q_1;y_0=q_0,y_1=q_1\right)=s\left(q_0+q_1\right)+d\left(q_0-q_1\right),$$

$$\text{where}\begin{cases} s\left(q_0+q_1\right)=\left[a-(1-b)c\right]\left(q_0+q_1\right)/(1-b) \\ \qquad -(1-n)\left(q_0+q_1\right)^2/4(1-b), \\ d\left(q_0-q_1\right)=-(1-n)\left(q_0-q_1\right)^2/4(1+b). \end{cases}$$

As explained in Ghosh and Mitra [5] and Matsumura and Ogawa [6], on the basis of the facts that $s'(\cdot)>0$ and $d'(\cdot)<0$, the effect of $d\left(q_0-q_1\right)$ on the equilibrium social welfare outstrips the effect of $s\left(q_0+q_1\right)$ when $n=0$; consequently, the equilibrium social wel-

[5]When $n=0$, the fact that such an equality holds is indicated in Ghosh and Mitra [5].

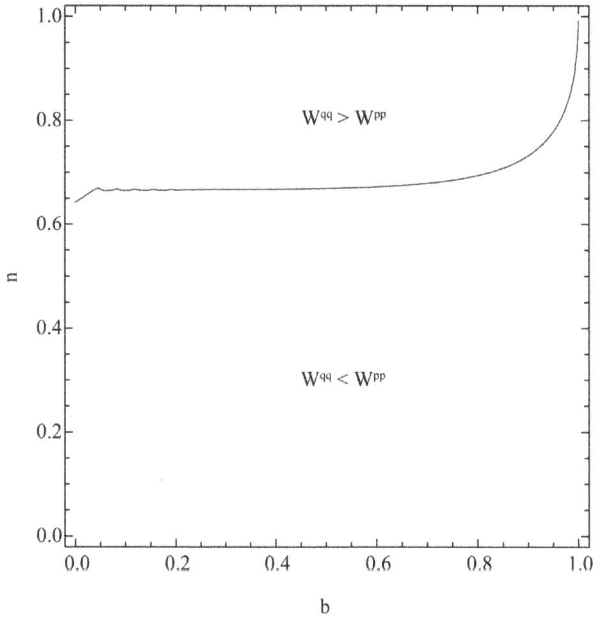

Figure 1. Comparison of the equilibrium social welfare between price-setting competition and quantity-setting competition.

fare is higher in price-setting competition than in quantity-setting competition if no network effects are considered. However, as n becomes higher, in a quantity-setting competition, the positive effect of $s(q_0+q_1)$ owing to $(q_0^{qq}+q_1^{qq})>(q_0^{pp}+q_1^{pp})$ on the equilibrium social welfare increases. On the other hand, the negative effect of $d(q_0-q_1)$ owing to $(q_0^{qq}-q_1^{qq})>(q_0^{pp}-q_1^{pp})$ on the equilibrium social welfare decreases. Therefore, the degree of the strength of network effects, n, reverses the order of the equilibrium social welfare between price-setting and quantity-setting competitions.

4. Conclusions

This study compared the equilibrium social welfare between price-setting competition and quantity-competition in a mixed duopolistic market with network effects. In Ghosh and Mitra [5] and Matsumura and Ogawa [6], where network effect is not considered, it was shown that the equilibrium social welfare is always higher in price-setting competition than in quantity competition[6]. However, in this paper, when the strength of network effects is sufficiently high, we found that the ranking order of the equilibrium social welfare between price-setting competition and quantity-setting competition is totally reversed. Thus, when network effects are explicitly considered, the superiority of price competition with regard to social welfare weakens in a mixed duopolistic market.

Furthermore, by following Matsumura and Ogawa [6], where public firm 0 and private firm 1 can choose their strategic variables (*i.e.*, their price levels or output levels), even if the network effects are explicitly introduced, we obtain the same results as those in their paper. Thus, in the two-stage game wherein both firms 0 and 1 simultaneously choose either their price contracts or their quantity contracts in the first stage, and accordingly engage in market competition in the second stage, we find that price-setting competition is a unique market competition structure led by dominant strategies such that both the firms take the price contracts[7].

REFERENCES

[1] M. Katz and C. Shapiro, "Network Externalities, Competition, and Compatibility," *American Economic Review*, Vol. 75, No. 3, 1985, pp. 424-440.

[2] S. Hoernig, "Strategic Delegation under Price Competition and Network Effects," *Economics Letters*, Vol. 117, No. 2, 2012, pp. 487-489.

[3] Y. Nakamura, "Capacity Choice in a Price-Setting Mixed Duopoly with Network Effects," *Modern Economy*, Vol. 4, No. 5, 2013, pp. 418-425.

[4] Y. Nakamura, "Endogenous Timing in Price-Setting Private and Mixed Duopoly with Network Effects," 2013, Mimeograph.

[5] C. Ghosh and M. Mitra, "Comparing Bertrand and Cournot in Mixed Markets," *Economics Letters*, Vol. 109, No. 2, 2010, pp. 72-74.

[6] T. Matsumura and A. Ogawa, "Price versus Quantity in a Mixed Duopoly," *Economics Letters*, Vol. 116, No. 2, 2012, pp. 174-177.

[7] J. C. Bárcena-Ruiz and M. B. Garzón, "Mixed Duopoly, Merger and Multiproduct Firms," *Journal of Economics*, Vol. 80, No. 1, 2003, pp. 27-42.

[6]Matsumura and Ogawa [6] found that the equilibrium social welfare becomes higher in price competition than in quantity competition regardless of the relation of goods produced by both the firms, that is, substitutable goods or complementary goods.

[7]Detailed discussions and proofs on the above are available upon request.

25

Economic and Emotional Rationality: An Application to Wealth Concentration

Jose Rigoberto Parada-Daza[1], Miguel Ignacio Parada-Contzen[2]
[1]Universidad de Concepcion, Concepcion, Chile
[2]Technische Universität Berlin (TUB), Berlin, Germany

ABSTRACT

This Paper presents a theoretical outline regarding the Emotional Well-being (EW) function as an extension of the economic utility function. EW includes habitual factors that are always present in everyday decision making. Firstly, an analytical-mathematical conceptualization of EW is carried out, followed by a study of the concept of emotional security, in order to define a new idea of emotional rationality as a complement to economic rationality. An explanation is put forth, as an application, of the concentration of wealth phenomenon according to the focus on economic and emotional rationality. The conclusion is that EW is a theoretical approach which can clarify the understanding of the decision making process in economics activities.

Keywords: Utility Function; Emotional Well-Being; Economic Rationality; Emotional Rationality; Concentration of Wealth

1. Introduction

The relation between levels of wealth and utility can be explained conceptually, from an exclusively economic point of view, by adopting the economic utility function concept, based on the theory of rational investment decisions measured in utilitarian units. This is the foundation of the argument for financial and economic decision making theory. However, this vision can change if variables are incorporated that are not completely explained by rationality of economic man when the interpretation of a particular economic fact is attempted. Sometimes it is not completely convincing that the person or persons behave solely as economic agents when making economic decisions.

As such, following the economic utility function, new variables can be incorporated into the analysis in order to explain the relation between wealth and utility. In this perspective, Parada-Daza [1], a function is developed that incorporates the economic rationale adding an element to interpret other variables that influence in making decisions during an economic act. This new factor includes factors such as: ethics, social responsibility and other characteristics related to people. This function has been titled the Emotional Well-being Function. The EW function has been used in literature to evaluate corporate social responsibility Parada-Daza [2], the sustainable development of small and medium enterprises, Brilius [3] and to evaluate the economic and non-economic behavior of various countries, Parada-Daza [4].

In this paper analytically distinct characteristics of the EW function are developed. Emphasis is placed on two new concepts; *emotional rationality and emotional security* to propose an application of the Emotional Well Being function that allows understanding, from a different perspective, what motivates the concentration of wealth and the perception that the actions of rich and poor citizens must be separated.

2. Prior Definitions and Literary Analysis

To substantiate the propositions of this paper, some concepts must be defined. These are extrapolated from consulted literature and new concepts incorporated here.

2.1. Emotional Well-Being

Personal Emotional Well-being (EW) is understood as the level of satisfaction that is felt when undertaking any act of daily life. This includes economic and global emotional satisfaction. This is evaluated by emotional pleasure. Higher the level of emotional pleasure, higher the level of emotional wellbeing. It is considered here that EW is a variable that is dependent on an individuals' wealth.

2.2. Relative Wealth

Let $w_{a,i}$ be the wealth of individual i, valued in absolute monetary units a, in an economy comprised of n individuals and W the total wealth in the economy in the following form:

$$\sum_{i=1}^{n} w_{a,i} = W$$

Thus, a variable is defined as $w_{r,i} \in [0,1]$ which represents the relative wealth of an individual i as:

$w_{r,i} = \frac{w_{a,i}}{W}$, such that $\sum_{i=1}^{n} w_{r,i} = 1$.

The relative wealth of the individual i permits the grouping of people as more wealthy and less wealthy. Therefore if an individual i has a wealth relative to 0.9 it indicates that, of the entire wealth of a society of n individuals, this individual i has accumulated 90% and the rest of the $n - 1$ individuals, possess 10% of the total wealth.

2.3. Utility Function and Its Literary Discussion

2.3.1. Economic Utility

In economic decision making theory, the utility function is used as the basis of analysis for explanation under risky conditions. A set of axioms has been developed to explain the choice or decision theory, Copeland and Weston [5] established a quadratic utility function as well as the logarithmic utility function that has been widely used in literature. Theories have been developed based on this type of function that reflect the behavior of people from an economic rationality standpoint, giving understanding as to why people are essentially maximizers and only move through this type of function.

Using the concept of relative wealth, for the purposes of this paper a utility function is defined as:

$U : [0,1] \to \mathbb{R}^+$ and $w_r \mapsto U = U(w_r)$.

Thus, U is differentiable up to at least second grade and is strictly increasing. *i.e.*

$$\frac{dU}{dw_r} > 0, \forall w_r \in [0,1]$$

In this approach, mathematically, utility is a function of wealth and it is supposed that the greater the wealth, the greater the utility. Each point shows the value that corresponds to each level of wealth. Economic man moves over the combination of these points. In regards to the previously mentioned it is assumed that the utility function is both increasing and limited. This implies that the greater the wealth, the greater the degree of economic satisfaction. The fact that it is limited means that certain levels exist where people consider a certain amount of satisfaction is acceptable.

Another characteristic of this function is that there is a diminishing marginal utility. That is, compared to an increase of wealth, an augment in utility will be gradually decreasing. Mathematically this is represented by a negative value of the second derivative of the utility function of which corresponds graphically to a convex function:

$$\frac{d^2U}{dw_r^2} < 0, \forall w_r \in [0,1]$$

Some utility functions commonly used in economic and financial literature are: logarithmic function, quadratic function, exponential negative function and potential function, Marin & Rubio [6]. In continuation, the two most common functions used in the economic literature are detailed.

2.3.2. Logarithmic Function

$$U(w_r) = a\ln(w_r + 1) + c, \text{ with } a, c \in [0, +\infty] \quad (1)$$

D. Bernoulli (1730-1731) applied the logarithmic utility function, *i.e.* $U(w) = \ln(w)$. Given that this paper utilizes relative wealth, which is defined between zero and one, the use of a logarithmic function is not possible because the function would take negative values. To avoid this problem, the argument of the logarithmic function is augmented in one unity as shown in Equation (1). The logarithmic function is used because it is increasing throughout its domain, is convex and has no relative maximum point or inflection.

Figure 1 shows the graph of this function. The dotted line represents the utility function value when $w_r = 1$.

2.3.3. Quadratic Function

$$U(w_r) = a(w_r - 1)^2 - a, \text{ with } a < 0 \quad (2)$$

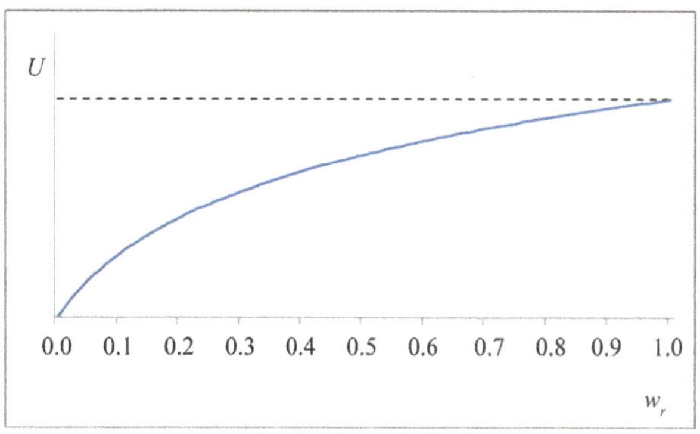

Figure 1. Function $U(w_r) = \ln(w_r + 1) + c$.

The quadratic function has been used by several authors such as R. Merton [7], Copeland-Weston [5], R. Jarrow [8]. W. Sharpe [9], Also represents the utility function by a quadratic function. The main feature of this is that it presents a maximum point of utility for a level of wealth. Beyond this point the function graph decreases and, therefore, the utility decreases with increasing wealth. Regarding this, W. Sharpe [9] said: this is clearly unacceptable. This is explained following the concept of economic rationality which is an intersection between a normative and a positive approach, as there are people in real life who behave according to this standard however others will not. Thus their everyday economic actions are not fully explained by the assumption of economic rationality and the ethic that this standard implies. **Figure 2** shows the graph of this function.

2.3.4. Discussion

Thus, personal economic performance reduces when maximum utility is obtained. This is methodologically explained through the mathematic maximization of the desired utility of an event various alternative propositions. The expected utility implies that, faced with two possibilities of obtaining compensation for a decision that is made, that which has a higher expected utility is appropriate. The aforementioned is that which is defined as the expected utility hypothesis which represents the "rational behavior" of a person faced with uncertainty. With respect to this, Lafont [10] poses the following:

a) The definition of the utility function with these normative assumptions is a working hypothesis and therefore it is necessary to deduce verifiable empirical implications. If the empirical study doesn't dismiss, it can be concluded that people act as if they will maximize the expected utility.

b) The utility function is a normative interpretation that consists of demonstrating that rational agents "should maximize" their expected utility.

The concept of rational behavior rests within the previously mentioned postulations and is defined as the ability to choose as if it were a lottery characterized by various paths of retribution. This interpretation is an economic definition and the rational concept should not be understood as a synonym for terms such as: reasonable, prudent, just and fair amongst others. Thus, a being is "rational" only if they behave according to the economic rule or standard, which from a Theory of Knowledge point of view, is based on a rational and empirical model. These two aspects of regulation and maximization are essential for understanding and reasoning what, under these suppositions, implies the concept of rational economic man.

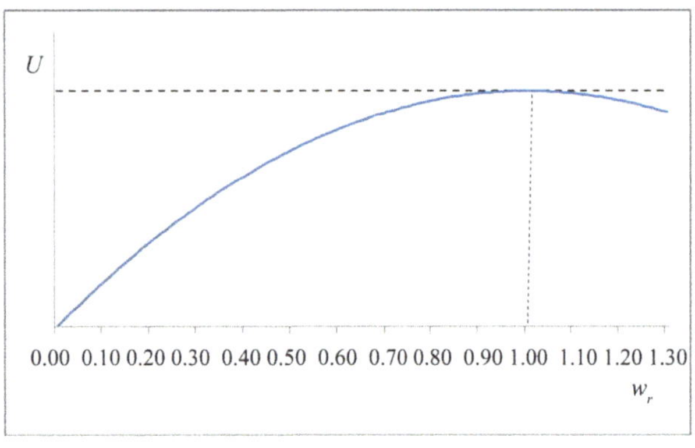

Figure 2. Function $U(w_r) = a(w_r + 1)^2 - a$.

Carroll [11] follows Max Weber in "*The Protestant Ethic and the Spirit of Capitalism*", which explains that people's search for wealth is for their own use and possession, and that this is the main cause of both the system and of individuals. Robinson [12] indicates that the maximization of profit is a metaphorical concept of impenetrable circularity. Debreu [13] shows that there are continuous and non-continuous utility functions. Markowitz [14] based his approach on the utility function. Pratt and Arrow [15] establish ways of measuring risk reward. "Powerful utility functions" have been developed with complex mathematical formulas under the same normative principles as indicated in Ait-Sahalia & Brandt [16], Ang [17], Mehra & Prescott [18], Friend & Blume [19].

Hwang and Satchell [20] elaborate from the Utility function, how much should be paid in order to acquire information. The utility function has been used to explain donations and signal that these have a similar behavior to luxury goods. Inhaber and Carroll [21] signal that luxury goods are generally associated with assets such as art, jewelry, sporting equipment, etc. Which are always goods in an economic sense and therefore, assimilable to any other economic good. Carroll [11] indicates that the love of wealth as motivation is assuredly an extreme position; there are other types of motivation such as: job satisfaction, status, philanthropic ambition, power, etc.

Considering the aforementioned, the utility function theory has a conceptual and philosophical foundation but is also regulative, forcing the understanding of people's behavior exclusively as rational economic entities. In this way, the utility function explains any other type of non-economic motivation which would be well represented under its assumptions. From a Theory of Knowledge stand point, the utility function theory is a mix between rationalism and empiricism, where an intersection can be made between the normative and the positive. The rationalism and empiricism approach is present in financial theory.

The interpretation of an economic act from a solely rational economic point of view and its methodological representation through the utility function can at times give partial results. For which, these acts should be analyzed from a view point that encompasses both rational economic standards and their implicit ethics, as with other ethic views that can fulminate distinct decisions to those that would suggest an analysis from a purely economic view point.

3. Emotional Well-Being Function

3.1. Definition

From the postulations of Sharpe (Op.Ci.), who indicates that no investor is located on the descending part of the utility function curve, a more global function of economic utility is discussed here. This new function explains the performance of people and businesses simultaneously incorporating both the facets of man with economic rationality and the view of people and businesses that also act motivated by other ethical values, Parada [1]. This same model has been used to explain the economic crisis in small and medium businesses and their sustainable politics, Brilius [3], in order to assess the social responsibility of the business, Parada-Daza [2], and by this same author in order to evaluate the economic behaviour of people in different countries, Parada-Daza [4].

An Emotional Well-being (EW) function considers that there are economic sacrifices in exchange for benefits provoked by different reasons and exclusively economic motives. This is translated mathematically in that the function is not necessarily strictly increasing throughout its domain.

$$\begin{aligned} &U:[0,1]\rightarrow\mathbb{R}^{+} \\ &w_r \mapsto U = U_r(w_r) + U_e(w_r, f) \end{aligned} \tag{3}$$

where $U_r(w_r)$ corresponds to a classic utility function as previously described. The term $U_e(w_r, f)$ joins all cultural, ethical, social, emotional or practical characteristics of a distinct nature to the strictly economic, that can cause the individual to be separated from the behavior of an economic man. Unlike the original article of Parada-Daza [1], an innovation is introduced here, making a generalization of both components and incorporating the f parameter to synthesize the non-economic characteristics mentioned.

For analysis, the following function is considered because the conclusions derived from it are easily generalizable to the types of functions described above.

$$\begin{aligned} &\mathrm{EW}:[0,1]\rightarrow\mathbb{R}^{+} \\ &w_r \mapsto U = \mathrm{EW}(w_r) \\ &= a\ln(w_r+1) + b\sin(2\pi f\cdot w_r) + c \end{aligned} \tag{4}$$

With $a, b, c, f \in \mathbb{R}$ parameters of the function and $a + b = 1$.

Parameters a and b are interpreted as the relative importance that people or organizations submit to economic rationality and the respective emotional component. In effect, if $a = 1$, then $b = 0$, a classic utility function is obtained as previously expressed. The parameter c represents the minimum satisfaction that is independent from the level of wealth of each person or business. This could be zero, in which case it is implied that emotional well-being only depends on wealth. The coefficient c is interpreted as a "Satisfaction of Belonging" for being an integral part of a business or society that provides emotional satisfaction to the person, independent to their wealth. This enjoyment can be explained by such factors as: social and business prestige, business and social history and tradition, social and business culture and other specific factors and characteristics of each person or business.

The parameter f is interpreted as the frequency with which the person or organization allows the aversion of strictly economic rationality. Distinct values of f involve distinct types of behavior. While higher the value of f, higher will be the oscillation of the emotional variable with respect to a purely economic component.

The approach of (4) is an extension of the Emotional Well-being function introduced by Parada-Daza [1], because in this paper, the parameter f is considered permanently in $f = 1/2$ and, given that it was working with absolute wealth (in general, $w > 1$), the displacement of the algorithmic component was not considered. However, in this paper it has been decided to open the spectral analysis to include the parameter f and with it explain why the valor $f = 1/2$ has been previously used. Therefore, in contrary to the Parada-Daza [1] paper, in this contribution the relative wealth concept has been adopted, with $w_r \in [0,1]$, and the original approach has been modified adding 1 to the argument of the logarithmic function, in such a way to adjust it in order to work without the EW function assuming negative values, Mao [22].

3.2. Coordinates of Emotional Well-Being: Enveloping Functions

The family of curves (4), defined by the parameter f, includes superior and inferior enveloping functions. This is explained by the sinusoidal component of the EW function that has a bounded range in $[-1,1]$, independent of its argument.

A curve is said to be enveloping a family of plane curves if it is tangent with all the lines of said family, additionally each point of the enveloping function has contact with some of the lines of the family that is examined, Demidovich [23].

For a family of plane curves depending on the parameter α that complies with the following equation: $f(x, y, \alpha) = 0$.

The enveloping equation is determined by way of the equation systems: $f(x, y, \alpha) = 0$ and $f'_\alpha(x, y, \alpha) = 0$.

By eliminating the parameter α, a discriminating curve (Φ) is obtained that contains the envelopment of the family studied, stemming from the following relation: $\Phi(x,y) = 0$.

In the generic case of the EW function proposed in (3), parameter α corresponds to f and $x \equiv w_r$, $y \equiv U$, then:

$$\begin{aligned} f &: U - U_r(w_r) - U_e(w_r, f) = 0 \\ f'_\alpha &: -\frac{\partial U_e}{\partial f} = 0 \end{aligned} \qquad (5)$$

Considering, as in (4), an emotional component of sinusoidal characteristics,

$$U_e(w_r, f) = b\sin(2\pi f \cdot w_r),$$

from the second equation of the system (5) it is concluded that:

$$\begin{aligned} -\frac{\partial U_e}{\partial f} = 0 &\Leftrightarrow -\frac{\partial}{\partial f}\left[b\sin(2\pi f \cdot w_r)\right] = 0 \\ &\Leftrightarrow -2\pi b w_r \cdot \cos(2\pi f \cdot w_r) = 0 \\ &\Leftrightarrow 2\pi f \cdot w_r = \pm\pi/2 \\ &\Leftrightarrow f = \pm 1/4w_r \end{aligned}$$

Replacing these values in the first equation of the system (5), the following discriminating function is obtained:

$$\Phi : U - U_r(w_r) - b\sin(\pm\pi/2) = 0$$

Given that $\sin(\pm\pi/2) = \pm 1$, two enveloping curves are obtained which correspond to:

$$\begin{aligned} U^+(w_r) &= U_r(w_r) + b \\ U^-(w_r) &= U_r(w_r) - b \end{aligned}$$

Note that no matter the type of strictly economic function that is used (logarithmic, quadratic or other), for an emotional component of the sinusoidal characteristic, the enveloping curves are of the same form as the economic utility function. These are interpreted as the maximum and minimum value of the described Emotional Well-being function. U^+ corresponds to the behavior of an economic man as a whole while U^- is interpreted as the minimum accepted level of security, which is personal and can be represented by a minimum requirement. In other words U^+ indicates the economic expectations and aspirations of an agent and U^- the minimum requirements.

In earlier papers, Parada-Daza [1] the existence of enveloping functions exclusively for a function with a rational logarithmic part. In this section, said proof has been broadened to include any type of utility function (U_r) that will give origin to enveloping functions with the same characteristics as U_r.

In the particular case of the equation proposed in (4), $U_r(w_r) = a\ln(w_r + 1) + c$ is given.

Therefore, replacing the expressions earlier deduced, the envelopments are:

$$\begin{aligned} U^+(w_r) &= a\ln(w_r + 1) + b + c \\ U^-(w_r) &= a\ln(w_r + 1) - b + c \end{aligned} \qquad (6)$$

3.3. Emotional Well-Being Function Graph

Figure 3 presents a graph of the EW function according to that which has been outlined previously, the same as both enveloping functions. The Emotional Well-being function (continuous curve) is contained between both enveloping functions (segmented lines). This characteristic allows the affirmation that enveloping functions have tendency to increase, although, a as a product of the emotional component, clearly identifiable intervals exist where the curve is decreasing.

With this the following question arises: Is it valid to be located above the decreasing interval of the curve? If conventional economic rationality necessarily locates economic agents above the ascending part of the utility function, what would justify this behavior contrary to that habitually studied in economic theory?

Observe in **Figure 3** that the Emotional Well-being function is always above the minimum established by the inferior envelopment (U^-). That is to say that there is always a level of economic satisfaction limit that the individual, society or organization is not willing to compromise. On the other hand, it can be observed that there is an increasing level of economic aspirations (U^+) that coincides with the behaviour of any agent in real life.

The difference that exists between this normative model and the actions of a real economic agent is contrasted by the differences between the minimum level of security established and the real actions to explain the making of determined decisions. In other words, The EW model encompasses complex agents, with a much wider philosophical understanding than an exclusively economic entity. In addition to the utilitarian characteristics which are taken as a normative assumption, other ethical concepts are added (such as moderation, bravery, justice or liberty) that permit a more complete analysis of human tasks. These characteristics are intended to be reflected through the parameter f. Large values of this parameter indicate a tendency to recede repeatedly form the imposed normative model denoting certain emotional "instability". In turn, values that are too small, demonstrate excessive prudence that diminishes in the long run. In fact, when $f = 0$, then the EW curve coincides with the average between both limits of behavior (fine segmented line **Figure 3**).

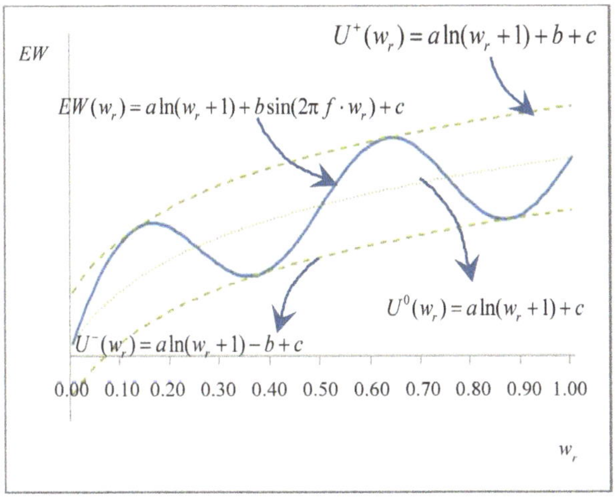

Figure 3. Emotional well-being utility function.

4. Measuring Emotional Rationality

4.1. Emotional Security Index (ESI)

Given the EW function, the Emotional Security Index (ESI) as the ration between that which is lost from economic earnings by paying attention to an emotion other than an economic one, divided by the excess earning ("Security cushion") with respect to the minimum desired profit for any point of relative wealth w_r.

That is to say, the numerator $U^{+}(w_r)-\mathrm{EW}(w_r)$ corresponds to lost earnings at a point w_r by paying attention to values different to denominator $\mathrm{EW}(w_r)-U^{-}(w_r)$, in turn, corresponds to excess earning ("Security cushion") with respect to minimum requirements at this point w_r.

The index is the following:

$$\mathrm{ESI}(w_r)=\frac{U^{+}(w_r)-\mathrm{EW}(w_r)}{\mathrm{EW}(w_r)-U^{-}(w_r)} \tag{7}$$

In the particular case of Equation (4), when $b = 0$, the index cannot be defined by the numerator as the denominator in the expression (7) would have a value equal to zero.

Replacing in (7), the expressions (4) and (6) and simplifying, for $b \neq 0$, the index takes the following form:

$$\mathrm{ESI}(w_r)=\frac{1-\sin(2\pi f\cdot w_r)}{1+\sin(2\pi f\cdot w_r)} \tag{8}$$

With $1+\sin(2\pi f\cdot w_r)\neq 0$. Note that always $\mathrm{ESI}(w_r)\geq 0$, due to the numerator and denominator are always positive.

Furthermore, ESI doesn't depend on parameters a and b but only of f. That is to say, it doesn't depend on how much importance is given to emotionality by each individual, organization or economic system, only the frequency f with which emotional behavior is accepted.

The index is interpreted as the relation between that which is not earned by not being an economic man with respect to the benefit obtained by over the minimum level of security. In order to correspond as close to reality as possible, this loss cannot be higher than the emotional benefit of situating over the minimum ("The Security Cushion"). As a consequence, a prudent form of behavior would yield a numeric value less than 1 for the ESI.

4.2. Emotional Rationality

A decision is defined as *emotionally rational* if the economic loss through emotional behavior is less than the benefits with respect to the minimum tolerated level. That is to say when:

$$\mathrm{ESI}(w_r)\leq 1 \tag{9}$$

In the context of (4), given that for any value of $2\pi f\cdot w_r$, both the ESI numerator and denominator are positive, thus:

$$\begin{aligned}&\mathrm{ESI}(w_r)\leq 1\\&\Leftrightarrow 1-\sin(2\pi f\cdot w_r)\leq 1+\sin(2\pi f\cdot w_r)\\&\Leftrightarrow 0\leq \sin(2\pi f\cdot w_r)\\&\Leftrightarrow 0\leq 2\pi f\cdot w_r\leq \pi\\&\Leftrightarrow 0\leq f\cdot w_r\leq 1/2\end{aligned}$$

As $w_r\in[0,1]$, in order to maintain emotional rationality on every level of wealth the following should be observed: $0\leq f\leq 1/2$.

For subsequent analysis, $f = 1/2$ is chosen which represents an extreme case. Thus, maximum frequency ensures *emotionally rational* behavior according to that which is defined in (9), for every level of wealth. Note that any inferior value would make the EW function seem similar to a pure utility function. In particular, if $f = 0$, then the EW function coincides exactly with average between both enveloping functions, that is:

$$\begin{aligned}\mathrm{EW}(w_r)&=a\ln(w_r+1)+c\\&=0.5\left[U^{+}(w_r)-U^{-}(w_r)\right]=U^{0}(w_r)\end{aligned}$$

With this, from this point onwards, Emotional Well-being and ESI functions will be implemented in the following form:

$$\begin{aligned}&\mathrm{EW}(w_r)=a\ln(w_r+1)+b\sin(\pi\cdot w_r)+c\\&\mathrm{ESI}(w_r)=\frac{1-\sin(\pi\cdot w_r)}{1+\sin(\pi\cdot w_r)}\end{aligned} \tag{10}$$

4.2.1. EW Function Properties under the Supposition of Emotional Rationality

1) Point of tangency with U^{+}

The EW function is tangent with U^+ in $w_r = 1/2$. Indeed, in order to have:

$$\mathrm{EW}(w_r) = U^+(w_r)$$

By (6) and (10) then:

$$a\ln(w_r+1)+b\sin(2\pi f\cdot w_r)+c$$
$$= a\ln(w_r+1)+b+c$$

Reducing, the following is obtained:
$\sin(2\pi f\cdot w_r)=1$.

This complies with the function domain only if:
$2\pi f\cdot w_r = \pi/2$.

Additionally, $f = 1/2$, thus: $w_r = 1/2$.

That is, the EW function reaches a superior level (U^+) at a solitary point within the domain when the emotional component reaches its maximum value. Additionally, at this point, the marginal growth rate for both functions is the same:

$$\frac{\mathrm{d}}{\mathrm{d}w_r}\left[\mathrm{EW}(w_r)\right]\Bigg|_{w_r=1/2}$$
$$= \frac{a}{w_r+1}\Bigg|_{w_r=1/2} + \pi b\cos(\pi\cdot w_r)\Bigg|_{w_r=1/2}$$
$$= \frac{a}{w_r+1}\Bigg|_{w_r=1/2}$$
$$= \frac{\mathrm{d}}{\mathrm{d}w_r}\left[U^+(w_r)\right]\Bigg|_{w_r=1/2}$$

These growth rates are interpreted as marginal emotional and economic wellbeing. That is, for this point, the marginal emotional wellbeing is exactly the same as the marginal emotional wellbeing for an economic man.

2) Determining the maximum level of emotional wellbeing

Deriving EW with respect to relative wealth, the following is obtained:

$$\frac{\mathrm{dEW}}{\mathrm{d}w_r} = \frac{a}{w_r+1} + 2\pi f\cdot b\cos(2\pi f\cdot w_r)$$

On the other hand, the second derivative of the EW function corresponds to:

$$\frac{\mathrm{d}^2\mathrm{EW}}{\mathrm{d}w_r^2} = \frac{-a}{(w_r+1)^2} - 4\pi^2 f^2\cdot b\sin(2\pi f\cdot w_r)$$

The derived functions can be disassembled into two parts u_1 y u_2 such as:

$$\frac{\mathrm{dEW}}{\mathrm{d}w_r} = u_1 + u_2 \qquad (11)$$

With: $u_1 = \dfrac{a}{w_r+1}$ and $u_2 = 2\pi f\cdot b\cos(2\pi f\cdot w_r)$

The first expression of (11), u_1, is interpreted as the rate of change in EW as a product of the emotional component of the behavior. Note that this change is always strictly positive. That is to say, the economic component of the behavior is strictly increasing in all the domain and that in the behavior of individuals, organizations or economies that approach the paradigm of economic rationality (*i.e.* when $a \to 1$ and $b \to 0$), the EW function will have a maximum level only in the outer lying reaches of its domain when $w_r = 1$.

Moreover, the second component of (11), u_2, corresponds to the EW rate of change produced by the emotional component of the behavior. This change can be both positive or negative, so it can be presumed that within the defined domain, $w_r \in [0,1]$, the EW function can have a maximum or minimum point in w^* when:

$$\frac{\mathrm{dEW}}{\mathrm{d}w_r}\Bigg|_{w_r=w^*} = 0 \Leftrightarrow -u_1(w^*) = u_2(w^*)$$

Note that the value of w^* depends on the parameters of the function a, $b = (1 - a)$ and f. this equation does not have a direct analytical solution, for which an analysis of all possible parameter values is not carried out.

Furthermore, when $w_r \to 0$ the EW derivative is positive and therefore, the EW function is increasing in a vicinity of 0. Also, under the supposition of emotional rationality stated earlier ($f = 1/2$), the second derivative is negative throughout the EW domain, thus the EW function graph is convex. In other words, these properties ensure that there is a point where the function reaches its maximum value within the domain [0, 1].

Therefore the EW function will be increasing in the interval [0, w^*] and decreasing in the interval [w^*, 1]. In which case with the supposition of emotional rationality the w^* point complies with:

$$-\frac{a}{w^*+1} = (1-a)\pi\cos(\pi\cdot w^*)$$

The solution to this equation depends exclusively on the value of parameter a. An extreme case is given when $w^* = 1$. In this situation, the function will be strictly increasing throughout its domain. If the solution to the equation is such that $w^* > 1$, therefore the maximum value of EW will correspond to $\mathrm{EW}_{\max} = \mathrm{EW}$ ($w = 1$), since the function would be increasing throughout the entire domain. From the latter it can be deduced that a value limit exists for the parameter a for which a maximum wellbeing is reached for total wealth ($w_r = 1$). Indeed, making $w^* = 1$ from the last expression is obtained that: $a=\dfrac{2\pi}{2\pi+1}\approx 0.862$.

This means that, under the supposition of emotional rationality, for values of a superior to 0.862 the EW function will be strictly increasing throughout its domain and will reach maximum in $w^*=1$.

3) EW function graph

Figure 4 shows an EW function under supposed emotional rationality function (continuous blue line) together with both enveloping functions (continuous green lines). Note the tangent point in $w_r = 1/2$ and that the function have a maximum value close to $w_r = 0.7$.

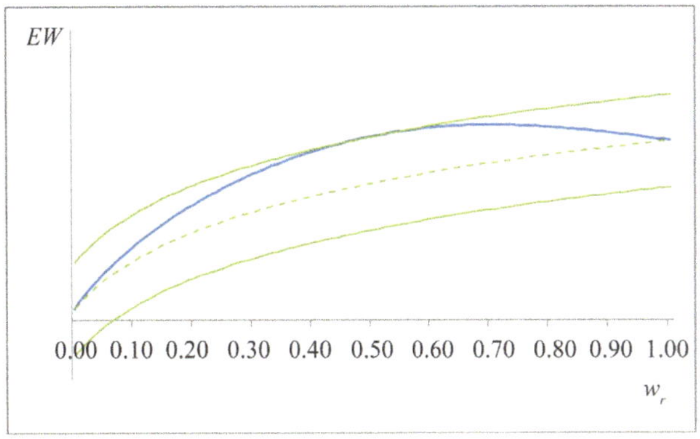

Figure 4. EW under supposed emotional rationality.

4.2.2. ESI Properties under Supposed Emotional Rationality

Note that the properties expressed in continuation are valid when $f = 1/2$.

1) Increasing and decreasing intervals

Considering that $w_r \in [0,1]$, the function is decreasing when:

$$\frac{\mathrm{d}}{\mathrm{d}w_r}\left[\mathrm{ESI}(w_r)\right]<0$$
$$\Leftrightarrow \frac{-2\pi\cos(\pi\cdot w_r)}{\left[1+\sin(\pi\cdot w_r)\right]^2}<0$$
$$\Leftrightarrow 2\pi\cos(\pi\cdot w_r)>0$$
$$\Leftrightarrow 0<\pi\cdot w_r<\pi/2$$
$$\Leftrightarrow 0<w_r<1/2$$

Analogous to the previous, the function is increasing when:

$$\frac{\mathrm{d}}{\mathrm{d}w_r}\left[\mathrm{ESI}(w_r)\right]>0\Leftrightarrow 1/2<w_r<1$$

2) Maximum and minimum points

The $w_r = 1/2$ point is a singular point, in effect:

$$\left.\frac{\mathrm{d}}{\mathrm{d}w_r}\left[\mathrm{ESI}(w_r)\right]\right|_{w_r=1/2}=0$$

Taking this into consideration as well as the increasing and decreasing intervals previously calculated, the maximum and minimum points of the function are given by:

$$\text{Maximum}: w_r=0\Rightarrow \mathrm{ESI}(w_r)=1$$
$$\text{Minimum}: w_r=1/2\Rightarrow \mathrm{ESI}(w_r)=0$$
$$\text{Maximum}: w_r=1\Rightarrow \mathrm{ESI}(w_r)=1$$

From this, it can be deduced that the ESI range corresponds to $\text{Range}\{\mathrm{ESI}(w_r)\}=[0,1]$.

3) Symmetry of the ESI

The ESI shows symmetric behavior in relation to the $w_r = 1/2$ point. This is demonstrated in continuation.

According to the definition of symmetry in differential calculus, a function $f(x)$ is symmetric with respect to x_0 when $f(x_0+x)=f(x_0+(-x))$.

Let $\delta > 0$, thus

$$\mathrm{ESI}(1/2+\delta)=\frac{1-\sin(\pi/2+\delta\pi)}{1+\sin(\pi/2+\delta\pi)}$$
$$=\frac{1-\left[\sin(\pi/2)\cos(\delta\pi)+\sin(\delta\pi)\cos(\pi/2)\right]}{1+\left[\sin(\pi/2)\cos(\delta\pi)+\sin(\delta\pi)\cos(\pi/2)\right]}$$
$$=\left.\frac{1-\cos(\delta\pi)}{1+\cos(\delta\pi)}\right|$$

$$\mathrm{ESI}(1/2-\delta)=\frac{1-\sin(\pi/2-\delta\pi)}{1+\sin(\pi/2-\delta\pi)}$$
$$=\frac{1-\left[\sin(\pi/2)\cos(-\delta\pi)+\sin(-\delta\pi)\cos(\pi/2)\right]}{1+\left[\sin(\pi/2)\cos(-\delta\pi)+\sin(-\delta\pi)\cos(\pi/2)\right]}$$
$$=\frac{1-\cos(-\delta\pi)}{1+\cos(-\delta\pi)}=\left.\frac{1-\cos(\delta\pi)}{1+\cos(\delta\pi)}\right|$$

Therefore $\mathrm{ESI}(1/2-\delta)=\mathrm{ESI}(1/2+\delta)$ and the function is symmetric with respect to $w_r = 1/2$. Precisely for $w_r = 1/2$, the EW function is tangent to its superior limit or utility function. That is to say, the loss produced by distancing from economic behavior is minimized at this point.

Note that if points are defined as $w_{r,1}$ y $w_{r,2}$, these two points are symmetric (that is, $w_{r,1} = 1/2 - \delta$ and $w_{r,2} = 1/2 + \delta$) if and only if $w_{r,1} + w_{r,2} = 1$. In other words, two different levels of wealth exist for which the ESI reaches the same value. These levels are such that together they represent all economic wealth, as it was previously defined that $\sum_{i=1}^{n} w_{r,i}=1$.

4) ESI Graph

It is necessary to note that the index is a relative measure and not absolute. In symmetric intervals, who has more wealth ($w_r \to 1$) has their EW balanced the same as those with less wealth ($w_r \to 0$), however with different levels of economic demands and expectancies. These levels of demands are given by U^- and exclusively economic expectancies by U^+. This implies that, even if they behave in different wealth dimension, both agents are equally satisfied because they share the same relationship between economic compromise and security cushion.

In order to explain the previous, the following example is used. Suppose that two individuals exist. One individual has 20% of the total wealth; on the contrary, the other individual has 80%. For symmetry, both individuals have the same level of emotional security. This is represented directly in **Figure 5**. In this case $\mathrm{ESI}(0.2) = \mathrm{ESI}(0.8) = 0.25962$. However, the individual who possesses 80% of the wealth has an EW value superior to the individual with 20% as can be observed in **Figure 4**. This is additionally accompanied by a higher level of minimum demand (U^-) and an economic expectancy of (U^+).

4.3. Concentration of Wealth

4.3.1. Differential Growth

In order to understand the way in which people behave between the two utility functions, U^+ y U^-, it is necessary to analyze the marginal growth of both curves for each given interval of wealth.

By *marginal growth* (*decline*) of a function $f(x)$ in the interval $[x_0, x_f]$, is understood the positive (negative) value calculated through the expression:

$$\Delta_f(x_0, x_f) = \frac{f(x_f) - f(x_0)}{f(x_0)} \tag{12}$$

4.3.2. Symmetric Interval Application

For the emotional Wellbeing Functions and their higher and lower levels, marginal growth can be calculated at a symmetric interval defined between w_r and $(1 - w_r)$, with $w_r < 1/2 < (1 - w_r)$, as:

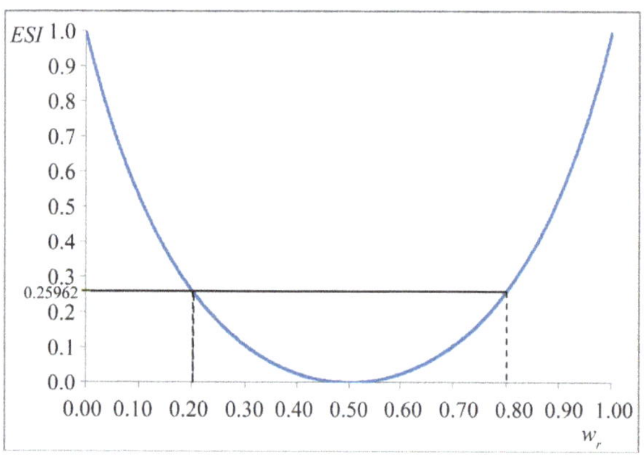

Figure 5. ESI(w_r) function under supposed emotional rationality.

$$\Delta_{U^+}(w_r, 1-w_r) = \frac{U^+(1-w_r) - U^+(w_r)}{U^+(w_r)} = \frac{a\ln(2-w_r) - a\ln(w_r+1)}{a\ln(w_r+1) + b + c}$$

$$\Delta_{EW}(w_r, 1-w_r) = \frac{\mathrm{EW}(1-w_r) - \mathrm{EW}(w_r)}{\mathrm{EW}(w_r)} = \frac{a\ln(2-w_r) - a\ln(w_r+1)}{a\ln(w_r+1) + b\sin(\pi\cdot w_r) + c}$$

$$\Delta_{U^-}(w_r, 1-w_r) = \frac{U^-(1-w_r) - U^-(w_r)}{U^-(w_r)} = \frac{a\ln(2-w_r) - a\ln(w_r+1)}{a\ln(w_r+1) - b + c}$$

The numerator of the second expression (Δ_{EW}) is obtained through simplification using the property:

$$\sin(\pi - \pi x) = \sin(\pi)\cos(-\pi x) + \sin(-\pi x)\cos(\pi) = -\sin(-\pi x) = \sin(\pi x)$$

Note that:

$$-1 \le \sin(\pi\cdot w_r) \le 1$$

$$\Leftrightarrow a\ln(w_r+1) - b + c \le a\ln(w_r+1) + b\sin(\pi\cdot w_r) + c \le a\ln(w_r+1) + b + c$$

$$\Leftrightarrow \frac{1}{a\ln(w_r+1) - b + c} \ge \frac{1}{a\ln(w_r+1) + b\sin(\pi\cdot w_r) + c} \ge \frac{1}{a\ln(w_r+1) + b + c}$$

$$\Leftrightarrow \frac{a\ln(2-w_r) - a\ln(w_r+1)}{a\ln(w_r+1) - b + c} \ge \frac{a\ln(2-w_r) - a\ln(w_r+1)}{a\ln(w_r+1) + b\sin(\pi\cdot w_r) + c} \ge \frac{a\ln(2-w_r) - a\ln(w_r+1)}{a\ln(w_r+1) + b + c}$$

$$\Leftrightarrow \boxed{\Delta_{U^-}(w_r, 1-w_r) \ge \Delta_{\mathrm{EW}}(w_r, 1-w_r) \ge \Delta_{U^+}(w_r, 1-w_r)} \tag{13}$$

Expression (13) implies that the increase in demand (Δ_{U^-}) is superior to the increase of EW (Δ_{EW}) and superior to the increase of economic expectations (Δ_{U^+}) through analysis of symmetric intervals. This implication is necessary in order to explain the following point.

4.3.3. Distribution of Wealth

Suppose an economy where only two agents exist who distribute wealth in an unequal manner. In such a way that the first agent has a relative wealth of w_r given by w_1 y and the second by $w_2 = 1 - w_1$. From symmetry, both agents have an equivalent ESI. That is, both have the same form of covering their economic expectations with respect to their level of security. It is assumed that the agent with a wealth of w_1 is less wealthy than the second agent with a wealth of w_2, ergo $w_1 < w_2$.

However, the second agent has a higher level of EW. In effect, if: $\mathrm{EW}(w_1) < \mathrm{EW}(w_2)$

Replacing and solving you have:

$$0 < \mathrm{EW}(1-w_1) - \mathrm{EW}(w_1)$$

Using (10):

$$0 < a\ln(2-w_1) + b\sin(\pi(1-w_1)) - a\ln(w_1+1) - b\sin(\pi w_1)$$

Reducing[1]: $0 < \ln\left[\dfrac{2-w_1}{w_1+1}\right]$

The following is obtained: $1 < \dfrac{2-w_1}{w_1+1} \rightarrow w_1 < 1/2$

This necessary in order to fulfill the premise of inequality between both agents. Additionally, in order to achieve this superior level of emotional wellbeing, the second agent has a higher level of demands (U^-) than the first agent. Furthermore, their economic expectations (U^+) are also higher.

The symmetric interval analysis of marginal growth in the EW function and its two enveloping Equation (13), concludes that the increase in U^- is higher than the increase in U^+. Thus, the quantitative difference between the rich agent and the poor agent is proportionally higher in the case of minimum demands (U^-) than in the case of economic expectations. This implies that as wealth increases, the richer agent becomes more demanding in relation to their economic expectations.

The latter is consistent with that which is observed in practice when individuals increase their wealth and, presumably for social reasons, their tastes and minimum standards become more demanding and refined. That is the case, even though the increase in economic expectations is not significantly as high as the increase in demand.

The concentration in wealth is explained through a numerical analysis in continuation. Take an economy of two individuals governed by an EW function with the following parameters: $a = 0.7$, $b = 0.3$, $c = 1.4$ and $f = 0.5$. **Figures 6** and **7** show graphs of each function of the associated ESI.

Supposing that the first economic agent concentrates 20% of their wealth and the second agent 80%, the previously mentioned figures mark the points that reach the EW and ESI in said concentrations of wealth. Numerically, BE(0.2) = 1.704 < BE(0.8) = 1.988 and ESI(0.2) = ESI(0.8) = 0.260.

It is clear that, even in the emotional rationality limit scenario ($f = 1/2$), the individual that concentrates the greater relative wealth has a higher level of EW, although both share the same emotional index security value. That is to say that, if both economic agents behave in a rational emotional way, then the accumulation of wealth will reward with a higher level of emotional wellbeing with at least the same level of emotional security for both.

On the other hand, if in addition to the previous, marginal variations are calculated for the EW function and its envelopments, the following are obtained:

$\Delta_{U^+}(0.2, 0.8) = 15.53\%$; $\Delta_{\mathrm{EW}}(0.2, 0.8) = 16.66\%$ and

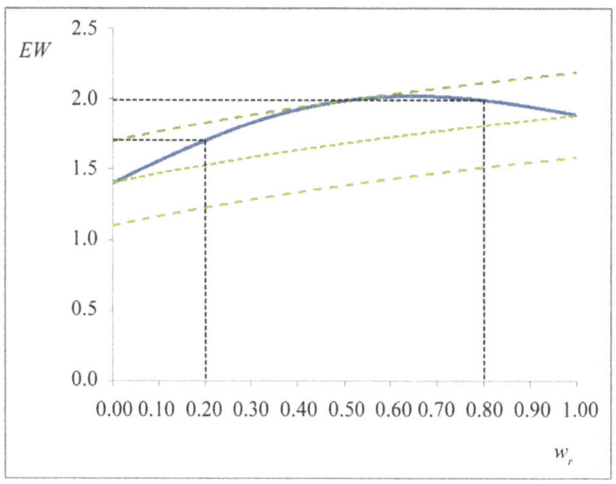

Figure 6. EW concentration of wealth.

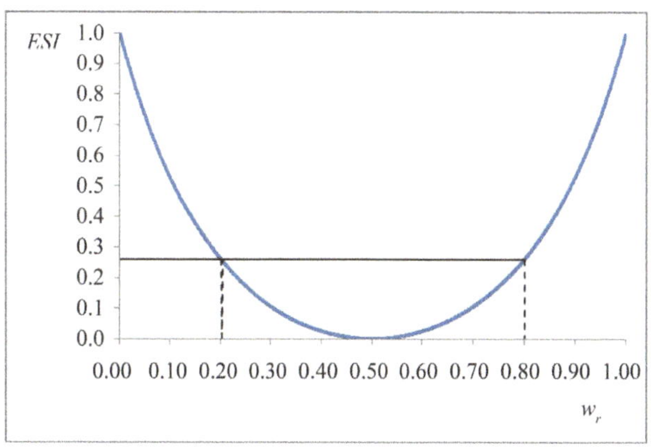

Figure 7. ESI concentration of wealth.

[1]Using:

$$\sin(\pi - \pi x) = \sin(\pi)\cos(-\pi x) + \sin(-\pi x)\cos(\pi) = -\sin(-\pi x) = \sin(\pi x)$$

$\Delta_{U^-}(0.2, 0.8) = 23.12\%$

This indicates that the change from a position of poverty to a position of relative wealth is accompanied by an increase of minimum demands by the agent. In this way indicating that the rich agent is comparatively more demanding that the poor agent and that continuing to concentrate wealth provides greater comfort.

5. Conclusions

This paper has presented a theoretic outline in reference to the Emotional Wellbeing function as an extension of the economic utility function. After analytical-mathematical conceptualization of the new function, a concept of *emotional security* has been developed which, in turn, is used to define a new idea of *emotional rationality* as a complement to *economic rationality*. This concept allows for the explanation of a more integrated vision with respect to economic decisions whether they are related to business or other everyday acts.

On the other hand, an analytical explication has been put forth of the concentration of wealth phenomenon through a function of rational emotional wellbeing.

In the introduction, it was stated that the economic utility function may represent a biased approach when trying to describe the behavior, for example, of a manager in the decision making process. Using a utility function can lead to an incomplete description of the process of economic decision. An Emotional welfare function, however, includes factors usually neglected by the economic rationalist approach, but always present in any business with or without a profitable outcome. Therefore it has been proposed that the role of Emotional Well-being may represent phenomenon related to both economic and non-economic satisfaction of agents who make decisions. In conclusion, this paper is an analytical attempt of integration between a rational economic approach and a management approach to explaining decision making in different daily acts, whether they are for business or other activities. Indeed, this paper uses an analytical language, typical of the utility function, to show that mathematical models are applicable to human behavior, and that they can collect various influences of ethical schools distinct to economic maximizing utilitarianism. In particular, the studied function of EW suggests that there are at least two ways to consider the influence of these other schools of thought on human behavior.

The first is the relationship between the a and b coefficients of the function. It is shown that through the consideration of these elements, a greater (or lower) relative importance an agent or company gives to both the economic maximizing component as well as the emotional component of their behavior. Furthermore, it is concluded that the parameter f represents the "type" of emotionality that the economic agent values in their decisions. This parameter is closely related to the concepts of emotional security and emotional rationality.

These aspects were synthesized through the inclusion and development of an emotional security index (ESI). Regardless of the values of a and b, this is an indicator of economic sacrifice in exchange for emotional satisfaction obtained for each level of wealth. Thus, this indicator is a periodic function that depends only on f. That is, the type of emotionality of the individual. This indicator corresponds to a theoretical novelty as it had not appeared before in literary references. This is an important finding because from the index develops the concept of emotional rationality, which allows for a more convincing justification of the strictly non-maximizing behavior of economic agents. This new concept of emotional rationality complements the economic rationality approach and allows an integrated view of the explanation of decisions to be generated.

A conclusion that is also relevant, thanks to the concept of relative wealth introduced in this paper, is that an application on the concentration of wealth is presented. Indeed, it is concluded as the proposed EW function helps to explain the phenomenon of concentration of wealth through an emotional incentive to do so. This will complement the analysis carried out to show the practical and conceptual validity of the proposition of EW.

This paper concludes that the function of EW has a new application, not thought of at first, that joins with other applications mentioned in literature. Another conclusion of the analytical work, that whatever the form adopted by utility functions most commonly used in economic literature (quadratic, logarithmic, power, negative exponential or other), they are also envelopments of an emotional wellbeing function. From this it can be concluded that the utility functions are an explanation of edge (or limit) behavior of people during their economic acts.

Lastly, a sinusoidal characteristic of the emotional part of the EW function is proposed here. However, the definition of EW function that has been given opens the option to use other features. In particular, it is only required that the emotional characteristic is a bounded function on its range to ensure the existence of enveloping functions. Thus it is possible to define other characteristics (Fourier series, stochastic functions, etc.) that can better represent a particular decision making process.

REFERENCES

[1] J. R. Parada-Daza, "The Utility Function and the Emotional Well-Being Function," *Electronic Journal of Business Ethics and Organization Studies*, Vol. 9, No. 2, 2004, pp. 22-29.

[2] J. R. Parada-Daza, "A Valuation Model for Corporate

Social Responsibility," *Social Responsibility Journal*, Vol. 5, No. 3. 2009, pp. 284-299.

[3] P. Brilius, "Economic Crisis and SMES Sustainability Policies: Application of Emotional Well-Being Function for Analysis," *Journal of Advanced Research in Management*, Vol. 1, No. 1, 2010, pp. 16-29.

[4] J. R. Parada-Daza, "Economic Ethics and Emotional Well-Being," *Journal of Behavioral Studies in Business*, Vol. 6, No. 1, 2012, pp. 1-12.

[5] T. E. Copeland and J. F. Weston, "Finantial Theory and Corporate Policy," 3rd Edition, Addison-Wesley Publishing Company, New York, 1992, p. 89.

[6] J. M. Marín and G. Rubio, "Economía Financiera," Antoni Bosch Editor, Barcelona, 2001, pp. 777-781.

[7] R. Merton, "Continuous-Time Finance," Blackwell Publishers Ltd., Oxford, 1996, p. 138.

[8] R. Jarrow, "Finance Theory," Prentice-Hall International Editions, Upper Saddle River, 1988, p. 199.

[9] W. F. Sharpe, "Teoría de Cartera y del Mercado de Capitales," Ediciones Deusto S.A., Bilbao,1976, p. 237.

[10] J.-J. Laffont, "The Economics of Uncertainty and Information," The MIT Press, Cambridge, 1995, p. 8.

[11] C. D. Carroll, "Why Do the Rich Save Much?" The Johns Hopkins University, Baltimore, 1998.

[12] J. Robinson, "Economic Philosophy," Aldine, Chicago, 1962.

[13] G. Debreu, "La Théorie de la Valeur," Dunod, Paris, 1966.

[14] H. Markowitz, "Portfolio Selection," Yale University Press, New Haven, 1959.

[15] J. W. Pratt, "Risk Aversion in the Small and in the Large," *Econometrica*, Vol. 32, No. 1-2, 1964, pp. 122-136.

[16] J. Ait-Sahalia and M. Brandt, "Variable Selection for Portfolio Choise," National Bureau of Economic Research (NBER), 2001.

[17] A. Ang, G. Bekaert and J. Liu, "Why Stocks May Disappoint?" EFA 0669, 2000.

[18] R. Mehra and E. Prescott, "The Equity Premium: A Puzzle," *Journal of Monetary Economy*, Vol. 15, No. 2, 1985, pp. 145-161.

[19] I. Friend and M. Blume, "The Demand for Risky Assets," *American Economic Review*, Vol. 65, No. 5, 1975, pp. 900-922.

[20] S. Hwang and S. Satchell, "Valuing Information Using Utility Functions: How Much Should We Pay for Lineal Factor Model?" *The European Journal of Finance*, Vol. 11, No. 1, 2005, pp. 1-16.

[21] H. Inhaber and S. Carroll, "How Rich Is Too Rich? Income and Wealth in America," Prarger Publisher, New York, 1992.

[22] J. C. T. Mao, "Quatitative Analysis of Financial Decision," The Macmillan Co., New York, 1969.

[23] B. Demidovich, "Análisis Matemático," Undécima Edición, Edit Paraninfo, Madrid, 1993, p. 247.

26

Elucidating General Equilibrium Multiplier Effects: A Differential Perspective

M. Alejandro Cardenete[1], Ferran Sancho[2]
[1]Department of Economics, Universidad Loyola Andalucía, Sevilla, Spain
[2]Department of Economics, Universitat Autònoma de Barcelona, Barcelona, Spain

ABSTRACT

Expenditure multipliers are routinely used to evaluate the effectiveness of government spending. When interested in disaggregated effects, interindustry models provide the necessary tools to be able to look at very detailed sectorial results. These models are theoretically simple and empirically operational, which makes them easily implementable and therefore popular with policy makers. They miss, however, quite a bit of the interaction that takes place at the micro level. On the one hand, they ignore the role exerted by supply constraints in primary factors; on the other hand, they look at the world as though it is fully linear. We overcome these limitations by using an opposite Walrasian general equilibrium model to compute marginal multipliers. By using differential calculus, we also offer some insights regarding the "under-the-hood" circuits of influence.

Keywords: Marginal Multipliers; General Equilibrium; Linear vs. Nonlinear Models

1. Introduction

Let us begin by considering the general setup of an economy described by m endogenous variables and k external exogenous variables, (say, policy instruments) affecting the equilibrium state. In this economy, multipliers connect exogenous injections x_i (I = 1,2 ⋯ k) with endogenous responses e_j (j = 1,2 ⋯ m). If the vector function $F : R^{m+k} \to R^m$ represents the equilibrium state $e = F(e,x)$, then it is possible to use differential calculus [1] to study the equilibrium dependence of endogenous variables e with respect to exogenous one x. In this case, we would have

$$de = \left(\partial F(e,x)/\partial e\right)de + \left(\partial F(e,x)/\partial X\right)dx\,.$$

Solving now for de would yield

$$\begin{aligned} de &= \left(\mathbf{I} - \left(\partial F(e,x)/\partial e\right)\right)^{-1}\left(\partial F(e,x)/\partial x\right)dx \\ &= \mathbf{M}(e,x)dx \end{aligned}$$

where $\mathbf{M}$ is a ($m \times k$) matrix whose generic element $\partial e_j/\partial x_i = m_{ji}(e, x)$ is an estimate of the (marginal) multiplier effect exerted by injection x_i upon endogenous variable e_j. Notice that in principle the multiplier matrix, $\mathbf{M}$ itself may be variable since it depends on the particular equilibrium state e induced by instruments x and the characteristics of the economy, as embodied in F. Since the vector function F is not usually directly observable, neither are its derivatives nor is matrix $\mathbf{M}$, hence there is the need for relying on some type of approximation. One such approximation is to linearize the economy; another is to use numerical methods for the evaluation of nonlinear equilibrium relationships.

2. Linear Multipliers

We now consider a linear economy of the interindustry type. For this type of economies we have n endogenous ($m = n$) and n exogenous variables ($k = n$). The endogenous variables correspond to total output in each of the n sectors, whereas the exogenous variables describe final demand. This includes discretional government demand for the goods and services of each of the n sectors. We will use the n-vector q to denote output (*i.e.* $e = q$ now) and keep x for the exogenous variables. The equilibrium state for this linear economy is represented, again using the vector function F, by $q = F(q, x)$. Thanks to the linearity assumption this can be seen to adopt the form $q = \mathbf{A}q + x$, where $\mathbf{A}$ is a $n \times n$ nonnegative, productive and homothetic technical coefficient matrix. From the equilibrium state we can quickly write the reduced form linking output with instruments as $q = (\mathbf{I} - \mathbf{A})^{-1}x = \mathbf{M}x$, with $\mathbf{M}$ representing the multiplier matrix of the linear economy. Because of the assumptions on $\mathbf{A}$, the matrix $\mathbf{M}$ is constant. Its entries are independent of the equilibrium state. Taking derivatives, it is quite simple now to relate changes in output with external changes in instruments

$$\Delta q = (\mathbf{I} - \mathbf{A})^{-1} \Delta x = \mathbf{M}\Delta x \qquad (1)$$

Multipliers are given directly by the cells in matrix $\mathbf{M}$, *i.e.* $\partial q_j/\partial x_i = m_{ji}$. All that is needed to compute (linear) multipliers is the coefficients matrix $\mathbf{A}$. Since this matrix is readily available from official statistics, this explains the popularity of linear models in policy oriented empirical economics. Even more, linear models are so simple that we need not worry about prices. Prices, in fact, can be seen to be completely independent from quantities in linear interindustry models. Notice that if quantities are not affected by prices, neither are multipliers. End of the story, all needed multiplier information is contained in matrix $\mathbf{M}$. But we know that the actual story is bit more complicated than that since, in general, prices and quantities are mutually dependent.

3. Applied General Equilibrium Multipliers

In a standard general equilibrium model the interactions of supply and demand determine, at the same time, prices and quantities. We use now a general equilibrium framework to elucidate multipliers and compare them to their linear counterpart. Endogenous variables include now n output levels q and n prices p, that is, $e = (q, p)$, so in total we have $2n$ endogenous variables. Let us consider again that the government decides how much to buy of each of the n goods and services; the government's demand levels are denoted by the vector x representing policy instruments. The structural function F representing the equilibrium state would now be of the type $F : R^{2n+n} \to R^{2n}$ which in turn can be split in two functions $F^q : R^{2n+n} \to R^n$ and $F^p : R^{2n+n} \to R^n$ determining quantities and prices, respectively. The complete general equilibrium state is represented by $(q, p) = F(q, p, x)$, or using the fact that $F = F^q \times F^p$, it can also be seen as

$$\begin{aligned} p &= F^p(q, p, x) \\ q &= F^q(q, p, x) \end{aligned} \qquad (2)$$

We perform comparative statics on the equilibrium state represented in Equation (2) considering an exogenous change dx in the instruments x. We would obtain

$$\begin{aligned} dq &= M_{qq}dq + M_{qp}dp + M_{qx}dx \\ dp &= M_{pq}dq + M_{pp}dp + M_{px}dx \end{aligned} \qquad (3)$$

where we use, in Equation (3), the notational convention $M_{qq} = \partial F^q(q, p, x)/\partial q$, $M_{qp} = \partial F^q(q, p, x)/\partial p$, and so on. Solving for dp in the second expression in Equation (3) and substituting the result in the first equation would yield

$$\begin{aligned} dq &= M_{qq}dq + M_{qp}dp + M_{qx}dx \\ &= M_{qq}dq + M_{qp}(I - M_{pp})^{-1}(M_{pq}dq + M_{px}dx) \\ &\quad + M_{qx}dx \\ &= \left(M_{qq} + M_{qp}(I - M_{pp})^{-1} M_{pq}\right)dq \\ &\quad + \left(M_{qx} + M_{qp}(I - M_{pp})^{-1} M_{px}\right)dx \end{aligned} \qquad (4)$$

Solving now for dq in Equation (4) we finally obtain

$$\begin{aligned} dq &= \left(I - \left(M_{qq} + M_{qp}(I - M_{pp})^{-1} M_{pq}\right)\right)^{-1} \\ &\quad \cdot \left(M_{qx} + M_{qp}(I - M_{pp})^{-1} M_{px}\right) = \mathbf{M}(q, p, x)\,dx \end{aligned} \qquad (5)$$

where $\mathbf{M}(q, p, x)$ stands for the general quantity multiplier matrix[1]. We now proceed to relate the linear multiplier matrix $\mathbf{M}$ in Equation (1) with the general multiplier matrix $\mathbf{M}(q, p, x)$ derived in Equation (5).

Recall first that in linear models quantities and prices are independently determined. Under this assumption the partial derivative matrices M_{pq} and M_{qp} would be such that $M_{pq} = M_{qp} = \mathbf{0}$ and then Equation (5) can be easily verified to reduce to

$$dq = (I - M_{qq})^{-1} M_{qx}dx \qquad (6)$$

The simplified expression that appears in Equation (6) is of course the differential version of the classical linear multiplier expression picked up in Equation (1) above, with $M_{qq} = \mathbf{A}$ and $M_{qx}dx = \Delta x$. The chains of interactions, however, can be seen to be quite more complex in Equation (5) than in Equation (1), in accordance with the higher complexity of nonlinear models vis-a-vis linear ones.

Figure 1 below depicts the way the model's interconnections work. Facing an external disturbance in x, the system first reacts with changes in prices and quantities through matrices M_{px} and M_{qx}. Price effects repeatedly self multiply through the loop M_{pp} along the cost structure which, in turn, are affected by cross effects M_{qp} from quantities to prices. Similarly, the initial effect of the disturbance on quantities gets itself multiplied by the chain reaction that moves directly from quantities to quantities, *i.e.* M_{qq}, and indirectly from quantities to looped prices and back to quantities via the combined

[1]A similar derivation, that we omit, would produce a general price multiplier matrix.

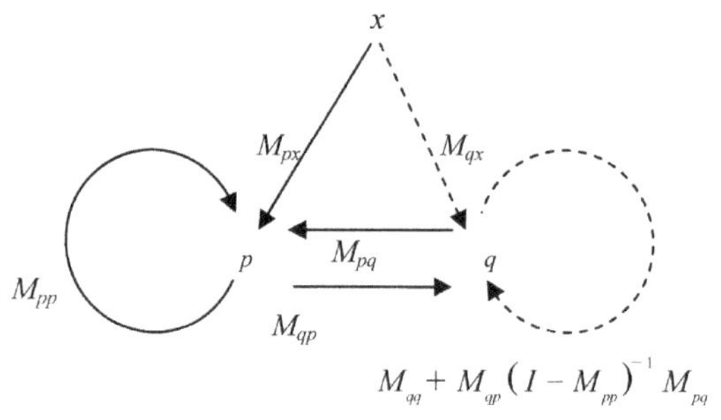

Figure 1. Example of the circuits of influence.

effect measured by

$$M_{qp}\left(I - M_{pp}\right)^{-1} M_{qp}.$$

Notice again the role exerted by cross effects, in this case from prices to quantities through M_{qp}. The dashed arrows show the only influence that would remain in the typical linear model where prices and quantities are independently determined. The linear model effects would be restricted to matrices M_{qx} and M_{qq}.

4. Some Numerical Results

We show now some results of implementing these two models, namely, a linear interindustry model first (see [2] for a reference of linear models), and then a Walrasian general equilibrium model (see [3,4] for examples and details of empirical general equilibrium models and their methodology). We use data from the Spanish economy [5] for 2006 to calibrate both models. Calibration entails the selection of parameters so as to reproduce the empirical data as an equilibrium under both models—the linear and Walrasian versions (see [6] for a step-by-step guide to calibration). The Spanish data distinguishes 26 productive sectors. For each sector we show the multiplier effects under the two models in **Table 1** below. For instance, the linear multiplier value of 1.4620 indicates the (positive) change in economy-wide production when a unitary exogenous demand for Agriculture is injected into the economy. The general equilibrium multiplier of −0.5341 tells a different story. Now overall production would go down, once all general equilibrium adjustments had taken place. Supply restrictions and interconnected price and quantity effects explain the different sign. The initial injection into Agriculture is not able to activate any overall output increase. The need for more primary factors to satisfy the extra demand for Agriculture requires siphoning them from elsewhere in the economy, triggering an economy-wide fall in production. The indirect output substitution effects more than compensate the direct output volume effect arising from the extra injection.

Table 1. Multiplier comparison.

Spanish Data	Multiplier Estimates		
	Economic Sector	Linear Multipliers	Gen. Equilib. Multipliers
1.	Agriculture	1.4620	−0.5431
2.	Fisheries	1.0394	0.3305
3.	Coal	1.0211	0.5179
4.	Petroleum and Gas	1.0056	0.9825
5.	Mining	1.0974	0.3106
6.	Oil Refining	2.0322	1.3076
7.	Electricity	3.1015	0.2129
8.	Gas	1.2480	0.8665
9.	Water	1.0640	−0.5126
10.	Foodstuffs	2.7998	0.4838
11.	Clothing	1.3781	0.7127
12.	Wood Products	1.5952	0.2936
13.	Chemicals	1.8607	0.6111
14.	Building Materials	2.0411	0.0953
15.	Iron and Steel	2.2508	0.5351
16.	Metal Products	2.0267	0.2699
17.	Machinery	2.1037	0.6224
18.	Vehicles	2.1284	0.8703
19.	Other Transport. Equip.	1.3384	0.5763
20.	Other Manufactures	2.2511	0.2646
21.	Construction	6.2904	−0.0082
22.	Commerce	3.5528	−1.7232
23.	Transport. and Comm.	2.8001	−03582
24.	Other Services	2.2807	−0.6793
25.	Services for Sale	2.2151	−1.1277
26.	Public Services	2.2962	−1-1607
	Total multiplier effect	**54.2805**	**3.7503**

Unlike the general positive multiplier effects of linear models, multipliers results can perfectly be negative in a Walrasian general equilibrium model. Moreover, the combined multiplier effects can be dramatically different in size. Under the linear model, aggregate output effects can be as high as 54.2805, meaning that an additional unitary demand for each and every of the 26 sectors would give rise, on average, to a multiplier effect of 54.2805/26 = 2.0877 new output units. The general equilibrium model, however, reduces this estimate drastically, with an average value of only 3.7503/26 = 0.1442 new units of output.

5. Conclusion

The interaction of demand and supply in goods, services and productive factors in response to external, policy oriented induced changes makes multiplier estimates be substantially smaller, and even negatively valued, in a general equilibrium model than in a linear model where price effects are disregarded and resource constraints are not binding. Expenditure policies designed upon optimistically estimated linear multiplier values should therefore be carefully reevaluated, and perhaps even abandoned. In fact the use of the name "multiplier" could even be a misnomer. Under general equilibrium, multipliers are not systematically above 1, or even positive in sign for that matter; hence output levels need not "multiply" over 1, as the standard linear models conclude. The tradition is however too strong to be changed, and we will still refer to the effects of external injections in endogenous output as "multipliers", provided the modeling assumptions under which they are estimated are explicitly laid out.

6. Acknowledgements

Support from research projects MINECO2009-11857 and SGR2009-587 is gratefully acknowledged. The usual caveat applies.

REFERENCES

[1] G. Debreu, "Economies with a Finite Set of Equilibria," *Econometrica*, Vol. 38, No. 3, 1970, pp. 387-392.

[2] R. E. Miller and P. D. Blair, "Input-Output Analysis: Foundations and Extensions," Cambridge University Press, Cambridge, 2009.

[3] J. Shoven and J. Whalley, "Applied General Equilibrium Models of Taxation and International Trade," *Journal of Economic Literature*, Vol. 22, No. 3, 1984, pp. 1007-1051.

[4] T. J. Kehoe, T. N. Srinivisan and J. Whalley, "Frontiers in Applied General Equilibrium Modeling," Oxford University Press, Oxford, 2005.

[5] J. M. Cansino, M. A. Cardenete, M. Ordóñez and R. Román, "Análisis de Los Sectores Clave de la Economía Española a Partir de la Matriz de Contabilidad Social de España 2006," University of Seville, Unpublished Mimeo, 2011.

[6] F. Sancho, "Calibration of CES Functions for 'Real-world' Multisectoral Modeling," *Economic Systems Research*, Vol. 21, No. 1, 2009, pp. 45-58.

Minimum Wage, Public Investment, Economic Growth

Minoru Watanabe
Graduate School of Economics, Kobe University, Kobe, Japan

ABSTRACT

This paper considers the relationship between economic growth and minimum wage. Minimum wage helps reduce poverty and maintain a minimum standard of living. However, it is also claimed that minimum wage has a negative effect on employment and GDP. This paper develops a simple two-period overlapping generation model with three economic policies, minimum wage, unemployment benefit, and public investment that improves labor productivity. The government imposes tax on firms to finance public capital and unemployment benefit under a balanced budget. We show that economic growth is promoted with an increase in minimum wage and the ratio of public investment to tax revenue.

Keywords: Minimum Wage; Public Investment; Economic Growth

1. Introduction

Minimum wage is an economic policy that helps reduce poverty and maintain a minimum standard of living. However, it is also claimed that minimum wage has a negative effect on employment and GDP. Therefore, earlier studies consider the relationship between minimum wage and economic growth in a dynamic framework. Cahuc and Michel [1] introduce human capital accumulation in an endogenous growth model. Ravn and Sorensen [2] consider skill formation accumulated by schooling and training. Askenazy [3] develops endogenous growth model with an open economy and R&D sector. Irmen and Wigger [4] consider minimum wage with a two-country endogenous growth model. Tamai [5] discusses the interaction between inequality and economic growth from the view point of political economy. The above papers assume two sectors or heterogeneous agents. Fanti and Gori [6] consider the relationship between economic growth and minimum wage under a simple one-sector overlapping generation model with [1]homogeneous agents. It is [2]uncertain whether minimum wage promotes economic growth in earlier papers.

This paper introduces public investment that improves labor productivity, for example, infrastructure and medical service. Public investment is an economic policy with an important role in macroeconomic performance. Barro [7], Futagami, Morita and Shibata [8] examine economic growth with public investment that improves labor productivity. Glomm and Ravicumar [9] discuss economic growth including public investment and human capital accumulation. Yakita [10] considers public investment in an aging society.

Following Fanti and Gori [6], this paper introduces public investment that enhances labor productivity and considers the relationship between minimum wage and economic growth. The results obtained in this study are presented below. First, an increase in minimum wage always promotes economic growth. Second, an increase in the ratio of public investment to tax revenue promotes economic growth.

The remainder of this paper is organized as follows. Section 2 presents our model. Section 3 describes the equilibrium. Section 4 summarizes the paper.

2. Model

2.1. Basic Structure

The economy in this paper is based on a basic two-period overlapping generations framework. There exist three agents, households, firms, and the government.

2.2. Households

Households live two periods, young and old and supply one unit of labor to the labor market. If they are employed they receive wages, and if they are not employed,

[1]They introduce heterogeneous agents in extension.
[2]Whether minimum wage promotes economic growth or not depends on parameters or assumptions in Cahuc and Michel [1], Ravn and Sorensen [2], Askenazy [3], Irmen and Wigger [4], and Fanti and Gori [6].

they receive unemployment benefit. The utility function in this paper is:

$$u_t^i = \log c_{y,t}^i + \beta \log c_{o,t+1}^i \tag{1}$$

where $c_{y,t}^i$ is the young-period consumption of household i, $c_{o,t+1}^i$ is the old-period consumption of household i; i is the index of both employment $(i = e)$ and unemployment $(i = u)$, and $\beta \in (0,1)$ is the constant discount factor. The budget constraint of households i is given as:

$$c_{y,t}^i + s_t^i - x_t^i \tag{2}$$

$$c_{o,t+1}^i = (1 + r_{t+1}) x_t^i \tag{3}$$

where x_t^i is the income in young period, s_t^i is the savings, and r_{t+1} is the interest rate. If the households are employed, they receive wags, and if they are not employed, they receive unemployment benefit. In this economy, minimum wages exist. Therefore the relation between minimum wage, $w_{m,t}$ and competitive wage, $w_{c,t}$, is given as:.

$$w_{m,t} = \mu w_{c,t} \tag{4}$$

where $\mu > 1$ is the constant mark-up rate that generates unemployment in the labor market. Households receive unemployment benefit b_t when they are not employed, and b_t is defined as:

$$b_t = \gamma w_{m,t} \tag{5}$$

where $\gamma \in (0,1)$ is the constant replacement rate. Therefore unemployment benefit is fraction of minimum wage. The optimal allocations of household i are given by:

$$c_{y,t}^i = \frac{1}{1+\beta} x_t^i \tag{6}$$

$$c_{o,t+1}^i = \frac{\beta}{1+\beta}(1 + r_{t+1}) x_t^i \tag{7}$$

2.3. Firms

This paper assumes [3]the production function as follows:

$$Y_t = A K_t^{\alpha} (G_t L_t)^{1-\alpha} \tag{8}$$

where K_t is the capital stock, G_t is the public investment, L_t is the labor input, A is the constant parameter, and $\alpha \in (0,1)$ is the constant parameter. This paper assumes neither depreciation nor population growth. Public investment and unemployment benefit are financed by tax revenue from firms. The profit maximizetion conditions are given as:

$$w_{m,t} = (1-\alpha) A K_t^{\alpha} G_t^{1-\alpha} L_t^{-\alpha} \tag{9}$$

$$(1+\tau_t) r_t = \alpha K_t^{\alpha-1} (G_t L_t)^{1-\alpha} \tag{10}$$

where τ_t is the contribution rate for firms to finance public investment and unemployment benefit. In the competitive equilibrium, $L_t = 1$ and

$$w_{c,t}^* = (1-\alpha) A K_t^{\alpha} G_t^{1-\alpha}$$

hold. Using $w_{c,t}^*$ with Equation (5) and (9), L_t is presented as:

$$L_t = \mu^{-\frac{1}{\alpha}} \tag{11}$$

Because L_t is constant, the unemployment rate, $u_t = 1 - L_t$, is also constant for any period t.

2.4. Government

The government imposes tax on firms to finance public capital and unemployment benefit. Assuming a balanced budget, the budget constraint of the government is given by:

$$E_{g,t} = \tau_t r_t K_t \tag{12}$$

$$G_t = \lambda E_{g,t} \tag{13}$$

$$u_t b_t = (1-\lambda) E_{g,t} \tag{14}$$

$$\lambda \in (0,1)$$

where $\tau_t r_t K_t$ is the tax revenue from firms, $E_{g,t}$ is the government expenditure, G_t is the public investment, $u_t b_t$ is the total unemployment benefit, λ is the constant ratio of public investment to tax revenue, and $(1-\lambda)$ is the constant ratio of unemployment benefit to tax revenue. Using Equation (5), (9), (10), (12), (14), and $u_t = 1 - L_t$ the budget constraint of the government is described as follows:

$$\frac{u_t \gamma (1-\alpha)}{(1-\lambda)} A K_t^{\alpha} G_t^{1-\alpha} (1-u_t)^{-\alpha}$$

$$= \frac{\tau_t}{1+\tau_t} \alpha A K_t^{\alpha} G_t^{1-\alpha} (1-u_t)^{1-\alpha}$$

where

$$\frac{u_t \gamma (1-\alpha)}{(1-\lambda)} A K_t^{\alpha} G_t^{1-\alpha} (1-u_t)^{-\alpha}$$

is the total expenditure for unemployment benefit, and

$$\frac{\tau_t}{1+\tau_t} \alpha A K_t^{\alpha} G_t^{1-\alpha} (1-u_t)^{1-\alpha}$$

is the tax revenue. Hence τ_t is given by:

$$\frac{\alpha \tau_t}{1+\tau_t} = \frac{\gamma (1-\alpha) u_t}{(1-\lambda)(1-u_t)} \tag{15}$$

[3]Barro [7] and Futagami and Morita and Shibata [8] assume public investment in the production function and public investment increases labor productivity.

From Equation (9), (10), (12), (13), and (15), G_t is given by:

$$G_t = \left[\frac{\lambda A\gamma(1-\alpha)}{1-\lambda}\right]^{\frac{1}{\alpha}} u_t^{\frac{1}{\alpha}}(1-u_t)^{-1}K_t \quad (16)$$

Tax rate τ_t is an endogenous variable delivered by a balanced budget and this [4]assumption is the same as in Fanti and Gori [4]. Equation (15) shows that the tax rate is an [5]increasing function of the unemployment rate and the ratio of public capital to tax revenue. The intuition is described as follows. If unemployment rate increases, then minimum wage increases and interest rate decreases because labor force becomes relatively scarce to capital. On the other hand, unemployment benefit b_t also increases with an increase $w_{m,t}$ because unemployment benefit is fraction of minimum wage, and the total unemployment benefit $u_t b_t$ increases. We assume the ratio of total unemployment benefit to tax revenue is constant and balanced budget. From Equation (12) and (14), the relationship between total expenditure of unemployment benefit and tax revenue is denoted as $u_t b_t = (1-\lambda)\tau_t r_t K$. To satisfy balanced budget when total expenditure of unemployment benefit, $u_t b_t$, increases and interest rate, r_t, decreases with an increase in unemployment rate, τ_t should increase. Hence tax rate is an increasing function of unemployment rate.

From Equation (16), public investment is also an increasing function of unemployment rate; the reason for this is described as follows. When the unemployment rate increases, there are two effects to public investment. First, an increase in the unemployment rate increases τ_t from Equation (15), and this enlarges public investment because the tax revenue increases. Second, an increase in the unemployment rate decreases r_t because labor force becomes relatively scarce to capital, and this decrease public investment because the tax revenue decreases. Comparing the two effects, the first effect dominates the second effect.

3. Equilibrium

In a basic overlapping generations model, the capital stock in period $t+1$ is equal to the savings in period t. The relationship between capital and savings is:

$$K_{t+1} = (1-u_t)s_t^e + u_t s_t^u \quad (17)$$

where K_{t+1} is the capital in period $t+1$, $(1-u_t)s_t^e$ is the total savings of employees, and $u_t s_t^u$ is the total savings of unemployment. The dynamics of this economy is shown as follows:

$$\frac{K_{t+1}}{K_t} = \frac{\beta Z}{1+\beta}\left[u_t^{\frac{1-\alpha}{\alpha}} + \gamma u_t^{\frac{1}{\alpha}}(1-u_t)^{-1}\right] \quad (18)$$

$$Z \equiv ((1-\alpha)A)^{\frac{1}{\alpha}}\left(\frac{\lambda\gamma}{1-\lambda}\right)^{\frac{1-\alpha}{\alpha}}$$

where K_{t+1}/K_t is the growth rate in the economy. To satisfy sustained growth, a large A is assumed. From Equation (11), the unemployment rate, u_t, is constant and an increasing function of the constant mark-up rate μ. The derivative of growth rate with respect to μ gives:

$$\frac{dg_t}{d\mu} = \frac{dg_t}{du_t}\frac{du_t}{d\mu} > 0 \quad (19)$$

$$g_t \equiv K_{t+1}/K_t$$

Therefore the following proposition is established.

Proposition 1

An increase in the constant mark-up rate increases the minimum wage and promotes economic growth.

The total unemployment income $u_t b_t$ increases when μ increases. Therefore the savings of unemployment increases. On the other hand, an increase in μ has two effects on the total income of employees $(1-u_t)w_{m,t}$. First, an increase in μ directly decreases the total income of employees because unemployment increases. Second, an increase in μ increases $w_{m,t}$ because labor force becomes scarce and labor productivity is promoted. Comparing the two effects, the second effect dominates the first effect. Because the total income increases with an increase in μ, the savings in this economy also increase. Therefore economic growth is promoted with an increase in μ.

Finally, we focus on the effect of the ratio of public investment tax revenue on growth rate. Public investment increases with an increase in the constant ratio of public capital to tax revenue, from Equation (16). The derivative of growth rate with respect to λ gives:

$$\frac{dg_t}{d\lambda} > 0 \quad (20)$$

Therefore the following proposition is established.

Proposition 2

An increase in the ratio of public investment to tax revenue promotes economic growth.

An increase in the ratio of public investment to tax revenue, λ, promotes public investment, and this increases the minimum wage and unemployment benefit, from Equation (5). Therefore both the total wage income and total unemployment benefit increase with an increase in the ratio of public investment. This means that the

[4]Fanti and Gori [6] also consider the exogenous replacement rates in extension.

[5]From equation (15), the derivative of tax rate with respect to unemployment rate gives:

$$\frac{d\tau_t}{du_t} = \frac{\gamma(1-\alpha)(1+\tau_t)^2}{\alpha(1-\lambda)(1-u_t)^2} > 0$$

total expenditure on unemployment benefit described as $u_t b_t = (1-\lambda) E_{g,t}$ increases even if the ratio of unemployment benefit to tax revenue decreases.

4. Conclusion

This paper presents a simple endogenous growth model with minimum wage and public investment that improves labor productivity. Minimum wage is an economic policy that helps reduce poverty and maintain a minimum standard of living. However, it is also claimed that minimum wage has a negative effect on employment and GDP. The relationship between minimum wage and economic growth is uncertain in earlier papers. This paper shows that a rise in minimum wage always promotes economic growth. Moreover, this paper shows that a rise in the ratio of public investment to tax revenue promotes economic growth.

5. Acknowledgements

The author would like to thank Tamotsu Nakamura, Takeshi Koba, and Masao Yamaguchi for their helpful comments and suggestions. The author is responsible for any remaining errors.

REFERENCES

[1] P. Cahuc and P. Michel, "Minimum Wage Unemployment and Growth," *European Economic Review*, Vol. 40, No. 7, 1996, pp. 1463-1482.

[2] M. Ravn and J. Sorensen, "Schooling, Training, Growth and Minimum Wages," *Scandinavian Journal of Economics*, Vol. 101, No. 3, 1999, pp. 441-457.

[3] P. Askenazy, "Minimum Wage, Exports and Growth," *European Economic Review*, Vol. 47, No. 1, 2003, pp. 147-164.

[4] A. Irmen and B. Wigger, "National Minimum Wages, Capital Mobility and Global Economic Growth," *Economics Letters*, Vol. 90, No. 2, 2006, pp. 285-289.

[5] T. Tamai "Inequality, Unemployment, and Endogenous Growth in a Political Economy with a Minimum Wage," *Journal of Economics*, Vol. 97, No. 3, 2009, pp. 217-232.

[6] L. Fanti and L. Gori, "On Economic Growth and Minimum Wages," *Journal of Economics*, Vol. 103, No. 1, 2011, pp. 59-82.

[7] R. J. Barro, "Government Spending in a Simple Model of Endogenous Growth," *Journal of Political Economy*, Vol. 98, No. 1, 1990, pp. S103-S125.

[8] K. Futagami, Y. Morita and A. Shibata, "Dynamic Analysis of an Endogenous Growth Model with Public Capital," *Scandinavian Journal of Economics*, Vol. 95, No. 4, 1993, pp. 606-625.

[9] G. Glomm and B. Ravikumar, "Productive Government Expenditure and Long-Run Growth," *Journal of Economic Dynamics and Control*, Vol. 21, No. 1, 1997, pp. 183-204.

[10] A. Yakita, "Aging and Public Capital Accumulation," *International Tax and Public Finance*, Vol. 15, No. 5, 2008, pp. 582-598.

28

Consumption Tax, Nontraded Goods and Welfare

Wataru Johdo
Faculty of Economics, Tezukayama University, Nara, Japan

ABSTRACT

This paper studies the welfare effects of a consumption tax rise based on the two-sector small open economy model of Obstfeld and Rogoff (1995) and Lane (1997). The main findings of our analysis are that 1) in the case of free trade, the consumption tax rise has no effect on welfare, 2) when there is the nontraded goods sector, the consumption tax rise has a negative effect on welfare, and 3) the larger the share of nontraded goods in consumption is, the larger the negative welfare effect of consumption tax will be.

Keywords: Consumption Tax; Nontraded Goods; Trade Openness; Small Open Economy; Welfare

1. Introduction

In the new open economy macroeconomics literature pioneered by Obstfeld and Rogoff [1], the relationship between monetary expansions and aggregate economic activity has been studied extensively at the theoretical level.[1] This literature has focused on how the macroeconomic activity and welfare of multiple countries are influenced by unanticipated monetary shocks in one country under monopolistic distortions and price rigidities. The benchmark model of Obstfeld and Rogoff [1] shows that a domestic monetary expansion raises consumption in both countries by lowering the world interest rate, which results in an increase in world consumption demand, and thereby improves foreign and domestic welfare. At the same time, in the appendix, Obstfeld and Rogoff [1] also sketch a small open economy model that incorporates a nontraded goods sector and show the possibility of exchange rate overshooting. Then, Lane [5] extends the small open economy model in Obstfeld and Rogoff [1] to include government behavior and shows how variation in trade openness affects the welfare effects of expansionary monetary policy shocks. Furthermore, Cavallari [6] and Lee and Chinn [7] also take the two-sector small open economy model of Obstfeld and Rogoff [1] (or Lane [5]) and study how the current account and exchange rate are influenced by monetary policy shocks. Johdo [8] also generalizes the two-sector small open economy model of Lane [5] to include habit formation, and examine how the strength of habit formation affects the response of welfare to monetary policy shocks.

However, no studies have attempted to examine the welfare effects of an increase in a consumption tax by using the two-sector small open economy model. The purpose of this paper is to contribute theoretically to the new open economy macroeconomics literature by generalizing the small open economy model of Obstfeld and Rogoff [1] and Lane [5] to include a consumption tax rate and examining the question of how the degree of trade openness (or the share of nontraded goods in consumption) affects the response of welfare to an increase in the consumption tax rate.

The main findings of our analysis are that 1) in the case of free trade, the consumption tax rise has no effect on welfare, 2) when there is the nontraded goods sector, the consumption tax rise has a negative effect on welfare, and 3) the larger the share of nontraded goods in consumption is, the larger the negative welfare effect of consumption tax will be.

The remainder of this paper is structured as follows. In Section 2, we outline the features of the model. In Section 3, we present the symmetric equilibrium with flexible nominal prices. In Section 4, we present a log-linearized version of this model. In Section 5, we analyze the welfare effect of a permanent consumption tax rise and examine how the degree of trade openness affects the responses of welfare to the consumption tax shock. Section 6 gives the conclusion.

[1] For surveys of the new open economy macroeconomics models, see Lane [2], Sarno [3] and Lane and Ganelli [4].

2. A Two-Sector Small Open Economy Model

Following Obstfeld and Rogoff [1] and Lane [5], we consider a small open economy with two sectors, a traded goods sector and a nontraded goods sector, with nominal price rigidities. The traded goods sector is characterized by a single homogeneous endowment, and the price of traded goods is determined in perfectly competitive world markets. Meanwhile, the nontraded goods sector is a monopolistically competitive market with differentiated goods. In this model, a unit mass of agents is characterized as both consumers and producers, where each agent produces a unit of nontraded differentiated goods. The agents have perfect foresight, derive their utility from consuming a homogeneous good and a group of differentiated goods and from holding real money balances, and incur the cost of expending labor (or production) effort.

The intertemporal objective of a typical agent at time 0 is to maximize the following lifetime utility:

$$U_0 = \sum_{t=0}^{\infty} \beta^t \left\{ \delta \log C_{Tt} + (1-\delta) \log C_{Nt} + \chi \log \frac{M_t}{P_t} - \frac{\eta}{2} y_{Nt}(i)^2 \right\}, \tag{1}$$

where $\beta \in (0,1)$ is a constant subjective discount factor, $y_{Nt}(i)$ is the agent's output of nontraded goods in period $t, \delta \in (0,1)$ is the share of the consumption of traded goods, C_{Tt} is consumption of the traded good, and C_{Nt} is composite nontraded goods consumption, defined as:

$$C_{Nt} = \left(\int_0^1 C_{Nt}(i)^{(\theta-1)/\theta} \, \mathrm{d}i \right)^{\theta/(\theta-1)}, \tag{2}$$

where $\theta\,(>1)$ is the elasticity of substitution between any two differentiated goods and $C_{Nt}(i)$ is the consumption of nontraded good i. The second term in (1) represents real money balances (M_t/P_t), where M_t denotes nominal money balances held at the beginning of period $t + 1$, and P_t is the consumption price index, which is defined as:

$$P_t = \frac{(1+\tau_t) P_{Tt}^{\delta} P_{Nt}^{1-\delta}}{\delta^{\delta} (1-\delta)^{1-\delta}}, \tag{3}$$

where τ_t is the consumption tax rate and P_{Nt} is the price of nontraded goods and is defined as:

$$P_{Nt} = \left(\int_0^1 P_{Nt}(i)^{1-\theta} \, \mathrm{d}i \right)^{1/(1-\theta)}, \tag{4}$$

and P_{Tt} is the domestic currency price of traded goods. Because there are no trade costs, the law of one price holds for traded goods; *i.e.*, $P_{Tt} = E_t P_{Tt}^*$, where E_t is the nominal exchange rate and P_{Tt}^* is the exogenously determined world price. A typical agent faces the following budget constraint:

$$P_{Tt} B_{t+1} + M_t = P_{Tt} (1+r) B_t + M_{t-1} + P_{Nt}(i) y_{Nt}(i) + P_{Tt} y_T - (1+\tau_t)(P_{Tt} C_{Tt} + P_{Nt} C_{Nt}) + T_t, \tag{5}$$

where B_{t+1} denotes real bonds denominated in traded goods in period $t+1$, r denotes the world real interest rate in traded goods on bonds that applies between periods $t-1$ and t, and T_t denotes lump-sum transfers from the government. In the government sector, we assume that government spending is zero. Hence, the government budget constraint is $\tau_t (P_{Tt} C_{Tt} + P_{Nt} C_{Nt}) + M_t - M_{t-1} = T_t$. In addition, in this model, each agent is endowed with a constant amount of the traded good in each period. Therefore, as shown in (5), we can delete the subscript t from y_{Tt}, *i.e.*, $y_{Tt} = y_T, \forall t$.

At the first stage, agents maximize the consumption index (2) subject to a given level of expenditure on nontraded goods $P_{Nt} C_{Nt} = \int_0^1 P_{Nt}(i) C_{Nt}(i) \mathrm{d}i$ by optimally allocating differentiated nontraded goods. This static problem yields the following demand function for good i:

$$y_{Nt}(i) = \left(\frac{P_{Nt}(i)}{P_{Nt}} \right)^{-\theta} C_{NAt}, \tag{6}$$

where C_{NAt} is aggregate consumption. At the second stage, agents maximize (1) subject to (5). For simplicity, we assume $\beta(1+r) = 1$. Then, the first-order conditions for this problem can be written as:

$$C_{Tt+1} = C_{Tt}, \tag{7}$$

$$C_{Nt} = \left(\frac{1-\delta}{\delta} \right) \left(\frac{P_{Tt}}{P_{Nt}} \right) C_{Tt}, \tag{8}$$

$$\left(\frac{1}{1+\tau_t} \right) \left(\frac{\delta}{C_{Tt}} \right) = \chi \left(\frac{M_t}{P_t} \right)^{-1} \left(\frac{P_{Tt}}{P_t} \right) + \beta \left(\frac{P_{Tt}}{P_{Tt+1}} \right) \left(\frac{1}{1+\tau_t} \right) \left(\frac{\delta}{C_{Tt+1}} \right), \tag{9}$$

$$y_{Nt}(i)^{(\theta+1)/\theta} = \left[\frac{(\theta-1)(1-\delta)}{\theta \eta} \right] \left(\frac{1}{1+\tau_t} \right) \left(\frac{1}{C_{Nt}} \right) (C_{NAt})^{1/\theta}, \tag{10}$$

and the terminal condition is

$$\lim_{T=\infty} (1/1+r)^T \left[B_{t+T+1} + (M_{t+T}/P_{t+T}) \right] = 0 .$$

3. Steady-State Flexible Price Equilibrium

Henceforth, we assume that initial net foreign assets are zero ($B_0 = 0$). In the steady state, all exogenous variables are constant. Substituting (8) into (10) and considering the symmetric equilibrium $C_N = y_N = C_{NA}$, we obtain:

$$C_N = y_N = \left[\frac{(\theta-1)(1-\delta)}{\theta\eta}\right]^{1/2}\left(\frac{1}{1+\tau}\right)^{1/2}. \quad (11)$$

Equation (11) shows that all agents produce the same output of nontraded goods. Meanwhile, from (7) and a fixed endowment of traded goods output, the consumption of traded goods remains constant in each period; *i.e.*, $C_{Tt} = y_T, \forall t$. This implies that the current account is always balanced.

4. A Log-Linearized Analysis with Nominal Rigidities

To examine the effects of an unanticipated permanent consumption tax rise, we solve a log-linear approximation of the system around the initial, zero-shock steady state. Following Obstfeld and Rogoff [1] and Lane [5], we assume nominal price rigidities under which the price of nontraded goods in period t is predetermined at time $t-1$. In addition, the price of nontraded goods is assumed to be fully adjusted after one period. For any variable X_t, we use $\hat{X}_t\left(\hat{X}_{t+1}\right)$ to denote the short-run (long-run) percentage deviation from the initial steady-state value. The short-run percentage deviation is proportional to the degree of the nominal price rigidity under which the output of nontraded goods is determined by demand. In the long run, the price of nontraded goods adjusts perfectly to the new steady-state value to be consistent with the optimal conditions (10).

First, in the short run, as the price of nontraded goods is sticky, we obtain $\hat{P}_{Nt} = 0$. In addition, as the consumption of traded goods remains constant in each period, we obtain $\hat{C}_{Tt} = \hat{C}_{Tt+1} = 0$. By log-linearizing Equations (8) and (9), and considering $\hat{P}_{Nt} = 0$ and $\hat{C}_{Tt} = 0$, respectively, we obtain:

$$\hat{P}_{Tt} = \hat{C}_{Nt}, \quad (12)$$

$$-\hat{P}_{Tt} = \frac{\beta}{1-\beta}\left(\hat{P}_{Tt} - \hat{P}_{Tt+1}\right) + \left(\frac{1}{1+\tau}\right)\mathrm{d}\tau. \quad (13)$$

Equation (12) shows that the consumption of nontraded goods is affected positively by the price of traded goods in the short run. Equation (13) shows that the price of traded goods is affected by the consumption tax rise. With $\hat{P}_{Nt} = 0$, the short-run response in the consumption price index is

$$\hat{P}_t = \left(\frac{1}{1+\tau}\right)\mathrm{d}\tau + \delta\hat{P}_{Tt}. \quad (14)$$

In the long run, the economy reaches a steady state. Therefore, for the price of traded goods, we obtain $\hat{P}_{Tt+1} = \hat{P}_{Tt+2}$. Substituting $\hat{P}_{Tt+1} = \hat{P}_{Tt+2}$ into the long-run case of (13), we obtain:

$$\hat{P}_{Tt+1} = -\left(\frac{1}{1+\tau}\right)\mathrm{d}\tau < 0. \quad (15)$$

In addition, from the consumption price index, we obtain

$$\hat{P}_{t+1} = \left(\frac{1}{1+\tau}\right)\mathrm{d}\tau + \delta\hat{P}_{Tt+1} + (1-\delta)\hat{P}_{Nt+1}. \quad (16)$$

Furthermore, from (8), we obtain

$$\hat{P}_{Tt+1} = \hat{P}_{Nt+1} + \hat{C}_{Nt+1}. \quad (17)$$

Substituting (17) into (16), we obtain

$$\hat{P}_{t+1} = \left(\frac{1}{1+\tau}\right)\mathrm{d}\tau + \hat{P}_{Tt+1} - (1-\delta)\hat{C}_{Nt+1}. \quad (18)$$

From (11), we obtain

$$\hat{C}_{Nt+1} = \hat{y}_{Nt+1} = -\frac{1}{2}\left(\frac{1}{1+\tau}\right)\mathrm{d}\tau < 0. \quad (19)$$

Substituting (15) and (19) into (18), we obtain

$$\hat{P}_{t+1} = \frac{1}{2}\left(\frac{1-\delta}{1+\tau}\right)\mathrm{d}\tau > 0. \quad (20)$$

Equation (20) shows that the consumption tax rise always increases the consumption price index in the long-run. Meanwhile, in the small open economy model, because the world price of traded goods is determined exogenously and $P_{Tt} = E_t P_T^*$ always holds, we obtain $\hat{P}_{Tt} = \hat{E}_t$ in the short run. This implies that the price of traded goods reacts proportionately to the exchange rate. By substituting $\hat{P}_{Tt} = \hat{E}_t$ into (13), the short-run response of the exchange rate to a consumption tax rise is given by:

$$\hat{E}_t = -\left(\frac{1}{1+\tau}\right)\mathrm{d}\tau < 0. \quad (21)$$

Equation (21) shows that a rise in the consumption tax rate appreciates the exchange rate. Therefore, from $\hat{P}_{Tt} = \hat{E}_t$, (14) and (21), the consumption tax rise always increases the consumption price index in the short-run, $\hat{P}_t = \left[(1-\delta)/(1+\tau)\right]\mathrm{d}\tau > 0$. Finally, from (12) and (21), we obtain:

$$\hat{C}_{Nt} = -\left(\frac{1}{1+\tau}\right)\mathrm{d}\tau < 0. \quad (22)$$

Equation (22) shows that the consumption tax rise decreases the consumption of nontraded goods in the short run. In addition, from (6) and $P_N(i)/P_N = 1$, we obtain $\hat{y}_{Nt} = \hat{C}_{Nt}$. Therefore, by linking this to (22), we obtain:

$$\hat{y}_{Nt} = \hat{C}_{Nt} = -\left(\frac{1}{1+\tau}\right)\mathrm{d}\tau < 0. \quad (23)$$

Equation (23) shows that the consumption tax rise also decreases the output of nontraded goods in the short run.

5. Welfare Analysis

Our interest here lies in exploring the welfare effects of a consumption tax rise. Recalling that $\hat{C}_{Tt} = \hat{C}_{Tt+1} = 0$, we can rewrite Equation (1) as:

$$\Delta U = \Delta U_R + \Delta U_M, \tag{24}$$

where

$$\Delta U_R = (1-\delta)\hat{C}_{Nt} - \eta y_{N0}^2 \hat{y}_{Nt} + \frac{\beta}{1-\beta}\left[(1-\delta)\hat{C}_{Nt+1} - \eta y_{N0}^2 \hat{y}_{Nt+1}\right],$$

$$\Delta U_M = \chi\left(\hat{M}_t - \hat{P}_t\right) + \chi\left(\frac{\beta}{1-\beta}\right)\left(\hat{M}_{t+1} - \hat{P}_{t+1}\right),$$

where y_{N0} denotes the initial steady-state output of nontraded goods. The short-run and long-run results for nontraded consumption, output and price index can be used to derive the impact of a consumption tax rise on welfare. By substituting these results into (24), we obtain:

$$\Delta U = -\left(\frac{1-\delta}{1+\tau}\right)\left(1+\frac{\beta}{2(1-\beta)}\right) \times\left[\left(1-\frac{\theta-1}{\theta(1+\tau)}\right)+\chi\right]\mathrm{d}\tau < 0. \tag{25}$$

The first term of the right hand side in square brackets of Equation (25) reflects the net welfare effect, composed of the welfare loss from a decrease in the consumption of nontraded goods and the welfare gain from a decrease in the production effort of nontraded goods. From $\delta < 1$ and $\theta > 1$, we find that the first term of Equation (25) is always negative. The second term is the welfare loss from a decrease in the real balances through $\hat{P}_t > 0$ and $\hat{P}_{t+1} > 0$. Therefore, the impact of a consumption tax rise on welfare is always negative.

The intuitive explanation is as follows. The welfare effect is determined by two mechanisms. On the one hand, an unanticipated permanent consumption tax rise requires an instantaneous decrease in the price of traded goods to restore the traded goods market equilibrium for a given constant endowment of tradable output. With fixed nontraded goods prices, the decrease in the price of traded goods in turn raises the relative price of nontraded goods and thereby decreases the consumption of nontraded goods. The importance of this negative nontradable consumption effect depends positively on the share of nontraded goods in consumption, $(1 - \delta)$. On the other hand, the consumption tax rise also increases the price index and thereby decreases real balances. Here, recall from $\hat{P}_{Tt} = \hat{E}_t$, (14) and (21) that the impact of a consumption tax rise on the price index depends positively on the share of nontraded goods in consumption, $(1 - \delta)$, from $\hat{P}_t = \left[(1-\delta)/(1+\tau)\right]\mathrm{d}\tau > 0$. Therefore, the scale of this negative real balance effect depends positively on $(1 - \delta)$. Thus, for reasons mentioned above, the larger the share of nontraded goods in consumption, the larger the negative welfare effect of consumption tax.

Here, remember that the parameter $\delta(0 < \delta < 1)$ measures the degree of trade openness, where δ approaches one as the degree of trade openness increases and approaches zero when trade is extremely costly. Therefore, Equation (25) also shows that the larger the size of trade cost, the larger the negative welfare effect of consumption tax.

Incidentally, in the extreme case of free trade ($\delta = 1$), the impact of a consumption tax rise on welfare is:

$$\Delta U_{\delta=1} = 0. \tag{26}$$

Thus, under free trade, the consumption tax rise has no effect on welfare. Intuitive explanation of this result is as follows. First, the negative nontradable consumption effect disappears when $\delta = 1$ as shown in the above. Second, recall that the consumption tax rise has two opposing effects on the consumption price index. On the one hand, a rise in the consumption tax increases the price index directly from (3). On the other hand, the consumption tax rise decreases the price index through an appreciation in the nominal exchange rate (see (21)). Therefore, there are two conflicting price index effects of a consumption tax rise. However, from $\hat{P}_{Tt} = \hat{E}_t$, (14) and (21), when $\delta = 1$, these two changes in the price index offset each other, and hence, the negative real balance effect also disappears. Thus, under free trade, the consumption tax rise has no effect on welfare.

6. Conclusion

We have used the two-sector small open economy model of Obstfeld and Rogoff [1] and Lane [5] to consider the response of welfare to a consumption tax rise. The main findings of our analysis are that 1) in the case of free trade, the consumption tax rise has no effect on welfare, 2) when there is the nontraded goods sector, the consumption tax rise has a negative effect on welfare, and 3) the larger the share of nontraded goods in consumption is, the larger the negative welfare effect of consumption tax will be. In particular, the latter results indicate the following policy implication: when trade is costly, the consumption tax rate must be decreased from a welfare point of view. Further, the actual data suggest that the second result in the above is consistent with the impacts of a consumption tax rise in Japan and the UK. Indeed, in Japan, the consumption tax rate was raised from 3% to 5% in 1997, while the real GDP growth rate was 2.6% in 1996 but it fell to 1.6% in 1997 (IMF, 2013 [9]). In addition, recently, in the UK, the consumption tax rate was raised from 17.5% to 20% in 2011, while the real GDP growth rate was 1.8% in 2010 but it fell to 0.9% in 2011

(IMF, 2013, [9]). Therefore, the main result of this paper is supported with the actual data, because, in both Japan and UK, the real GDP growth rates fall after the consumption tax rise.

7. Acknowledgements

The author would like to thank an anonymous referee for valuable comments and suggestions. The author is also grateful to have received financial support from Tezukayama University.

REFERENCES

[1] M. Obstfeld and K. Rogoff, "Exchange Rate Dynamics Redux," *Journal of Political Economy*, Vol. 103, No. 3, 1995, pp. 624-660.

[2] P. R. Lane, "The New Open Economy Macroeconomics: A Survey," *Journal of International Economics*, Vol. 54, No. 2, 2001, pp. 235-266.

[3] L. Sarno, "Towards a New Paradigm in Open Economy Modelling: Where Do We Stand?" *Federal Reserve Bank of St. Louis Review*, Vol. 83, No. 3, 2001, pp. 21-36.

[4] P. R. Lane and G. Ganelli, "Dynamic General Equilibrium Analysis: The Open Economy Dimension," In: A. Altug, J. S. Chaddha and C. Nolan, Eds., *Dynamic Macroeconomic Analysis*, Cambridge University Press, Cambridge, 2003, pp. 308-334.

[5] P. R. Lane, "Inflation in Open Economies," *Journal of International Economics*, Vol. 42, No. 3-4, 1997, pp. 327-347.

[6] L. Cavallari, "Current Account and Exchange Rate Dynamics," *Economic Notes*, Vol. 30, No. 1, 2001, pp. 27-51.

[7] J. Lee and M. D. Chinn, "Current Account and Real Exchange Rate Dynamics in the G7 Countries," *Journal of International Money and Finance*, Vol. 25, No. 2, 2006, pp. 257-274.

[8] W. Johdo, "Does Monetary Expansion Improve Welfare under Habit Formation?" *Economics Bulletin*, Vol. 33, No. 3, 2013, pp. 1959-1968.

[9] International Monetary Fund, "World Economic Outlook Database," International Monetary Fund, Washington DC, 2013.

29

Why Does the US Prevent Parallel Imports?

Yih-Ming Lin
Department of Applied Economics, National Chiayi University, Chiayi, Taiwan

ABSTRACT

Most studies on parallel trade conclude that parallel imports, in general, benefit the importing country because it lowers the price of parallel imports and benefits to the consumers in the importing country. Richardson [1] explicitly indicates that there is no importing country not to permit parallel imports because they are discriminated against in its absence. However, an obvious counter example is observed in the US. In this paper, we propose a two-country model of parallel trade with innovation to explain why some countries, such as the US would like to prevent parallel imports. We show that the elasticity of innovation is crucial to the welfare of importing country and global welfare.

Keywords: Parallel Imports; Welfare; Innovation

1. Introduction

Most of the previous literatures, such as Malueg and Schwartz [2], Richardson [1], Maskus and Chen [3,4], and Chen and Maskus [5], on parallel trade conclude that parallel imports, in general, benefit the importing country because it lowers the price of parallel imported goods and benefits to the consumers. Among them, Richardson [1] explicitly indicates that there is no importing country not to permit parallel imports because they are discriminated against in its absence. However, an obvious counter example is observed in the US. For instance, the message "*This International Edition is not for sale in the United States of America, its dependencies or Canada.*" is common to be found in a copyright page or cover of the International Edition textbook, which indicates that the US does not allow new or used international edition textbooks to be circulated within the country. Therefore, this phenomenon raises the question: If parallel import is always in favor of the importing country, then why would the US government prevent parallel import?

Previous discussion on whether parallel trade should be prevented includes Maskus [6,7], Malueg and Schwartz [2], and so on. Maskus [6] summarizes the arguments which are in favor of preventing parallel trade. Among them, the most well-known explanation is that third-degree price discrimination may be beneficial to the global welfare, which will not necessarily happen but depend on whether the global output increases or not under each case (Varian [8]). Another argument opposing to parallel trade proposed by Malueg and Schwartz [2] is that some markets will become unserved due to a uniform price, the direct consequence of parallel trade. However, the above arguments seem hard to explain why a country is willing to block parallel import if its government concerns its own welfare, instead of the global welfare. In particular, the above discussions are concentrated on the benefits of the entire world, instead of that of an individual country.

In this paper, we build in a two-country model with innovation to analyze the welfare effects of parallel imports from the viewpoint of an importing country. The welfare effects of parallel trade on the importing country and global welfare are also investigated by a simulation approach. We investigates the welfare effects and how parallel trade relates to the incentive of product innovation by employing a differentiated-goods model, which extends the models of Li and Maskus [9], Li and Robles [10], and Li [11,12]. It distinguishes from the previous studies, while only a single product model is used to demonstrate how parallel trade affects the welfare in most of existing literatures. See Malueg and Schwartz [2], Maskus and Chen [3,4], and Chen and Maskus [5] for examples.

The remainder of this paper is organized as follows. In Section 2, we demonstrate a conventional two-country model with linear demand. Following Section 2, we set up a two-country model of parallel trade incorporated with innovation to explain why a country would like to prevent parallel imports in Section 3. Section 4 gives conclusions.

2. The Single Product Case

In this section, we describe a simple, conventional, two-country model of parallel trade with a single product. Consider an economy with two countries, North and South, denoted by n and s, and a monopolistic manufacturer. The monopolist manufacturer produces and sells identical products in both countries. Further, we follow Malueg and Schwartz [2] to assume that the demand function is linear such that he inverse demand function of the market i has the form

$$p_i(q_i) = a_i(1-q_i), \quad i = n, s, \tag{1}$$

where p_i and q_i represent the price and consumption in country i, respectively. Both countries have horizontal intercepts at 1, but different vertical intercepts at a_i. Without of loss of generality, we may assume that $a_n = 1 + x$ and $a_s = 1 - x$, where $x < 1$.

The monopolist determines the price in both markets to maximize its profits. Suppose that the markets are segmented so that the producer can set different prices according to the demand elasticity in both countries in order to make its profit maximized, which is a standard case of third degree price discrimination. Moreover, suppose that the marginal production cost is constant and the same in the two countries. Without loss of generality, we may assume that marginal production cost is zero and there is no transaction cost for simplicity. Therefore, the monopoly price in the North, $p_n^m = \frac{1+x}{2}$, is higher than the price in the South's market, $p_s^m = \frac{1-x}{2}$, which implies that the North is the importing country if parallel trade is exhibited.

As long as there exists a price difference, there are incentives for arbitrage. If parallel trade is allowed, the optimization problem of the monopolist is

$$\text{Max } \pi(p) = p\left[\left(1-\frac{p}{1+x}\right)+\left(1-\frac{p}{1-x}\right)\right],$$

where p is the uniform price, $1-p/(1+x)$ and $1-p/(1-x)$ are the quantities consumed in the North and the South, respectively. Taking derivative with respect to p, we obtain

$$\frac{\partial \pi(p)}{\partial p} = 2 - 2p/(1+x) - 2p/(1-x).$$

and the optimal price is $p^* = (1-x^2)/2$.

Note that p^* is greater than p_s^m, but less than p_n^m.

Next, we investigate the welfare effects of parallel trade. First, assume that the two markets are segmented, and let W_i represent the welfare of country i ($i = n, s$), which is equivalent to the sum of consumers' and producer's surplus of the country. Then $W_n = 3(1 + x)/8$ and $W_s = 3(1 - x)/8$ and the global welfare $W_n + W_s = 3/4$. Next, let's consider the case where parallel trade is allowed. solving the firm's problem gives the optimal price $p^* = (1 - x^2)/2$ and $W_n = (1 + x)^2(3 - x)/8$ and $W_s = (1 - x)^2(3 + x)/8$, respectively. The global welfare $W_n + W_s = 3/4 + x^2/4$ in this case. Consequently, we can conclude that the global welfare in the case of parallel trade is greater than in the case of segmented markets. In particular, global welfare is increasing in x.

Furthermore, if the monopolistic manufacturer is from the North, the welfare of the South decreases once parallel trade is allowed which makes the price of goods higher in the South. Thus, the welfare of the North improves. Moreover, if the monopolist is from the South, it is easy to show that the welfare of the North improves because the price in the North decreases. Therefore, we can conclude that global welfare and the welfare of the North improve if parallel trade is allowed. Consequently, we may generalize the above linear demand model to different market size and can still conclude the same for importing country. In particular, the above conclusion for importing country holds under the model of Varian [8] as well as the multi-country model of Malueg and Schwartz [2]. However, for simplicity, we shall still focus on the case of a two-country model with the same market size but generalize our analysis to a multiple-products setting.

3. The Welfare Effects of Parallel Trade Incorporated with Innovation

In this section, we develop a two-country model with innovation. Similar to the previous setting, we consider an economy with two countries, named South (s) and North (n), and a firm that develops new products in the North. But, here we assume that there are two sectors in a firm, including a homogenous good sector and a differentiated products sector. Following Deardorff [13] and Scotchmer [14], innovation is incorporated in to the model through a two-stage model; *i.e.*, the firm chooses the number of differentiated products to be produced in the first stage and then sells the products in both countries in the next stage.

Consumers in the same country are assumed to have identical preferences but consumers in different countries may have different preferences. Consumer i chooses z and $x(j)$ to maximize his utility function $u_i(\cdot)$, where $u_i'(\cdot) > 0$ and $u_i''(\cdot) < 0$ and $i = n, s$. The problem can be written as

$$\text{Max} \int_0^N u_i\left(x_i\left(j\right)\right)dj + z_j\,, \tag{2}$$

Subject to $\int_0^N p_i\left(j\right)x_i\left(j\right)dj + z_j = Y_i$,

where j is the index of differentiated goods, N is a measure of differentiated products in the North, $x_i(j)$ is the consumption of a differentiated good j in country i, z_i is the consumption of the homogenous good, and Y_i represents the income of an individual in country i.

Solving the first order condition of the consumer's problem yields $x_i(j) = x_i(p(j))$, where $x_i = (u_i')^{-1}$, which suggests that the demand for the numeraire good is $z_i = Y_i - \int_0^N p_i\left(j\right)x_i\left(j\right)dj + z_j$ Furthermore, the indirect utility function can be written as

$$U = \int_0^N S_i\left(p_i\left(j\right)\right)dj + Yi,$$

where $s_i(p_i(j)) = u_i(x_i(p_i(j))) - p_i(j)x_i(p(j))$, is the consumer surplus associated with a representative differentiated product.

The equilibrium of the two-stage model can be thought of as that representing the steady state of an infinite horizon general equilibrium model in which a firms innovates in every period and products have an exogenously given useful life, as has been shown by Grossman and Lai [15]. In order to make a comparison, we assume that the demand function for each differentiated product is the same as that in Equation (1) for a different country.

For the monopolistic manufacturer, we may, without loss of generality, assume that the production of one unit of all varieties of differentiated products has the same constant marginal cost c, where c is set to be 0, similar to the assumption imposed in the previous section. Furthermore, we follow Grossman and Lai [15] and assume that the innovation cost function is specified as

$$C\left(N\right) = N^{\alpha}, \tag{3}$$

where $\alpha > 1$. Note that we rule out the case$\alpha \leq 1$, where both the marginal and average innovation cost are nonincreasing in N. Equation (3) implies that the innovation cost is convex in N. Next, we define

$$\gamma = C'\left(N\right)/\left(NC''\left(N\right)\right)$$

to be the elasticity of innovation with respect to an increase in the profit from innovation. Our specification of innovation cost function has a constant elasticity of innovation, which has the same properties as the innovation cost function in Grossman and Lai [15].

The firm's problem is to choose the number of the new differentiated products, N, and the price in both markets to maximize its profit. Since the p_s and p_n are determined as in Section 2, the optimal N^* is determined by marginal profit and the marginal innovation cost of innovating a new differentiated good. Thus,

$$C'\left(N^*\right) = \pi_n\left(p_n\right) + \pi_s\left(p_s\right),$$

where the right hand side is the marginal profit generated by an additional differentiated product.

The welfare of the North is a composition of the profit of the firm in the North and the South, the consumers' surplus in the North, and the innovation cost.

$$W_n\left(N\right) = N\left(\pi_n\left(p_n\right) + \pi_s\left(p_s\right) + s_n\left(p_n\right)\right) - C\left(N\right).$$

Moreover, since the firm is in the North, the welfare of the South includes only the consumers' surplus generated in the South.

$$W_s\left(N\right) = Ns_s\left(p_s\right).$$

Furthermore, the global welfare is the sum of two countries welfare.

Next, we utilize a simulation approach to investigate the welfare effects of parallel trade for the North and the global welfare effects. The welfare effects of parallel trade is examined by numerical simulation for $x \in [0, 0.5]$ under different innovation cost functions. Here, we concentrate on the cases only when $x \in [0, 0.5]$, because no parallel trade will happen when $x > 0.5$. Similar results for different cases of the innovation cost function are obtained, therefore, we use two representative cases of γ in **Figures 1** and **2** to illustrate the results. In **Figures 1** and **2**, the *x-axis* is defined as x and the *y-axis* is defined as the relative welfare of the North and relative global welfare.

Two cases of elasticity of innovation, $\gamma = 5$ and $\gamma = 10/11$ are illustrated in **Figures 1** and **2**, respectively. The former represents the cases of high elasticity of innovation and the latter represents the cases of low elasticity of innovation. We define the "W_n *ratio*" as the North welfare with the occurrence of parallel trade divided by that of the North without the occurrence of parallel trade. Then "W_n *ratio*" > 1 means that the North welfare is improved when parallel trade exists. Analogously, we can also define the global welfare ratio, denoted by "*GW ratio*" and the global welfare with an occurrence parallel trade improves when "*GW ratio*" > 1.

Figure 1 shows that the two ratios are concave in x. They are increasing in x first, and then decreasing in x. We can find that there exists a $x = 0.117$, which makes the North obtain the maximal W_n *ratio*, *i.e.*, the maximal welfare improvement for the North from parallel imports. For $x \in [0.117, 0.5]$, W_n *ratio* is decreasing in x. In addition, when $x = 0.231$, we have W_n *ratio* = 1, *i.e.* the North welfare of parallel trade is equal to that without parallel trade. It suggests that if x is big enough, parallel importation is not beneficial to the importing country. Furthermore, it also shows that *GW ratio* is no greater than 1, and is decreasing in x for all x when $\gamma = 5$. It suggests that when the elasticity of innovation is relatively high then the global welfare will decrease due to parallel import-

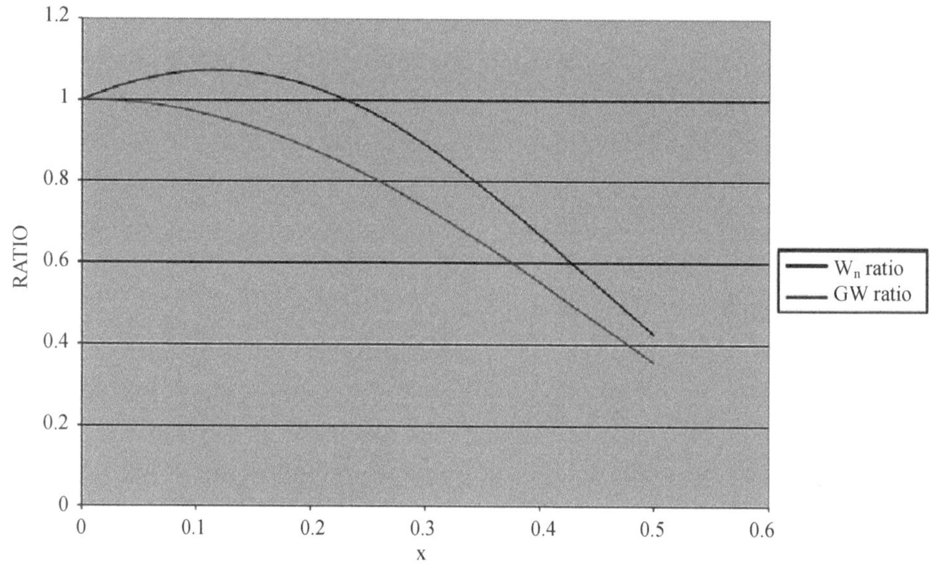

Figure 1. Relative welfare, $\gamma = 5$.

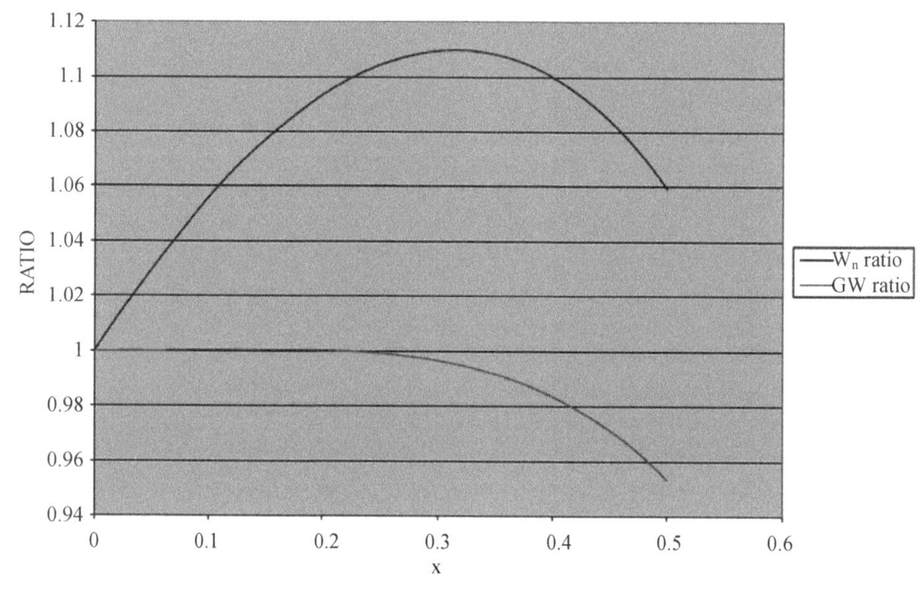

Figure 2. Relative welfare, $\gamma = \frac{10}{11}$.

ing.

Next, the simulation results of the relative welfare of the North and the global welfare for the case of $\gamma = 10/11$ is shown in **Figure 2**. It indicates that the welfare of North and global welfare are analogous to the case of $\gamma = 5$. The main difference is that global welfare may be improved because of parallel trade which, however, may not be significant. Furthermore, it also shows that the North welfare of parallel imports is always greater than that under the banning of parallel trade.

To sum up the results, **Figure 3** is constructed under various elasticities of innovation. The y-axis is defined as the elasticity of innovation, γ, and the x-axis is the difference between the slope of demand function in different market, x. **Figure 3** contains three regions: A, B, and C. The points (x, γ) falling into the area A represent the cases where parallel trade will reduce both of W_n and global welfare. In particular, when both γ and x are high, parallel trade lowers the welfare of the North and the whole world. Moreover, the points in region C of **Figure 3** represents the cases that both of W_n and global welfare are better off. When elasticity of innovation is low, parallel trade will increase the North's and global welfare. Finally, region B means the North's welfare increases but global welfare decreases if parallel trade exists. Therefore, we conclude our results in Proposition 1.

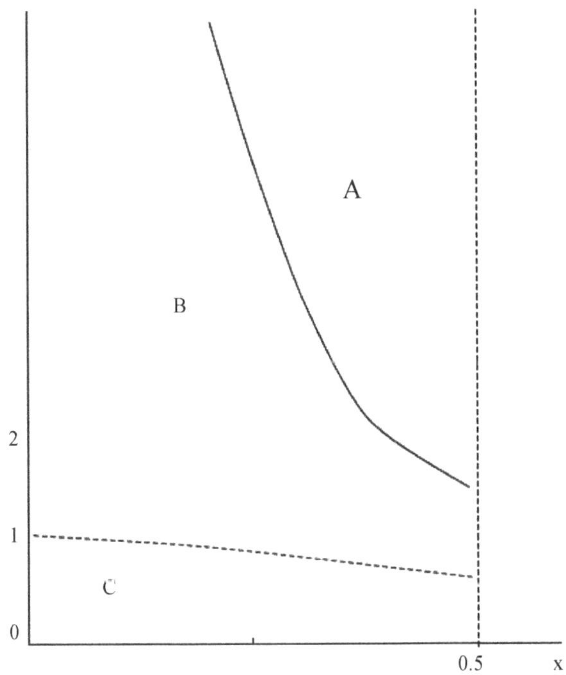

Figure 3. The relation between elasticity of innovation, γ and x.

Proposition 1:

1) When elasticity of innovation is high, the innovating country welfare increases in x first, and it decreases in x when x is getting large. Global welfare decreases in x.

2) When elasticity of innovation is low, the innovating country welfare and global welfare increase in x first, and they decrease in x when x is getting large.

3) When elasticity of innovation and x are high, parallel trade decreases the innovating country welfare as well as global welfare.

4) When elasticity of innovation is low, parallel trade will improve the innovating country welfare as well as global welfare. However, the increase in global welfare is limited.

Proposition 1 indicates that parallel imports can usually make the North's welfare improve whenever the difference between the North and the South is small. On the other hand, if the difference between the two markets is significant, parallel imports will make the North worse. Thus, Proposition 1 provides a reasonable interpretation of why some countries permit parallel importing, but some do not.

Another finding is that global welfare decreases under the case of high elasticity of innovation at any given values of x, which is quite different from the results in section 2, where global welfare always increases under a single product model with linear demand function. It is mainly resulted from the reduced number of innovations which is accompanied with the reduced profit. For the case of low elasticity of innovation, global welfare is improved if the difference between the two markets is not significant. The profit of monopolist is reduced which is a direct consequence of parallel trade reduces. Therefore, parallel trade reduces the incentives for innovation, which results in a decreasing number of innovations. Although parallel trade in a single product case improves the welfare of the importing country and global welfare concluded in Section 2, the welfare effects of parallel trade become ambiguous in the more general model.

4. Conclusion

We introduce a model of parallel trade with innovation to explain the phenomena why there exist various policies on parallel trade in the real world. One reasonable interpretation is that allowing parallel imports may reduce producers' incentives for innovation, and thus reduce the number of new innovation. We show that the welfare effect is not only related to the difference between the two markets, but also related to the elasticity of innovation. Parallel trade improves the welfare of importing country, which, however, also reduces the incentives to innovate new products. Overall, the welfare effects of parallel imports are ambiguous. It provides an interpretation for why some countries allow parallel import but some do not. Furthermore, when elasticity of innovation and x is high, parallel trade decreases the innovating country welfare as well as global welfare. When elasticity of innovation is low, allowing parallel trade improves the welfare of the innovating country as well as global welfare. However, the increase in global welfare is not significant.

REFERENCES

[1] M. Richardson, "An Elementary Proposition Concerning Parallel Imports," *Journal of International Economics*, Vol. 56, No. 1, 2002, pp. 233-245.

[2] D. A. Malueg and M. Schwartz, "Parallel Imports, Demand Dispersion, and International Price Discrimination," *Journal of International Economics*, Vol. 37, No. 3-4, 1994, pp. 167-195.

[3] K. E. Maskus and Y. Chen, "Parallel Imports in a Model of Vertical Distribution: Theory and Evidence and Policy," *Pacific Economic Review*, Vol. 7, No. 2, 2002, pp. 319-334.

[4] K. E. Maskus and Y. Chen, "Vertical Price Control and Parallel Imports: Theory and Evidence," *Review of International Economic*, Vol. 12, No. 4, 2004, pp. 551-570.

[5] Y. Chen and K. E. Maskus, "Vertical Pricing and Parallel Imports," *Journal of International Trade and Economic Development*, Vol. 14, No. 1, 2005, pp. 1-18.

[6] K. E. Maskus, "Intellectual Property Rights in the Global Economy," Institute for International Economics, Washington DC, 2000.

[7] K. E. Maskus, "Parallel Imports," *The World Economy*, Vol. 23, No. 9, 2002, pp. 1269-1284.

[8] H. Varian, "Price Discrimination and Social Welfare," *American Economic Review*, Vol. 75, 1985, pp. 870-875.

[9] C. Li and K. E. Maskus, "The Impact of Parallel Imports on Investments in Cost-Reducing Research and Development," *Journal of International Economics*, Vol. 68, No. 2, 2006, pp. 443-455.

[10] C. Li and J. Robles, "Product Innovation and Parallel Trade," *International Journal of Industrial Organization*, Vol. 25, No. 2, 2007. pp. 417-429.

[11] C. Li, "Vertical Product Innovation and Parallel Imports," *Singapore Economic Review*, Vol. 50, No. 1, 2005, pp. 35-46.

[12] C. Li, "Competition, Parallel Imports and Cost-Reducing Innovation," *Scottish Journal of Political Economy*, Vol. 53, No. 3, 2006, pp. 377-397.

[13] A. V. Deardorff, "Welfare Effects of Global Patent Protection," *Economica*, Vol. 59, No. 233, 1992, pp. 35-51.

[14] S. Scotchmer, "The Political Economy of Intellectual Property Treaties," *Journal of Law, Economics, and Organizations*, Vol. 20, No. 2, 2004, pp. 415-437.

[15] G. M. Grossman and E. L. C. Lai, "International Protection of Intellectual Property," *American Economic Review*, Vol. 94, No. 5, 2004, pp. 1635-1653.

Two-Player Lopsided Contests under Different Timing Assumptions

Kyung Hwan Baik
Department of Economics, Sungkyunkwan University, Seoul, South Korea

ABSTRACT

I study contests in which two asymmetric players compete with each other by expending irreversible efforts to win a prize. I consider three types of games, which are distinguished by their different timing assumptions: the simultaneous-move game, the sequential-move game, and the game with endogenous timing. I compare the outcomes obtained under the different timing assumptions.

Keywords: Contest; Rent Seeking; Timing Assumptions; Underdog; Favorite

1. Introduction

A contest is a situation in which players compete with each other by expending irreversible efforts to win a prize. Examples include rent-seeking contests, patent contests, sporting contests, competition among candidates for office, litigation and tournaments.

The purpose of this paper is to study contests with two asymmetric players under different timing assumptions. The asymmetries between the players arise because of the players' different valuations for the prize or their different abilities to convert efforts into probability of winning or both. Using the model in Baik [1], I consider three types of games, which are distinguished by their different timing assumptions: the simultaneous-move game, the sequential-move game, and the game with endogenous timing. I compare the outcomes obtained under the different timing assumptions.

This paper is related to Dixit [2], Baik and Shogren [3], Leininger [4], Nitzan [5], Baik [1], Morgan [6], Malueg and Yates [7], and Baik and Lee [8], which study asymmetric contests, with or without endogenous timing.

2. The Model

Two risk-neutral players, 1 and 2, compete with each other by expending their irreversible effort to win a prize. The probability that a player wins the prize is increasing in his own effort level, and decreasing in the rival's effort level. Player 1 values the prize at αv, and Player 2 at v, where $\alpha > 0$. Each player's valuation for the prize is positive and publicly known.

Let x_i for $i = 1, 2$, represent the effort level expended by player i. Each player's effort level is positive, and is measured in units commensurate with the prize. Let $p_i(x_1, x_2)$ denote the probability that player i wins the prize when Players 1 and 2 expend x_1 and x_2, respectively, where $0 \le p_i(x_1, x_2) \le 1$ and $p_1(x_1, x_2) + p_2(x_1, x_2) = 1$. I assume that the contest success function for Player 1 is

$$p_1(x_1, x_2) = \sigma h(x_1) / \{\sigma h(x_1) + h(x_2)\}, \qquad (1)$$

where $\sigma > 0$ and the function h has the properties specified in Assumption 1 below. The parameter σ represents the relative abilities of the players to convert effort into probability of winning.

Assumption 1. I assume that $h(0) \ge 0$, and h is increasing in x_i. I assume also that h is twice differentiable, and $h''(x_i) \le 0$, where h'' denotes the second partial derivative of the function h.

It follows from Equation (1) and Assumption 1 that each player's probability of winning is increasing in his own effort level at a decreasing rate, given a value of σ and an effort level of the opponent. It follows also that each player's probability of winning is decreasing in his opponent's effort level at a decreasing rate, given a value of σ and his own effort level.

Let π_i represents the expected payoff for player i. Then the payoff function for Player 1 is

$$\pi_1 = \alpha v p_1(x_1, x_2) - x_1,$$

and that for Player 2 is

$$\pi_2 = vp_2(x_1, x_2) - x_2.$$

I consider three types of games, which are distinguished by their different timing assumptions: the simultaneous-move game, the sequential-move games, and the game with endogenous timing. In the simultaneous-move game, both players choose their effort levels simultaneously, and this order of moves is given exogenously. In a sequential-move game, one player chooses his effort level, and then after observing it, the other player chooses his effort level; this order of moves is given exogenously. In the game with endogenous timing, each player first decides independently whether he will choose his effort level in the first period or in the second period. The players announce their decisions simultaneously. Then, after knowing his opponent's decision, each player chooses his effort level in the period which he announced.

I assume that all of the above are common knowledge between the players. I employ Nash equilibrium as the solution concept for the simultaneous-move game, and subgame-perfect equilibrium as the solution concept for the sequential-move games and the game with endogenous timing.

3. Preliminaries: Previous Results and Definitions

As proved in Szidarovszky and Okuguchi [9], the simultaneous-move game has a unique pure-strategy Nash equilibrium. Let (x_1^N, x_2^N) denote the Nash equilibrium. Based on the analyses in Baik [1] and Baik and Lee [8], I obtain Lemma 1[1].

Lemma 1. a) If $\alpha\sigma h'(x_1^N) < h'(x_2^N)$, then Player 1's probability of winning is less than 1/2 at the Nash equilibrium, b) If $\alpha\sigma h'(x_1^N) > h'(x_2^N)$, then Player 1's probability of winning is greater than 1/2, c) If $\alpha\sigma h'(x_1^N) = h'(x_2^N)$, then each player's probability of winning equals 1/2.

In Parts a) and b), the players' probabilities of winning are not the same at the Nash equilibrium. I call these cases lopsided contests, to which I restrict attention in this paper.

Next, consider the first stage of the game with endogenous timing in which the players decide and announce when to expend their effort. Based on the analyses in Baik and Shogren [3] and Baik and Lee [8], I obtain Lemma 2.

Lemma 2. a) If $\alpha\sigma h'(x_1^N) < h'(x_2^N)$, then Player 1 announces the first period while Player 2 announces the second period, b) If $\alpha\sigma h'(x_1^N) > h'(x_2^N)$, then Player 1 announces the second period while Player 2 announces the first period.

Studying two-player contests, Dixit [2] defines the underdog as the player who has a probability of winning less than 1/2, and the favorite as the player who has a probability of winning greater than 1/2, at the Nash equilibrium of a simultaneous-move game. I define the terms, the underdog and the favorite, for each of the three types of games.

Definition 1. a) The simultaneous-move underdog [favorite] is defined as the player who has a probability of winning less [greater] than 1/2, at the Nash equilibrium of the simultaneous-move game. b) The sequential-move underdog [favorite] is defined as the player who has a probability of winning less [greater] than 1/2, in the subgame-perfect equilibrium of a sequential-move game. c) The endogenous-timing underdog [favorite] is defined as the player who has a probability of winning less [greater] than 1/2, in the subgame-perfect equilibrium of the game with endogenous timing.

Using Lemma 1 and Definition 1, I can restate Lemma 2 as follows: In every lopsided contest, the simultaneous-move underdog announces the first period while the simultaneous-move favorite announces the second period. Importantly, this implies that the outcomes—the players' equilibrium probabilities of winning, effort levels, and expected payoffs—of the game with endogenous timing are exactly the same as those of the sequential-move game with the simultaneous-move underdog as the leader. Consequently, henceforth I restrict attention to just three games: the simultaneous-move game, the sequential-move game with the simultaneous-move favorite as the leader, and the game with endogenous timing.

4. Comparison of the Three Games

I compare the outcomes—the players' equilibrium probabilities of winning, effort levels, and expected payoffs—in the three games. **Table 1** summarizes the outcomes of the three games, and Propositions 1, 2 and 3 below describe the comparison of these outcomes[2]. The superscripts *SM*, *SQ*, and *EN* in **Table 1** indicate the outcomes of the simultaneous-move game, those of the sequential-move game with the simultaneous-move favorite as the leader, and those of the game with endogenous timing, respectively. I begin by comparing the players' equilibrium probabilities of winning in the three games.

Proposition 1. In every lopsided contest, the simultaneous-move favorite, the sequential-move favorite, and the endogenous-timing favorite are the same player.

As **Table 1** shows, Player 2 is always the favorite regardless of the timing assumption of the contest if

[1]For concise exposition, I do not provide the proofs of the lemmas and propositions presented in Sections 3 and 4. They are available from the author upon request. For the proof of Lemma 2, see also Leininger [4].

[2]If $\alpha\sigma h'(x_1^N) = h'(x_2^N)$, then I have $x_i^{SM} = x_i^{SQ} = x_i^{EN}$ for i = 1,2, so that I have $\pi_i^{SM} = \pi_i^{SQ} = \pi_i^{EN}$.

Table 1. Comparison of the outcomes of the three games.

	$\alpha\sigma h'(x_1^N) > h'(x_1^N)$	$\alpha\sigma h'(x_1^N) > h'(x_1^N)$
Simultaneous-Move Favorite	Player 2	Player 1
Sequential-Move Favorite	Player 2	Player 1
Endogenous-Timing Favorite	Player 2	Player 1
Effort Levels	$x_2^{EN} < x_2^{SM} < x_2^{SQ}$	$x_1^{EN} < x_1^{SM} < x_1^{SQ}$
	$x_1^{SQ} < x_1^{SM}$	$x_2^{SQ} < x_2^{SM}$
	$x_1^{EN} < x_1^{SM}$	$x_2^{EN} < x_2^{SM}$
Expected Payoffs	$\pi_2^{SM} < \pi_2^{SQ}$	$\pi_1^{SM} < \pi_1^{SQ}$
	$\pi_2^{SM} < \pi_2^{EN}$	$\pi_1^{SM} < \pi_1^{EN}$
	$\pi_1^{SQ} < \pi_1^{SM} < \pi_1^{EN}$	$\pi_2^{SQ} < \pi_2^{SM} < \pi_2^{EN}$

$\alpha\sigma h'(x_1^N) < h'(x_2^N)$, while Player 1 is so if $\alpha\sigma h'(x_1^N) > h'(x_2^N)$, In this contest, the players' valuations for the prize and their relative abilities determine the players' strength. A player with less strength tries to overcome his competitive disadvantage given a timing assumption. Unfortunately, however, any timing assumption does not help in putting him in better position.

Next, I compare the equilibrium effort levels of each player in the three games.

Proposition 2. a) In every lopsided contest, the favorite expends the least effort in the game with endogenous timing, and expends the most effort in the sequential-move game with the simultaneous-move favorite as the leader. b) In every lopsided contest, the underdog expends the most effort in the simultaneous-move game.

Proposition 2 implies that, in every lopsided contest, each player expends less effort in the game with endogenous timing than in the simultaneous-move game, so that the equilibrium total effort level is less in the game with endogenous timing than in the simultaneous-move game[3]. Proposition 2 can be explained as follows. In the sequential-move game with the simultaneous-move favorite as the leader, the favorite expends more effort than in the simultaneous-move game to preempt the opponent with less strength. In response to this preemptive behavior, the simultaneous-move underdog steps back by expending less effort than in the simultaneous-move game. On the other hand, in the game with endogenous timing (or, equivalently, in the sequential-move game with the simultaneous-move underdog as the leader), the underdog expends less effort than in the simultaneous-move game to avoid a big fight against the opponent with more strength. This in turn allows the simultaneous-move favorite to ease up and expend less effort than in the simultaneous-move game.

Finally, I compare the equilibrium expected payoffs of each player in the three games.

Proposition 3. a) In every lopsided contest, the favorite has the least expected payoff in the simultaneous-move game. b) In every lopsided contest, the underdog has the most expected payoff in the game with endogenous timing, and has the least expected payoff in the sequential-move game with the simultaneous-move favorite as the leader.

Proposition 3 implies that, in every lopsided contest, each player's equilibrium expected payoff is greater in the game with endogenous timing than in the simultaneous-move game, so that the sum of the players' equilibrium expected payoffs is greater in the game with endogenous timing than in the simultaneous-move game. The intuition behind Proposition 3 is as follows. In the sequential-move game with the simultaneous-move favorite as the leader, the favorite earns more expected payoff, due to the first-mover advantage, than in the simultaneous-move game, whereas the simultaneous-move underdog earns less expected payoff, due to the second-mover disadvantage, than in the simultaneous-move game. On the other hand, in the game with endogenous timing (or, equivalently, in the sequential-move game with the simultaneous-move underdog as the leader), both the simultaneous-move favorite and the underdog engage in less competition, and thus end up with greater equilibrium expected payoffs, than in the simultaneous-move game.

5. Conclusion

I have studied contests in which two asymmetric players compete with each other by expending irreversible efforts to win a prize. I have compared the outcomes in the three games: the simultaneous-move game, the sequential-move game with the simultaneous-move favorite as the leader, and the game with endogenous timing. I have found that, in every lopsided contest, the same player becomes the favorite across the three games. However, I have found that, in every lopsided contest, the equilibrium effort levels of each player differ across the three games; the equilibrium expected payoffs of each player differ across the three games.

REFERENCES

[1] K. H. Baik, "Effort Levels in Contests with Two Asymmetric Players," *Southern Economic Journal*, Vol. 61, No. 2, 1994, pp. 367-378.

[2] A. Dixit, "Strategic Behavior in Contests," *American Economic Review*, Vol. 77, No. 5, 1987, pp. 891-898.

[3] K. H. Baik and J. F. Shogren, "Strategic Behavior in Contests: Comment," *American Economic Review*, Vol. 82, No. 1, 1992, pp. 359-362.

[4] W. Leininger, "More Efficient Rent-Seeking—A Münch-

[3]Baik and Shogren [3], Leininger [4], Nitzan [5] and Baik [1] obtain this result.

hausen Solution," *Public Choice*, Vol. 75, No. 1, 1993, pp. 43-62.

[5] S. Nitzan, "More on More Efficient Rent Seeking and Strategic Behavior in Contests: Comment," *Public Choice*, Vol. 79, Nos. 3-4, 1994, pp. 355-356.

[6] J. Morgan, "Sequential Contests," *Public Choice*, Vol. 116, Nos. 1-2, 2003, pp. 1-18.

[7] D. A. Malueg and A. J. Yates, "Equilibria and Comparative Statics in Two-Player Contests," *European Journal of Political Economy*, Vol. 21, No. 3, 2005, pp. 738-752.

[8] K. H. Baik and J. H. Lee, "Endogenous Timing in Contests with Delegation," *Economic Inquiry*. In press.

[9] F. Szidarovszky and K. Okuguchi, "On the Existence and Uniqueness of Pure Nash Equilibrium in Rent-Seeking Games," *Games and Economic Behavior*, Vol. 18, No. 1, 1997, pp. 135-140.

Permissions

The contributors of this book come from diverse backgrounds, making this book a truly international effort. This book will bring forth new frontiers with its revolutionizing research information and detailed analysis of the nascent developments around the world.

We would like to thank all the contributing authors for lending their expertise to make the book truly unique. They have played a crucial role in the development of this book. Without their invaluable contributions this book wouldn't have been possible. They have made vital efforts to compile up to date information on the varied aspects of this subject to make this book a valuable addition to the collection of many professionals and students.

This book was conceptualized with the vision of imparting up-to-date information and advanced data in this field. To ensure the same, a matchless editorial board was set up. Every individual on the board went through rigorous rounds of assessment to prove their worth. After which they invested a large part of their time researching and compiling the most relevant data for our readers. Conferences and sessions were held from time to time between the editorial board and the contributing authors to present the data in the most comprehensible form. The editorial team has worked tirelessly to provide valuable and valid information to help people across the globe.

Every chapter published in this book has been scrutinized by our experts. Their significance has been extensively debated. The topics covered herein carry significant findings which will fuel the growth of the discipline. They may even be implemented as practical applications or may be referred to as a beginning point for another development. Chapters in this book were first published by Scientific Research Publishing Inc.; hereby published with permission under the Creative Commons Attribution License or equivalent.

The editorial board has been involved in producing this book since its inception. They have spent rigorous hours researching and exploring the diverse topics which have resulted in the successful publishing of this book. They have passed on their knowledge of decades through this book. To expedite this challenging task, the publisher supported the team at every step. A small team of assistant editors was also appointed to further simplify the editing procedure and attain best results for the readers.

Our editorial team has been hand-picked from every corner of the world. Their multi-ethnicity adds dynamic inputs to the discussions which result in innovative outcomes. These outcomes are then further discussed with the researchers and contributors who give their valuable feedback and opinion regarding the same. The feedback is then collaborated with the researches and they are edited in a comprehensive manner to aid the understanding of the subject.

Apart from the editorial board, the designing team has also invested a significant amount of their time in understanding the subject and creating the most relevant covers. They scrutinized every image to scout for the most suitable representation of the subject and create an appropriate cover for the book.

The publishing team has been involved in this book since its early stages. They were actively engaged in every process, be it collecting the data, connecting with the contributors or procuring relevant information. The team has been an ardent support to the editorial, designing and production team. Their endless efforts to recruit the best for this project, has resulted in the accomplishment of this book. They are a veteran in the field of academics and their pool of knowledge is as vast as their experience in printing. Their expertise and guidance has proved useful at every step. Their uncompromising quality standards have made this book an exceptional effort. Their encouragement from time to time has been an inspiration for everyone.

The publisher and the editorial board hope that this book will prove to be a valuable piece of knowledge for researchers, students, practitioners and scholars across the globe.

List of Contributors

Wen-Shai Hung
Department of Business Administration, Providence University, Taichung, Chinese Taipei

Sofia B. Villas-Boas
Department of Agricultural and Resource Economics, University of California, Berkeley, USA

George Judge
Department of Agricultural and Resource Economics and Graduate School, University of California, Berkeley, USA

Shunsuke Sekiguchi
Ishinomaki Senshu University, Ishinomaki, Japan

Kengo Nutahara
Department of Economics, Senshu University, Kanagawa, Japan
The Canon Institute for Global Studies, Tokyo, Japan

Kerstin Pull
School of Economics and Business, Eberhard Karls University Tuebingen, Tuebingen, Germany

Hendrik Bäker
Mathematics, Eberhard Karls University Tuebingen, Tuebingen, Germany

Agnes Bäker
School of Economics and Business, Eberhard Karls University Tuebingen, Tuebingen, Germany
Department of Economics, University of Warwick, Coventry, UK

Jeremy Berkowitz
Department of Finance, Bauer College of Business, University of Houston, Houston, USA

Xiaoning Lv and Xuezhi Qin
Faculty of Management and Economics, Dalian University of Technology, Dalian, China

Tao Sun
School of Mathematics, Liaoning Normal University, Dalian, China

Junji Kageyama
Department of Economics, Meikai University, Urayasu, Japan

Susanne Fuchs-Seliger
Institut für Volkswirtschaftslehre Karlsruher Institut für Technologie, Karlsruher, Deutschland

Patrick de Lamirande
Financial and Information Management, Cape Breton University, Sydney, Canada

Masayuki Otaki
Institute of Social Science, University of Tokyo, Tokyo, Japan

Swapnika Reddy Rachapalli and Praveen Kulshreshtha
Department of Humanities and Social Sciences, Indian Institute of Technology Kanpur, Kanpur, India

Barry R. Cobb and Atin Basuchoudhary
Department of Economics and Business, Virginia Military Institute, Lexington, USA

Gregory Hartman
Department of Mathematics and Computer Science, Virginia Military Institute, Lexington, USA

Luis-Felipe Arizmendi
GPI Asset Management S.A., Lima, Perú
Center for International Policy Studies, Department of Economics, Fordham University, New York, USA

Yasuhiko Nakamura
College of Economics, Nihon University, Tokyo, Japan

Yasuhiko Nakamura
College of Economics, Nihon University, Chiyoda, Japan

Damien Gaumont
Pantheon-Assas, Sorbonne Universities, ERMES EAC 7181 CNRS, CRED, Institute for Labor Studies and Public Policies, Paris, France

Daniel Leonard
Flinders Business School, Flinders University, Adelaide, Australia

André de Palma
Economics and Management Department, ENS Cachan, France and KU Leuven, Belgium

Soumyanetra Munshi
Economics and Social Science Area, Indian Institute of Management Bangalore (IIMB), Bangalore, India

Maria Teresa Bosch-Badia, Joan Montllor-Serrats and Maria Antonia Tarrazon
Department of Business Economics, Autonomous University of Barcelona, Barcelona, Spain

Kangsik Choi
Graduate School of International Studies, Pusan National University, Pusan, South Korea

Minhwan Lee
Division of Global Finance and Banking, Inha University, Incheon, South Korea

Ruey-Ji Guo, Yenpao Chen and Chun Chen Lee
Department of Accounting, Soochow University, Taipei, Taiwan

José Alberto Molina Chueca
Departamento de Análisis Económico, Facultad de Economía y Empresa, Universidad de Zaragoza, Zaragoza, Spain
Institute for the Study of Labour-IZA, Bonn, Germany

Joaquín Andaluz Funcia and Miriam Marcén
Departamento de Análisis Económico, Facultad de Economía y Empresa, Universidad de Zaragoza, Zaragoza, Spain

Jose Rigoberto Parada-Daza
Universidad de Concepcion, Concepcion, Chile

Miguel Ignacio Parada-Contzen
Technische Universität Berlin (TUB), Berlin, Germany

M. Alejandro Cardenete
Department of Economics, Universidad Loyola Andalucía, Sevilla, Spain

Ferran Sancho
Department of Economics, Universitat Autònoma de Barcelona, Barcelona, Spain

Minoru Watanabe
Graduate School of Economics, Kobe University, Kobe, Japan

Wataru Johdo
Faculty of Economics, Tezukayama University, Nara, Japan

Yih-Ming Lin
Department of Applied Economics, National Chiayi University, Chiayi, Taiwan

Kyung Hwan Baik
Department of Economics, Sungkyunkwan University, Seoul, South Korea